Democracy and Decentralisation in South Asia and West Africa
Participation, Accountability and Performance

This book is an in-depth empirical study of four Asian and African attempts to create democratic, decentralised local governments in the late 1980s and 1990s. The case studies of Ghana, Côte d'Ivoire, Karnataka (India) and Bangladesh focus upon the enhancement of participation; accountability between people, politicians and bureaucrats; and, most importantly, on whether governmental performance actually improved in comparison with previous forms of administration. The book is systematically comparative, and based upon extensive popular surveys and local fieldwork. It makes an important contribution to current debates in the development literature on whether 'good governance' and decentralisation can provide more responsive and effective services for the mass of the population – the poor and disadvantaged who live in the rural areas.

RICHARD CROOK is Senior Lecturer in the Department of Politics at the University of Glasgow. He was Joint Editor of the *Journal of Commonwealth and Comparative Politics* between 1980 and 1990, and the author (with A. M. Jerve) of *Government and Participation: Institutional Development, Decentralisation and Democracy in the Third World* (1993).

JAMES MANOR is a Professorial Fellow at the Institute for Development Studies, University of Sussex. He was Director of the Institute of Commonwealth Studies and Professor of Commonwealth Politics at the University of London between 1993 and 1997. His recent books include *Nehru to the Nineties: the Changing Office of Prime Minister in India* (edited, 1994), *Power, Poverty and Poison: Disaster and Response in an Indian City* (1993), and *Rethinking Third World Politics* (edited, 1991).

Democracy and Decentralisation in South Asia and West Africa

Participation, Accountability and Performance

Richard C. Crook and James Manor

CAMBRIDGE
UNIVERSITY PRESS

CAMBRIDGE UNIVERSITY PRESS
Cambridge, New York, Melbourne, Madrid, Cape Town,
Singapore, São Paulo, Delhi, Mexico City

Cambridge University Press
The Edinburgh Building, Cambridge CB2 8RU, UK

Published in the United States of America by Cambridge University Press, New York

www.cambridge.org
Information on this title: www.cambridge.org/9780521636476

© Richard C. Crook and James Manor 1998

This publication is in copyright. Subject to statutory exception
and to the provisions of relevant collective licensing agreements,
no reproduction of any part may take place without the written
permission of Cambridge University Press.

First published 1998

A catalogue record for this publication is available from the British Library

Library of Congress Cataloguing in Publication Data
Crook, Richard charles.
Democracy and decentralisation in South Asia and West Africa: participation, accountability and performance / by Richard C. Crook and James Manor.
   p. cm.
Includes bibliographical references and index.
ISBN 0 521 63157 2
1. Decentralisation in government – South Asia.
2. Decentralisation in government – Africa, West.
3. Local government – South Asia.
4. Local government – Africa, West.
5. Comparative government.
I. Manor, James.   II. Title.
JS6970.C76   1998
352.2'83 – dc 21   97–52669   CIP

ISBN 978-0-521-63157-0 Hardback
ISBN 978-0-521-63647-6 Paperback

Cambridge University Press has no responsibility for the persistence or
accuracy of URLs for external or third-party internet websites referred to in
this publication, and does not guarantee that any content on such websites is,
or will remain, accurate or appropriate. Information regarding prices, travel
timetables, and other factual information given in this work is correct at
the time of first printing but Cambridge University Press does not guarantee
the accuracy of such information thereafter.

This book is dedicated to Lizzie, Alastair and Hugh

Contents

List of maps		*page* ix
List of tables		x
Acknowledgements		xiv
1	Introduction	1
2	India (Karnataka)	22
	The background	22
	Participation	26
	Institutional performance	52
	Concluding remarks	80
3	Bangladesh	85
	The background	85
	Participation	89
	Institutional performance	111
	Concluding remarks	132
4	Côte d'Ivoire	136
	The background	136
	Participation	148
	Institutional performance	176
	Concluding remarks	199
5	Ghana	202
	The background	202
	Participation	213
	Institutional performance	247
	Concluding remarks	267

6	Conclusions	271
	Assessing participation	271
	Assessing performance	281
	Explaining performance	283
	Comparing explanations of performance: a cross-national analysis	289
	Democratic decentralisation in comparative perspective	292
	Methodological appendix	305
	References	320
	Index	331

Maps

1 Karnataka: the districts, showing location of case
  studies *page* 24
2 Bangladesh: the districts, showing location of case-
  study sub-districts 88
3 Côte d'Ivoire: the Prefectures, showing location of case-
  study communes 142
4 Ghana: the District Assemblies, showing location of case
  studies 206

Tables

2.1	Results of District Council elections	*page* 28
2.2	Results of Mandal Council elections	29
2.3	Attendance at officially sponsored meetings	31
2.4	Consultations with villagers about projects	32
2.5	Frequency of councillors' consultations	32
2.6	Contacting of councillors	33
2.7	Contacting of bureaucrats	33
2.8	Proactive participation	34
2.9	Participation in associations	34
2.10	Socio-economic characteristics of participators, by selected activities	35
2.11	Scheduled Castes' participation in associations	36
2.12	Scheduled Castes' ability to name councillors	37
2.13	Scheduled Castes' proactive participation	37
2.14	Ability by gender to name councillors	40
2.15	Involvement in council election campaigns	41
2.16	Proactive forms of participation, by gender	41
2.17	Funding of development projects	71
2.18	Projects and needs identified by villagers	72
2.19	Levels of satisfaction with projects	72
2.20	The nature of responses to contacts	73
2.21	Levels of satisfaction with elected councils	73
3.1	The fairness of council elections	91
3.2	Participatory activities between elections	94
3.3	Contacted elected councillors	94
3.4	Participation in associations	95
3.5	Frequency of councillors' availability	95
3.6	Consultations with villagers about projects	95
3.7	Socio-economic characteristics of participators, by selected activities	96
3.8	Ability, by gender, to name elected councillors	97
3.9	Proactive political activity, by gender	98

List of tables   xi

3.10	Associational activity, by gender	99
3.11	Types of projects identified	124
3.12	Projects and needs identified by respondents	128
3.13	Levels of satisfaction with projects	128
3.14	The nature of responses to contacts	129
3.15	Levels of satisfaction with elected councils	129
4.1	Côte d'Ivoire, commune elections, 1990 and 1996	149
4.2	Electoral turnout in the four case-study communes	150
4.3	Direct participation by citizens, group and individual activities, by commune	153
4.4	Sex and age group of participators, by selected activities, compared with profile of total population (four communes)	156
4.5	Educational and occupational characteristics of participators, by selected activities, compared with profile of population of southern communes (Affery and Yakassé)	156
4.6	Educational and occupational characteristics of participators, by selected activities, compared with profile of population of northern communes (Mbengué and Dikodougou)	157
4.7	Participation rates in selected activities, by sex	158
4.8	Participation rates in selected activities, by age group	158
4.9	Participation rates in selected activities, by education	158
4.10	Participation rates in selected activities, by occupational group	158
4.11	Social composition of the four commune councils	162
4.12	Type of consultation reported by respondents for main projects mentioned, by commune	164
4.13	Political knowledge: % respondents who can name elected councillor and/or the mayor, by commune	164
4.14	Frequency with which councillors hold meetings with their constituents, by commune	165
4.15	Community leaders:participation and relationships with commune councillors	165
4.16	Development expenditure as a proportion of total expenditure in the four-case study communes	178
4.17	Commune of Mbengué: breakdown of actual development expenditure by kind of project, 1986–92	179
4.18	Commune of Affery: breakdown of actual development expenditure by kind of project, 1986–92	180
4.19	Commune of Yakassé: breakdown of actual development expenditure by kind of project, 1986–92	181
4.20	Commune of Dikodougou: breakdown of actual development expenditure by kind of project, 1986–92	182

xii   List of tables

4.21	State grant as a proportion of total actual revenue in the four case-study communes	183
4.22	Respondents' perceptions of funding of main projects mentioned, by commune	187
4.23	Popular perceptions of commune and sub-prefecture performance	187
4.24	Rank order of most frequently mentioned popular needs by commune	189
4.25	Rank order of most frequently mentioned popular needs, by sex	189
4.26	Rank order of most frequently mentioned needs, respondents with no education	189
4.27	Elite survey: rank order of most frequently mentioned needs, by commune	190
4.28	Top three development priorities of the four communes in Three Year Plans, 1986/7–1994/5	191
4.29	Four main areas of cumulative expenditure, 1986–92, by commune	192
4.30	Responsiveness ratings of the four communes	194
5.1	Direct participation by citizens, group and individual activities	217
5.2	Relationships between elected councillors and their constituents	219
5.3	Direct participation by community leaders	220
5.4	Occupational groups of Assembly members elected in 1989, Ghana	224
5.5	Educational level of Assembly members in East Akim and East Mamprusi	225
5.6	Occupational characteristics of Assembly members in East Akim and East Mamprusi	226
5.7	East Akim DA: socio-economic characteristics of participators, by selected activities, compared with the profile of the total population of the district	228
5.8	East Mamprusi DA: socio-economic characteristics of participators, by selected activities, compared with the profile of the total population of the district	229
5.9	Participation rates in selected activities, by sex	230
5.10	Participation rates in selected activities, by age group	230
5.11	Participation rates in selected activities, by education	230
5.12	Participation rates in selected activities, by occupational group	230
5.13	Central government contribution to revenue: East Akim District Council and Assembly, 1986–91	248

List of tables   xiii

5.14 Central government contribution to revenue: Mamprusi
     District Council and East Mamprusi District Assembly,
     1986–91   249
5.15 East Akim District Assembly and District Council
     compared: expenditure on development 1986–91   249
5.16 East Mamprusi District Assembly and Mamprusi District
     Council compared expenditure on development, 1986–91   250
5.17 East Akim District Council and Assembly: selected
     expenditure patterns, 1986–91   252
5.18 Mamprusi District Council and East Mamprusi District
     Assembly: selected expenditure patterns, 1986–91   252
5.19 Popular perceptions of Assembly performance   255
5.20 Elite survey: perceptions of project funding   256
5.21 Elite survey: perceptions of District Assembly performance   256
5.22 Rank order of most frequently mentioned popular needs, by
     district   257
5.23 Rank order of most frequently mentioned needs, respondents
     with no formal education   259
5.24 Rank order of most frequently mentioned needs, by sex   259
5.25 East Akim District Council and Assembly: breakdown of
     development/capital expenditure 1986 – 1991   261
5.26 Mamprusi District Council/East Mamprusi District
     Assembly: breakdown of development/capital expenditure
     1986–1991   261
 6.1 Summary of measures of popular participation and
     relationships with elected councillors, by country   273
 6.2 Comparing popular performance assessments   283
 6.3 Factors explaining performance   290

Acknowledgements

This book could not have been written without the generous support of the British Overseas Development Administration (now the Department for International Development), through ESCOR, its committee on social and economic research. They first enabled us to do a full-scale examination of the secondary literature and to develop a proposal for field research. They then underwrote both our field investigations and our efforts to develop them into this detailed study.

A great many people provided us with vital help in the field and thereafter. It is impossible to mention them all, but it is essential to identify some. In Karnataka (India), we received valuable assistance from colleagues at the Institute for Social and Economic Change, Bangalore, many of whom have actively studied decentralisation for years. We are especially indebted to T. R. Satish Chandran, B. S. Bhargava, Abdul Aziz and G. K. Karanth. We received invaluable help from two institutions which provided research teams for grassroots survey work. The first was the Institute of Social Studies Trust, Bangalore, where Devaki Jain and Revathi Ramachandran gave generously of their time. The second was the Institute of Development Studies, University of Mysore where the Director, V. K. Natraj was immensely helpful.

We owe special thanks to E. Raghavan and his colleagues in the *Times of India* organisation, most crucially M. Ahiraj and M. B. Maramkal. M. Madan Mohan of *The Hindu* showed again why he is one of the most esteemed journalists in South India. Many civil servants who had worked in this system offered subtle, informative comment including Messrs Sreenivasa Murthy, A. Ramaswamy and the man who presided over Karnataka's decentralisation experiment, S. S. Meenakshisundaram. Others including L. C. Jain, George Mathew, Anand Inbanathan and David Arnold also offered generous assistance.

In Bangladesh, we were fortunate to be associated with the University of Dhaka and Talukder Maniruzzaman. Two institutions there provided teams of researchers for field studies. The first was the impressive non-governmental organisation, Proshika, where M. Shahabuddin and Farouque Ahmed were exceedingly helpful. The second was the Rural Development Academy, Bogra – most especially its Director, Ashrafuddin Ahmed. Two young men proved to be patient and perceptive translators – Nasir Hussain of Proshika in Manikganj and Tariq Ahmed in Bogra.

We are also indebted to colleagues at the National Institute of Local Government and the Bangladesh Institute of Development Studies – particularly Atiur Rahman. Mohammad Mohabbat Khan, Kamal Hussain and Minhaj Uddin Khan who offered valuable insights. We would have achieved far less in our field research without the crucial assistance of David Chiel of the Ford Foundation.

Our research in Ghana would not have been possible without the kind permission of the Ministry of Local Government and the co-operation of the University of Ghana. We should like to thank the PNDC Secretary for Local Government (as he then was), Mr Kwamena Ahwoi, for his interest and co-operation; also Mr K. Agama of the MLG Research Branch, and Mr K. Owusu of the Local Government Inspectorate. At the University we are particularly indebted to Professor K. Ninsin and Professor J. Ayee of the Department of Political Science and to Mr S. N. Woode (then Acting Director) and Dr S. Asibuo of the School of Administration. Other organisations which gave valuable assistance were the World Bank office in Accra, NORRIP (Gambaga) and the Baptist Medical Centre (Nalerigu). In Gambaga, the DAO and staff of the District Assembly gave unstintingly of their time and we are especially grateful to them and to our team of interviewers who cycled many miles and forded many rivers to complete the questionnaires! In Kibi, the Acting DAO, the District Treasurer and his staff were also most helpful and again we should like to thank our interviewers, some of whom had to endure difficult conditions in the remoter villages. Last but not least, thanks are due to Mr Kofi Asare of Royal Rentals, Accra, without whose driving, mechanical and diplomatic skills the field research could literally not have been accomplished.

In Côte d'Ivoire, we are grateful to the Ministry of Scientific Research which gave such prompt permission for the research and to the Ministry of Interior, in particular M. Koné (Sous-Directeur, Budgets) of the DGCL (Department of Local Government) who gave his full and friendly co-operation. Academically and organisationally, the research would not have been possible without the collaboration and assistance of colleagues at ORSTOM (Petit Bassam) who provided Dr Crook with a base for his work in Côte d'Ivoire. We should like to thank all of the staff there, and to give a special thanks to M. Bernard Contamin (Director of the Centre) and to Mme. Dominique Couret, who gave so generously of their time. Professor K. Nguessan at ENSEA provided invaluable assistance in the recruitment and training of interviewers and M. J. Saint-Vil of the DCGTx helped enormously with documentation. Other organisations which provided assistance, information and advice were the World Bank (West Africa HQ) in Abidjan, and USAid. In the four communes of Affery, Yakassé-Attobrou, Mbengué and Dikodougou it is impossible to mention all the different individuals who helped, but a special thanks should go in each case to the administrative staff, the mayors and assistant mayors of each commune for their time and their courtesy. We are also extremely grateful to Professor Richard Stren of the University of Toronto, Canada, whose willingness to share his unrivalled knowledge of Francophone local government and of the Côte d'Ivoire in particular, made the field trip in Côte d'Ivoire so much more profitable and pleasant.

Numerous colleagues outside our four case-study countries also helped us greatly. David Leonard assisted us in developing key concepts and a field research strategy. Harry Blair in America, William Miller (University of Glasgow), Kirsten Westergaard and Ole Therkildsen in Denmark, Alain Dubresson (University of Paris X) and Donal Cruise O'Brien (University of London) all offered vital assistance. Joel Barkan, Njuguna N'gethe and their colleagues in a Ford Foundation project assessing five African cases provided valuable comparative insights. We are also indebted to Mahmuda Khan for translations of documents in Bangla (Bengali), and to the researchers who helped us process our survey findings – Tessa Peasgood in Brighton and Ray MacDonald and James Murray in Glasgow.

Some parts of Chapters 4 and 5 were originally published in *Public Administration and Development*, 14 (1994), pp. 339–64 ('Four years of the Ghana District Assemblies in operation') and *Public Administration*, 74 (1996), pp. 695–720 ('Democracy, participation and responsiveness: a case-study of relations between the Ivorian communes and their citizens'). Some sections of Chapter 6 are based upon an article originally published in the *Journal of Commonwealth and Comparative Politics*, 33 (1995), pp. 309–34 ('Democratic decentralisation and institutional performance compared: four Asian and African experiences compared'). We are grateful to the editors of those journals for permission to reproduce this material.

1 Introduction

During the 1980s, many influential people in African, Asian and Latin American governments, in international development agencies, and in academic life became enthusiastic about decentralisation in less developed countries. A recent World Bank study noted that: 'out of 75 developing and transitional countries with populations greater than 5 million, all but 12 claim to be embarked on some form of transfer of political power to local units of government'.[1] The devolution of power, responsibility and sometimes resources on to democratically elected councils at local or intermediate levels appealed to very different sets of people who often disagreed on other issues. Economists who had been influenced by neo-liberal ideas saw it as a way of shifting power away from the centralised state which had discredited itself in their eyes through voracious rent-seeking and other abuses. Advocates of pluralist, competitive politics regarded it as a device for prying open closed systems, to give interest groups space in which to organise, compete and otherwise assert themselves. Enthusiasts for efforts by village communities to achieve things through co-operation rather than competition viewed it as a means to that end. The leaders of some autocratic regimes in Asia and Africa saw it as a substitute for democratisation at the national level, as a safe way to acquire much-needed legitimacy and grassroots support. Democratic politicians in less-developed countries regarded it as a way to make government more responsive to local needs and preferences. Taken together, these diverse groups represented a potent coalition for change.

It was in some ways surprising that decentralisation should arouse such interest, since an earlier wave of experiments with it in Africa and Asia had largely foundered a generation earlier. Beginning in the 1950s in South Asia and in the 1960s in Africa, various attempts had been made to 'bring government closer to the people' and to tap the creativity and resources of local communities by giving them the chance to

---

[1] Dillinger (1994), p. 8.

participate in development. But by the early 1970s, most of these initiatives had been vitiated by distrust and interference from above, and by infighting and shortages of resources and expertise in elected councils and local communities.

Some recent decentralisers have been unaware of these earlier episodes. Others have argued that those problems could be overcome if more genuine and generous efforts to decentralise were made. Enough had gone wrong with centralised governments to make people want to believe this. In the 1980s, unlike the 1960s, every sort of critique of the state – Friedmanite, Gandhian or whatever – seemed plausible.[2] In this new climate, it was not hard to believe that decentralisation combined with democratisation (usually in its electoral, representative form) might provide greater transparency, accountability, responsiveness, probity, frugality, efficiency, equity and opportunities for mass participation – or enough of these to justify fresh attempts at reform. Decentralisation deserved another chance.[3] Nor has interest in decentralisation abated. At this writing, both the World Bank and the US Agency for International Development (USAID) have launched major investigations of decentralisation in both its democratic and purely fiscal and administrative forms. Perhaps because of the collapse of Communism, however, the potential contributions of decentralisation to the enhancement of participation, good governance and democratisation have received most emphasis, pushing the more long-standing concern with its role in economic development into second place.

Our research sought to determine empirically how realistic these various expectations about decentralisation were. At the outset, we neither shared nor dismissed these. Decentralisation, after all, does not even necessarily imply democracy. The outcomes of a decentralisation policy will depend not just on the relative weights of devolution and deconcentration in the institutional and fiscal structures, but also on their combination with two other important elements: the kind of legitimation and accountability adopted (e.g., participatory, electoral, religious, monarchical) and the principles according to which the area (and hence size and character) of a decentralised authority are determined. We therefore selected for close study four recent cases of

---

[2] See Jain (1993) for a statement of the communitarian Gandhian view; Olowu and Wunsch (1990) Ostrom (1989) Ostrom *et al.* (1993), and Bennett (1990, 1994) for 'New Right' views based on public choice theory.

[3] See, for example, the argument that there is a close connection between the policy objective of 'good government' (defined as government which has the capacity to build and sustain an 'enabling environment' for economic development) and decentralisation, in: Healey and Robinson (1992); Moore (1993); World Bank (1989, 1992).

decentralisation, all specifically based on the principle of *representative* democracy, with elected councils and executives but differing in their institutional character according to three criteria: the scope of their devolved powers, the mix of deconcentration with locally accountable administration, and scale or closeness to the grassroots. Because of the world-wide character of the 'second wave' it was considered desirable to select cases from at least two of the great continental groupings of less-developed countries, sub-Saharan Africa and South Asia. This allowed us to make comparisons, of a kind only rarely attempted, of the experiences of democratic decentralisation across these very different political, socio-economic and cultural worlds. Our aim was to assess how these different systems performed in practice.

Our four cases, chosen according to these criteria, were Bangladesh, the Indian state of Karnataka, Ghana and Côte d'Ivoire. In each of these areas, it was possible to study democratic decentralisation in action within the same time-frame, since in each place a new system of elected councils standing somewhere above the village level was created in the mid- or late 1980s. In each case, the new councils were fully operational and obtained one or two electoral mandates between the mid-1980s and 1992 or later.

Ghana (in 1989) and Karnataka (in 1987) each introduced a system which has become increasingly common in Asia and Africa in recent years – the 'mixed' authority which combines deconcentration of central ministries with democratic control by an authority invested with varying degrees of devolved revenue-raising powers. Such a system dissolves the Anglophone distinction between local government and field offices of central ministries, by allocating the central agencies and their staff to a single governmental authority for the agreed territorial divisions of the state. It aspires both to solve the traditional problem of lack of good quality staff for local government, and to decentralise planning and budgeting. Ghana's District Assemblies were based (with some subdivisions) on the existing administrative districts with populations of between 100,000 and 240,000 (except for the big city Metropolitan Assemblies). The Karnataka District Councils (*zilla parishads* – also based on existing administrative districts) were authorities for populations averaging around two million people, but were the superior tier of a two-tier system based on local councils (*mandal panchayats*) with average populations of between 8,000 and 12,000 people.

In both Ghana and Karnataka, rural society is well organised and politically conscious, being rooted in a relatively prosperous and commercialised peasant agriculture. But these societies are set in very different political contexts. The former has a history of extreme instability and alternating civil and military rule, whilst the latter has long experienced liberal, stable multi-party politics.

In Ghana, the revolutionary military government of Jerry Rawlings transformed itself into a party-based civilian regime after multi-party elections at the end of 1992. The District Assemblies elected in 1989 remained in office until after the inauguration of the new government, and the main outlines of the decentralised system were incorporated into the 1992 Constitution. Minor changes were made to the structure of the District Assemblies by the Local Government Act of 1993 in order to reflect the more democratic spirit of the new regime, and a second set of elections took place in 1994.

In Karnataka, the District Councils and the lower-level Mandal Councils were elected in January 1987 and continued through a five-year term. They were then effectively suspended at the end of 1991 by a new state government, pending new legislation to bring the state laws into conformity with a 1993 amendment to the Indian Constitution.

In Bangladesh the system adopted in 1985 was a much more restricted version of deconcentration with local democratic control, and was part of an attempt by H. M. Ershad's military regime to gain legitimacy and to build its own mass party, the Jatiyo Party. The Bangladesh experiment was to show that substantial local democratic control was feasible even under an authoritarian national regime. A broad range of relatively low-level functions were deconcentrated to the main sub-District Councils (*upazila parishads*) which had only minimal revenue-raising powers and were in practice dependent upon (very generous) central financing and staff allocated from line ministries. The sub-District Councils, with average populations of around 245,000, were indirectly elected from the lower-tier Union Councils based on areas with around 20,000 inhabitants, but their chairmen were directly elected by all voters in the sub-district. The cautious character of the reform was perhaps related to a social context of extreme inequality combined with mobilised conflict and a history of political instability. After the fall of Ershad and the election to power of the Bangladesh National Party in 1991, the sub-District Councils were abolished and power was reconcentrated in the new, indirectly elected District Councils. But the lower-tier Union Councils continue more or less unchanged, at least in legal terms.

Côte d'Ivoire is unusual in that it presents one of the few current examples in Africa and Asia of a devolved local government system. Set firmly within the Francophone tradition of a highly centralised prefectoral administration with supervisory powers, Côte d'Ivoire's rural communes based on single settlements or small towns are nevertheless intended to be legally quite separate from the central government

Introduction 5

machinery. They do not have control over any deconcentrated central line ministries or agencies. Because of their small scale and community basis (the average commune created by the 1985 reforms has a population of 16,000), they are important as an example of a local government authority very close to the grassroots.

Unlike Ghana and Bangladesh, the Ivorian communes created in 1985 were introduced into a political context of stable single-party rule and were associated initially with an attempt at political renewal and liberalisation within the ruling party.[4] The new communes survived the 1990 political crisis which ushered in multi-party elections (very few of which were won by the opposition) and a second set of competitive elections was successfully carried out in early 1996, with similar results. In 1993, the country also coped peacefully with the death of President Houphouët-Boigny, ruler for nearly forty years, when the presidency passed to his constitutionally designated successor, the Speaker of the National Assembly, Henri Konan Bédié.

THE RESEARCH DESIGN

The principal aim of the study was to investigate three specific questions in each of the selected countries. First, how had patterns of popular political participation changed as a result of decentralisation? Second, how had the performance of governmental institutions changed? Finally, were changes in participation and changes in institutional performance interrelated, or were other factors such as the form of decentralisation more important in explaining performance? It was expected that comparison amongst the four countries would help to illuminate the final question, whilst recognising the inevitable limitations of using such a small number of widely varying cases to explain an outcome as complex and multi-causal as institutional performance.

Although our unit of analysis was, therefore, the legally constituted, decentralised authority within each system our approach was, by necessity, that of the 'comparative case-oriented method'.[5] We therefore carried out a detailed study of the context, institutions and processes of democratisation and decentralisation in each case, aimed at establishing configurations or patterns of relationships amongst the main variables identified for study within each country. (Such an analysis virtually

---

[4] The first stage of the communalisation reform in 1980 created thirty-seven fully democratised communes, including ten in the City of Abidjan; the total number leapt to 135 in 1985 with the creation of 98 new authorities covering most of the small towns of the interior.
[5] Ragin (1987).

requires that the researchers are already well acquainted with the history and culture of the cases; Richard Crook was therefore responsible for the studies of Ghana and Côte d'Ivoire, and James Manor for the studies of Karnataka and Bangladesh.) It is an approach particularly well suited to grappling with the undoubted causal complexity of any supposed connection between democratic decentralisation and the beneficial outcomes expected by its advocates. Most crucially, it recognises that the outcomes of different forms of decentralisation are likely to be explicable only by combinations of a multiplicity of factors.

Having established combinations of causes in each case, any subsequent comparison using this method proceeds by first establishing types of outcome – in our case, positive or negative performance ratings – and then looking either for similar patterns of factors associated with particular outcomes, or, more revealing, for a particular combination associated with a clearly different or 'deviant' outcome.[6] In this way the method avoids attempts to make direct comparisons of measures derived from different systems, which may not be equivalent because of a host of contextual factors.[7] Clearly, no findings of statistical significance can be generated by such comparisons; at the most, they can generate hypotheses or suggested explanations which are persuasive to the extent that other experts with knowledge of different cases can find useful parallels and insights. Although the comparative analysis developed in our conclusion (Chapter 6) is therefore inevitably limited by the cases upon which it is based, it does, we argue, have a more general interest and application.

In order to facilitate comparisons amongst our cases, we not only asked the same questions but used the same concepts and a similar methodology, with measures adapted to local circumstances. We also developed a model of what we expected would be the relationship between participation and other relevant factors on the one hand, and institutional performance on the other.

Our key terms and concepts are defined in the following way: *decentralisation* within government is taken to mean a transfer of power away from a central authority to lower levels in a territorial hierarchy. It can take two forms, deconcentration and devolution, each of which has a different logic. Deconcentration tends to extend the scope or reach of central government and to strengthen its authority by moving executive agencies controlled by the centre down to lower levels in the political system. In other words, with deconcentration, the central government is

---

[6] Cf. the comparative study of decentralisation by Graham (1991) in which cases are grouped into types by outcome.
[7] Cf. Ashford (1975); Mayer (1989).

not giving up any authority; it is simply *relocating* its officers at different levels or points in the national territory.[8] Devolution has the opposite effect, since it cedes control of such agencies and resources to political actors and institutions at lower levels. It is always a form of power-sharing between central government and sub-national authorities.[9] A devolved authority is granted legal personality and legally defined areas of competence within which it has autonomy to tax and spend, and may even have limited or minor legislative competence. Some of the systems that we studied are in practice mixtures of these structural principles.

Participation is defined as citizens' active engagement with public institutions, an activity which falls into three well-defined modes: voting, election campaigning, and contacting or pressuring either individually or through group activity,[10] including non-violent protests.[11] We exclude attitudes towards participation from our definition, which some others include, because – for the sake of conceptual clarity – attitudes are best seen as sources of participation (or as impediments to it) rather than as forms of participation.[12] We also exclude 'participation in rural development efforts'.[13] We do so because we focus on representative institutions which, while they often mount rural development projects, often provide a range of services and exercise governmental authority. So when we speak of active engagement with these representative institutions, we refer to something which stands adjacent to 'participation in development efforts' – indeed, there is a limited amount of overlap between them – but for the most part, it is not the same thing. Participation in the 'benefits'[14] which flow from decentralisation is excluded, partly because we regard it as a passive experience that fails to qualify as an 'activity', and partly because it cannot influence government institutions. More importantly, including it would be illogical, given the design of our research project. Our main concern is the interaction of participation and institutional performance, and the benefits which flow from institutions need to be placed on the 'performance' side of the ledger.

---

[8] Smith (1985), p. 11.   [9] Mawhood (1991).
[10] We drew most heavily here upon the *locus classicus* for the study of political participation (Verba, Nie and Kim (1978)). We also make much use of another valuable source (Parry and Moyser (1992)). For a fully developed discussion of our concepts, the literature and our research methods, see Crook and Manor (1991), and the Methodological Appendix.
[11] Verba *et al.* exclude it. We include it for reasons similar to those given in Parry and Moyser (1992), p. 18.
[12] See Parry and Moyser (1992), pp. 46–7. They do not mention attitudes' potential role as impediments to participation. See also Huntington and Nelson (1976), pp. 4–5, on how the study of attitudes requires different research techniques from those needed to study activities or behaviour.
[13] Cohen and Uphoff (1977), p. 6.   [14] Cohen and Uphoff (1977), p. 7.

In addition, we include directly taking part in community-level activities in so far as they articulate with the representative, communicatory or feedback structures of the local government authorities. Where relevant, therefore, we view willingness to pay taxes or local levies as an input on the participation side, although clearly there is a reciprocal or feedback relationship between performance and willingness to contribute (see below). Finally, we look at the scope of participation, in terms both of the social composition of participants and of the absolute numbers involved, and at whether greater power to affect particular issues is available to citizens.[15]

Changes in the *performance* of decentralised institutions have tended to be studied principally in terms of financial performance or revenue mobilisation.[16] Our focus, by contrast, was much more on their performance *as organisations*, both internally and in relation to their public outputs. The concept of institutional performance is, however, widely recognised to be both multi-dimensional and difficult to measure.[17]

Both local and central government administration in the industrialised countries have witnessed an enormous growth over the past decade in the use of formal and highly elaborated 'performance indicators'.[18] But such devices cannot be imposed by external researchers in the absence of internal collection and monitoring systems which assume a well-founded and well-resourced administrative machine. In this study, we are dealing with institutions which frequently lack even the most basic 'bureaucratic hygiene', let alone the middle management and technostructure necessary for routine collection of statistics purporting to measure the quantity or quality of outputs.[19] (Even where such a capability exists, serious problems have arisen from the temptation to 'measure the measurable' or to manipulate results in order to create 'self-fulfilling prophecies'.[20]) For these reasons we eschew any attempt to use internally generated performance indicators to measure output effectiveness. The 'low technology, low resources' context of rural government in poor countries demands instead relatively simple measures of achievement which, it may be argued, are adequate in situations where what is usually at stake is the

---

[15] We therefore pay attention to changes in participation rates among vulnerable groups – notably poor, low-status groups and women. We consider attempts at designing decentralisation to encourage 'broadened' participation, and the success of those attempts, which mainly occurred in India.
[16] See, for instance Smoke and Olowu (1992); Thomas (1987); Sanda *et al.* (1989); Blair (1989).
[17] See, for instance, the interesting discussion in Chapter 3 of Putnam (1993).
[18] See Likierman (1988); Schick (1990).
[19] Leonard (1987); Moris (1991); Uphoff (1986); Dichter (1989).
[20] Leonard and Prewitt (1974); Burkhead and Hannigan (1978); Likierman (1988).

Introduction 9

difference between *no* provision and *some* provision of a school, clinic or feeder road.[21]

Our analysis of performance is therefore organised according to three heuristic sub-categories: *effectiveness, responsiveness* and *process*.[22] *Effectiveness* is narrowly defined in our study as the quantity of tangible 'outputs' (development projects and services) measured in relation both to official objectives or targets and to previous (pre-reform) levels of output.[23] It therefore includes an assessment of whether the pattern of resource allocations reflects the priorities implied by official goals or functions. Organisational factors such as the role commitment of officials, internal accountability mechanisms and budgetary processes are likely to be important as explanatory factors for this dimension of performance in so far as they help to explain what gives an institution the *capacity to be* effective.[24]

'Total performance measurement' nevertheless requires some assessment of the quality and impact of even the very limited, mainly infrastructural outputs with which we were concerned.[25] The problems experienced with the validity of quantitative output measures in the industrialised countries ('number of arrests per policeman', 'number of potholes filled') have led many administrative theorists to advocate public or 'client group' assessments, or the 'perceived quality' of outputs as the most reliable way of judging this aspect of performance.[26] This shifts the focus to the question of the extent to which the activities or expenditures of a public institution are valued by the public, and underlies our choice of the concept of *responsiveness*.

Under the heading of *responsiveness* we investigate not just the degree of congruence between community preferences (citizens' perceived needs)

---

[21] As Leonard and Marshall put it: 'The important thing is to do the job' (Leonard and Marshall (1982)); see also Maddock (1990).

[22] See Robbins (1990); Harmon and Mayer (1986); Hatry (1978). Efficiency is normally included as a fourth sub-category, but this was excluded from our study because of the technical difficulty of establishing the production functions necessary to measure the ratios of inputs to outputs; see: Israel (1987); Likierman (1988). Some analysts are in any case sceptical of the possibility of establishing reliable efficiency measures for public service bodies because of the difficulty posed by 'multiple reciprocal externalities' (Burkhead and Hannigan (1978)).

[23] Cf. Blunt *et al.* (1989).

[24] Blunt *et al.* (1989); Uphoff (1986); Moris (1991).

[25] Hatry (1978); Marsden and Oakley (1990); Schick (1990).

[26] Becker and Selwyn (1975); Brudney and England (1982); Burkhead and Hannigan (1978); Carter (1991); Harmon and Mayer (1986); Hatry (1978); Rose and Peters (1981); Schick (1990). As Becker and Selwyn observe, this is the only way to compare the 'quality' of services of a very different nature such as a state opera house and a rubbish collection service. Otherwise one could end up comparing 'tons of garbage collected' with 'number of arias sung in tune'.

and government policies,[27] but also the issue of which sections of the community are being responded to. We also pay attention to the speed and quality of responses from government.

The *process* dimension concerns means rather than ends. Here we look at the legal and political norms embodied in the modes of operation of decentralised institutions. It is an element of performance in so far as the levels of fairness, probity, transparency, due process and political accommodation embodied in institutional procedures form an important part of public perceptions of the value and quality of those institutions.[28] Although difficult to study, it is very important, for instance, when judging the way in which officials of decentralised institutions deal with members of the public when providing services, implementing consultation procedures or dealing with grievances. Corrupt or oppressive behaviour by officials, even a tendency to adhere to the letter rather the spirit of the law, are factors which can undermine public acceptance of the legitimacy of a local government authority. Internal procedures for allocating resources and imposing taxes must also be accepted by the public as legitimate and fair, otherwise there may be adverse consequences for performance in the areas of resource mobilisation and public willingness to support the programmes of the government. Ultimately the legitimacy of an authority derives from the manner of its creation and we therefore also look at the fairness of the elections which ushered in these new decentralised institutions.

Using the above concepts, we developed a model of the main factors which might determine institutional performance, attempting first of all to isolate and focus on our principal interest – the *impact of democratic participation on the performance of decentralised institutions*. We theorised the relationship between participation and performance principally in terms of *notions of accountability*.

Administrative theorists have always emphasised that bureaucratic performance is to a large extent related to the effectiveness of mechanisms for encouraging or sanctioning organisational commitment and role performance.[29] The variety of ways in which officials can be held responsible for their actions has been summarised by Thynne and Goldring into a four-fold typology of external and internal/ formal and

---

[27] Fried (1980), p. 7.
[28] We draw here on Harmon and Mayer (1986), p. 43; our concept of process is different from that used by Putnam, who defines it as the efficiency of internal organisational procedures as measured by such indicators as promptness in agreeing budget estimates Putnam (1993), p. 67.
[29] See, for instance Blau and Scott (1963), p. 163; Dunsire (1978), pp. 26–7; Harmon and Mayer (1986), p. 47; Blunt *et al.* (1989, 1990).

informal modes of accountability.[30] But accountability to 'external actors', who can control behaviour through political, legal or intra-organisational means, emerges from the literature as one of the most favoured methods of ensuring good institutional performance. O'Loughlin even operationalises the term accountability as the 'degree of responsiveness to external actors', whilst Moris emphasises the importance of an 'agency ideology', *combined with* realistic objectives and accountability to client groups.[31]

The impact of participation in a representative democracy is mediated most obviously through elections, which impose very general public accountabilities on elected representatives who have to submit their record to the electorate at periodic intervals – and, in addition, may have to report back to or meet with electors on a regular basis between elections. At the institutional level, however, elections create a more intense formal accountability by rendering bureaucrats responsible to elected officials and to political bodies which, depending on their social and political character, can be crucial in maintaining commitment to 'goal-directed actions' (implementing policy). More subtly, they can influence the development of internal and informal modes of accountability, based either on specific organisational commitments or various political and social norms including, at their very broadest, the idea of 'public service'. Indeed, some analysts of the problems of Third World bureaucracies have argued that their central problem is the lack of a legitimate and respected political class genuinely rooted in the society and capable of exercising a disciplined control over the administration.[32]

Whatever the problems which political control may bring in terms of possible conflict with professional or legal-rational norms, the responsiveness aspect of performance is undeniably connected to the existence of such social and political articulations between administration and society. There is no guarantee that even the most appropriate and autonomous formal structures and the most plentiful resources will be translated into better performance unless those in charge of the new

---

[30] Thynne and Goldring (1987), p. 11.
[31] O'Loughlin (1990), p. 282; Moris (1991). Smith (1991) notes that many elements of the Thynne and Goldring model are likely to be absent in developing countries, where external public controls are weakly developed and internal mechanisms are vitiated by clientelism, or excessive formalism; cf. Jabbra and Dwivedi (1989), Chapter 9.
[32] Koehn (1990), p. 295) writes: 'making bureaucracy more responsive in Nigeria awaits the arrival of informed, reliable, forceful and effective representation of the rural and urban poor'. It might be added that in countries with a relatively effective administration the political elite is also committed to technocratic values; cf. Crook (1989), p. 225; Leonard (1991); T. Smith (1991).

authorities are more responsive to popular needs and can actually ensure the implementation of those more sensitive or appropriate policies. Recent empirical work in the Third World field suggests that the emphasis of mainstream or 'Western' public administration theory on 'representative bureaucracy' has little relevance in such a context. What is required are precise mechanisms of accountability linking bureaucrats and elected officials to the public who, in the case of decentralised or local administration, are a specific and readily identifiable client group.[33]

Using these theories of accountability, we therefore investigated the connection between participation and performance by tracing empirically the extent to which the demand for accountability affected institutional processes and behaviour and hence institutional policies and outputs. Our principal hypothesis was that the quality of accountability relationships would have a crucial impact on performance at two levels: first, relations between elected representatives and the public, and second, relations between local bureaucrats, other government agencies and executive officials on the one hand, and elected representatives on the other. We also expected a feedback effect between performance and willingness to participate, particularly in the African cases where there was an emphasis on local resource mobilisation combined with a very negative history of local government.

In addition, we attempted to isolate the impact of the democratisation reforms on performance by making *longitudinal comparisons* between participation and performance indicators immediately before and after the introduction of democratic decentralisation in each country.[34] This was possible since democratic decentralisation was a specific reform associated either with a transformation of existing authorities or with the creation of new ones in the mid- to late 1980s.

Our primary interest in the impact of participation on performance was situated within a more general model, according to which we systematically considered the political and social context, the formal administrative, legal and political structures of decentralised institutions and their relationships with higher levels of the political system, and resources including administrative capacity and funding systems.

The *degree of social and political mobilisation* in a country (or strength of civil society) is manifested in such features as the number of parties and associations, whether there is free electoral or party competition, a

---

[33] Uphoff (1986), p. 202.
[34] Cf. Ragin (1987), p. 73; the 'interrupted time series design' is discussed by Collier (1991), p. 19, and Casley and Lury (1982).

free press and so on. These, when linked with broader cultural or social expectations concerning the behaviour of holders of political or bureaucratic power, can have a determining impact on the extent to which newly elected decentralised authorities are monitored and held accountable to the public. Social structures at the local level also have an obvious relevance to the empirical question of whether the introduction of electoral politics reinforces or challenges the dominance of local elites, both economic and social.[35]

The *political context* refers both to the nature of the regime and to the political objectives underlying the creation of a decentralised system. These are usually the determining factors in the choice of what kind of decentralised system is adopted – for instance, the degree to which the system is predominantly one of deconcentration or devolution, the scale and the principles according to which the areas of the new authorities are delimited, the scope of the functions allocated, the resources granted, and the methods by which councils and executive authorities are chosen. The extent to which the national political elite wishes to gain the support of local elites, and whether those elites are antagonistic to demands for popular empowerment may determine the degree of autonomy given to the new local authorities.[36] Military regimes in particular may go for support-building exercises in which they want the 'benefits of popular participation without paying the costs of power-sharing'.[37] The general political context is also relevant in so far as it determines economic policy and the state of public finances; the existence of a Structural Adjustment Programme or of severe retrenchment in the public service is bound to have an impact on the fate of a decentralisation reform.

Once decided upon, the *formal structure of the decentralised system* is likely to have an impact on a number of factors important to performance, such as administrative and technical capacities, costs, the degree to which accountability and legitimacy can be established, resources, managerial and budgetary autonomy and even the 'implementability' of the

---

[35] Although our emphasis on the interaction between civil society and political institutions has some similarities with the 'social capital' theory used by Robert Putnam and his colleagues to analyse the differences between regional governments in Italy (Putnam (1993), p. 199), our analysis focuses more on the traditions and the characteristics of political institutions in each country than it does on 'social capital' *per se* (see our comparative conclusions in Chapter 6).

[36] Leonard and Marshall (1982), pp. 15–20; Smith (1985), p. 191.

[37] Mawhood (1983), p. 252. Barkan and Chege even propose that in ethnically plural underdeveloped countries there is a systematic relationship between the power base of the regime and the probability that decentralisation will serve its interests. Thus an ethnic minority regime of 'have nots' is likely to favour a deconcentrated form of decentralisation in order to enforce ethno-regional redistribution (Barkan and Chege (1989), p. 21).

reform itself. These structural factors can be broken down into the following more specific elements:

(i) The size and 'level' of the new authorities (in relation to the existing system of territorial administration) are likely to have an important effect on their administrative and revenue viability, and also on accountability factors such as the closeness of relations between representatives and the population, the number of competing communities represented, and the status and power of elected officials in relation to bureaucrats.

(ii) The mix of deconcentrated and devolved administrative institutions will affect the degree to which there are problems of multiple, competing hierarchies and hence can also affect managerial efficiency, administrative capacity, staff morale and commitment.

(iii) The sufficiency of the resources available to a newly decentralised system is one of the most important of factors likely to affect performance. It is most directly a function of the financial and fiscal arrangements set up to fund the new authorities, although the macro-economic situation and the local resource base also matter. In all our cases (as more generally with decentralised systems outside wealthy urban centres), it was clear that the *adequacy* of resources was overwhelmingly determined by central government decisions on transferred funds – even in cases where local resource mobilisation was supposed to play an important role. We therefore paid particular attention to the extent to which the funding system provided assured stability of financing, and autonomy in the access to and management of funds.

(iv) Whatever the level of resources, a further factor arising from the structure of the decentralised system is the degree of budgetary, managerial and political autonomy enjoyed at the operational level by any particular authority. This autonomy is a function of variations in the tightness of the political, legal and administrative controls normally exercised by central government. These variations can have an important influence on performance in so far as they limit the *capacity* of an authority to pursue local objectives, provide services and, especially, respond to local demands.

(v) Differences in the method of electing both councils and executives can have an important impact on the quality of the accountability which develops between councillors and the public on the one hand, and between councils, the executive and bureaucrats on the other. The impact of electoral systems on the character of local councils can also affect the way allocative decisions are made and thus the process dimension of performance.

METHODOLOGY

Our measures of participation and performance were based on a wide range of indicators, collected using a variety of complementary methods. In each of the four countries we selected a small number of local authorities for intensive case study. (The method of selection and the character of the authorities chosen are described in the first part of each country chapter.) In each of our local case studies we pursued field inquiries at two levels: semi-structured elite interviews and surveys among ordinary citizens and community leaders at the grassroots.[38] The elite interviews were conducted with elected councillors, bureaucrats who oversee and work with or under the councils, and with other elite informants knowledgeable about council affairs. At the institutional level, qualitative analyses were made of the participation of elected representatives in council business and of the extent to which they could either monitor, sanction or exercise executive power. This information was obtained by observation, by studying documents concerning council activities, and by gathering case histories of particular projects, local issues and conflicts – in short, by making a full study of the local political context. Such information on local politics enabled us to make qualitative judgements on the operation of local institutions and on their relationships with the electorate.

We also developed a method of gathering information at the grassroots which enabled us to supplement and, at times, to correct elite-level misperceptions and misrepresentations.[39] After randomly selecting groups of villages in each of our local authority areas, stratified according to their degree of remoteness, we administered a common questionnaire to both a representative quota sample of ordinary villagers and to a smaller sample of community or opinion leaders in each village. On the participation side, we asked respondents to recall specific occasions on which they or their neighbours had engaged in various types of participation. Using replies from 2,030 interviews, we developed a profile of participation telling us who participated, how and how much they participated, and how effective the participation of various groups had been. We asked them these questions about the period before democratic decentralisation took place, and about the period after. This revealed how patterns of participation had changed after the creation of elected, decentralised councils.

On institutional performance, we asked villagers for information

[38] For a fuller discussion of all of this, see the Methodological Appendix.
[39] We adapted a method developed by David Leonard and Fenno Ogutu at the University of California (Ogutu (1989)).

about specific development projects undertaken in their villages by governmental institutions – again in the periods before and after decentralisation. What types of projects were undertaken? How many were undertaken and completed and how long did completion take? How much influence did ordinary villagers or organised interests at the village level have on such projects? We asked them about service provisions and invited them to talk about what they themselves felt to be the main development priorities of their communities. We also sought more general comments on how local people perceived the performance of the new authorities. The answers to these questions revealed much about governmental outputs and the responsiveness of institutions. This combination of methods enabled us to gather data for a range of measures upon which we could base our assessment of changes in participation and changes in performance. Our *measures of participation* can be grouped into the following areas:

(i) Electoral participation

In each country, elections were held to set up the new authorities, followed in most cases by second or even third sets of elections as determined by events at the national level or the formal expiry of terms of office. We gathered official and unofficial statistics on turnout and competitiveness, comparing the results in our local case studies with previous local and national elections and with national aggregate data. We also noted rates of renewal or turnover of office-holders, taking this as a measure of the degree to which popular dissatisfaction with the record of local councils was able to express itself. The popular survey provided figures on the percentage of respondents who said they had joined in campaigning for candidates, an activity which we took as evidence of a high level of participatory zeal.

(ii) Direct contacting or pressuring activities

Our survey data was the main source of measures of the extent to which individual citizens actively engaged with local political institutions, either as individuals or through a group activity. At the group level, we used two main measures: (a) the percentage of respondents who had attended an official consultation meeting organised by their local representative, or who had attended a community-level institution such as a village council, village development committee, or other meeting organised by the political authorities (these institutions took various forms in the different countries); (b) the percentage of respondents who had attended

Introduction 17

an 'unofficial' meeting whose purpose was to raise a public issue or problem. The significance of these simple attendance measures was deepened by asking whether attenders at such meetings had been able to make a contribution.[40] For participation of a more individual kind, we used a further two measures: (a) the percentage of respondents who had contacted either an elected representative, a council official or an official of any other government agency to raise a problem, and (b) the percentage who had signed a letter or petition.

(iii) Indirect participation

We expected that much of the active participation such as attendance at meetings would take place within the context of, or be organised by, particular associations or groups as well as by more general community organisations. We therefore measured the extent of our respondents' associational membership, supplementing this information with local case-history material on the activities of various groups and parties.

(iv) The relationship between elected representatives and their constituents

An essential element in both encouraging and sustaining active participation by citizens in local public affairs is the quality of the relationship between elected representatives and the electorate. To what extent are representatives known by the population and regularly in touch with them? How do representatives see their own role, and how are they judged by their constituents? Our three principal measures here were: (a) assessments of the frequency of councillors' meetings with their constituents, drawn from three different sources – interviews with councillors themselves, the popular survey and the community elites survey. In the case of the popular survey, we interpreted a majority of respondents agreeing that councillors met with them at least once since they had been elected (i.e. with a frequency greater than zero), to be a positive sign; (b) the extent to which representatives were known by their constituents, as tested by a simple knowledge rating – the percentage of respondents who could give the name of their councillor (or, in the Ivorian communes, the mayor and/or a councillor); (c) the contacting indicators already mentioned under (ii), which were used to measure this relationship as well.

---

[40] Two other minor measures of group activity were taking part in protests or demonstrations and holding a meeting to thank representatives.

(v) The character and scope of participation

We were particularly interested to discover whether democratic decentralised government had helped to broaden the scope of participation to include hitherto disadvantaged or marginalised groups such as the poor, younger age groups, women, inhabitants of remoter or more rural areas and (in India) lower castes. All of the above indicators could therefore be broken down by demographic criteria of age, sex, socio-economic status, area and caste to give measures of the character of those participating. In addition, we analysed the socio-economic composition of elected councils and office-holders in order to assess their representativeness in terms of locality, interest group and the foregoing demographic criteria. Finally, we made qualitative analyses of the extent to which representatives of 'disadvantaged groups' (in so far as they could be identified) played an active role in the affairs of the new councils or associated lower-tier institutions.

Our *measures of performance* were grouped into the following sub-categories:

(i) Output effectiveness

We used a combination of official budgetary data, where available, and survey material to generate two sets of measures of output. (a) Patterns and trends of actual revenues and expenditures for each case-study authority were collected, and then compared with official objectives (legal, planned, budgetary or other) and with the expenditures patterns of the immediately preceding forms of local administration. Where the data were sufficient (which was not always the case) these figures enabled us to determine whether there had been improvements in overall levels of development and/or service expenditure, and whether patterns of allocation had changed. (b) The village surveys provided evidence on the numbers and types of actual projects commenced in those particular villages; identification by respondents of the source of funding of these projects yielded an 'unofficial' measure of the extent to which the new decentralised authorities had actually implemented projects at the village level, compared to the previous system or to other agencies or sources of development finance.

(ii) Responsiveness

The main focus of our performance assessment was on responsiveness, defined as the degree of congruence between policies, outputs and popular preferences. Our four main measures of this aspect of performance were: (a) a rank ordering of popular preferences, derived from respondents' own assessments of what they considered to be the main development needs of their areas. These popular priorities were compared with official policies and with the actual output record of the case-study authorities; (b) respondents' answers to the general question of whether they considered the new system to be an improvement on the previous one; (c) the percentage of respondents giving a positive answer to the question of whether they felt the new council could satisfy their (expressed) needs; (d) satisfaction ratings in respect of particular projects mentioned in particular villages. A fifth, additonal set of measures concerned the extent to which the role commitment of council staff had improved as demonstrated by the speediness and effectiveness of job performance, reductions in absenteeism, and the willingness of councils to discipline staff in response to public complaints. Data for these measures were derived from elite interviews with senior officials, absenteeism rates (where available), popular survey assessments and documentary sources.

(iii)   Process

Assessing and measuring such a concept (as defined here) inevitably involved elements of subjective judgement as well as reliance on qualitative information. The issue of corruption, for instance, was clearly relevant to whether the procedures of the new councils and the behaviour of their officials were considered fair and legitimate. Measuring actual corruption was dependent upon 'insider' information. But how it was perceived by the electorate was susceptible to measurement by questions in our surveys. Our measures of the quality of institutional procedure therefore included the following types of data: (a) the percentage of respondents who considered the electoral process to have been free and fair; (b) the answers given by those who had engaged in contacting activities to the question of whether they found representatives or government officials 'fair and helpful'; (c) qualitative or case-history data on the extent to which services and project implementation were speedier under the democratised authorities; and (d) case-history and financial data on the extent to which local people were willing to contribute to official development efforts, either through paying local levies or taxes, or contributing their time and labour.

The kind of information which we obtained from these methods of research is seldom if ever available even to people in decentralised institutions. By conducting our inquiries at both the elite and the popular levels, we were able to expose the links between popular participation, actual development effort at the village level and institutional processes. We could then assess whether changes in institutional performance were mainly produced by changes in participation, by changes in intra-organisational relationships, or by other factors.

THE STRUCTURE OF THE ARGUMENT

In each country chapter we first consider, under the heading of 'popular participation', accountability to the electorate through the analysis of both elections and the quality of inter-election contacts between representatives and their constituents. After assessing the extent to which the level and the social character of popular participation have changed, we ask, how much consultation and contact is there between councillors and the public? To what extent are they capable of expressing or representing public demands, and from which sections of the public in particular? Are legally prescribed mechanisms of report-back and accountability working? Do the public have any knowledge of or interest in the decentralised system? If accountability at this level fails, then there is little hope of democratic participation in a representative democracy having much impact on institutional performance. This is the beginning of the process through which greater power to affect local issues becomes available to citizens.

Second, under the heading of 'representation through institutions', we examine the extent to which elected representatives or elected officials were able to express popular demands and translate them into policies and outputs. The functioning of the new bonds of accountability at the institutional level is traced by assessing changes (for better or worse) in the role commitments of officials, and by examining the working relationships between elected councillors and the executive (both official and elected). We follow the processes of policy-making, budgeting and planning and attempt to establish the extent to which councillors are able to influence these processes and to monitor and sanction policy implementation by the executive. We also show how aspects of the decentralised structure itself – dual or triple hierarchies, relations between different tiers of the local system, rivalries between different officials, the degree of financial or fiscal autonomy of the new authorities and the power of the central civil service – can all affect the establishment of genuine local accountability.

In the third part of each chapter, we measure and assess institutional performance, subdivided into our three sub-categories of effectiveness, responsiveness and process. Our purpose here is to measure, using tests which are independent of our analysis of accountability mechanisms, the quantities of outputs, the degree to which patterns of resource allocation are responsive to popular demands and the extent to which locally acceptable norms of due process are observed. We then assess and give a rating to the overall performance of each decentralised system, on the basis of whether it is an improvement on the previous system which it replaced, our responsiveness ratings and popular judgements of its record (see above for a description of the measures used). Finally, we attempt to explain the performance rating by relating it to our analyses of participation, accountability processes, and the other factors considered in our analytical model.[41]

Our comparative analysis of the results from the four countries is taken up in Chapter 6. Here, we summarise the participation and performance data for each case, and rate each system on a simple three-point scale (good, mixed and poor). Our assessments and our explanation of why each decentralisation experiment performed in the way it did are based on our detailed, 'within-system' measurements. We then compare *explanations* of performance across the four countries, in order to identify or isolate the most important factors and, in particular, to judge whether enhanced participation could be said to have had a consistent effect on performance. We argue that in these four important cases of African and Asian democratic decentralisation, whilst increased participation had a positive impact on the performance of decentralised institutions, adequate resources for councils were also essential, and – as we shall see – the social and political contexts within which decentralisation was undertaken also influenced outcomes. But the most critical determinant was the existence of a combination of all these factors with effective mechanisms of institutional and popular accountability. It is those mechanisms which provided – and are likely to provide more generally – the crucial link between enhanced participation and enhanced institutional performance.

---

[41] It should also be acknowledged that there is a feedback element here. Performance and participation have a reciprocal influence in so far as improved performance can in turn affect willingness to participate. This can have practical consequences for resource mobilisation, and is particularly relevant in systems which are trying to encourage local self-reliance. But given the dismal history of most local government systems at least in Africa, we would argue that the better performance has to come first in the establishment of such a virtuous circle.

2 India (Karnataka)

THE BACKGROUND

The structure of decentralisation

At an election in 1983, the Janata Party won control of the government in the Indian state of Karnataka[1] at a time when the Congress Party held power at the national level. Janata leaders wanted to demonstrate that they were more imaginative and radically democratic than their Congress rivals, to revive their party's fortunes nationally. They also had next to no party organisation in the state, and they believed that a new system of elected councils at the district level and below would provide a framework for party-building. They therefore undertook a programme of decentralisation which gave elected councillors control of more than half of the state's bureaucrats and responsibility for nearly every field of development.

Elected councils were created at two levels – the district and the lower, Mandal level. A Mandal Council covered a group of adjacent villages with a population of between 8,000 and 12,000 and consisted of around thirty members. Each of them was directly elected from a distinct territorial constituency averaging just under 400 voters. 2,536 Mandals were established, with 55,188 members. The small size of the Mandals, in relation to the much larger and far more powerful District Councils (*Zilla Parishad*), made them the less important of the two elements in the system. This was apparent from the power of the District Council to approve the annual budget estimates of the Mandals, to investigate their annual accounts and administration reports, to intervene in the event of irregularities, and to appoint and control their administrative staff.

There were nineteen District Councils in Karnataka. Members were directly elected by distinct territorial constituencies with an average

---

[1] We decided to examine a single state in the Indian federal system, partly because decentralised systems vary in different states, and partly because this state (with a population of 43 million) is comparable in size to most nation-states in Asia and Africa.

population of 28,000 (except in one small, eccentric district), and the number of elected members of these councils varied between twenty-three and sixty-four, depending on population. The members of the state Legislative Assembly and Legislative Council (the upper house), and of the Indian Parliament from the district also sat on the District Council with voting rights, but they were greatly outnumbered by elected councillors.

District councillors elected a president and vice-president. The latter had the status of a deputy minister in the state government. The former had the status of a junior minister and since he headed a council that controlled nearly all government agencies in the district, his actual power matched his status. He supervised and largely controlled a formidable staff of senior administrators deputed from line ministries, which was headed by a chief secretary drawn from the elite, generalist Indian Administration Service (IAS). The result was usually a system characterised both by managerial competence and by the ascendancy of elected representatives. In an indication of the power of the District Council, the chief secretary was senior to another IAS officer who served as the deputy commissioner – the figure who for over a century had dominated district administration, but who now dealt only with non-developmental activities.[2] In Indian terms, this represented a radical devolution of power on to elected councils.

To ensure adequate influence for less powerful groups, 25 per cent of the seats on all councils were reserved for women, and a minimum of 18 per cent for members of the Scheduled Castes (ex-untouchables) and Tribes. Provision was also made for the 'Backward Classes' – the groups standing above the Scheduled Castes, but below the higher castes in the traditional hierarchy. When no members of those groups were elected to a council, two such persons are appointed members by the government.

The Karnataka experiment lasted only for the first five-year term of the councils, from January 1987 when the Councils were first elected until the end of 1991, when a Congress state government hostile to decentralisation abandoned the system.

The socio-economic context

Society in Karnataka has long been more tranquil than in most Indian regions, partly because disadvantaged groups have not experienced the severe alienation that is common elsewhere. This is not to say that this region is devoid of inequities. They are ubiquitous. Poor, low caste

---

[2] Ray (1991), p. 24.

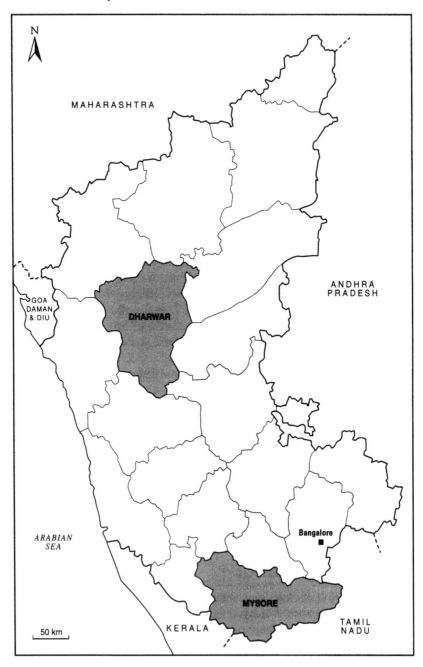

Map 1 Karnataka: the districts, showing location of case studies

people have long faced serious indignities. But disparities of wealth, status and power in the villages have been less marked than in most other parts of South Asia – certainly including Bangladesh.[3]

Except in certain eccentric areas, the distribution of land and resources tends to be relatively equitable in rural areas. 'Middle farmers' or owner-cultivators predominate. Indeed, in the southern half of the state, they constitute close to 80 per cent of the rural population, a huge proportion. That area also has the lowest incidence of landlessness in the subcontinent. The amounts of other key resources – for example, the number of cattle – possessed by tenants and landless labourers have long exceeded the all-India average.[4]

This is not a stagnant socio-economic order of the kind found in Bangladesh and parts of North India. The middle farmers have sought, with no little success, to maximise incomes by developing the land in partnership with the state. The resulting agricultural growth 'has had a significant spread effect', so that modest benefits have reached the rural poor.[5] Post-independence governments have also introduced moderate agrarian reforms, with moderate success. Both the character of these changes and the pace at which they have occurred have reinforced and not threatened the stability of the agrarian order.

As a consequence, many of the hierarchical attitudes associated with the caste system survive in rural Karnataka, where the landowning, cultivating castes still dominate daily life. But enough resources have long been available to the poor to enable them to avoid the kind of vicious exploitation and systematic humiliation that one sees in regions like Bihar. This has also made it possible for state-level politicians to mobilise poorer groups without provoking violent conflict, so that since 1972 no state government has been able to exclude such groups from very substantial shares in political spoils. In other words, landed groups still dominate at the village level, but not at the state level.[6]

Karnataka has a lively civil society (organised interests enjoying some autonomy from the state) and many active non-governmental organisations. In some Indian states, such groups have suffered attempts by state governments either to suppress or to control them, but this has never been seriously attempted here. Instead, since 1972, multi-party competition has served as an important catalyst for such groups.[7]

---

[3] This is explained in great detail in Manor (1989).
[4] See for example ibid., pp. 323 and 329.
[5] This comes from an observer who is by no means uncritical – Ray (1991), p. 25.
[6] Note the stability of the statistics on pp. 179–83 and 222–45 of Karnataka (1974). See also Manor (1988) pp. 331–5 and 342–53. For a little context, see Manor (1977b).
[7] Manor (1980a) and Manor (1984).

Karnataka has an assertive and sophisticated electorate. Witness the elections to the Indian parliament in late 1984 and then the state legislature in early 1985. In a period of just nine weeks, voters in 105 of the 224 state assembly constituencies shifted majority support from the Congress Party, which won the first election, to the Janata Party which won the second. Only an awakened, discerning electorate could have effected a swing on that extraordinary scale.

The choice of case studies for field research

Our field research concentrated mainly on two districts in the state of Karnataka – Dharwar and Mysore. We paid particular attention to two sub-districts (taluks) within each,[8] which meant that our research here roughly paralleled that in the other three countries under study.

Karnataka can be disaggregated into various sub-regions on various criteria, but the main divisions most commonly used are: old Mysore (roughly the southern half of the state, which before independence in 1947 was a princely state), Bombay Karnataka (which were formerly directly administered by the British as part of Bombay Presidency), Hyderabad Karnataka (formerly ruled by the Nizam of Hyderabad). Of these, old Mysore and Bombay Karnataka are the largest and most important. We therefore selected one district from the former (Mysore) and one from the latter (Dharwar).

Rural politics and village life in the state are dominated by two landowning caste-clusters, the Lingayats and Vokkaligas. They tend, with some overlap, to occupy two distinctive sections of Karnataka. Dharwar District is a Lingayat area. Mysore District is subdivided into areas of Lingayat and Vokkaliga power, but we did our field research in two Vokkaliga-dominated sub-districts there. Dharwar is located far from the political and economic capital of the state, Bangalore, while Mysore lies close to it and to the rich sugar-growing district of Mandya. Both are thoroughly mainstream districts in terms of education levels, the distribution of land and resources, etc.

PARTICIPATION

The first section ('Popular Participation') below deals with changes in patterns of political participation by individuals and groups as a result of democratic decentralisation.The second section ('Representation and Institutional Accountability') extends the discussion beyond that. If

---

[8] In Dharwar District, these were Hubli and Kundagol, while in Mysore District, they were Heggadedevankote and Hunsur.

'inputs' from those at the grassroots are to have an impact on government institutions, they must be transmitted through elected representatives to civil servants who execute policy. If that does not occur, citizens' participation can increase without having any tangible effect. So the second section assesses relations between elected politicians and bureaucrats, and the performance or non-performance of institutions as transmitters of information and influence from below.

Popular participation

Electoral participation

Elections to the District and Mandal Councils were held on separate days in January 1987. Local elections had been something of a rarity in Karnataka,[9] but civil servants there had abundant experience at conducting free and fair legislative and parliamentary elections. That tradition was maintained on these occasions. Turnout was high – 60 per cent for the District Councils and 75 per cent for the Mandal Councils. That compares favourably with the average turnouts in this state of 60.4 per cent at national elections and 46.5 per cent at state elections.[10]

We interviewed a total of 288 villagers in four sub-districts who were a representative sample of the rural population there according to age, gender and education levels. A remarkably high proportion of respondents stated that they had not only voted, but had taken some part in council election campaigns. 23.1 per cent said that they had campaigned for candidates seeking election to the localised Mandal Council, and surprisingly, a slightly higher number – 24.5 per cent – said that they had worked for candidates to the more distant District Councils. These figures probably overstate the amount of actual campaigning, since some respondents appear only to have witnessed election processes. But there was still a very high participation rate in the campaigns.

The overwhelming majority of successful candidates stood as representatives of one of the two parties which then predominated in the state, Congress and Janata. This extended the already well-advanced process by which factional rivalries at the local level were given a party political character. Conflict among rival groups in rural areas intensified as a consequence and a modest amount of violence occurred at and after elections, but this did not pervert the results. Our survey of villagers

---

[9] They had only occurred on three previous occasions, in 1960, 1968 and 1978. State governments had preferred to allow local councils to expire after their terms of office ended, and to do without them for periods of several years before holding fresh elections.

[10] These figures are for nine parliamentary elections between 1952 and 1989 and seven state elections between 1962 and 1989 Butler *et al* (1991) pp. 177–8.

Table 2.1. *Results of District Council elections*

	Votes	Percentage of votes	Seats	Percentage of seats
Janata	5,502,967	45.64	450	50.73
Congress	5,371,399	44.45	395	44.45
BJP	237,497	1.96	5	0.56
CPI(M)	61,611	0.51	1	0.11
Lok Dal	1,989	0.01	0	0.00
Independents	811,043	6.80	34	3.83[1]

[1] Institute of Social Sciences (1992), p. 130.

found that fully 95.4 per cent saw these elections as 'completely fair'; 3.6 per cent regarded them as 'fair with some problems'; and only 1 per cent stated that they were 'very unfair'.

District Council candidates sometimes received limited amounts of money from parties, while those standing for Mandal Councils had to raise their own. But money played only a marginal role in these elections – partly because uncertainty about how much power the new councils would have made politicians cautious about spending, and mostly because voters have long been too sophisticated to be swayed by inducements.[11] Mandal Council candidates often stated that they distributed liquor and others gifts in the customary manner during election week, but they knew that nearly all who accepted these made their decisions on the merits of competing candidates and parties.

At the time of the council elections, Karnataka had in effect a two-party system, involving the Janata and Congress parties. The aggregate statewide results of the District Council election appear in Table 2.1. This brought the Janata Party to power in sixteen districts, and the Congress in three. Janata held power in both of the districts in which we did intensive fieldwork – Mysore and Dharwar.

Party affiliations were less important in the Mandal Council election than local factors such as factional and caste alignments, but they still mattered (see Table 2.2).

This gave majorities to the Janata Party in 1,323 Councils (53.17 per cent of the total), to the Congress in 687 (27.82 per cent) and to others in 183 (7.41 per cent). No party had a majority in 182 cases.[12]

Once the members of District Councils had been chosen, they were called upon to elect council presidents and vice-presidents. These contests

[11] Manor (1993).   [12] Ibid., p. 132.

Table 2.2. *Results of Mandal Council elections*

	Seats won	Percentage of seats
Janata	27,333	50.27
Congress	20,679	38.03
Other	6,359	11.70

involved little chicanery. Councillors voted along party lines after candidates for these posts had been selected via consultation between the state-level party leaders and councillors in each district. Both parties made some effort to ensure that representatives of non-dominant social groups gained some of these posts – a custom in state-level politics since the early 1970s.

The process by which Mandal councillors elected their chairmen differed from this in several ways. State-level leaders found it logistically impossible to influence 2,535 councils. They therefore left decisions to the new councillors. The logic of local politics therefore prevailed, and local caste and factional alignments allowed locally dominant groups – Lingayats and Vokkaligas – to capture a disproportionate share of these chairmanships.[13]

Many aspiring Mandal chairmen engaged in frantic pampering and bribery of councillors, and even in what one described as 'friendly kidnapping'. This entailed taking councillors who promised support on holidays in city hotels until election day, lest other candidates should offer more lavish enticements. But the amounts of money that changed hands were quite limited. One Mandal chairman stated that the going rate among councillors who were not members of his faction was a mere Rs.500. He added that in subsequent elections, councillors' awareness of the sizeable powers available to Mandal chairmen would have inspired them to ask for as much as Rs.20,000.[14] But the refusal of the state government to hold fresh elections when the Councils' first term expired in 1992 meant that this hypothesis was never tested.

Village meetings (Gram Sabhas)

Each Mandal Council in Karnataka was legally required to hold twice-yearly meetings in every village within its boundaries, to which all

---

[13] A study of 45 Mandal Councils across the state found that they held 51.11 per cent of chairmanships. They also held 31.35 per cent of the seats on those councils. Lingayats and Vokkaligas together constitute 27 per cent of the state's population (Institute of Social Sciences, n.d., p. 21).

[14] These comments are based on interviews with Mandal Council chairmen in four districts (Mysore, Mandya, Bangalore and Dharwar) in March–April 1993.

residents were welcome. These gatherings, or Gram Sabhas, were the main device to ensure councils' accountability to citizens between elections and had two main purposes. They allowed people to seek information and air their views on the work of the Council, and they were to identify the most deserving recipients of assistance from anti-poverty programmes.

Neither of these things appealed to Mandal councillors. Villagers demanded explanations for unfulfilled election promises, and councillors' answers often produced heated reactions. Popular pressure sometimes forced politicians to abandon private arrangements with clients. In one such case, villagers demanded genuinely open competition for the sale of fishing rights in a local tank, and this resulted in an increase in council revenue from Rs.12,000 to 75,000.[15] As one observer put it, 'People got the power in their hands and they said whatever they liked – earlier the system was not like that'.[16] Informants who witnessed many such meetings stated that the formal nature of the occasion made it necessary for councillors to tolerate these reactions politely. One Mandal chairman, a master of understatement, said that he found all of this 'discouraging'. Others stated that they regarded these inquisitions as humiliating and beneath their dignity. Most chairmen also resented what they saw as the Gram Sabha's usurpation of their 'right' to allocate benefits from government programmes.

As a result, councillors in most places abandoned Gram Sabha meetings after the first year or two.[17] Some resorted to subterfuge – holding unannounced meetings at times when most villagers were away at work or at market, or staging Gram Sabha 'meetings' in the Mandal office. Many did not even bother with such charades. This spared them painful encounters with constituents and allowed chairmen and councillors to draw up lists of beneficiaries – including their clients' names at the expense of the deserving poor.

The failure of the Gram Sabhas to serve as an effective formal device to promote grassroots participation was apparent from responses to our survey of a representative cross-section of villagers in four sub-districts. Table 2.3 sets out their responses to questions about whether they had attended officially sponsored meetings, and if so, whether they had spoken there. If only 17 per cent of all villagers interviewed had attended such meetings, they clearly did not serve the purpose that was intended.

---

[15] Hegde (1994), p. 22.
[16] Interview with an activist from the India Development Service, a local non-governmental organisation, Dharwar, 6 April 1993.
[17] See in this connection, for example, *Times of India*, 4 and 6 September 1990.

Table 2.3. *Attendance at officially sponsored meetings*

	Full sample (%)	Scheduled castes (%)
Attended and spoke	6.5	3.8
Attended, stayed silent	10.5	0.0

Nor does the tiny proportion of Scheduled Caste respondents that attended inspire confidence in the Gram Sabhas.

District councillors and officials had so many Mandals to deal with that they found it difficult to check either the lists of beneficiaries or assurances that Gram Sabhas had actually met. Some of them – including a few outstanding district chief secretaries (seniormost bureaucrats) – toured villages and talked with citizens in ways that would have been inconceivable before decentralisation. This sometimes persuaded bureaucrats at the sub-district level to do the same. They sought evidence of irregularities and acquainted villagers with their entitlements, urging them to press for these. In a few areas, local non-government associations did likewise.

More often, citizens who had been deprived of their rights to question councillors in Gram Sabhas accomplished the same thing by attending Mandal Council meetings – to complain, raise questions or simply to see whether things that they wanted or had been promised would be delivered.[18] But this happened too infrequently to compensate for the damage done to popular participation by the abandonment of Gram Sabhas.

How and to what extent did people participate in the political process which developed round the new councils? One finding of our survey of villagers indicates a high level of popular awareness, which might in turn suggest high levels of participation. We asked respondents to name their councillors. Not surprisingly, the number of those able to do so was higher (75.0 per cent) for the more localised Mandal Council which usually serves a circle of villages, but it was also quite high (54.5 per cent) for the District Councils.

To get at forms of participation more directly, we employed a number of devices. We investigated opportunities which elected politicians provided for participation in two ways. We first asked respondents how often, and by what means, councillors had consulted them about development projects in their localities. Table 2.4 summarises their answers. We then asked villagers how often elected representatives had taken the initiative in consulting them. Table 2.5 sets out their replies.

---

[18] This discussion is based on interviews with a large number of Mandal chairmen and councillors, journalists and non-governmental organisation activists in three districts (Mysore, Mandya and Dharwar), March and April 1993.

Table 2.4. *Consultations with villagers about projects*

	Percentage of projects with consultation
At a public meeting	18.3
At a small group meeting	0.7
Our leader was consulted	0.9
Unspecified consultations	20.0
None	61.1

Table 2.5. *Frequency of councillors' consultations*

	Mandal Councillors (%)	District Councillors (%)
Once/month or more	17.1	7.7
Once/3–6 months	20.3	4.6
Once/6–12 months	6.1	6.7
Once/12–24 months	9.5	8.8
Other	10.4	12.7
Never	36.6	59.5

These figures again indicate a reluctance among councillors to engage their constituents. The number of consultations by Mandal councillors may seem reasonably high, but we must remember that they lived cheek by jowl with constituents. Given that proximity, the figures look rather low. This meant that people were often compelled to seek out councillors. This is the nub of the matter. To what extent did it occur?

We asked respondents whether they had taken the initiative to contact a member of the District or Mandal Council about a matter of personal concern to them. Their replies are set out in Table 2.6. To have nearly a quarter of our sample engaged in contacting is quite impressive. Mandal councillors, who were so close at hand, were clearly easier to reach, but the figure on contacts with District councillors is also respectable.

We then asked them whether they had ever contacted public employees. Their answers are aggregated in Table 2.7. These figures are less striking, but we were often told that villagers understood that under the decentralised system, councillors possessed the leverage to persuade bureaucrats to act. After four decades of representative government, they also understood that elected councillors had an obligation to constituents – and they believed that councillors knew this too (as indeed they did). Citizens therefore proceeded straight to the person who was most likely to be helpful.[19]

[19] See Table 2.20 under 'responsiveness' on the extent to which councillors and bureaucrats were seen to be helpful.

India (Karnataka)

Table 2.6. *Contacting of councillors (%)*

Yes, District Councillor	6.0
Yes, Mandal Councillor	15.6
Yes, unspecified	3.0
No	75.4

Table 2.7. *Contacting of bureaucrats (%)*

Yes	17.7
No	82.3

We also asked respondents whether they had engaged in a number of other forms of proactive participation. Their replies are summarised in Table 2.8. These levels of participation are very high. And given the remoteness of state legislators prior to decentralisation – there were far fewer of them than District councillors after 1987, and they were often away in the state capital – most of these proactive doings would not have occurred had the councils not been created.

Our survey also asked people to identify organisations in which they had been active. Their responses are summarised in Table 2.9. These figures are less impressive than those in Table 2.8. Our interviews with elites suggest that most people operated more (and quite extensively) through informal networks (especially factions or local notables' patronage networks) or through direct contacting than in formal associations.

We then asked whether they had been active in these organisations prior to decentralisation in 1987. 43.8 per cent of them had been active before, and 56.2 per cent had joined associations since then. Interviews with local leaders (external to the representative sample) indicated a similar or perhaps more marked increase in involvement in informal factional/patronage networks. We also found that 86.0 per cent of those who had contacted bureaucrats had done so, for the first time, after the creation of the elected councils – mainly because they believed that the existence of councils with leverage over bureaucrats gave them a chance of success when dealing with the latter. These figures indicate that democratic decentralisation in Karnataka played a significant role in catalysing proactive participation.

Participation by disadvantaged groups
We address the issue of disadvantaged groups' participation in two ways. First, we analyse *all* of those who participated in three types of political

Table 2.8. *Proactive participation (%)*

Campaigned in Mandal election	23.2
Campaigned in District election	25.3
Signed a petition	20.3
Attended non-official meeting	14.0
Attended officially organised meeting	17.0
Joined in protest	7.1
Expressed thanks to elected representative	11.8

Table 2.9. *Participation in associations*

	Percentage of sample active
Village development association	4.5
Youth association	4.5
Caste association	1.0
Women's association	9.3
Farmers' association	3.8
Professional association	0.7
Trade union	0.3
Others	5.2

activity to see how large a role various disadvantaged groups played in each. The main categories in Table 2.10 which may be regarded as 'disadvantaged' are women and those with no education – the 'None' line under 'Education'. The latter serves well as a proxy for poor people. Second, we consider in more detail the range of activities which were engaged in by women and, more especially, Scheduled Castes – ex-untouchables (15.1 per cent of the state population), which is a category unique to India.

When we examine the composition of all participators (Table 2.10), we see that men predominated heavily among those who contacted councillors and those who attended group meetings and spoke there, but that more than one-third of those present at such meetings were women – a reasonably high figure. (Participation by young people was sufficiently high that it is possible to regard them as less than disadvantaged.)

More crucially, people with no education (and those with only primary education) were remarkably active in contacting councillors. More of those without education engaged in contacting than those with secondary education, and uneducated people were only slightly outnumbered by those with secondary education in the overall attendance at meetings – although the latter were much more inclined to speak there. This

Table 2.10. *Socio-economic characteristics of participators, by selected activities (%)*

	Contacted councillor (N=82)	Attended official meeting (N=56)	
		All attenders	Attended and spoke
Sex			
Men	81.4	64.3	82.6
Women	18.6	35.7	17.4
Age			
18–29	31.7	25.0	30.4
30–44	40.2	44.6	47.8
45–64	25.7	26.8	21.8
65+	2.4	3.6	0.0
Education			
None	36.2	40.0	18.2
Primary	20.0	9.1	9.1
Secondary	31.3	43.6	59.1
Higher	12.5	7.3	13.6

indicates that in Karnataka, disadvantaged groups were far less inhibited participators than we might have expected. Better educated – which is to say more prosperous and high-status groups – clearly did not dominate participation in this system.

We arrive at a more ambiguous but broadly similar conclusion when we consider political awareness and the *range* of participatory activities in which the Scheduled Castes and women engaged. (The benefits that they received or failed to receive are assessed in the third part of this chapter, where the story is rather different.)

In Karnataka, as in most of India, the upper and/or middle-ranking caste groups that control the lion's share of the land (and the better land) dominate life in the villages. They once dominated politics at the state level as well, but over the last twenty years or so, poor groups have become sufficiently organised, discerning and assertive to demand substantial concessions from state governments. As a result, in many states landed groups need to draw at least some poorer groups into political coalitions at the state level to have any chance of winning elections. Karnataka was one of the first states to witness this change, in 1972, and the Scheduled Castes (thanks in part to their numerical strength) gained as a result.[20] So if elite caste dominance exists at the village level but not at the state level, what of the District and Mandal levels, at which elected

---

[20] See in this connection Manor (1977c) Manor (1980a) and Manor (1989).

Table 2.11. *Scheduled Caste participation in associations*

	Percentage of sample active
Village development association	3.7
Youth association	3.7
Women's association	7.4
Farmers' association	3.7
Professional association	3.7

councils were created? This key question looms large both here and, especially, in the discussion of 'responsiveness' in the third part of this chapter.

Our survey of villagers found that in all types of elections, Scheduled Caste respondents had voted in only slightly fewer numbers than members of other groups. All groups tended to overstate their rate of turnout (judging by reliable official voting statistics), so the precise figures are misleading enough not to be quoted. But our survey data and our earlier studies of nine state and national elections in Karnataka all indicate that voting levels among the Scheduled Castes are high – almost as high as among prosperous groups.

Scheduled Caste respondents believed that elections were fair: 14.8 per cent ventured no opinion on fairness, but 100 per cent of the rest stated that elections were 'completely fair'. They had slightly more faith in elections than did our total sample, of which 95.4 per cent took that view.

Members of the Scheduled Castes were nearly as active in associations as were people in other groups. This is set out in Table 2.11. Since no Scheduled Caste respondent belonged to more than one organisation, this meant that 22.2 per cent of them participated in associations, as against 25.3 per cent of the total sample. When we consider the huge disadvantages that they face, this is remarkable.

Precisely half of those members of Scheduled Castes who were active in organisations had joined them since decentralisation in 1987. This was a slightly smaller proportion than in the total sample, but it still suggests that decentralisation galvanised associational activity, even among the most disadvantaged groups. Their level of political awareness was not far short of that of the total sample. This is apparent from their ability to name members of the localised Mandal Council and of the District Councils, set out in Table 2.12.

To what extent did they engage in proactive forms of participation? Table 2.13, based on our survey data, answers this. This adds up to a mixed picture. It is surprising that the Scheduled Castes were more active

India (Karnataka) 37

Table 2.12. *Scheduled Castes' ability to name councillors*

	Mandal councillor (%)	District councillor (%)
Scheduled castes	70.4	40.7
Total sample	75.0	54.5

Table 2.13. *Scheduled Castes' proactive participation*

	Sch. Castes (%)	All groups (%)
Campaigned in Mandal election	18.5	23.2
Campaigned in District election	19.2	25.3
Signed a petition	22.2	20.3
Attended non-official meeting	0.0	14.0
Attended officially organised meeting	3.8	17.0
Joined in protest	4.3	7.1
Expressed thanks to elected representative	4.3	11.8

than the generality of villagers at petitioning. Our evidence indicates that this usually entailed efforts to obtain legal entitlements. However, our discussions of Gram Sabhas (above) and of official responses to social groups (below, under 'Responsiveness to Whom?') indicate that these efforts seldom bore fruit.

The other form of proactive participation in which they engaged at a relatively high level was election campaigning. Local politicians needed their votes and thus had good reason for systematically encouraging them to participate – in contrast to other times when they were discouraging. Scheduled Caste campaigners usually operated separately from campaigners from other castes, in the spatially distinct sections of villages where their caste fellows lived. The other types of participation in the list above all entailed Scheduled Castes mixing with others – which the others discouraged. It is thus not surprising that participation rates among the Scheduled Castes should be so low. Their total exclusion from meetings organised by non-officials in the villages is especially striking.

The figures above on political awareness and levels of participation, when the Scheduled Castes were not actively discouraged from doing so, indicate what politicians in Karnataka have long known. These groups may be poor, ill-educated and subject to severe discrimination, but they are neither ignorant nor inert politically. This sets up a cruel irony, since – as we shall see later – they gained little from democratic decentralisation.

Let us now consider participation by elected Scheduled Caste councillors. The law required that a minimum of 18 per cent of seats in every district be reserved for Scheduled Caste and Scheduled Tribe candidates, but that more be provided when they constituted a greater share of the population. (In such constituencies, all adults voted, but only Scheduled Caste candidates could stand.) Since they exceeded 18 per cent in some districts, and since few won non-reserved seats, they were over-represented in seventeen of the nineteen districts. Statewide, they held 20.4 per cent of all seats.[21]

This did not mean, however, that Scheduled Caste District councillors achieved much – individually or collectively. An energetic individual from a disadvantaged group could make a modest difference. In meetings of the Dharwar District Council, a forceful woman from a Scheduled Tribe often tackled bureaucrats and the district president in a rustic manner about inadequate help to poor groups. Her interventions were so unvarnished and entertaining to most councillors that she often got her way. In Gulbarga District, a Scheduled Caste councillor with Communist cadre training and long experience as a health worker at the sub-district level was less ostentatious but similarly effective. The same can be said of a Scheduled Caste councillor in Mysore District who had a university education, long experience and excellent contacts in the Congress Party. But such people were extreme rarities.

Nor did they undertake much collective action on District Councils. The main exception was in Mysore District where Scheduled Caste councillors from both main parties once grew so frustrated with the District president that they boycotted a Council meeting and held a demonstration chanting appeals for his resignation. This persuaded the president to give ground on their demands[22] and they then received a

---

[21] The two locally dominant landowning caste groups, the Lingayats and Vokkaligas (who constitute 27 per cent of the state's population) were also over-represented. They held 50.61 per cent of seats (Institute of Social Sciences (1989), pp. 17–28).

The reservation of seats for Scheduled Caste representatives was done, as it has been in state and national elections in India for decades, by declaring that certain constituencies could elect only members of Scheduled Castes to the council. The voters in such constituencies come from all sections of society, but only Scheduled Caste candidates may stand for office.

It should be noted that well-connected local politicians were able to exploit their links with legislators, prior to the election of the District Councils, to ensure that the District Council constituencies where they wished to stand for election were not reserved for Scheduled Caste candidates. This tended to result in disadvantages for the Scheduled Castes, since it brought members into District Councils who were less sympathetic to them.

[22] They were pressing him to go beyond a state government policy whereby funds for certain programmes to assist the Scheduled Castes were to be spent only in state legislature constituencies which were reserved for Scheduled Caste representatives. They asked that funds be spent in every part of the district. Interviews with the District president and one Scheduled Caste councillor, Mysore, 13 and 14 April 1993.

more sympathetic hearing in council meetings where they occasionally lobbied for advantages. But that demonstration was a unique event. In most other districts, the Scheduled Castes (and other poor groups) never constituted an effective lobby. They almost never received assistance from other disadvantaged groups. Even in Mysore District, it was exceedingly unusual for groups who stood just above them in the traditional hierarchy to support them. When they did so, the link was often quickly broken. Since these groups were even less inclined than the Scheduled Castes to assert themselves in the councils – where they were under-represented[23] – poorer groups achieved little at the district level.

In one district, Hassan, a Scheduled Caste man was elected president of the District Council. But he could accomplish little for his caste because his election was arranged by a powerful dominant caste politician – elected Karnataka's Chief Minister in late 1994 – whose son sat on the council and ensured that resources went mainly to that dominant group. This was in one sense an admirable attempt by the Janata Party to signal its empathy with the Scheduled Castes, but in practice, it amounted to tokenism.

In a small number of districts like Bangalore Rural, the Scheduled Castes did not need forceful representatives to obtain justice because leaders from other social groups who dominated the councils treated them generously. But that did not represent effective participation by Scheduled Caste councillors. In general, they managed only minimal achievements at the district level.

What of the lower-level Mandal Councils? These stood so close to the village level, where the traditionally dominant castes still exercise overwhelming power, that it was virtually impossible for Scheduled Caste representatives to influence events. Other poor groups, who lacked reserved seats on Mandal Councils, were poorly represented there. Scheduled Caste members of Mandal Councils seldom had much education and often their election was due to a dominant caste patron. Since the Mandal Councils played a decisive role both in implementing many district programmes and in selecting beneficiaries, they often prevented poorer groups from gaining even from enlightened District Councils.

The whole cultural milieu in those local arenas weighed against assertiveness from low-status groups. On several occasions, chairmen of Mandal Councils told us how they had prevented Scheduled Caste councillors from influencing decisions and obtaining resources earmarked for the Scheduled Castes. They said this as if this were the most

---

[23] These groups (including Muslims and other religious minorities) held only 17.97 per cent of District Council seats (Institute of Social Sciences (1989), pp. 17–28). They constituted roughly 30 per cent of the state's population.

Table 2.14. *Ability by gender to name councillors*

	Women (%)	Men (%)
Named Mandal councillor	63.5	86.3
Named District councillor	37.1	72.0

natural thing in the world – as indeed it is at that level. (They frequently expressed similar views about women councillors.) Others stated that Scheduled Caste representatives 'obviously' could not question decisions by other councillors or make suggestions. They were, in the main, utterly passive. The most that could be expected were occasional requests that their caste fellows receive the percentage of funds due to them under law.[24]

As we shall see in the third part of this chapter ('Institutional Performance'), most Mandal Councils systematically prevented such funds from reaching the Scheduled Castes and discriminated against them in other ways. So decentralisation to Councils located so close to the grassroots where landed castes dominate meant that power was being taken from higher levels where Scheduled Castes gain a little justice, and injected into arenas where that is almost impossible. It is thus naive to expect the devolution of power on to councils at such localised levels to serve the causes of poverty alleviation or social reform, whatever its other virtues.

What of participation by women and other disadvantaged groups? Our survey of rural dwellers found that in council elections, as in parliamentary elections, women probably turned out in slightly lower numbers than men. When we asked respondents to name their elected councillors, we got ambiguous results. Women were not far behind men in their ability to name members of the localised Mandal Council, but they were far less able to name their District councillor than were men. This suggests a marked difference in the two groups' awareness of supralocal politics (see Table 2.14).

Let us now consider proactive participation. Far more men than women stated that they had taken some part in council election campaigns, as Table 2.15 indicates.

We then asked about other forms of proactive participation (see Table 2.16). Note that when women contacted councillors, they tended far more strongly than men to confine themselves to Mandal councillors

---

[24] The comments in this entire section are based on extensive interviews with Scheduled Caste and other councillors, and with knowledgeable outsiders like local journalists and community leaders in six districts (especially in Mysore and Dharwar Districts), March–April 1993.

Table 2.15. *Involvement in council election campaigns*

	Women (%)	Men (%)
Mandal Council election	9.8	36.4
District Council election	12.9	35.7

Table 2.16. *Proactive forms of participation, by gender*

	Women (%)	Men (%)
Engaged in protest	4.8	8.1
Attended non-official meeting	8.6	18.4
Attended officially organised meeting	12.4	21.8
Met to thank elected representative	10.4	11.5
Contacted Mandal councillor	12.0	19.3
Contacted District councillor	2.4	9.6
Contacted bureaucrat	10.2	25.5

who lived locally. Men spoke much more often at officially organised meetings – 52.8 per cent of men who had attended such meetings, as opposed to 20.0 per cent of women. Overall, these findings indicate a modest but significant level of proactive participation by women villagers.

Evidence on women's involvement as elected councillors is, rather surprisingly, less inspiring, although the potential for great participation there over time was apparent. Women had 25 per cent of the seats reserved for them. (Again, the entire electorate votes, but only women may stand.) No woman candidate won a seat in an unreserved District Council constituency.[25] A tiny number won unreserved seats in Mandal elections, but nearly all of them appear (as in Bangladesh) to have been closely related to influential men. The same can be said of the handful of women elected to chair Mandal Councils, but some of the small number of women who were chosen as vice-presidents of District Councils were formidable, respected figures in their own right.

Since reservations for women were an innovation – unlike reservations for the Scheduled Castes, the norm in legislative elections since 1952 – they caused greater controversy than the latter. Similarly, it had long been common for Scheduled Caste issues and grievances to be addressed in legislatures and public discussions more generally, but women's grievances arose far less often. It is therefore not surprising that District

---

[25] Institute of Social Sciences (1989), p. 6.

Councils paid much greater heed to the former than the latter – though both got short shrift in the Mandal Councils, where village-level parochialism held sway.

It is perhaps more surprising that Scheduled Caste members of District Councils raised issues that mattered to their caste-fellows more often than female councillors raised issues of concern to women – although in both cases, such initiatives were extreme rarities. On most District Councils, women spoke less often than the Scheduled Castes, and when they spoke they tended to address matters of concern to all constituents rather than to women – unlike the latter who often raised caste questions. (The same was true, on a much smaller scale, on Mandal Councils.) There were some notable exceptions to this pattern, particularly in those few cases where women with tertiary and especially professional education held District Council seats. They also managed some modest achievements in districts where women councillors held nearly all of the seats on the Standing Committee for Women's and Child Welfare. But in general, women District councillors performed more timidly and ineffectually than male councillors from the Scheduled Castes.[26]

After the first two years or so of the councils' existence, women began to assert themselves slightly more than before – especially in a small number of districts like Dharwar where they had a confident, well-educated female role model in their midst. But then, as before, they were far more active on behalf of constituents generally than for women in particular. Many bureaucrats were more inclined to respond to pleas from women councillors than from men, because they believed that women were far less likely to be corrupt or to concoct false stories about constituents' needs.[27]

Representation and institutional accountability

This section deals with the extent to which information and influence from the grassroots were transmitted through institutions, especially elected councils, to those exercising power and implementing policy. The record of Karnataka's decentralised system here was mixed, but often quite positive.

---

[26] The comments in the preceding paragraphs are based on extensive interviews with women and men councillors and with other knowledgeable observers in six districts (especially Mysore and Dharwar Districts), March–April, 1993.

[27] This point initially emerged in an interview with a former District chief secretary, New Delhi, 26 March 1993. It was echoed repeatedly in subsequent discussions with bureaucrats in five districts.

Relations between bureaucrats and politicians

This topic is relevant to discussions of both institutional performance and participation. If good working relationships exist between politicians and civil servants, institutional performance (including 'outputs' from government) should be enhanced. But if bureaucrats are genuinely accountable to elected representatives, it means that the 'inputs' will often be transmitted from participating citizens, through elected councillors to bureaucrats executing policy. Since its importance seems greater on the input side, this topic is mainly discussed here, under 'Participation'.

It was bound to be difficult for elected councillors and bureaucrats to develop a constructive working relationship under the new system. Each group regarded the other with suspicion after many years in which civil servants had operated at the district level and below with considerable autonomy. The patterns which gradually emerged were variegated and ambiguous, but in general, the two sides eventually adjusted uncomfortably but tolerably well.

District Council meetings, particularly in the early years, were often marked by councillors' strident criticisms of bureaucrats. In several places, the president's commanding presence or precautions by the chief secretary[28] (the senior civil servant), or both, minimised this. But press reports frequently refer to a 'hue and cry' here, a 'scathing attack' there, a 'tirade against the callousness of officials', 'scenes wherein the dignity and decorum of the meeting were thrown to the winds', etc.[29] In one

---

[28] For example, one imaginative chief secretary managed to minimise conflict in District Council meetings by arranging for the councillors who headed the various Standing Committees rather than civil servants to report on matters which came under their purview. This meant, first, that bureaucrats in various departments usually sorted problems out with councillors prior to the monthly meeting of the full District Council and, second, that controversy in those meetings often occurred between councillors rather than between them and civil servants.

Other chief secretaries offered considerable protection to bureaucrats by consulting them just before monthly council meetings to anticipate criticisms that would arise and to prepare responses to them which would remind over-zealous councillors of the rules within which civil servants were required to work. In a few districts, chief secretaries arranged to obtain questions which councillors would raise in advance of monthly meetings. This made it possible to muster more helpful answers and largely prevented severe conflict between councillors and civil servants at the meetings. Interviews with former chief secretaries, New Delhi, 27 March 1993 and Bangalore, 20 and 21 April 1993. Chief secretaries' efforts to east conflict did not always work. See for example, *Times of India*, 20 June 1987.

One prominent bureaucrat at the district level, the chief accounts officer who was the main financial adviser, was fully protected by law from councillors' pressure. His advice had to be both sought and followed by councils.

[29] Quotations are from *Times of India*, 11 April and 6 September 1990; 12 and 22 January 1991. See also, amid many other examples, *Times of India*, 20 June 1987 and 4 January

case, criticism grew so fierce that bureaucrats boycotted council meetings in protest.[30]

The logic which led to these scenes changed over time. In the early years, they were often inspired by councillors' naive over-estimates of their powers over bureaucrats. Later, when councillors grasped that more senior civil servants could only be disciplined by state-level ministries which were disinclined to intervene, they seized upon the sole avenue left to them – public embarrassment of allegedly errant officials. But in either case, life was often distinctly unpleasant for bureaucrats.

One perceptive chief secretary who had served as a deputy commissioner (senior district-level official) before decentralisation said that in that previous period, the deputy commissioner's 'control' over line ministry personnel was only 'notional'. They were 'practically independent' within the budget and enjoyed 'huge discretion'. 'Real accountability was to their state department heads', but the distances which separated most of them from the state capital meant that they were beyond effective control from there as well.[31] They therefore operated with something like a free hand.

A forestry officer in a sub-district, for example, would decide what sorts of projects should be implemented and (often) where they should be located. He would then inform the generalist development officer in charge of the sub-district who seldom disagreed, and they would inform the generalist deputy commissioner at district level. These proposals would be discussed at a monthly district-level meeting of these officers with legislators, but the latter were so sketchily informed that they tended to approve anything as long as their constituencies got a reasonable share of resources. This allowed most line ministry officials an untroubled life.

Decentralisation changed things dramatically for these people. It brought many more elected representatives into the process, and Mandal councillors demanded fair distribution of resources on a far more disaggregated basis. They then closely monitored the quantity and quality of work actually done, and reported problems early and often to higher authorities. Line ministry officials faced relentless enquiries and pressure to work harder, longer and more scrupulously. They found it far

---

1988; *The Hindu*, 2 March and 8 June 1989; and especially, E. Raghavan's column in *Times of India*, 1 November 1987.

[30] This owed much to bungling by the chief secretary and to 'virulent attacks' on councils by the Congress Party's Minister of Panchayati Raj. *Times of India*, 24, 26, 28 and 30 July 1991.

[31] Interview with the official in question, Bangalore, 21 April 1993.

more difficult to get away with corrupt acts or to falsify records on the amount of time spent in the field.

One result of this, which enhanced the effectiveness of government institutions, was a distinct improvement in the co-ordination of civil servants working for different government departments at and below the district level. Former chief secretaries were virtually unanimous on this point. Because they and the district presidents had greater influence over line ministry personnel, they were better able to draw them into collaborative efforts to ensure that – for example – the insights of specialists in irrigation, forestry, soil erosion and engineering works would inform the design and implementation of a project involving tree planting and irrigation channels.

Line ministry bureaucrats also faced a difficult system of dual accountability. They were rendered accountable to the chief secretary and hence the District Council. But they also remained partially accountable to their department chiefs in the state capital, and the main power to discipline the more senior officials among them resided with those chiefs (although bureaucrats could be temporarily suspended by district presidents). State department chiefs often refused to take the views of District Councils seriously, and this eased somewhat the pressures on line ministry bureaucrats. But dual accountability sometimes pulled them painfully in opposite directions and impeded their effectiveness in the eyes of councillors.

Within every district, bureaucrats at all levels were made considerably more accountable to elected politicians than they had ever been before. This was true to varying degrees from district to district and from time to time – as district presidents and chief secretaries changed.[32] Some chief secretaries stated that, as one put it, civil servants within their districts were 'really scared' of the councillors and performed more effectively and responsively as a result.[33] Others argued that this over-states the change, but not by much. District councillors, journalists and other informed non-officials agreed that accountability improved markedly, and that bureaucrats – many of whom had earlier been almost 'totally non-functioning' – became far more energetic and amenable to councillors.[34]

A small minority of the bureaucrats working for line ministries in the

---

[32] In some cases, District presidents gave chief secretaries a free hand in dealing with subordinate bureaucrats and the chief secretaries permitted the latter to engage in corrupt acts. But such cases were rare. Interview with a knowledgeable journalist, Mysore, 12 April 1993.

[33] Interview with A. Ramaswamy, New Delhi, 28 March 1993.

[34] These comments are based on discussions with a wide range of politicians, bureaucrats and informed non-officials. The quotation comes from a highly knowledgeable journalist, Mysore, 19 April 1993.

districts eventually came to like the new system. This was particularly true of senior figures in some development departments who found that if they co-operated with councillors on the district standing committee which oversaw their work, the latter would lobby on their behalf in the District Council for resources. Some found that councillors' links to citizens could be exploited to explain to villagers why certain projects – inoculations and other forms of preventive medicine, for example – were being undertaken, so that the uptake improved. This also helped to defuse popular resentment at the temporary inconvenience caused by certain construction projects. It helped to acquaint people with the limitations on what government departments could achieve, minimising unrealistic expectations. It also drew villagers into projects at crucial stages – for instance, into watch and ward arrangements to protect newly planted saplings from destructive animals.[35]

But most line ministry officials were traumatised by the changes and, as one chief secretary stated, 'never came out of it fully'. They adjusted grudgingly, under duress. Most eventually developed an uneasy *modus vivendi* with councillors. This became easier as many of the latter realised that they could often gain more from bureaucrats through gentle persuasion than caustic criticism in council meetings. Civil servants were also reassured by the fact that the chief secretary and not the district president wrote most of the annual confidential report which went into their permanent career file.[36] But in the main, their relationship with elected office-holders remained tense and prone to conflict.[37]

For most chief secretaries, it was a very different story. The adjustment to the new role was difficult, but in time, the majority of them became advocates and even ardent enthusiasts for decentralisation. When they were initially appointed, nearly all felt trepidation and frustration. There was, for example, the question of status. In theory, the chief secretary was senior to the deputy commissioner – the long-standing senior figure in the district who continued to handle law and order, revenue collection and some other tasks. But in practice, this was far from clear. The deputy commissioner continued to receive the traditional deference paid to him while the chief secretary had to operate in roughly equal partnership with an elected district president who was often less polished and educated

---

[35] This is based on numerous interviews with department heads in Dharwar, Mysore and Bangalore Districts.

[36] The remainder of the report, the section dealing with their technical competence, was written by their state-level department head. District presidents could add comments to these reports, but most did not bother.

[37] This is based on interviews with a large number of bureaucrats in six districts during March and April 1993.

than any senior civil servant. Many chief secretaries also faced rustic, truculent councillors with an inflated sense of their own importance.

Their new job lacked glamour. The deputy commissioner unfurled the national flag on Independence Day and retained his grant bungalows while the chief secretary searched for rented accommodation. The former had access to better quality vehicles and to telecommunications equipment linking them to the state capital which was denied to the chief secretary. This was hard for the latter to swallow, especially since many had once been deputy commissioners themselves. Several could not adjust and had to be transferred.

Most, however, developed reasonably congenial, constructive relations both with the deputy commissioner and – more crucially – with the District Council and its president. They found it far easier than bureaucrats who served under them to develop a liking for the next system. As one put it, 'we suffered culture shock' because 'we had to shed our past' and now 'we were only asked to obey', but in most cases 'we took to it'.[38] A large minority of chief secretaries performed impressively and eventually became passionate advocates for decentralisation. They took risks in career terms by bargaining aggressively with state-level officials and by encouraging councils to be assertive.

Chief secretaries' relations with District Council presidents were potentially tense because the latter were empowered to write yearly assessments of the former. But this was eased by an informal decision that the main annual report would be penned by the state-level civil servant in charge of the decentralised system. The president's document was appended to it.

A district president possessed higher status and greater authority than his chief secretary, but he lacked the power to demand outright obedience. Some presidents did so anyway, and this led to serious conflict. But most chief secretaries who faced such demands found diplomatic solutions to the problem. Most wisely maintained a low profile and did a lot of listening. Things worked best if they 'appeared willing to abdicate' decision-making powers and exerted influence by 'helping to crystallize a consensus' among councillors.[39] They also reminded councillors and presidents of laws and regulations when the latter proposed things which violated these, and such warnings were usually heeded.

If a chief secretary treated a district president with due respect, their relationship usually flourished. One made a point of rising when the president or a councillor entered his office, of getting out of his car to

---

[38] Interview with a former chief secretary, Bangalore, 19 April 1993.
[39] Interview with a former chief secretary, Bangalore, 18 April 1993.

talk to them, of allowing them to enter a car first and permitting their cars to precede his when travelling. He knew to do these things because he was senior enough to have served not only as a deputy commissioner (and 'uncrowned king') of a district, but also in the secretariat in the state capital where he had learned this etiquette in dealing with ministers and legislators.[40]

Some chief secretaries, who lacked this man's subtlety and secretariat experience, neglected these courtesies. Such intangibles may sound unimportant, but their omission created tensions with district presidents. A few even adopted a commandist approach and triggered damaging conflicts, but this was highly unusual. So *hauteur* among senior civil servants was not a significant impediment to democratic decentralisation here.

In most respects, the division of responsibilities between chief secretaries and councils on one side and deputy commissioners on the other was clear, but a few anomalies caused problems. This was most evident when drought – a frequent occurrence – had to be tackled. The deputy commissioner was responsible for monitoring the development of droughts and alerting the state government to severe problems. But the District Council managed the services which tackled the problem. This led to some confusion.

The difficulty was compounded by deputy commissioners' tendency to play down the seriousness of drought (to give the impression that all was well in their districts) and councillors' inclination to exaggerate it to seek extra funds. Such problems were never adequately resolved.[41] They grew far worse after the Congress Party took power in 1989 and a minister who was hostile to decentralisation assumed charge and began fomenting conflict between deputy commissioners and District Councils.

Conflicts between civil servants and Mandal councillors were less serious. Mandal Councils employed just one bureaucrat, a secretary who was very junior and highly subservient. Council meetings were therefore largely devoid of the 'noisy scenes' familiar at the district level. Councillors interacted frequently with civil servants at the sub-district (taluk) level just above them, who helped to design and implement projects. Mandal chairmen found some of these officials corrupt or inefficient, but they often got help from their representative on the District Council to deal with this. Most chairmen and civil servants had few complaints about the relationship which then evolved. Such bureaucrats mainly

---

[40] Interview with A. Ramaswamy, a former chief secretary, New Delhi, 28 March 1993.
[41] Interview with M. Ahirzj, *Times of India*, Hubli, 6 April 1993.

resented district councillors who applied pressure to get them to cooperate with Mandal Councils.

Decentralised planning

In Karnataka, decentralisation was supposed to foster planning from below to enable citizens' views to shape official policy.[42] It was, however, largely unsuccessful – here as in the other countries covered by this study. Indeed, so many difficulties stand in the way of decentralised planning, that it is unwise to expect much advance on this front in any Asian or African setting.

Some of the problems that arose may have been transitory, but there is reason to suspect that others might persist. District officials' main job had always been implementing policies handed down from above. After decentralisation, they still had to do that, but they were also asked to absorb from below ideas which might go into a plan. They needed to collect other data on local facilities and problems, which were in short supply given the virtual absence of a district planning tradition. They found both of these tasks difficult, since they had little experience of either.

Once such information had been amassed, bureaucrats had to consider the feasibility of various projects, seek to balance requests from various areas, form judgements about how disparate inputs might be coordinated, and finally distil variegated proposals into a coherent whole. These tasks would have been taxing even if they had done this before, but for these people, they were well nigh impossible. Elected councillors were supposed to assist, but their main preoccupation was – understandably – to maximise resources for their constituencies. So, far from easing the bureaucrats' problems, they compounded them and left most civil servants 'at a loss'.[43]

The main elements of district plans were selected because councillors favoured them for political rather than developmental reasons. That was inevitable and in some ways healthy, but many plans became fragmented lists of pet schemes rather than integrated sets of mutually reinforcing proposals. Nor did councillors pay much attention to existing local resources or to ways of building plans around them. This doomed many projects to failure. For example, a councillor pressing for a dairy might not recognise the need to reinforce it with inputs like fodder provision and arrangements for outputs like a butter- and ghee-making facility. Without this, a dairy on its own was unlikely to succeed. Such poorly

---

[42] See in this connection Hegde (1994), pp. 19–28.
[43] I am especially grateful to V. K. Nataraj of the Institute of Development Studies, Mysore, for insight into these problems.

conceived plans gave bureaucrats at the state level an excuse to disregard district plans, which many of them were happy to do.[44]

They were assisted in this by the practice of earmarking a huge proportion of the funds passed down to the councils from above for specific programmes. In some countries – notably Bangladesh – Councils got round this by ignoring guidelines. In Karnataka, the rules had to be adhered to quite closely. This left councils with just two options. They could, to a limited degree, interpret or bend the rules in ways that enabled them to accomplish a little of what they preferred. Or their president and chief secretary could lobby the state government to allow them greater freedom. This latter tactic produced modest benefits, but neither rescued decentralised planning from the constraints of earmarking.

In the early years, District Councils often sent the state government plans seeking far more money than was available. They did so mainly because they felt unable to say no to proposals from the Mandal level. They soon realised, however, that this was politically unwise, since the state-level authorities would cut plans drastically, often in priority areas. They therefore learned to ask for slightly more than was fiscally possible, to give the government fewer opportunities to slash key programmes. This led to fewer unwelcome surprises, but it did little to improve decentralised planning. It continued to suffer from multiple afflictions: the incapacity of bureaucrats to adjust to planning tasks, the huge number of Mandals per district, inadequate linkage between Mandal and District levels, the inadequacy of Mandal staffing, and unhelpful interventions by District councillors and other notables.

Early warnings of disasters

Perhaps the most crucial service which elected representatives can perform for their constituents is to transmit urgent messages to government agencies about problems which might develop into disasters – droughts, floods, outbreaks of disease or shortages of food, drinking water or other essentials. Scholars have rightly stressed the role which India's free press plays in providing early warnings of such disasters.[45] But decentralisation in Karnataka provided a far more effective system of early warnings than the press could.

This point was made most forcefully by journalists in northern

---

[44] The preceding two paragraphs are derived from conversations with Abdul Aziz of the Institute of Social and Economic Change, Bangalore, who has researched the subject thoroughly (Aziz (1993)).

[45] See for example Dreze and Sen (1989), ch. 5; and Dreze and Sen (1990), especially chs. 2 and 3, by Dreze.

Karnataka who, before decentralisation, had raised the alarm when disasters loomed. They insisted that their conditions of employment make them an undependable source of warnings. Most reporters in that drought-prone area are stringers for newspapers in the state capital. Stringers receive around Rs.250 per month, which means that this is necessarily a part-time job. The need to do other work stops them from moving very far or very often outside the district headquarters. Since most use a motor scooter for transport and receive no allowance for hiring other vehicles, their ability to roam widely within their districts (some of which are huge) is further limited. This seriously undermines their effectiveness at discovering and investigating emerging calamities, most of which arise far from the main towns. Even the few who are proper, full-time 'staff reporters' have difficulties with transport. Since most publishable stories emerge from the headquarters towns, reporters rarely venture into remoter areas.

They also seldom look beyond the boundaries of their districts, since this means trespassing on the bailiwick of a colleague on the same newspaper. And yet the full seriousness of a drought or outbreak of disease may only become apparent when borders are crossed. Only *one* journalist in northern Karnataka routinely ranges over more than one district. This has enabled him to deliver early warnings on several occasions, but he stresses that the press is not a satisfactory safeguard.[46]

Even when district-level bureaucrats are directly informed by citizens of impending calamities, they often fail to respond. To ensure that such messages trigger prompt action, some means must exist to put political pressure on civil servants. District and Mandal Councils provided the means.

We might expect state legislators to play a role in raising the alarm and pressing for action. But most spend too much time politicking in the state capital or elsewhere to do this effectively. There was a time, long ago, when the Congress Party organisation in the districts was sufficiently strong and penetrative to help with this. But it has decayed severely.

Before decentralisation, legislators and bureaucrats from each district conferred every three months. Information at these meetings mainly flowed in one direction, from the deputy commissioner to legislators. The latter mostly asked questions about what was being done at the grassroots and received what reporters call 'cursory' answers. Most legislators

---

[46] Local papers in the districts lack the resources to assist much. I am grateful to M. Madan Mohan of *The Hindu*, Hubli; E. Raghavan, Associate Editor of the *Times of India*, Bangalore; to M. Ahiraj, *Times of India*, Hubli; and M. B. Maramkal, *Times of India*, Mysore and formerly Gulbarga, for information on these matters, provided in interviews in April 1993.

were too ill-informed to see how inadequate these were. As a result, the drought relief programme remained mainly on paper.

Decentralisation changed things dramatically. Coming from much smaller constituencies, District councillors were extremely well-versed on conditions in the villages. The law gave them sufficient powers and status to make them assertive in monthly council meetings, which were always well attended. Hardened journalists found it 'thrilling' to attend these, not least because of the avalanche of information on grass roots problems that emerged.[47]

In these circumstances, civil servants and representatives of statewide newspapers learned early and in great detail about water shortages, outbreaks of disease and flooding in rural areas. Councillors' formidable powers gave them the clout to force prompt action from bureaucrats. If a council president was slow to respond to reports of distress, the presence of opposition councillors guaranteed that he would be forced to act. It is not surprising, then, that journalists regarded District and Mandal Councils both as a virtually foolproof source of early warnings, and an effective means of ensuring that warnings were heeded.

INSTITUTIONAL PERFORMANCE

We now turn to the other main concern of this study: the changes produced by decentralisation in the performance of government institutions. We first assess the 'effectiveness' of institutions, and then discuss 'responsiveness' and changes in the political and administrative 'process'.

Effectiveness

The autonomy, powers and resources of the councils

In Karnataka, decentralisation was attended neither by the reductions in development spending by higher levels of government seen in Ghana nor by the increase seen in Bangladesh. The state government spent roughly the same amounts after decentralisation as before. But it gave elected councils substantial control over these funds and over a huge array of subjects including agriculture, animal husbandry, fisheries, rural development, primary and secondary education, health and family welfare, the welfare of Scheduled Castes and Tribes, rural employment schemes,

---

[47] These comments are based on discussions with dozens of former presidents and members of Zilla Parishads, district-level bureaucrats and journalists, in Dharwar, Mysore, Uttara Kannada, Mandya, Bangalore and Kolar Districts. The quotation comes from an interview with M. Madan Mohan, Hubli, 5 April 1993.

sericulture (as important subject in this state), village and small industries, and civil supplies.[48]

This gave councils charge of nearly all state development funds – including those to pay salaries of development ministry employees at the district level and below (a relatively small proportion of the total outlay[49]) and those used for goods and services. Thus, they received roughly 40 per cent of the stage budget, a huge concession. And since they also had considerable control over personnel from the line ministries, this represented a genuinely radical devolution of authority and resources.

We found very little discontentment among members of District and Mandal Councils, either with the amount of resources available or with the manner in which they were distributed among various councils and councillors' constituencies. The state government was legally required to allot resources to various districts according to a complex formula which prevented it from favouring certain areas for partisan reasons.[50] District Councils were further required to allocate resources internally on a similar basis to all areas within the district – a provision which meant that distribution proceeded more fairly than before decentralisation when state legislators controlled it. Since these requirements were broadly adhered to, most councillors felt reasonably content with their lot.[51] This helped to maintain remarkably civilised relations between parties in most councils.

District Council leaders sometimes expressed regret that they (unlike Mandal Councils) lacked tax-raising powers,[52] but this was not a major

---

[48] They did not gain control of law and order, revenue collection, public works, irrigation, horticulture or forests. Co-operatives, which were initially given to them, were subsequently withdrawn (Karnataka 1989, p. 8).

[49] The Chief Minister who presided over the creation of the system has given the example of one district where 16 per cent of the funds went on establishment costs while the rest went on development (Hegde (1994), p. 22). The share going to establishment costs was greater in many other districts, but not vastly so.

[50] The criteria used to determine the division of the untied grant were as follows: 50 per cent on population, 5 per cent on backwardness in agriculture, 7 per cent on backwardness in irrigation, 5 per cent on backwardness in industrial output, 5 per cent on road and rail mileage per 100 sq km per 100,000 of population, 2 per cent on backwardness in financial infrastructure, 5 per cent on backwardness in medical facilities, 5 per cent on backwardness in power supply, 4 per cent on the problems of the 'weaker sections' of society, and 12 per cent for hilly and drought-prone areas. Further funds came from the central government, as we shall see. Ibid., pp. 25–6.

[51] Numerous Mandal chairmen behaved less even-handedly and distributed excessive resources to their own clients and backers. At that level, personal and factional networks were usually more important than party loyalties.

[52] They had the power to charge licence fees, collect rents from property and, with the approval of the state government, raise loans (Karnataka (1989), pp. 11–12; and Karnataka (1985), chs. 1, 19, 33 and 35).

concern. As one District president stated, 'We had enough money. Why should we take the burden of raising taxes?'[53] District councillors knew that to impose fresh taxes was to risk unpopularity (a major reason why Mandal Councils seldom made full use of their limited taxation powers). They also understood that the government had been astonishingly generous – by the standards of previous practice across India – in empowering councils. Most District Councils also had Janata Party majorities which had been persuaded by Janata ministers at the state level that the government had given them all of the powers and resources that were possible in the face of budgetary stringency and the resentment of state legislators at such substantial decentralisation.[54]

Despite this, most District presidents and councillors were unhappy with the state government's earmarking of most funds for specific programmes. They were supposed to be able to influence earmarking through a bottom-up planning process, but as we saw earlier, this system often failed to work effectively.

District Councils were permitted to transfer up to 10 per cent of funds under any single budget heading to any other. But most found this far too low a figure. Some found it difficult to spend all of the money allotted to unpopular programmes. They also resented the requirement that they obtain permission from the state government before making such transfers, and its refusal on a sizeable minority of occasions to oblige. The state-level official who oversaw the decentralising process believes that the government was generous in approving transfers of 10 per cent and, on occasion, even more.[55] But his view is not shared by those who were active in the districts.

In at least one case, the president and chief secretary of an important District Council were sufficiently frustrated by this that they conspired to transfer, furtively, far more than 10 per cent of funds earmarked for low-priority programmes. They did so on the assumption – which in law was highly dubious – that Council resolutions were 'infallible' and that the state government 'had no business to meddle'. They covered their tracks well enough to get away with this repeatedly,[56] but such actions were very unusual.

Another chief secretary took advantage of ambiguities about whether certain projects fell under one or another budgetary heading. 'I told them

[53] Interview with K. N. Puttubuddhi, Mysore, 1 April 1993. He had earlier contradicted this view in an interview with the *Star of Mysore*, 16 February 1991, but he dismissed that press interview as empty posturing.
[54] This came across vividly, for example, in an interview with Singari Gowda, Mandya District President, in Nagamangala, 10 April 1993.
[55] Interview with S .S. Meenakshisundaram, New Delhi, 15 April 1993.
[56] Interview with a former District Council chief secretary, Bangalore, 20 April 1993.

to pass a resolution placing it under a heading where they were inclined to spend less, and then I would wait for the state government to haul me up' – something which occurred only rarely.[57] In most cases, however, councils complied strictly – if grudgingly – with the rules and concentrated on persuading the state government in the subsequent planning round to change allocations. They made only limited progress with this, however, and earmarking remained a major annoyance.

Mandal Councils faced a similar 10 per cent limitation, but many of them disregarded legal restrictions far more often and more extensively than District Councils. They often falsified spending records. One Mandal chairman said that he would propose an expenditure of, say, Rs.600,000 for a project which he knew to cost only Rs.400,000, so that he could spend the remaining Rs.200,000 on other things.

When this sort of concealment failed to deceive the district-level officials who checked their records once or twice a year, or when the records showed a refusal to comply with priorities, Mandal chairmen usually dared their visitors to do something about it. Partly because there were so many Mandals to deal with – an average of 130 per district – disciplinary action seldom followed. So as one Mandal chairman stated, they found it 'easy going' to ignore the rules in this and – as we shall see – in other ways.[58]

In the first two years of the councils' existence, the District Councils had control over very substantial resources for two major national programmes to provide rural employment. In 1989, however, Prime Minister Rajiv Gandhi integrated these and other initiatives into something called the Jawahar Rozgar Yojana (JRY). Under this heading, massive funds were channelled from New Delhi directly to institutions at or near the village level. When more than one tier of decentralised government existed, the lion's share of JRY resources was to go to those closest to the grassroots. Thus in Karnataka, the Mandal Councils received 80 per cent of these funds, while the District Councils – which had previously controlled all of them – retained only 20 per cent. Some District Councils delivered somewhat less than they were required to,[59] but in the main, they complied with the rules.

This represented a huge increase in resources at the Mandal level. One typical Mandal chairman explained that after the inauguration of the JRY he had access to the following resources in any single year: Rs.120,000 from the state government per capita grant;

---

[57] Interview with a former District Council chief secretary, Bangalore, 19 April 1993.
[58] Interview with a Mandal chairman in Dharwar District, 7 April 1993. This paragraph draws on numerous interviews with Mandal councillors and district-level officials.
[59] Interview with a former District Council chief secretary, Bangalore, 19 April 1993.

Rs.350,000–400,000 from the JRY; Rs.50,000–100,000 from the Integrated Development Programme. This gave his Mandal Council, which presided over about 10,000 constituents, upwards of Rs.620,000 per year. By any standard, that is a great deal of money. The chairman in question reckoned that it was a nine-fold increase over the funds available before decentralisation.[60]

The Mandal Council also has great freedom to decide how to spend this money. Officially, councils were free to decide how to spend only 20 per cent of JRY funds. But in practice, they did what they liked with most of it and nearly always got away with it.

Councils at both levels did next to nothing to supplement their revenues by investing in enterprises which would yield surpluses, since the state government was empowered to recover all profits which they derived from the use of state grants. Thus the example of the Bangalore Rural District Council investing in a fisheries project, of which much has been made by some writers, was unusual. Chief accounts officers in the districts – financial advisers to the councils – stated that they counselled against such investments since the councils could expect no returns from them.

Decentralised systems in which most resources are provided from above are often condemned by analysts for giving councils no autonomy. The same analysts often presume that this also gives higher levels of government control over the councils and wrecks democratic decentralisation. The evidence from Karnataka (and from Bangladesh) shows these complaints to be baseless. As long as substantial resources are passed down to councils (as they were not in Ghana), and as long as they are not greatly reduced or cut off (as they were with disastrous effect in Côte d'Ivoire), councils which have considerable autonomy and decentralisation will be genuine.

Mandal Councils' problems and relations with District Councils

The Mandal Councils, which stood only slightly above the village level, were the main agencies responsible for implementing development projects and mobilising local resources. Very little was accomplished on that latter front, since councillors found that levying taxes and pressing people for voluntary contributions made them unpopular.[61] They concentrated instead on spending the substantial funds received from above on projects. The District Councils' tasks were to oversee and co-ordinate them, to provide staff to assist them in project implementation, and to link the Mandals with the state government.

---

[60] Interview with N. R. Ranganarasimhiah, Hanchikuppe, 21 April 1993.
[61] Our findings are at variance with comments in Karnataka (1989), p. 12.

The Mandal Councils had such limited staff resources that there was 'a gross mismatch' between their developmental duties and their capabilities.[62] At best, a Mandal Council possessed only a single, poorly trained secretary to keep records and accounts. And since these bodies were created anew in 1987, long delays occurred before many of them acquired even one functionary. This left them far too dependent on District Councils for staff to help with implementation, and the latter had too many Mandal Councils to serve to respond adequately.

The decision by Karnataka's decentralisers to establish elected councils at only these two widely separated levels – with no elected body in between[63] – made it difficult for District Councils to assist, communicate with, monitor or co-ordinate the doings of Mandal Councils, or to be informed and lobbied by them. These problems were exacerbated by the failure to arrange regular meetings between Mandal Chairmen and key district officials.[64] These districts are huge, with an average population in 1991 of 2.4 million. Distances between the district headquarters and many Mandals were enormous, and the sheer numbers of Mandal Councils per district (130 on average) meant that this was one of the few serious flaws in this system.

Some District presidents and councillors stated that they eased this problem by touring extensively. But most knowledgeable observers saw this as woefully inadequate. They argue convincingly that the only way to integrate the two levels was to obtain sustained help from the sub-district level in between, where the key figure was a bureaucrat, the block development officer (BDO). It was difficult, however, to mobilise BDOs, for two reasons. First, they and the level at which they worked had lost status and power when decentralisation was introduced. They went from being the main focus of rural development efforts to a marginal role, as levels above and below were empowered.

Second, the BDOs were closely associated with state legislators who were the other major losers from decentralisation. The state government had created bodies at the sub-district level as 'an ego-satisfying institution' for the legislators who headed them.[65] But these had so little power

---

[62] Ibid., p. 22.
[63] The decision to adopt this approach owed much to the preference of the Janata Party's state government (which instituted the system) for the model of decentralisation that had been devised by the Ashok Mehta Committee, appointed by the Janata government in New Delhi during the 1970s (India (1978)). This preference was not merely the result of partisan feeling, however, since by adopting the Mehta model, the state government avoided the time-consuming business of establishing their own committee to conduct a prolonged investigation into decentralisation.
[64] Karnataka (1989), p. 34.
[65] These words were attributed to Ramakrishna Hegde, the Chief Minister who presided

that many legislators took this as an affront. Their antagonism to the new councils reinforced that of the BDOs who were thus unenthusiastic link-men between district and Mandal levels. So Mandal Councils were never effectively integrated with the district level.

This gave them immense autonomy[66] which was sometimes put to beneficial effect. But it also meant that Mandal leaders often got away with violations of laws and regulations – see the discussion below of their failure to meet obligations to the Scheduled Castes. Mandal leaders either concealed these omissions by creative accounting or they openly admitted them on the usually safe assumption that no punitive action would follow. Mandal Councils' misdeeds were also supposed to be checked by mass meetings (Gram Sabhas). But we have seen that Mandal leaders soon abandoned these.

District Councils gained a little influence over certain Mandals by providing administrative support for development projects. But in the main, they felt unable to maintain contact with most of them, 'like postmen' whose main task was merely to pass funds down to the Mandals.[67] They sometimes acted as spoilers, preventing Mandal Councils from operating effectively. But in general little influence, oversight or co-ordination was exercised by the District Councils.[68]

Absenteeism and work-rate among government employees

The effectiveness of institutions is undermined if government employees absent themselves from work while taking their salaries, or do little when they turn up. The Karnataka government sees this as a significant

---

over decentralisation, who uttered them in the presence of a District Council chief secretary, interviewed in Bangalore, 19 April 1993.

[66] Mandal Councils' autonomy was derived partly from the informal practicalities of politics outlined in the text, and partly from formal provisions. For example, they received their main block grants on the basis of population within the Mandal, so that neither the state government nor the District Council could influence them much via discretionary payments. Their resources were rather limited until 1989, when the Rajiv Gandhi government created the Jawahar Rozgar Yojana programme that delivered 80 per cent of central development funds directly from New Delhi to the lowest tier of local government. Mandal Councils then gained immense new resources at the expense of District Councils which retained only 20 per cent.

They had to obtain District Council approval for projects on which this money was spent, but the worst problem that they usually experienced on that front was a delay of one to two months. They also had to gain approval of lists of beneficiaries for various projects, but they were usually able to arrange the lists in ways that prevented the overburdened and under-informed district authorities from undermining their decisions. Interviews with numerous Mandal chairmen in four districts, March and April 1993.

[67] Interview with a former District councillor, Mysore, 18 April 1993.

[68] These remarks are based on a large number of interviews with journalists, bureaucrats and District and Mandal councillors in three districts (Dharwar, Mysore and Mandya) in March and April 1993.

problem.⁶⁹ Advocates of decentralisation there have argued that absenteeism declined radically after the creation of elected councils – by as much as 91 per cent.⁷⁰ Our research indicates that such figures exaggerate the change somewhat, but that considerable progress was made none the less.

The creation of elected councils vastly expanded the number of people in authority to whom citizens could complain about government employees. Villagers had 'many masters to ask', as one councillor put it.⁷¹ Members and chairmen of Mandal Councils could also see these things with their own eyes. They often took action themselves, by pressuring workers in the local school or medical dispensary. If they needed additional leverage, they could contact their representative on the District Council. Bureaucrats at the district and sub-district levels who now toured more extensively also reported such things to the District Council, lest their failure to do so be reported up through the system.⁷²

When Mandal councillors were ineffective or inclined to connive in dereliction of duty by government employees, other people from their area could pass the word to District councillors. After hearing a number of such stories, one District president suspended nine government doctors for non-attendance at work. This was a calculatedly draconian action, *pour encourager les autres*, and he found thereafter that employees in all twenty-seven of the departments under his supervision 'got more responsible'.⁷³

Such action had to come from the District Council, since the Mandal Councils lacked the authority to suspend such officials. But moral pressure from Councils at both levels was always more important than formal disciplinary action. The power of even the District Councils to move formally against civil servants was limited. They could in most cases suspend but not dismiss people. As a result, councillors' main tactic in pressuring bureaucrats was to threaten to embarrass them by publicising their misdeeds.

The results varied considerably both between and within districts. But

---

⁶⁹ *Times of India*, 10 November 1993.
⁷⁰ This figure, which refers to primary school teachers and health workers, was cited by L.C. Jain in a Ford Foundation symposium (Ford Foundation 1992, p. 35). For unquantified comments in a similar vein, see Karnataka (1989, pp. 9–10 and 24–25) and the statement by Abdul Nazir Sab, the Minister concerned (*Deccan Herald*, 8 July 1987).
⁷¹ Interview with D. R. Patil, opposition leader of the Dharwar District Council, Hubli, 4 April 1993.
⁷² Interview with a former District Council Chief Secretary, 27 March 1993. Corroborating evidence came from interviews with numerous people who had knowledge of several districts.
⁷³ Interview with K. N. Puttubuddhi, former Mysore District President, Mysore, 13 April 1993.

modest and sometimes marked changes occurred in the behaviour even of doctors, nurses and paramedics – all of whom had greater status, self-confidence and insulation from pressure than teachers and employees of some other line ministries. Among these latter groups, the change was more substantial. All manner of government employees 'were now made to work' because they were for the first time 'under the supervision of the questioning public mind'.[74]

This should not be over-stated. The changes were seldom dramatic. Our village surveys and elite interviews indicate that the main result was not less absenteeism – it declined 'remarkably' in certain areas,[75] but usually only moderately – but more assiduous, more responsive and less corrupt behaviour by those who were on the job. Many were compelled to work longer hours. They also faced pressure to bend bureaucratic rules – usually to enhance service delivery rather than to facilitate corruption.

District Councils also reduced urban bias in the administration, not least because they were elected almost entirely by rural dwellers. In several districts, new routines were introduced to get officials out of the larger towns and cities. For example, one District president decreed that officials working out of his office had to spend twenty days per month on tour, and required them to keep diaries which were randomly checked.[76] Variations on this theme were found in several other districts, and reports of inflated reports on the number of villages visited often emerged from the Mandal level.[77]

It was also common for District Councils to transfer significant numbers of employees – especially teachers – from urban to rural areas.[78] (This and the power which councils had over discipline and personnel records of junior government employees like teachers would be seen as radical in an African context.) Such transfers were not always altruistic. Employees have long proffered payments to politicians to ensure good postings, and councillors sometimes accepted bribes after threatening transfers. But across most of the state, there was nevertheless at least a modest shift of personnel from urban to rural areas as a result of decentralisation – despite state government resistance.

Taken overall, these changes produced a limited but still significant

---

[74] Interview with the head of a district health department of northern Karnataka, 7 April 1993.
[75] Interview in Bangalore with a former Chief Secretary in a southern district, 19 April 1993.
[76] Interview with K. N. Puttubuddhi, Mysore, 13 April 1993.
[77] Interview with a former District Council Chief Secretary, 27 March 1993.
[78] See for example, *Star of Mysore*, 16 February 1991, on the transfer of 500 teachers at once.

enhancement of the effectiveness and responsiveness of government institutions – at no extra cost to the taxpayer or the state exchequer. It is also widely believed – with good reason – that if decentralised institutions had been allowed to survive, further improvements of this kind would have occurred.

Declining corruption and its impact on effectiveness
Where corruption is a serious problem, the effectiveness of government institutions is impaired. If politicians and/or bureaucrats steal money from development programmes, citizens receive fewer benefits. If they demand bribes before delivering goods and services, citizens gain less. It is therefore appropriate in a discussion of institutional effectiveness to consider the changes which decentralisation wrought in patterns of corruption.

Our discussion of corruption here is more extensive than in chapters on the other three countries, for two reasons. Information was easier to come by there, but more crucially, this experiment generated greater change – and for the better – than did the others.

Decentralisation in Karnataka yielded paradoxical results. The number of people involved in corrupt acts increased significantly. But the overall amount of money stolen almost certainly decreased – at least modestly. We cannot offer absolute proof of this latter point, but the evidence to support it is strong.

The growth in the numbers of people engaged in malfeasance was inevitable. This should be understood wherever democratic decentralisation is contemplated. When power was dispersed into the hands of (on average) nearly 3,000 elected councillors in every district, the number of people with influence to peddle naturally rose. Little more than a score of legislators, bureaucrats and others in each district had previously had access to state power. Therefore the villagers who told us that the creation of District and Mandal Councils entailed 'a decentralisation of corruption' were correct.[79] But those (and there were many) who then drew the further conclusion that decentralisation entailed an increase in the overall amount of money illegally diverted were mistaken. In most districts – there were perhaps two exceptions out of nineteen – corruption was more apparent, but it declined in scale.

Decentralisation made the political process much more transparent, and the theft of funds and the sale of influence far more visible. A lively two-party system ensured that it was not left to citizens to detect and

---

[79] They made similar observations to an Institute of Social Sciences team headed by Anand Inbanathan. Interview with him, Bangalore, 9 April 1993.

protest against corrupt acts. Opposition parties seized every opportunity to sound the alarm, even on flimsy evidence.

Our argument about the decline in the overall amount of corruption rests on an understanding of the logic of corruption before decentralisation. Consider first the state level under the old system where ministers and legislators exercised immense influence over the flow of development funds. Their ability to conceal how those funds were managed, and the spectacular levels of corruption which prevailed at that level after 1972, ensured that a large (but unknowable) proportion of development resources was siphoned off before it reached lower levels. When the new councils were given control of development programmes, this became immensely more difficult.[80]

Consider next the 'taluk' or sub-district level which stands between the district and Mandal levels. The key institution here in former days[81] had been the Taluk Development Board. It consisted of directly elected members, but it was far weaker than the District and Mandal Councils, and its members had far less information about and influence over development programmes. This lack of information was central to the old system of corruption. Taluk Board members never knew how much money passed from New Delhi and the state capital down to their level in any given year. Only four or five persons had access to this information: the chairman of the board, the taluk's state legislator (who sat on the board), the block development officer (chief developmental bureaucrat), the chief engineer, and sometimes an accounting officer. The first four of these people had such tight control over development funds, and operated in such secrecy, that they could divert large amounts to themselves, their friends and clients without being found out. It is impossible to say how much was stolen under the old system. But when old Taluk board members got elected to the new Councils in 1987, they were amazed at the amounts of funds provided to district and Mandal levels. When they learned that the government had not increased such

---

[80] Interviews with E. Raghavan, Bangalore, 10 April 1993, and with numerous senior bureaucrats in development departments.

[81] In the period after 1960, the reluctance of most state-level leaders to permit decentralized councils to exercise influence caused them to hold elections to the Taluk Development Boards rather irregularly. This meant that when the Boards' official term (four and then five years) ended, their functions were turned over to the bureaucrats. As a result, these Boards actually existed only about half of the time between their creation in 1960 and the election of District and Mandal Councils under the new system in 1987. When the boards did not exist, a taluk's legislator and one or two civil servants exercised virtually complete and highly secretive control over the funds which came to the Board. Even when they did exist, elected members of the Board were unable to learn how much money was available for various programmes.

India (Karnataka) 63

provisions, they saw immediately that substantial amounts must have gone astray under the earlier system.

Many new councillors stole funds and took bribes. But the new system was so open that a large number of people – councillors, journalists, senior and junior bureaucrats, informed citizens – knew how much money was available. Party competition made councillors eager to pounce on the misdeeds of opponents. Pounce they did, and journalists seized avidly on the merest sign of scandal. Press reports of District Council meetings are saturated with accounts of 'heated exchanges' over alleged profiteering.[82]

Corruption among councillors was also checked both by tight official auditing procedures at the district level, and by the vigilance of journalists and leaders of voluntary associations. Corruption among bureaucrats, which in many districts appears to have exceeded that among elected politicians (particularly at sub-district levels), was restrained by the vigilance of councillors and their constituents (especially where voluntary groups were strong).

Serious cases of corruption could only occur when bureaucrats and councillors colluded or when one side acquiesced in the other's misdeeds. But the social distance between these two groups severely limited the number of such cases.

Attempts to profiteer became public knowledge in a variety of ways. Most District Council presidents toured extensively. They encountered constituents who often complained of corruption in front of witnesses at organised meetings, formal visits or random stops along the road. Since action against corruption gained them popular support, they investigated the complaints. One District president spoke of a visit to a school where he found that the cereals being offered in student meals were inferior to agreed standards. He terminated the supplier's contract forthwith, and when the contractor took this as a request for a bribe, the president berated the man publicly.[83]

Most District Presidents tried to check on Mandal chairmen, partly because laxity could inspire criticism from District councillors. When misdeeds were unearthed, they could threaten Mandal chairmen with the loss of discretionary grants, suppression or prosecution. The last two threats were very seldom carried out, and there were so many Mandals that such oversight had limited effect, but it sometimes produced results. District *councillors* provided more comprehensive oversight. Since exposing murky doings enhanced their standing, District Council meetings

[82] I am grateful to M. Madan of *The Hindu* for explaining this. Interview, Hubli, 6 April 1993.
[83] *Star of Mysore*, 16 February, 1991.

seldom passed without at least one such allegation. These nearly always found their way into press reports.

At the Mandal level, inadequate remuneration – nothing for councillors, Rs.300 per month for chairmen, Rs.150 for vice-chairmen – encouraged profiteering.[84] Corruption there mainly entailed sharing percentages skimmed off of construction projects. The system, which varied little from district to district, was cheerfully explained by several former chairmen.

They frequently gave Mandal councillors contracts to execute projects, even though this was illegal. The largest item by far in project budgets was 'labour charges'. It was from this that funds were mainly diverted. The usual rake-off was around 20 per cent of the budget. Roughly half of this had to be paid to a minor civil servant who was the project engineer. Another quarter went to the contractor, and the remainder was used to bribe higher officials who approved the work. Contractors often managed to extract further modest profits by using sub-standard materials and by spending a little less on labourers' wages than they claimed. Mandal council chairmen were sometimes able to take a cut similar to that of the contractor. But this was often difficult if the former was politically obliged (for his election as chairman) to the councillor/contractor. This constraint meant that chairmen made most of their money by taking percentages from funds to purchase supplies.[85]

Despite all of this, the high visibility of corruption at Mandal level imposed restraints upon it. As one knowledgeable bureaucrat said, 'The veil of secrecy, almost a steel curtain, that had hidden things before the councils had now been removed.' In villages, we and others found that 'everyone was talking about corruption',[86] usually in a well-informed manner. Many Mandal councillors said that villagers learned about virtually every underhand deal, and that this checked corruption. Citizens routinely protested against it at periodic village meetings. When councillors stopped holding these, they were angrily assailed at public celebrations. It was virtually impossible for them to budget for a project and then not build it. When they used sub-standard materials, they often encountered trouble. One group of villagers who spotted a bridge builder using inferior quality cement levelled the structure to the ground. All of

---

[84] (Karnataka 1989, p. 31).
[85] These comments are based on numerous interviews with Mandal councillors, Chairmen and other knowledgeable informants in Dharwar, Mysore, Bangalore and Mandya Districts.
[86] The quotation comes from a conversation with B. S. Bhargava who has studied the Mandal-level very extensively.

this meant that, after decentralisation, it was extremely difficult for people at this level to steal much.

What of corruption at the district level? Knowledgeable sources believe that nearly all efforts at profiteering there were uncovered. Examples are legion. In Mysore District, health officials attempted a major scam by falsely claiming to have achieved 100 per cent of their family planning target, while pocketing Rs.15 million. One District councillor learned from constituents that little work had actually been done. His protest pried open the scandal and other councillors made similar enquiries to show their concern for clean government. Severe action was taken against these bureaucrats and most of the money was recovered.

Councillors elsewhere made allegations that materials for borewell construction were missing from government stores, that seeds for farmers had gone astray, that officials had embezzled funds for well-digging, medicines and primary health care.[87] Some exposés were particularly telling, as when inferior materials caused leaks to appear in an irrigation project even before it was inaugurated. Others were ghastly. One Council learned that after doctors refused treatment to patients who would not provide bribes, a pregnant women and three cholera victims died.[88] The Mysore District Council heard of Social Welfare Department officials' 'involvement' in a gang rape in a council Scheduled Caste hostel.[89]

Allegations usually triggered investigations by councils, so that press reports are full of accounts of probes into the non-payment of workers in a forestry project, the diversion of wood from a housing scheme, and so on. If the District President delayed or refused an investigation, major ructions followed.[90]

Councils also uncovered corruption at higher and lower levels. In Dharwar, a councillor unearthed a major scam at the state level whereby nearly 40 per cent of the funds for the purchase of cloth for one million school uniforms had been stolen. In Tumkur, it was discovered that councillors in one Mandal had sold pipes intended for a local drinking water scheme.[91]

Press reports also assisted by publishing allegations of corruption which councillors investigated. For this reason, several District presidents had the newspapers scanned each morning.[92] The press was sometimes

---

[87] *Times of India*, 19 April and 13 November 1987; 11 April and 8 September 1990; and *The Hindu*, 8 June 1989.
[88] *Times of India*, 13 November 1987 and 12 June 1989.
[89] *Times of India*, 20 July 1991.   [90] See for example, *Times of India*, 4 January 1988.
[91] *Times of India*, 16 April and 13 September 1990. See also, 24 September 1990.
[92] This is clear from ibid. and from interviews with three other District Presidents.

threatened with libel actions over these reports, but the editors usually stood by their stories, almost all of which were well founded, and corruption was duly curbed.[93]

When it was discovered, as it almost always was, that a District president was conspiring with bureaucrats to divert development funds, a bipartisan uproar would ensue. In one district, for example, it was shown that borewells which had supposedly been dug were non-existent and that the president was involved. Councillors from both parties threatened his removal and prevented the theft.[94]

Corruption was most serious in Gulbarga District. This was a problem council from the start, whether the issue was probity, political murder (an extreme rarity in this state) or just ordinary business.[95] In mid-1989, councillors held the District President responsible for the misuse of over Rs.10 million intended for flood relief. They requested a criminal investigation. A councillor's simultaneous appeal for the annulment of purchases made by the chief secretary indicated their belief that he had colluded.[96]

Later estimates placed the amount diverted at Rs.16 million, and many councillors and observers thought that collusion had occurred. The council lacked the power to discipline the chief secretary who, reportedly anticipating trouble, obtained a transfer to New Delhi.[97] An enquiry later exonerated him, although reliable sources claim that this occurred because he covered himself by getting the president to approve the illegalities in writing. The president also went unpunished. He protested his innocence and announced that he would seek exoneration from the voters.

It is clear from this and another case,[98] and from discussions with numerous witnesses, that some corruption went unpunished. There were two main reasons for this. First, the security of tenure which IAS officers enjoy – to insulate them from unwarranted political intrusions – impeded

---

[93] Interview with E. Raghavan, *Times of India*, 10 April 1993. Interviews with various District and Mandal councillors indicate that it was more difficult to stop certain unscrupulous District Presidents (a minority of the total) obtaining money by taking 'commissions' on purchases of supplies and bribes from civil servants to obtain or avoid transfers. Most (though not all) Chief Secretaries were regarded as clean. District councillors could make modest amounts for awarding sizeable contracts.
[94] Interview with a former District councillor, Mysore, 13 April 1993.
[95] See for example *Times of India*, 10 June and 30 November 1987. The former deals with the Council's inability to conduct business, and the latter with a murder of a councillor, apparently as a result of a feud within the Janata Party. On corruption, see also *Times of India*, 13 January 1991.
[96] *Times of India*, 3 June 1989; and *The Hindu*, 5 June 1989.
[97] Interview with a journalist familiar with the case, Bangalore, 21 April 1993.
[98] *Times of India*, 30 July 1991.

anything more than transfers of errant members. Second, after November 1990, when the Congress Party changed its Chief Minister, Karnataka suffered its most flagrantly corrupt government. With bureaucrats being pressed to assist state-level politicians in looting the exchequer, it was immensely difficult to discipline wayward district officials. But such cases were rare enough that the overall level of corruption almost certainly declined as a result of decentralisation.

One unexpected check on corruption deserves attention. Every civil servant, male councillor and journalist that we interviewed – many of whom were hard-eyed realists – stated that they knew of no instance when a woman councillor indulged in corrupt acts. Since they held 25 per cent of the seats, this had an impact on the incidence of corruption. We are sceptical of statements that admit no exception; on occasion, this generalisation was surely disproved. But the evidence shows that the number of such occasions was exceedingly limited. As the years passed, some women councillors almost certainly acquired the profiteering habits of their male colleagues, but their standards of conduct were so high that it is safe to expect that they would have continued, in the main, to be a force for probity.

The result of all this was a much lower level of corruption than in Bangladesh, where as much as 40 per cent of development funds were stolen. Such estimates are necessarily approximate but the evidence is consistent enough to lend this figure considerable credence. The actual levels of corruption in Karnataka varied from district to district and from time to time. The arrival in a district of a new chief secretary who lacked the skill and determination to curb malfeasance among bureaucrats, or a change of council president (a much rarer occurrence) which ushered in a man who was dishonest or inept at tackling councillors' misdeeds, would allow the level to rise. Problems were less serious in districts which (i) had effective voluntary associations (ii) had a strong local press and – less crucially – (iii) were nearer the state capital. In such districts (roughly half the state), it is reliably estimated that corruption consumed only 5–10 per cent of council funds. In most other districts, the figure probably exceeded 10 per cent only slightly. In perhaps two or three, like Gulbarga – remote, devoid of strong voluntary associations, poorly led and with a weak local press – the figure may have reached 25 per cent. But even in such places, that only occurred in bad years and it nearly always became public knowledge.

By the standards of the other three countries in this study, or of Karnataka itself prior to decentralisation, this is an impressively low level of corruption. Since the councils lapsed in late 1991, corruption is reliably reported to have soared. Tens of millions have been stolen by one means alone – persons filing bills for work that was not done, something that was exceedingly difficult while the councils existed.[99]

Escaping political paralysis at the state level

Decentralisation here had one further advantage which contributed to the effectiveness of government institutions. The councils did not suffer from a type of political paralysis which has gripped state governments (in Karnataka and in many other Indian states) at most times over the last twenty years or so.

This paralysis first became apparent in Karnataka after the post-Emergency parliamentary election in February 1977. It appeared to many legislators in the ruling Congress Party there that they might be swept from power at an early state election, like the Congress in that parliamentary election. With time so short before a possible end to their careers, many frantically pressed the Chief Minister to allow them to enrich themselves illegally. To get his attention, they often threatened to defect to another party or to destabilise his government. He had to spend most of his time attending to their demands, merely to keep himself in power. The machinery of state government seized up, and policy implementation virtually stopped.

Congress was re-elected in 1978, but then Indira Gandhi began fomenting dissidence in her party to prevent state-level leaders from becoming too powerful. Paralysis set in again. In 1980, a new Chief Minister took power who was extravagantly loyal to Mrs Gandhi. Dissidence ceased, but since the new Chief Minister was mentally incapable and monumentally corrupt, his regime was brutish and utterly unresponsive to elected representatives.

The voters replaced it with a Janata Party government in 1983 which was both creative and free from paralysis. But by 1986, legislators' efforts to enrich themselves and factional infighting paralysed that government as well. It was succeeded in 1989 by a Congress government which suffered paralysis for similar reasons until Janata won an election in 1994.[100] Paralysis has thus become almost endemic, the 'normal' condition of state-level politics here and in many other Indian states. Karnataka's District and Mandal Councils did not suffer from this affliction, and for complicated reasons, it is unlikely that decentralised councils will be overtaken by it in the future. Therefore, the devolution of

---

[99] This is based on interviews with two skilled investigative journalists and two well informed and perceptive former District Council Chief Secretaries.

[100] For a devastating account of the impact of this paralysis on this government's development policies, see Imran Qureshi's article, *Times of India*, 12 October 1993.

power to lower levels enhances the effectiveness of government at implementing development programmes.

Outputs

How many and what sort of tangible benefits, in the form of development projects or 'outputs', did the councils deliver? Our survey of villagers yielded information on several hundred local-level projects. These will be discussed more fully in the section on 'responsiveness' below, but four points are worth noting here about their contribution to institutional effectiveness.

First, only 10.8 per cent of the projects identified to us had been implemented by the government prior to decentralisation in 1987, as against 73.4 per cent which had been wholly or partially funded by the councils. Although council projects were fresher in respondents' minds, the evidence clearly indicates a marked increase in micro-level development 'outputs' as a result of decentralisation.

Often and without prompting, villagers stated that more development had taken place during the councils' five years than in the forty years before that. This view is clearly inaccurate, but it is a revealing misperception. It highlights four important things.

First, the decentralisation of decision-making about development heightened citizens' awareness and, therefore, made development projects more visible – even though opportunities for villagers to participate in decisions did not increase dramatically. Second, the bias of successive state and national governments before decentralisation had caused micro-level development to suffer far greater neglect than most politicians and bureaucrats realised.

The third point emerges from councillors' strong bias towards the construction of physical facilities. It is that more micro-level, infrastructural projects were completed than were intended by the state and central governments that earmarked funds passed to the councils. Earmarking was often ignored, especially by the Mandal Councils. As a result, the provision of services suffered, although this was somewhat counterbalanced by a reduction in absenteeism and an increase in hours worked and work rates among bureaucrats.

Finally, this increase in micro-level projects occurred even though spending on development did not increase with decentralisation (as it did in Bangladesh). This is partly explained by the bias of councillors for such projects, but the increase was so marked that it also owed something to the decrease in corruption. Development funds that had earlier been stolen now found their way into actual projects.

Responsiveness

Democratic decentralisation plainly enhanced the responsiveness of government institutions in Karnataka, to a much greater extent than in our other three cases. This was true in three senses. Virtually all of our sources agreed that the speed of response increased enormously. Nearly all agreed that significant improvements occurred in both the quantity and the quality of responses. That is, institutions responded far more often than before, and their responses were deemed to be more satisfactory and to have conformed more closely to the felt needs of villagers. Let us consider each of these changes.

The speed of responses

The increased speed at which responses emerged is partly explained by an acceleration in the rate at which felt needs were communicated to people in authority. Councillors were quick to pass requests for official action to key government offices at and below the district level. Since District councillors had substantial influence over what went on in those offices, civil servants tended to be prompt both in their replies and in reporting problems to elected officials. Things would have worked even better had Mandal Council chairmen been able to meet District Council personnel on a regular basis, but this fault in the system[101] did not prevent a significant acceleration of responses.

The autonomy of the councils provides the rest of the explanation for this. Officials at the district and sub-district levels no longer needed approval from the state capital for development projects. In former days this usually delayed things by weeks, even when urgent action was needed.[102]

The quantity and quality of responses

We begin this discussion by considering the data from our survey of a representative sample of villagers. We then examine how and why decentralisation changed things. We asked villagers to name the sources of funding for the various development projects which they recalled in their localities (see Table 2.17).

These answers probably over-state somewhat the number of projects

---

[101] (Karnataka 1989, p. 34.)
[102] Under the decentralized system, non-urgent projects proposed by Mandal Councils which were to be funded by money which the Government of India provided under the Jawahar Rozgar Yojana programme were subject to approval by the District Council. Mandal Chairmen estimate that this usually entailed a delay of one to two months. Projects funded by other programmes did not require such approval from the district level.

Table 2.17. *Funding of development projects (%)*

Government before decentralisation	10.8
Government since decentralisation	4.0
District Councils	3.0
Mandal Councils	58.7
District and Mandal Councils	2.6
Mandal Council and NGOs	1.7
District Council and NGOs	0.3
Government and Mandal Councils	5.1
Self-help	0.2
Government and self-help	0.2
NGOs	9.3
Government and NGOs	0.3
Mandal Council and NGOs	1.7
District Council and NGOs	0.3
Others	0.1
Don't know	1.7

funded by the Mandal Council to the detriment of the District Council, since the former usually implemented the decisions of the latter. Some projects credited to the government since decentralisation may also have been the work of councils. But even if we take the figures as they stand, 73.4 per cent of projects were seen to have received at least partial financial support from the councils – a mightily impressive total.

We asked for information on the status of development projects which they identified. They indicated that 79.7 per cent of all projects had been completed, while 7.5 per cent had been abandoned unfinished, and 12.8 per cent were still in progress. This evidence demonstrates Councils' strong inclination to see projects through.

Let us now compare council projects mentioned by villagers in our survey with villagers' comments on their communities' needs. For complicated methodological reasons, this comparison can only yield rather crude indications of responsiveness, but it is worth considering none the less. Table 2.18 lists the types of projects and needs, one or both of which was mentioned on thirty-five or more occasions. (Villagers were encouraged to mention multiple projects and needs.)

In no case did councils implement significant numbers of projects of a type that villagers did not regard as genuinely needed. Councils tended to see direct aid to social groups or associations as lying outside their remit. The interest in houses and house sites arose because earlier government programmes had promised these, but such schemes had been largely discontinued and councils thus felt unable to move on that front. Beneficiaries of those programmes had mainly been poor families, and

Table 2.18. *Projects and needs identified by villagers*

	Projects	Needs mentioned
Water (wells, pipes, trucks)	233	161
Health facilities/programmes	181	148
Road building or repair	187	122
Sanitation (drains, latrines, etc.)	65	86
Education facilities/programmes	45	69
Electricity	155	53
Agricultural inputs, equipment, etc.	19	53
Transport facilities, services	48	52
Assistance to social groups, associations	0	37
Houses, sites for houses	0	38
Poverty alleviation projects	0	36

Table 2.19. *Levels of satisfaction with projects (%)*

Very satisfied	32.1
Somewhat satisfied	51.1
Dissatisfied for unspecified reasons	6.4
Dissatisfied, project unfinished	3.3
Dissatisfied, project not usable	0.7
Dissatisfied, project too expensive	0.2
Dissatisfied, poor quality	4.0
Dissatisfied, bad maintenance	1.0
Dissatisfied, poorly equipped	1.2

the inaction of councils here is partly explained by their disinclination to provide assistance to poorer groups. (See the next section of this chapter.) Villagers were somewhat unfair to councils here, since some projects identified by them under other headings were targeted on vulnerable groups.

Our survey found that villagers were, with some reservations, reasonably satisfied with the projects implemented by councils. Their views are summarised in Table 2.19. A total of 16.8 per cent of comments registered dissatisfaction, but the Councils were clearly substantially successful.

Our earlier discussion of 'participation' indicated that a significant minority of the respondents had contacted councillors and bureaucrats (24.6 per cent and 17.7 per cent respectively) about matters of concern. We asked them whether they had found these people 'honest and fair' and 'helpful'. Their answers are summarised in Table 2.20. The figures on the honesty of councillors and bureaucrats are reasonably good, when we consider that corruption was much more visible after decentralisation.

India (Karnataka)

Table 2.20. *The nature of responses to contacts*

	Councillors (%)	Bureaucrats (%)
Honest, fair	64.3	67.9
Dishonest, unfair	35.7	32.1
Helpful	54.9	67.7
Unhelpful	45.1	32.3

Table 2.21. *Levels of satisfaction with elected councils*

	Mandal Councils (%)	District Councils (%)
Very satisfied	12.2	40.4
Satisfied to some extent	54.3	28.8
Not at all satisfied	33.5	30.8

But they still reveal significant popular reservations. Their reservations plainly indicate that the performance of councillors could have been better. But it needs to be stressed that they also owe something to villagers' high expectations.

Similar reservations were apparent from the qualified answers which villagers gave to a question about their satisfaction with the councils' overall performance (see Table 2.21). District Councils received reasonably high ratings, but people were more sceptical about the more visible Mandal Councils. These answers were provided by members of an electorate which has, since the 1970s, shown itself to be increasingly impatient with elected representatives. In that context, the percentages in Table 2.21 are less than damning – councils received a grade of 'B-minus'. The long-term implications of these figures are far from discouraging. They indicate that villagers were developing a realistic understanding of what could be expected from decentralised institutions. Thus, when the state government revives such institutions, as it is required to do under a 1993 constitutional amendment, councils will not face a potentially threatening naivety about what they can accomplish.

How and why did these changes in responsiveness occur? The relative lack of responsiveness before decentralisation resulted from hauteur and procrastination among some bureaucrats, state legislators and ministers, the predominance of development programmes designed at national and state levels, etc. But that is only part of the story. Many politicians and civil servants in the state capital and district headquarters genuinely wanted to respond to the grassroots, but had been impeded by an inadequate flow of information from below. It is clear from their comments, however, that until decentralisation, they were unaware of how poorly informed they had been. It was only when the new system massively increased the flow of information that they grasped the limitations of the old system.

The remarks of one civil servant illustrate the point. Before decentralisation, he had served as deputy commissioner (chief civil servant) of a district. After the creation of the Councils, he then became chief secretary in another district. He was astonished at the difference between these two experiences.

As deputy commissioner, he had heard next to no complaints about government performance unless something went badly wrong. Very occasionally, he would chance upon something while touring rural areas. But most districts are so huge and he had so little time for touring that it was a hopelessly hit-and-miss method, 'not at all satisfactory' in his view. A typical day on tour entailed stops in perhaps ten villages, with roughly thirty minutes for each village. The immense psychological distance between villagers and the deputy commissioner made it hard for him to break through their deference, even when they were exasperated with a problem.

So news of problems often reached him only after they had simmered for extended periods. He recalled that one village had been without water for two years because of a broken pump before he learned of it. It was virtually impossible to obtain warnings early enough to nip things in the bud.

All of this changed after decentralisation. As chief secretary, information about problems great and small was constantly fed to him by councillors, their clients and constituents – including Mandal councillors. His sources had multiplied exponentially. There were on average forty-three District councillors and a staggering 2,905 Mandal councillors in each district, as opposed to twelve state legislators per district (who were often away in the state capital) before decentralisation. The councillors were also far better informed than the 'blissfully unaware' legislators, who usually took the deputy commissioner's word on 'blind faith'.[103]

Visits to villages produced greater information than before, partly because the presence of Mandal councillors (about whom villagers often complained) eroded the psychological distance between this senior official and common folk, and partly because decentralisation yielded much more information to villagers about government projects.

The chief secretary's problem was thus not too little information but

---

[103] The quotations in this sentence are from M. Madan Mohan, correspondent of *The Hindu*, Hubli, 5 April 1993.

too much. When troubles arose, he usually heard about them within a matter of days – often, as another stressed, within twenty-four hours. 'Even if I did not want to hear about a problem, I would hear anyway.' He was now expected, and often pressured, to respond.[104]

And respond they often did. District presidents frequently set deadlines for responses by various departments – in Mysore District, seven days for borewell repairs, three for pipes bearing tap water, etc. District councillors toured rural areas to monitor work by departments under their standing committees (health, education, social justice, etc.). If they found bureaucrats falling short, they often told them to mend their ways within a specified period. If they did not comply, it went to the district authorities. These injunctions did not always produce results, but it happened often enough to transform the old, ossified system.

Two other qualitative gains were often stressed by informants. First, the suitability of technical work improved considerably, because elected representatives closely tied to villagers frequently advised on design and implementation. Prior to decentralisation, this kind of input had only rarely come from state legislators. After decentralisation, councillors who nearly all lived locally were able to achieve far more. Second, and for the same reason, decisions about locating projects were much more fully informed by local knowledge and dialogues with villagers than before.

Mandal Council chairmen stressed that there was greater equity in geographical terms. Before decentralisation, if a legislator took a dislike to a set of villages, they could be starved of resources from government. Once councils were created, any semi-assiduous Mandal chairman could ensure that his area was not excluded. Even with an ineffectual chairman, a Mandal received substantial resources commensurate with its population, as a matter of right.

The district authorities heard pleas from remote villages that had seldom received development projects, and their responses clearly undercut urban bias. They also heard from disadvantaged groups that had seldom had assistance (though rural elites dominated the system) concerning problems that had arisen. Subsidised fertiliser and farm implements occasionally went to poor farmers in remote villages as well as to prosperous cultivators. A fisherfolk sub-caste within a low-status caste

---

[104] Interview with M.R. Sreenivasa Murthy, Bangalore, 2 April 1993. The supplementary comment was provided by A. Ramaswamy, New Delhi, 27 march 1993. The material in these paragraphs is consistent with that provided by many other former Chief Secretaries. Numerous sources indicated that touring by civil servants at and below the district level – especially Block Development Officers at the sub-district or taluk level – also increased markedly.

cluster that had never received much funding, because other groups in the cluster lobbied only for help to agriculture, gained access to village ponds and aid from the fisheries department. And so it went on.

Given the radical increase in the amount of information and appeals for assistance that poured forth from the state's lively civil society, and given that 'local grievances which had been hidden all those years were now vented',[105] the new councils inevitably failed to do enough to satisfy many people. Popular exasperation was especially evident over a few issues on which the councils were impeded by the state government. Nowhere was this more apparent than in the government's refusal (for financial reasons) to permit District Councils to hire more primary school teachers – to which villagers everywhere attached high priority. But enough was accomplished on most fronts to earn the system high marks for responsiveness.

This was vividly illustrated by the way in which District and Mandal councillors' bias towards projects that entailed construction – buildings, road, etc. – took a somewhat different shape in Karnataka than in our other three countries. In those countries, while this bias was in part a response to a popular desire for such projects, it was mainly driven by the inclinations of politicians. In Karnataka, the appetite for such projects among citizens counted for more.

This was true partly because Karnataka's system was more open to pressure from voters and organised interests, and because civil society there was reasonably lively – although the latter was also true in Bangladesh and Ghana.[106] The main reason, however, was that the citizens in Karnataka were accustomed to and skilled in the business of representing their concerns to elected representatives. Decentralisation multiplied their opportunities to do so. Councillors in Karnataka repeatedly stressed that they were under relentless, insistent pressure from voters to deliver such projects. Their decisions to do so were less a matter of their own preferences than of the need to respond to pressure.

Responsiveness to whom? – vulnerable groups

We must also consider which groups received responses. Elites made gains, but democratic decentralisation in Karnataka did little to benefit vulnerable groups – poor people, Scheduled Castes (ex-untouchables) and women. Indeed, its net effect – particularly at the lower Mandal level – was to enhance the share of resources going to prosperous groups at

---

[105] Interview with M. Ahiraj, correspondent of the *Times of India*, Hubli, 6 April 1993.
[106] On Bangladesh, see the statistic on associational membership in chapter three of this study. For an analysis of the contrasting condition of civil society in Ghana and Côte d'Ivoire, see Crook (1991).

India (Karnataka) 77

the expense of the poor. It placed the Scheduled Castes in a less advantageous position than previously, even though it was supposed to help them. We should therefore not expect democratic decentralisation in India to assist in poverty alleviation over the short to medium term, unless the decentralised system is dominated by a leftist party, and that seems possible only in the state of West Bengal.

The Karnataka government's efforts to assist vulnerable groups unwittingly caused problems for them in two ways. First, its guidelines stated that the Scheduled Castes were to receive 18 per cent of Council resources, but it was unclear whether this meant 18 per cent of plan funds, total development funds, projects or whatever. This played into the hands of those who preferred not to assist the Scheduled Castes. Second, the state government was supposed to monitor the District Council's management of anti-poverty programmes, but it largely failed to do so. This left things to the Councils, and actual performance varies.

We saw earlier that elected Scheduled Caste members of District Councils seldom asserted themselves. This did not, however, destroy any chance that they might gain something from these councils. In a small number of cases, where one landowning caste group[107] had influence and where it was led by persons unsympathetic to the poor, vulnerable groups had little hope of concessions. In many cases, however, district-level politicians had internalised enough of the state-level penchant for bargaining between rich and poor groups to permit some accommodation. In a small number of districts, enlightened politicians from the dominant castes led the fight on behalf of low-status groups.[108] Karnataka's two-party system also helped, since opposition councillors often complained about inadequate help to the poor and Scheduled Castes. They did so mainly to embarrass the ruling party, but this still produced modest benefits.

It is widely believed – within and beyond India – that bureaucrats are more committed to the poor than are elected politicians from elite backgrounds. In Karnataka, however, this was often untrue. In Dharwar District, civil servants were reliably reported to be especially inclined to pilfer funds intended for the Scheduled Castes or to leave such money unspent. This 'played havoc with schemes to help the needy'. In Mysore

---

[107] It is more precise to say not 'caste group', but 'jati-cluster'. A jati is a endogamous caste group. Each of the so-called 'dominant castes' of Karnataka – the Lingayats and the Vokkaligas – in fact consists of a cluster of jatis. The two clusters tend to occupy distinct parts of the state, although there is some overlap. See Manor (1977a and Manor 1998).

In some districts, where one jati-cluster is found almost exclusively, it is easier for it to exercise great influence.

[108] This was true, for example, one leading Congress politician in Dharwar District who was a Lingayat. Interview with M. Madan Mohan, Hubli, 5 April 1993.

District, reliable sources argued that 'the key' to ensuring that programmes for Scheduled Castes worked was the control of corruption and inaction among bureaucrats.[109] In several districts, enough control was exercised over bureaucrats, and enough councillors wanted the Scheduled Castes to gain something that modest efforts were made to achieve that. They were more limited than the law or natural justice required, but they were not insignificant.

Legal requirements that Scheduled Castes be assisted were, however, widely flouted by Mandal Councils. They tended to spend money intended for the Scheduled Castes in ways that mainly or wholly benefited prosperous groups while claiming that it went to Scheduled Castes. Numerous Mandal chairmen explained to us how this was done. A council would, for example, mount a project to provide electricity and lighting to an entire village. This might extend into the Scheduled Caste quarter, but even if it did, 90 per cent of the benefit would go to others. But the entire sum spent was listed among the 18 per cent of funds devoted to Scheduled Caste uplift. Projects for village road repair, water supplies, etc., were handled similarly. Such deception was practised systematically in every part of the state, and next to nothing was done to curtail it.

We also saw earlier that women District councillors largely failed to assert themselves. This did not mean, however, that nothing was done at that level to assist women. Bureaucrats whose task was to implement programmes for women's and child welfare indicated that service delivery sometimes improved as a result of decentralisation. The existence of women councillors gave these civil servants useful links to women at the grass-roots and made it easier for them to understand women's needs. Responses from the district level occurred more quickly than before. The most significant gains were when the (often mainly female) bureaucrats in these government departments persuaded elected councillors (of both genders) to publicise opportunities for immunization, family planning, etc. But these changes seldom occurred on the initiative of women representatives. Rather they were the result of general improvements in services and communication with citizens.[110]

Apart from this, only very limited tangible benefits for women materialised. The best that women's leaders in the districts could say was that by the end of the councils' five-year term, a greater willingness

---

[109] Interviews with M. Ahiraj and M. Madan Mohan, Hubli, 6 April 1993, and with M. V. Maramkal and V. Nagaraj, Mysore, 13 April 1993.

[110] This is based on interviews with bureaucrats working in this field in Dharwar, Mysore and Bangalore Rural Districts.

had developed among prominent women to fight future council elections.[111]

It has been argued that, in time, vulnerable groups will become more confident, assertive and impatient in councils such as these, and that councils' failure to respond adequately to such groups will therefore be a temporary problem.[112] This argument is similar to that which one of us has made about state-level politics in India (based on data from Karnataka),[113] but the evidence from the Mandal level raises doubts.

It is not naive to expect such things at the district level where the state-level culture of power-sharing between elites and disadvantaged groups was in evidence. But when elected bodies are created at or just above the village level – as in the case of Mandal Councils – it is very difficult to break down the dominance (in both gender and caste terms) of conservative men from landowning castes. Women councillors who press their claims at that level risk embarrassment and intimidation, and the Scheduled Castes risk harassment and violence.

Nor can low-caste voters be confident about remaining anonymous when they vote in such a localised council election – as they can when they and thousands of others elect a legislator. In a constituency with only 400 voters, if the Scheduled Castes combine to defeat a candidate who is the favourite of dominant groups, their action will be apparent and violent retribution may follow. We therefore remain concerned that, despite its many virtues, democratic decentralisation to very localised levels empowers arenas where social justice is much harder to achieve than at higher levels. And this may not change much any time soon.

Process

How did decentralisation in Karnataka affect the processes through which government and society interacted, and the popular perception of these processes?

Elections were extremely fair, but since that had long been true here, it produced little change in citizens' views. The political process became much more transparent than before. However, this did not earn the system the popular appreciation it deserved because people could more clearly see the shortcomings of government as well as its achievements. In Karnataka, ironically, although corruption declined as a result of decentralisation, most people believed that it had increased because it was now more apparent than under the old, opaque system.

---

[111] This was the consensus view that emerged from interviews with numerous women councillors and women's leaders in Karnataka, March and April, 1993.
[112] Blair (1988).   [113] Manor (1980b).

The increased speed of government responses was clearly perceived and welcomed by ordinary folk, as was the marked increase in the number of those responses. They also regarded the quality of most projects as good, and the types of projects implemented conformed quite closely to their felt needs. All of these things facilitated creative interactions between the state and local society, and made the political process appear more congenial and worthwhile.

Decentralisation also created a huge number of opportunities for would-be politicians, and eased frustration among them. However, the introduction of inter-party competition into local arenas tended to embitter local rivalries further – a cause of some popular dismay. And the failure of the councils to meet their legal responsibilities to the Scheduled Castes caused resentment among some. But in most respects, this more open, effective and responsive system made government appear more tractable and legitimate to most villagers.

CONCLUDING REMARKS

The preceding discussion is saturated with references to the political process, but this story would not be complete without an assessment of important political themes.

The impact of a change of government

In April 1989, the Indian government deposed Karnataka's state government and imposed direct rule from New Delhi. During eight months of that, the authorities curtailed the powers of councils – especially at the district level. District Councils were deprived of their powers to transfer teachers and to distribute crucial agricultural inputs. This created friction between District Councils and their chief secretaries, since the latter were ordered to ensure that councils did not exercise these powers. The authorities also refused to publish the report of a high-powered committee which praised the councils.[114]

Things grew worse after a state election in December 1989 brought the Congress Party to power. The new minister for decentralisation was extremely hostile to it. He favoured District Councils controlled by his party, although the law restricted his actions there. He also undermined the powers of *all* councils. They suffered successive funding cuts. In the eleventh month of the financial year 1989–90, their budgets for that year

---

[114] This is based on numerous interviews with councillors and civil servants, but see also, for example, *The Hindu*, 4 and 8 June 1989, and *Times of India*, 8 and 10 June 1989.

were slashed by more than Rs.10 million per district. Then, all District Council purchases of materiel were banned, blocking hundreds of millions of rupees worth of transactions. Tens of millions owed to District Councils were withheld.[115] The minister also transferred important powers and functions of chief secretaries to deputy commissioners who were outside council control.

The non-release of funds to District Councils prevented them from implementing certain poverty programmes. The government announced that it was considering depriving them of control over those programmes because implementation had failed! It took over the hiring of subordinate officials. Attempts were made to divest councils of sericulture, irrigation and education. They were deprived of their right to transfer even 10 per cent of funds from one budget heading to another. The number of uncompleted development projects soared.

This approach by the Congress government often angered Congress councillors as much as their Janata counterparts. Unanimous protests ensued.[116] But party loyalty divided many councils, and it was mainly left to Janata councillors to complain that 'deliberate mischief', 'calculated harassment' and the 'autocratic temperament' of the minister were 'throttling' Councils.[117]

Higher-level politicians' resentment

The Congress government's hostility was also bound up with a problem that affects virtually all experiments in democratic decentralisation – the jealousy of power-holders at higher levels in political systems. Even before the Congress Party took power, most Janata Party ministers and legislators had resented the Councils' powers.[118]

The two Janata ministers responsible for decentralisation argued that ministers' proper role was to make high policy, to which legislators could contribute in debates in the House. This may sound uncontroversial to readers in some Western systems, but in India it deprived these politicians of prized powers to distribute patronage in their constituencies.

So for example, we find the Janata Party's Education Minister

---

[115] *The Hindu*, 12, 26 and 28 March 1990.
[116] See for example, *Times of India*, 8 June 1989, 11 April 1990, and 1 and 13 January 1991.
[117] *Times of India*, 2 and 23 April 1990, and 26 July 1991.
[118] Decentralisation had been opposed even by leading ministers from the caste clusters (Lingayats and Vokkaligas) who dominate most villages in the state, despite the fact that a devolution of power to Mandals, which stand near to the village level, would empower their fellow castemen. They thus put the interests of the state-level political elite, in which they enjoyed prominence, ahead those of their caste clusters. This point emerged from my discussions with E. Raghaven.

protesting that he was unable even to decide on the location of a single school in his own constituency. Legislators found that bureaucrats in their constituencies who had once agreed to their every suggestion now paid greater heed to councillors.[119] The change was so dramatic that many politicians thought that a District Council President possessed greater power than a minister. That was not true if ministers' powers to make policy were considered, but politicians were so preoccupied with patronage distribution that many still thought this way.[120]

As one District councillor put it, the legislators 'really became legislators and not development implementors'.[121] If legislators had supported councillors within their constituencies, they could have constructed transitional networks that would have ensured their own re-election. (Indeed, this sometimes occurred.)[122] But legislators and ministers had long stood atop networks of support consisting of favoured backers. They were reluctant to draw several dozen new and younger faces into the political establishment in each district, since this might weaken their grip. This anxiety and their resentment at their loss of power to the new bodies prevented most of them from building new support bases among councillors. Most preferred to obstruct councillors.

In so doing, ministers and legislators were reacting against two constructive aspects of decentralisation. The first was the creation of a huge number of fresh opportunities for (mainly) young people in politics. Before decentralisation, between twelve and twenty politicians had a virtual lock on positions of power in each district. Skilled activists in their twenties and thirties – of which there was no shortage – were almost entirely shut out. This caused massive frustration which encouraged normless behaviour and destructive infighting in all parties. Decentralisation opened up new avenues for such people – mostly under the age of forty[123] – to play creative roles.

The second constructive aspect was the opportunity offered to political parties to strengthen their organisations. The simple need to find candidates for council elections enabled a party to forge ties to over 50,000 people. However, the resentments which state-level politicians felt towards the councils prevented them from seizing this chance to reinforce their parties.[124]

[119] Interview with M. Madan Mohan of *The Hindu*, Hubli, 6 April 1993.
[120] Interview with a former District Council Chief Secretary, New Delhi, 27 March 1993.
[121] Interview with the D. R. Patil, opposition leader on the Dharwar District Council, Hubli, 4 April 1993.
[122] Interview with a former District Council Chief Secretary, Bangalore, 20 April 1993.
[123] Stats. on age from ISS doc.
[124] Legislators pressured the state-level leadership of the Janata Party (which won control of most District Councils) to insert men of their choosing into the Presidencies of

When those seeking to protect decentralisation from the jealousy of higher level politicians made modest concessions to their opponents, it served only to encourage them to cripple them further. This tends to be a problem everywhere that decentralisation is attempted. If it is embedded in a nation's constitution, it can provide some extra protection. But even this may not have much effect in countries where constitutions are taken less seriously than in India.[125]

We have no easy, reliable answer to this problem, but would-be decentralisers need to keep it constantly in mind as they design and then implement their experiments.

Generalising from the Karnataka case

Democratic decentralisation in Karnataka achieved considerable success. But we must be cautious about inferring from this that decentralisation can produce similar benefits elsewhere. Many of the gains here resulted from things external to the experiment, from socio-political conditions which are often absent elsewhere.

Karnataka had a reasonably lively civil society. The resilience of caste and other social institutions meant that society was not dependent upon or structured by groups' access to the state, as is true in parts of Africa.[126] Since organised interests had had decades of experience with democracy, their leaders and activists possessed many of the bargaining, organising and lobbying skills necessary to make open, decentralised politics work creatively. Karnataka was largely free of extreme socio-economic inequalities which can generate oppression, desperation and vicious conflicts that make it difficult for liberal institutions to function.

Social forces here were also accustomed to working through political parties. Competition between parties was lively but moderate in char-

---

various District Councils. However, they succeeded only in a small number of cases, and despite this, most District Presidents possessed sufficient powers to operate largely as their own men.

The comments in the preceding three paragraphs in the text owe much to numerous discussions with E. Raghavan.

[125] The constitutional amendments requiring Indian states to create elected councils in rural and urban areas, which came into force in March 1993, have not fully solved this difficulty. Since 'panchayati raj' is a subject reserved to state governments under the Indian Constitution, there are limits on what the central authorities can prescribe in this vein. The amendments require states to establish several tiers of councils and to hold elections for them regularly. They also provide for semi-autonomous Finance Commissions to decide on the resources that will be provided to such councils. But the legislation now being prepared in several states to fulfil their constitutional obligations does not appear to empower these councils adequately.

[126] This becomes clear from a comparison between material provided in Chabal (1985) and in Manor (1989).

acter, thanks in part to one thing that was internal to the system of decentralisation – the requirement that most resources be distributed among councils according to population. That prevented politicians at higher levels from starving opposition-controlled councils. It was quite common for councillors from both parties to unite when confronting corruption or serious mismanagement, or when a Council's interests were threatened.[127]

Both main parties were strongly enough represented on District Councils to ensure spirited interplay between them. This contributed to greater transparency – to revelations that unearthed and impeded corruption, to investigations into budgets, policies and project implementation, and to early warnings of potential disasters. Party competition yielded similar benefits on many Mandal Councils too. Party connection tenuously integrated many Mandal Councils with higher levels in the political system in ways that proved creative, especially since the formal institutional links between the Mandals and higher levels were inadequate.

Karnataka also enjoyed the advantages of a free and assertive press, and a bureaucracy which was used to working under elected politicians and which tends to comply both with politicians' wishes and with the law. It is unusual to find so many of these factors robustly present elsewhere in Asia, Africa, Latin America or Eastern Europe.

[127] Examples of this are plentiful. See for example, *The Hindu*, 14 August 1989, and 7 March 1990; and *Times of India*, 10 April and 6 November 1987, 12 January 1988, 11 June 1989, 11 and 30 April 1990, and 1, 12 and 13 January and 24, 25 and 30 July 1991.

3 Bangladesh

THE BACKGROUND

The structure of decentralisation

The Bangladeshi experiment in democratic decentralisation was the creation of H. M. Ershad who had seized power in a military coup in 1982. His government created new elected councils at the sub-district (upazila or thana) level (with an average population of 245,000), and linked them to long-standing elected councils at the Union level much closer to the grassroots (with an average population of 20,000). There are 495 sub-districts and 4,401 Unions in Bangladesh. This system operated from 1985 until it was disbanded in 1991 after the fall of Ershad.

The sub-District Councils were more powerful than any such elected authorities in the history of Bangladesh. Their chairmen were directly elected while the other voting members included the heads of the eight to ten Union Councils within the sub-district's borders, plus four appointees: three women and a former freedom fighter. Non-voting members included the sub-district's chief civil servant and bureaucrats who oversaw the broad array of activities entrusted to the councils: agriculture, primary education, health and family planning, rural water supply, sanitation, Food for Work programmes, co-operatives and social welfare. The sub-District Councils served five-year terms and had modest revenue-raising powers, but they made limited use of them because the regime channelled abundant resources to them.

At the lower level in the system, the Union Councils (Parishads) consisted of a chairman and nine members, all of them elected for five-year terms, plus two women appointed by the central government. They were charged with maintaining law and order, and with mounting various development projects. Their resources were extremely limited, but this was compensated for by their chairman's membership on the well-funded sub-District Council. In theory, approval from the sub-District Council had to be obtained by a Union Council for its budget and taxes levied. The sub-District Council also decided what development projects (if any) were passed down to Union level. But since most voting members of the sub-District Council were heads of Union Councils, they obtained substantial resources.

Bureaucrats in development departments had previously been concentrated in the district headquarters, but they were deconcentrated to the sub-district level when councils there were created. The sub-District Council chairman, rather than the line ministries in Dhaka, was supposed to control these officials and integrate their work. Sub-District Councils were also meant to oversee the Union-level councils under its wing, and the formulation of a broad development plan. This entailed formidable problems of co-ordination, both among specialist bureaucrats working in diverse fields and between levels in the political system.

The socio-economic context

Scholars tend to use words like 'semi-feudal' to describe the socio-economic order in rural Bangladesh. They point to a lack of dynamism – in terms both of agricultural development and social reform – in rural society. They speak of serious inequalities and the dominance which the landed elite exercises uncompromisingly over their landless and land-poor neighbours. This is not to say that Bangladesh is without 'middle farmers' – that is, owner-cultivators with modest landholdings who seek to raise productivity in order to increase their incomes. But these people are less numerous than in more dynamic regions of South Asia (such as Karnataka). One study reckons that they constitute about one-sixth of rural households. They are greatly outnumbered by the landless, the functionally landless (with less than half an acre) and the owners of uneconomic farms (of less than two acres) – three groups who constitute perhaps 70 per cent of the rural population.[1]

Efforts by middle farmers and others to enhance productivity have been largely frustrated by the landed elite which is prepared to sacrifice wealth generation in order to sustain its control over the poor. They achieve this by money-lending, physical intimidation, and by maintaining low wages, share-cropping and other devices that ensnare the poor. They have nearly always been assisted in this by regimes at the national level and whose main concern has been to keep order in the countryside.[2]

This does not necessarily imply, however, that 'civil society' (organised interests which possess some autonomy from the state) is inert. This is

---

[1] World Bank (1983). Comments on the current regime are based on discussions with Harry Blair and field investigations.
[2] Blair (1988) and Jahan (1980), especially chapter 9.

the only country in the Commonwealth to have accomplished the overthrow of the post-colonial political order from below.[3] It has also experienced numerous elections at both national and lower levels. Such events tend to catalyse the awareness of citizens and the development of organised interests. This is a 'participation-oriented political culture'.[4] Various regimes in Dhaka have often visited repression on organised interests. But despite this and the repeated inability of democratic regimes to survive for long, civil society has not been crushed. In this respect, Bangladesh bears a certain resemblance to Ghana and offers a clear contrast to Côte d'Ivoire where organised interests have never been allowed to emerge in strength.

Other developments at and near the grassroots have also fostered civil society in Bangladesh. The extensive activities of non-governmental organisations (NGOs) and political parties count for a great deal. The fact that the last two military rulers of Bangladesh – Ziaur Rahman and H. M. Ershad – have felt it necessary to create their own party organisations argues for the durability of rival parties. The decentralisation experiments undertaken by those two rulers, partly to facilitate the creation of their own parties, have also encouraged organised interests. Persistent conflict between groups within Bangladeshi villages, some of it severe, has also impelled people to organise themselves for mutual protection. Our survey research found remarkably high levels of associational membership in rural Bangladesh. So the contrast between India (Karnataka) and Bangladesh should not be seen as analogous to that between Ghana and Côte d'Ivoire where the former country has a lively civil society while the latter tends towards quiescence.

The choice of case studies for field research

Our field research concentrated on two districts: Manikganj and Bogra. We paid particular attention to two sub-districts within each, and in each case these included both the sub-district round the district headquarters and a sub-district further afield.[5] The two districts contrasted with one another usefully, in several ways. Manikganj has been the scene of intensive work by several NGOs, while Bogra had seen little such activity. This helped us to determine whether an NGO presence made

---

[3] The only other possible candidate is Zimbabwe, but it should probably be excluded for several reasons.
[4] Maniruzzaman and Banu (1983).
[5] In Manikganj District, we worked mainly in Manikganj Sadar (round the headquarters town) and Saturia sub-districts; in Bogra District, we worked in Bogra Sadar (round the headquarters town) and Sherpur sub-districts.

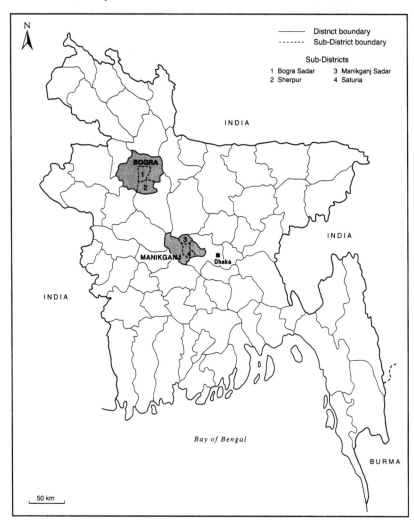

Map 2 Bangladesh: the districts, showing location of case-study sub-districts

much difference in the way that decentralisation developed. Manikganj is comparatively close to the capital, Dhaka – an eighty-minute drive – while Bogra lies far from the capital, in the northwest.

Both Manikganj and Bogra fall well within the mainstream of Bangladeshi districts in terms of levels of economic development, social composition, the availability of natural resources, literacy rates, the distribution of wealth, etc. Neither is an extreme or eccentric case.

PARTICIPATION

Before we begin an assessment of the changing patterns of participation which resulted from decentralisation, two preliminary comments are in order. First, generalisations are more difficult to make about Bangladesh than our other three cases, since there were more variations from place to place and time to time there. The Ershad regime which seized power in a military coup in 1982 was so preoccupied with using the system to obtain political allies in rural areas that it permitted council chairmen enormous latitude to do as they wished. So while an elaborate set of laws and formal regulations was drawn up for this decentralised system, its operation in any particular place or period depended heavily upon the personalities of council chairman and, to a lesser degree, prominent bureaucrats. Nevertheless, our inquiries indicate that the patterns which prevailed most of the time in the four sub-districts which we studied in depth were reasonably typical of the predominant tendencies nationwide.

Second, the regime's permissive approach towards council chairmen undermined whatever hope it may have had of controlling the councils. Several analysts have argued that 'control' was exercised from on high – especially over the sub-District Councils which were the key element in the system.[6] Another has claimed that the councils 'act virtually as agents of Central Government'.[7] But such interpretations rest on the incorrect assumption that the government made full use of its considerable powers to intervene in the operation of the councils and on an unwarranted belief that the formal laws and rules provide a reliable guide to the functioning of the system. Our study of actual political practice indicates that what the regime got from the councils was half-hearted acquiescence

---

[6] I have profited greatly from discussions of this with, among others, Mohammed Mohabbat Khan and Kirsten Westergaard, both of whom argue along these lines. (Khan (1987)). See also in this vein Akhter (1990) and (Haque (1985)). That latter article was published in the year the sub-District Council chairmen were first elected, when it was far too early to know how the system would work in practice. It concluded that the government would 'control' the councils by presuming that the government would fully exercise its powers over them. It did not.

[7] Faizullah (1989a), p. 3.

rather than control. Indeed, the national leaders were so indulgent in their dealings with council chairmen that it is difficult to believe that they ever expected to control them.

Popular participation

Electoral participation

Council elections occurred on four occasions under Ershad. Union Councils were elected in 1983–4 and 1988, and sub-District Council chairmen were elected in 1985 and 1990. Few statistics exist on turnout at council elections, and those which do vary sufficiently to be distrusted. Our survey of a cross-section of the rural population in four sub-districts indicates that at three of the four occasions mentioned above (excluding 1988, discussed below), people voted in similar or somewhat greater numbers than at the parliamentary election of 1992, when the turnout was accurately reported at 55.35 per cent.[8]

Remarkably high proportions of our representative sample of the rural population in four sub-districts stated that they had taken some part in council election campaigns: 37.9 per cent in the more localised Union Council campaigns and 31.4 per cent in those for sub-District Council chairmen. There is evidence to suggest that much of this participation was limited – perhaps no more than attending an election meeting or observing a procession. But the figures are quite high, none the less.

There were marked variations in the fairness of elections from place to place and, especially, from time to time. The most serious and widespread abuses – which undermined the legitimacy both of the regime and of decentralisation – occurred during the 1988 election of Union Councils, whose chairmen serve as voting members of the sub-District Councils one level up. On that occasion, the authorities in Dhaka made massive use of coercive force – including elements of the military and, more often, groups of toughs personally linked to supporters of Ershad's Jatiyo Party – to intimidate people from voting and to secure the 'election' of persons preferred by the regime, often by rigging results. The extent to which such abuses occurred varied somewhat among regions, but they occurred on a vast scale, far in excess of any other occasion since the creation of Bangladesh. When analysts refer to this as a 'voterless' election, they exaggerate only slightly.[9]

The Ershad regime adopted these tactics not because it felt threatened by the popularity of opposition parties, but for the opposite reason. It believed that it could get away with anything, especially after the failure

---

[8] Maniruzzaman (1992), p. 211.   [9] H. Z. Rahman (1990).

Table 3.1. *The fairness of council elections (%)*

Completely fair	68.6
Some problems occurred	12.8
Very unfair	6.9
Don't know	11.7

of an opposition agitation in 1987.[10] The abuses of 1988 were an act of political imbecility. National leaders apparently did not see that they were undermining the credibility of their decentralisation experiment, which held some promise for the regime. There is little doubt that broadly fair elections would not have threatened their influence.

This becomes clear when we consider the other three elections to decentralised bodies under Ershad. All of them were attended by significant abuses, in isolated pockets where they were almost always locally inspired. But they were much fairer than in 1988, as Table 3.1, which deals with these other three elections, indicates. (Here and throughout this chapter, aggregate figures are given because the variations among the four sub-districts were too small to justify disaggregation.)

While the Jatiyo Party never fared particularly well at these elections, it consistently managed to persuade many successful candidates to join it or co-operate with it after results were announced.

The first such elections were to Union Councils in 1983–4. These were marked by moderate levels of impersonation, bribery, and violence – more than at the exceedingly peaceful Union elections of 1977 before Ershad's coup, but not much more than at the first Union elections after the creation of Bangladesh in 1973.[11] Most respondents regard the 1983–4 elections as largely fair, and they stress that such violence as occurred (attacks on canvassers, intimidation of voters on election day, the occasional seizure of ballot boxes from polling stations, etc.) was mainly the result of conflicts between local rivals rather than an attempt by the central government to impose its preferred candidates as in 1988. Here as in the two elections assessed below, our inquiries indicated that varying levels of electoral abuses cannot be correlated with particular regions or with distances from urban centres. They were largely random in character.

Respondents took a similar view of the first elections of sub-District Council chairmen in 1985. A survey of 130 of the chairmen elected in

---

[10] Interviews with journalists and politicians, Bogra and Manikganj Districts, January–February 1993, and with a senior civil servant privy to the process, Dhaka, 31 January 1993.
[11] H. Z. Rahman (1990).

1985 showed that, in an election which was only theoretically partyless, candidates affiliated to the Jatiyo Party won only 18–19 per cent of those contests. They did less well than candidates associated with the Awami League which won more than 30 per cent of the posts (precise figures are unavailable), and not much better than those linked to the Bangladesh National Party (BNP) who appear to have won around 9 per cent. (Many winners had no party affiliations.) However, soon after the elections, around 55 per cent of the new chairmen defected from other parties to become at least nominal members of Ershad's Jatiyo Party, giving it nearly three-quarters of all chairmen.[12] Many others, who did not formally become members, proved amenable to the regime.

They were under heavy pressure to do so. They feared that if they remained loyal to opposition parties, their councils would receive only limited resources from Dhaka. (This sanction appears to have been used only infrequently, and its impact was mitigated by the fact that all sub-District Councils received significant sums as minimum statutory grants.) Chairmen also knew that if they remained linked to opposition parties, they were likely to find that the government would back the senior bureaucrats in the council offices against them. This would cripple them politically and make it impossible for them to enrich themselves and close associates. This was a decisive consideration in the minds of many. Some chairmen also feared that loyalty to opposition parties might ultimately lead to their arrest by the military which was well known for brutality to prisoners.[13]

At the second election of sub-District Council chairmen in March 1990, public employees often came under heavy pressure to work in the re-election campaigns of incumbent chairmen – although few did so assiduously enough to have much effect. Those supervising polling stations were sometimes asked to permit large-scale impersonation, although this also produced a patchy response. There was limited rigging of the count in certain segments of some sub-districts, and candidates often attempted to buy votes. But that election was attended by only moderate levels of violence, compared to the massive abuses of 1988.[14] The 1990 violence mainly grew out of conflicts at the sub-district level. This often involved members of the Jatiyo Party – which attracted both upright and unsavoury elements, but enough of the latter to generate

---

[12] A. Rahman (1988), pp. 138–9. A different set of figures, drawn from the newspaper *Ittefaq*, 13 June 1985, is given in Ahmed (1990), note 9. But our investigations suggest that Rahman's figures are more accurate than that press report.

[13] These comments are based on interviews with sub-District Council chairmen and members, and journalists, Bogra and Manikganj Districts, January–February 1993.

[14] These comments are based on interviews with large numbers of journalists, public employees and politicians in Bogra and Manikganj District, January–February 1993.

more than its share of thuggery. But other parties and, especially, individual candidates were also responsible for this.

The Ershad regime was more restrained at this election because the emergence of popular protests and opposition parties over the preceding months had thrown it on to the defensive. This also emboldened citizens in many, though not all, areas to organise themselves prior to polling day and to protest loudly against abuses. Most respondents regarded this as a largely fair election. Malpractices had little effect, since the electorate rejected the overwhelming majority – well in excess of 90 per cent – of incumbent chairmen.

Even though it was increasingly hemmed in by protests and mass opposition, which would bring it down in November of 1990, the regime still managed to gain the acquiescence of many of the new sub-district chairmen immediately after this election. It is clear from this that the abuses to which Ershad and company resorted at the 1988 Union Council elections were unnecessary and vastly counter-productive. To make matters worse for the regime, the Union chairmen elected in 1988 proved to be faint-hearted supporters when the control of the country was threatened in 1990. Most attempted (often successfully) to shift their loyalties to the BNP after it won the 1991 parliamentary election.

It was obvious throughout the Ershad years that all but a few of these 'recruits' stopped well short being activists or loyalists for the Jatiyo Party. Their link to it was merely nominal. Most regarded party membership cynically as an inconvenience that was necessary to obtain a free hand on their councils. In that sense, their view of the regime was probably quite similar to Ershad's view of them.

If the BNP government that came to power after the fall of Ershad and the admirably free parliamentary elections in February 1991 had paid more attention to sub-district and Union councillors' lack of enthusiasm for the Jatiyo Party, it might not have abolished the sub-District Councils later that year. Most council chairmen and members were eager to be co-opted, as they had been under the old regime. But Ershad's illiberal ways discredited this decentralised system in the eyes of the new government.

So despite its considerable promise, the system was abandoned when the sub-District Councils were abolished. The Union Councils – which predated both Ershad and Bangladesh itself – were allowed to survive. But without an elected council higher up at the sub-district level to integrate them into the supra-local political system, they were too small and isolated to enable rural dwellers to influence government institutions in any meaningful way. The new system of indirectly elected councils at the district level, which has replaced the old sub-District Councils, has far less promise than the former system.

Table 3.2. *Participatory activities between elections (%)*

Signed a petition	16.9
Joined a protest	5.6
Attended meeting to thank elected leader	9.1
Attended other non-official meeting	12.5
Attended officially organised meeting	23.5

Table 3.3. *Contacted elected councillors (%)*

Contacted Union councillor	10.9
Contacted sub-District councillor (Union Chairman)	6.3
Contacted unspecified councillor	6.6
Total	23.8

Direct participation between elections

Our survey found that limited but significant numbers of people had been politically active between elections during the lifetime of the councils (see Table 3.2). Of those who attended officially sponsored meetings, 20 per cent had spoken at least once. We then asked if they had contacted a councillor on a matter of personal concern to them (see Table 3.3). Respondents contacted councillors more than bureaucrats – an activity in which only 14.4 per cent engaged. But more people contacted bureaucrats after decentralisation than before – by a margin of 84.1 per cent to 15.9 per cent. So the new system encouraged encounters with elected representatives *and* government employees.[15]

We asked villagers to identify organisations in which they had been active (see Table 3.4). The figures represent a remarkably high level of associational activity – well above that in Karnataka (India). This lends support to those who argue that, despite repeated breakdowns of democracy, Bangladesh has a lively civil society.

We then asked whether respondents had been active in these associations prior to decentralisation: 52.9 per cent had been, and 47.1 per cent had joined since then. Decentralisation clearly played a significant catalysing role (though a somewhat lesser role than in Karnataka).

We also gathered survey data on opportunities provided by councillors to citizens to participate between elections. This emerged in two ways.

---

[15] The nature of the responses which they received from councillors and bureaucrats is examined under 'Responsiveness' in the third part of this chapter.

Table 3.4. *Participation in associations*

	percentage of sample active
Village association	8.9
Youth association	10.7
Grameen Bank association	17.8
Women's association	31.4
Farmers' association	3.6
Professional association	1.8
Trade union	3.0
Cultural/religious associations	3.0
Others	16.0

Table 3.5. *Frequency of councillors' availability*

	Sub-District Councillor (%)	Union Councillor (%)
Once/month or more	17.9	31.3
Once/3–6 months	17.6	21.5
Once/6–12 months	7.5	4.4
Once/12–24 months	1.9	2.2
Other	5.3	2.8
Never	49.8	37.7

Table 3.6. *Consultations with villagers about projects*

	percentage of projects with consultation
At a public meeting	7.5
At a small group meeting	0.8
Our leader was consulted	7.4
Unspecified consultations	63.7
None	20.6

We first asked how often their councillors had made themselves available to villages (see Table 3.5). Union councillors were clearly more easily available than those who sat in the sub-District Council. But the latter were the chairmen of the localised Union Council and usually lived locally. Given this, it is clear that both sets of councillors stood aloof from ordinary people much of the time. Opportunities to engage them were far more limited than we might expect.

We also asked how and how often villages had been consulted concerning council development projects (see Table 3.6). The figure for unspecified consultations is extraordinarily high, even if it often refers to

Table 3.7. *Socio-economic characteristics of participators, by selected activities (%)*

	Contacted councillor (N= ?)	Attended official meeting (N= ?)	
		All attenders	Attended and spoke
Sex			
Men	80.5	84.0	86.7
Women	19.5	16.0	13.3
Age			
18–29	19.6	21.2	10.5
30–44	50.0	33.3	57.9
45–64	26.1	17.2	10.5
65+	4.3	28.3	21.1
Education			
None	52.2	46.3	25.0
Primary	10.9	14.9	8.3
Secondary	30.4	32.8	50.0
Higher	6.5	6.0	16.7

councillors going through the motions. The system appears to have worked remarkably well on this front.

Participation by disadvantaged groups

Here, as in Chapter 2, we consider two types of evidence, to assess participation by disadvantaged groups – women, young people and those without education. Table 3.7 contains data on the composition of all participants. In Bangladesh, men dominated all of the three types of participation, to a degree not found in Karnataka. This is not surprising, since roughly 80 per cent of the women in our two Bangladeshi districts had never been to school. As in India, young people – adults under 30 years of age – participated less often than their elders. But they were sufficiently active for us to view them as less than severely disadvantaged.

The most surprising and revealing data, however, appear under 'Education' in Table 3.7. People with no education (mainly men) were a good deal more active than we might expect, given the poverty and inequality that afflicts them. They comprised the largest single group among those attending meetings. One-quarter of those who spoke at meetings had no schooling, so that even there they were not entirely dominated. And it is remarkable that uneducated people outnumber those with secondary education among contactors of councillors.

Few countries which have attempted democratic decentralisation have

Table 3.8. *Ability, by gender, to name elected councillors*

	Women (%)	Men (%)
Can name Union councillor	84.8	95.3
Cannot name Union councillor	15.2	4.7
Can name Sub-District councillor	88.7	95.3
Cannot name Sub-District councillor	11.3	4.7

higher levels of impoverishment than Bangladesh, and more extreme inequalities. These figures indicate that substantial participation, at least by men who lack education and wealth, can be expected in decentralised systems even amid apparently unpromising conditions.

Let us now turn to the data on the range of participatory activities in which disadvantaged groups, particularly women and the poor, engaged. Women (and poor people) voted in sizeable numbers in council elections. Our survey indicated that the turnout among women voters stood a few percentage points lower than that for men at both parliamentary and council elections. Such modest differences are perhaps surprising given the *exceedingly* limited educational opportunities available to women. The differences in basic political awareness were again less marked than we might expect, as Table 3.8 indicates.

How much did women participate between elections? To ensure that they were represented in the new system, the government provided for the nomination of three women members to each sub-District Council. However, this did next to nothing to enhance genuine participation in council business. As nominees, they were not permitted to vote. Without exception, knowledgeable witnesses in both districts studied stated that women nominees almost always remained silent and were invariably powerless. Many seldom attended meetings. On those rare occasions when they spoke, it was to support the chairman in disputes, since they owed their nominations to him. We found no evidence that women members influenced the priorities of sub-District Councils.

A tiny number of women won elections to head the lower-level Union Councils which meant that they also served as elected members of sub-District Councils, with voting rights. A 1987 study identified six, out of nationwide total of 4,401. All of them had male ancestors or relatives who had previously been Union Council chairmen. Five of the six were, in effect, 'stand-ins' for their husbands – two for chairmen husbands jailed for crimes, one for a chairman husband who had been murdered, another for a chairman husband who had been removed for malpractices, and one for a husband who could not seek the chair because he was a

Table 3.9. *Proactive political activity, by gender*

	Women (%)	Men (%)
Signed a petition	17.0	21.0
Engaged in protest	5.8	8.6
Attended non-official meeting	12.7	18.9
Attended officially organised meeting	23.7	37.7
Met to thank elected representative	9.2	15.2
Contacted councillor personally	23.8	30.8
Contacted bureaucrat	14.4	18.3

government official. Only one woman claimed to have stood for office in her own right, but since her brother-in-law had previously been chairman for twenty years, she may also have been a 'stand-in'.[16] These minute numbers and their role as 'stand-ins' raise serious doubts about the gains that this represented for women.

At the first of two elections for the leadership of the 495 sub-District Councils in 1985, eight women stood as candidates. All lost. In December 1986, by-elections were held to fill thirty-one of these posts. On that occasion, two women won, although once again they were apparently 'stand-ins' for husbands who had become members of parliament.[17] No conclusive figures exist for the second election of sub-District Council heads, but it appears that they were all men.

If we consider women's involvement in proactive political activity, the differences with men are less marked. Tables 3.9 and 3.10, based on our survey, set this out in detail. When we consider these figures in the light of the impediments which confront women in this society, they are well-nigh heroic and suggest that decentralisation did much to encourage their participation in the political system.

The figures on women's involvement with associations are less impressive. Apart from membership in local women's groups and the associations of the Grameen bank which systematically seeks them out, they left such doings largely to men, as Table 3.10 shows.

Our findings, taken overall, add up to a mixed picture. The data on women's ability to name councillors and on proactive participation are impressive. The rest are far less encouraging. Our interviews with large numbers of people familiar with council operations strongly indicate that the efforts at proactive participation yielded few results for women. But it appears possible that, if strong decentralised structures are revived in

[16] Alam (1987). [17] Ibid.

Table 3.10. *Associational activity, by gender*

	Women (%)	Men (%)
Village association	0.7	8.3
Youth association	nil	10.7
Grameen Bank association	7.9	10.7
Women's association	34.4	0.6
Professional association	nil	1.8
Trades unions	nil	3.0
Cultural/religious associations	nil	3.0
Other associations	16.0	2.0

Bangladesh (an open question), their proactive doings may eventually have some impact.

What of the poor? The only occasion in the history of Bangladesh on which poorer people won a significant number of seats at a local council election occurred in 1973, immediately after the liberation war and the creation of the country. The struggle had seriously disrupted the rural socio-economic order across much of the country, and in many areas prominent members of the locally dominant landed elite had been discredited after collaborating with the old Pakistani regime. However, by the next local election in 1977, moneyed rural groups had reasserted their dominance. They have maintained it ever since.[18]

It is not just the substantial proportion of the population which is landless that was largely excluded from the councils. In more prosperous districts, only an extremely limited number of 'middle farmers' or owner-cultivators gained places on the lower-level Union Council. Scarcely any became Union chairmen and thus gained seats on the sub-District Council. In less prosperous districts, they had only slightly greater opportunities. Since decentralisation created significant new openings for village elites to influence government institutions, its overall impact was to intensify already extreme inequalities.[19]

---

[18] These comments emerge from many conversations in Bangladesh, but I am grateful to Kazi Afsanul Saqui and Aftabuddin Khan at the National Institute for Local Government for first stressing this. See also A. Rahman (1988) and Holtsberg (1990), p. 15.

[19] Zarina Khan of Dhaka University, after doing research on local councils both in the late 1970s and early 1980s, and again in 1992, found that local elites dominated councils throughout the period covered by her work. The decentralisation experiment under study here brought no change on this front. Interview, Dhaka, 9 January 1993.

Non-governmental organisations (NGOs) and disadvantaged groups

Any assessment of the experience of disadvantaged or vulnerable groups necessarily involves a discussion of indigenous NGOs. Poor people and women face massive disadvantages in rural Bangladesh – as a result of severe poverty and social discrimination, extremely high levels of illiteracy, intimidation, fragmentation (social and spatial) and dependence upon elites. They therefore find it almost impossible to generate collective appeals to government institutions, unless they have previously been organised by NGOs working at the grassroots. In areas where NGOs had not been active, we found *no* evidence of concerted action by vulnerable groups.

NGOs loomed larger here than in our other South Asian case, Karnataka, not because they did more in absolute terms – it is unclear which place has more energetic NGOs – but because the poor and women in Bangladesh had far greater need of NGO assistance. We are not implying that Bangladeshi society is more quiescent than Karnataka's. Conflicts in Bangladesh are often more severe and more marked by desperation. But elites (mainly wealthy males) exercise greater dominance there. NGOs were important because they occasionally enabled poorer groups and women to achieve minimal inputs into the decentralised system. For this reason we compared one Bangladeshi district where NGOs had been particularly active (Manikganj) with another (Bogra) where this was much less true.[20]

When villagers who had been organised by NGOs mounted moderately strident protests, they tended not to succeed, even in districts with a strong NGO presence. This was apparent in Manikganj District from, for example, the collapse after two days of an attempt by women labourers who had been unpaid by a contractor to gherao (imprison in his office) the defaulter. But on a very limited number of occasions, more restrained appeals to power-holders produced results.[21] This takes some explaining.

Several well-organised NGOs had been working in Manikganj District for over fifteen years, mainly at the village level among poor, usually landless people. Their methods varied, but they encouraged poor villagers to form associations for their collective good – with men and women in separate associations, as befits social practice here. These groups

---

[20] The NGO Proshika has been quite active in one sub-district of Bogra (Shibganj), but we intentionally conducted field surveys in two other sub-districts, in order to understand the contrast with Manikganj District.

[21] These comments are based on extensive discussions with activists from two NGOs – BRAC and Proshika – in Manikganj District, January 1993.

pooled meagre resources and efforts and received from NGOs resources and instruction on their use, on methods of collective action, on their rights under law, and on the workings of the legal and political systems.

Some NGOs organised co-ordination committees at the Union level to which village associations sent representatives to monthly meetings, and sub-district-level committees (one level further up) to which each Union committee sent a few representatives for meetings each month. These committees were created to exchange information from different localities, to build a sense of collective strength and to monitor resource distribution by government to various social groups (mainly elites) in the area, rather than to lobby political authorities. However, decentralisation opened up new opportunities for lobbying to which these groups responded on a small number of occasions.

It is important that we not exaggerate their lobbying efforts. Even in Manikganj District, which has witnessed some of the most intense NGO efforts in all of Bangladesh, significant lobbying occurred in only one sub-district – Manikganj Sadar (round the headquarters town, one of the two that we studied closely). On two or three occasions during the years in which this decentralised system operated, the sub-district committee organised by NGOs there became concerned over the tendency of sub-district councillors to distribute benefits mainly to their prosperous clients. One example was the right to develop fisheries projects in small, commonly owned village ponds. On one or two other occasions, the committee sought concessions which were not being allotted to anyone – for example, permission to lease the unused verges of rural roads for tree planting.

When strong feelings developed on such issues, the committee mustered polite gatherings of between 100 and 200 people outside the sub-District Council offices (a rare event), and representatives of the group met the council chairman or chief bureaucrat (UNO) to request a favourable response. On three or four occasions (the precise figure is unclear) their efforts were rewarded.[22] Lower key lobbying at the Union Council level, closer to the grassroots, occurred more often – in most sub-districts of Manikganj District and in two sub-districts of Bogra District (not accidentally, in the only two Bogra sub-districts where NGOs were present in strength). This produced helpful responses on a small but not insignificant number of occasions.

It is also clear from extensive interviews with politicians, bureaucrats and NGO activists that in areas where NGOs have done intensive work, a sizeable minority of council chairmen had recognised that vulnerable

[22] Ibid.

groups were sufficiently aware of the logic of representative politics and well enough organised to vote against them at the next election if they became unhappy with their performance. These chairmen continued to channel most political spoils to prosperous clients, but they also made occasional modest concessions to vulnerable groups in the hope of gaining their support. Most NGO leaders reckon that this produced greater benefit than direct lobbying.

These leaders argue that these gains could not have been achieved had democratic decentralisation not occurred. But our evidence also indicates that organised inputs by vulnerable groups into the decentralised system occurred only very rarely, and that they triggered positive action by council chairmen only to a very limited extent. We found no evidence of such doings in the absence of prior NGO work at the grassroots. Such work is estimated to have reached no more than 20 per cent of the rural population, and even that figure is probably optimistic. This gives a comment by one prominent NGO leader an ominous ring. He said that where the poor are unorganised, having the government so close to the people is a problem (since nearly all benefits go to prosperous groups, exacerbating inequality), but where they are organised, it offers an opportunity.[23] Our findings strongly suggest that, despite the gains discussed above, it was a problem far more often than it was an opportunity.

Representation and institutional accountability

Chairmen of sub-District Councils – the key figures
For citizens and groups to influence decentralised institutions in Bangladesh, it was necessary that their elected representatives possess the authority and leverage to influence bureaucrats who implemented policy at the sub-district level and below. The most crucial elected official was the chairman of the sub-District Council. His importance stemmed partly from his direct election by the entire voting population of the sub-district. He had a more formidable mandate than councillors who sat there by virtue of being chairmen of the much smaller Union Councils. A leading authority on decentralisation in Bangladesh has stressed that the popular election of a sub-district chairman was 'something extraordinary in the history of this country', since the size of his constituency greatly exceeded that of any Member of Parliament, and he – unlike an MP – had substantial formal powers over policy implementation.[24]

---

[23] Interview with Kazi Farouque Ahmed, head of Proshika (an important NGO), Dhaka, 21 January 1993.
[24] Interview with Kamal Siddiqui, Dhaka, 22 January 1993.

But the main source of the sub-district chairman's power was his direct link to the Bangladeshi President, H. M. Ershad, who permitted and even encouraged chairmen to operate just as they pleased. He needed their political support, so he backed them strongly, even when they exceeded their authority.

They did so often. In theory, they were less formidable figures than, for example, their counterparts at the district level in Karnataka (India). But in practice, most of them – those with intelligence and tactical skills – made themselves more powerful than the latter. This was possible because the law and the rules of the system were adhered to less closely in Bangladesh, as we shall see. Evidence from a wide range of developing nations suggests that departures from the rules in the manner of Bangladesh are more common than Karnataka's broad adherence to them. It is useful to remember this when considering the frequent assertions in the literature on Bangladesh and elsewhere that the solutions to problems that afflict these institutions lie in devising tighter or more elaborate sets of laws and administrative rules.

The importance of the sub-district chairmen's link to Ershad at the apex of the political system naturally caused many of them to be more preoccupied with cultivating that link than they were with their links to constituents or even to powerful interests in their sub-districts. This undermined, to varying degrees, their ability and inclination to serve as representatives of the people who had elected them. It also seriously eroded the principle of their accountability to voters, on which the success of this experiment as an exercise in democracy rested. So while there can be no doubt about the clout wielded by elected sub-district chairmen, this system did not necessarily provide citizens or even powerful interests with major new opportunities to participate between elections or to make significant inputs into the policy process. This will become clearer from an examination of relations between the chairmen and bureaucrats within their sub-districts.

Relations between chairmen and chief bureaucrats

Let us first consider their interactions with senior officials. The formal rules governing this decentralised system included a set of checks and balances to prevent either the elected chairman or the senior bureaucrat in the council office from dominating. On paper, a form of dyarchy existed. We noted earlier that most developmental functions were formally 'transferred' to the chairman and elected members. At the same time, a more limited set of functions, including those pertaining to law and order, were formally 'retained' by the chief civil servant who was called the Upazila Nirbahi Officer or UNO.

The transferral of developmental functions entailed less a horizontal shift of power from bureaucrats to elected representatives at the sub-district level, than a devolution of responsibility for development from the district level (where bureaucrats had dominated) downward to the sub-district level. Before decentralisation, civil servants in sub-district offices mainly dealt with public order and revenue collection, tasks which they were supposed to retain under the new system.[25]

To sustain dyarchy, the law required decisions by the sub-District Councils and authorisations for the disbursement of funds to be signed both by the elected chairman and the UNO. There was some chance that this would lead to deadlock if the two disagreed, but the risk seemed worth taking since it appeared to provide a safeguard against one or the other exceeding his (or, very occasionally, her) authority.

Most of the time, however, the safeguard did not work and dyarchy did not actually operate. In a small but not insignificant minority of cases – where the elected chairman was poorly educated or inept – the UNO held his own or even predominated. This sometimes entailed intriguing with elected councillors and, in remote sub-districts, using the two-way radio link to district and national levels which he monopolized. A few UNOs had connections with powerful civil servants or politicians in Dhaka, which helped them to resist pressure from chairmen. Very occasionally, chairmen were content to work within the rules which supposedly limited their power. In a rather larger number of cases, deadlock occurred, some of the time.[26] But in a large majority of cases, chairmen exercised far more dominance over the councils and development activities than formal regulations permitted. In some cases, they even acquired influence over the police and the new sub-district courts which, in theory, stood outside their purview.[27]

The principal reason for this was the permissive attitude of the Ershad regime towards sub-district chairmen, especially those who ingratiated themselves with central authorities. Many chairmen were often in Dhaka forging close links to Ershad and his associates. We were given a list of five hotels in the capital which chairmen frequented, and checks there

---

[25] UNOs, the top civil servants at the sub-district level, were mightily pleased to see developmental responsibilities, resources and staffs grow so markedly as a result, and in the year or so prior to the election of sub-District Council chairmen in 1985, they greatly enjoyed the unfettered command of this new set of instruments. They were less happy to see them pass, in 1985, to elected representatives.

[26] These comments are based largely on interviews with UNOs, councillors, chairmen and others, Manikganj and Bogra Districts, January–February 1993. An extremely good source on this, and on the relationship between chairmen and UNOs more generally, is Ahmad and Alam (1991). On deadlock, see pp. 47, 50 and 54.

[27] This is based both on numerous interviews in Manikganj and Bogra Districts, and on Ahmad and Alam (1991), pp. 34, 57, 59–60.

confirmed that they had been habitual guests. Many of them also developed cordial ties with central government ministers and members of parliament, mainly by providing these people with shares of their considerable private profits.

This meant that most chairmen could bend or break laws and regulations at will. It opened the door to substantial corruption, as we shall see in the next part of this chapter, but it also gave rise to what one UNO criticised as his 'Chairman's excessive commitment to development activities'.[28] When the UNOs protested against the assertive doings of chairmen, the latter could say – in the words of one in Bogra District – 'Forget government instructions; I am the local government.'[29] Many UNOs who tried to stand out against their chairmen were transferred.

Some chairmen were occasionally pulled up by senior bureaucrats at the district level (one tier above them). But in the main, district officials monitored them in a cursory, intermittent manner. Many neglected them altogether for long periods. Such laxity owed much to bribes which many chairmen of sub-District Councils steadily provided to key district officials. These payments also ensured that district-level officials would not back bureaucrats in the sub-districts when they tried to stop chairmen from bending or breaking the rules.

Most chairmen were also adroit enough to cultivate support not only at the apex of the political system, but also at the base – the Union level. The key figures at that level were the Union Council chairmen who were sub-district councillors. It was usually easy to gain their backing by agreeing with their proposals for development projects (funded by the sub-District Council) in their bailiwicks, and by allowing them a free hand at the local level and opportunities to enrich themselves and their friends. Since Union Council chairmen sought to please important interests at the grassroots, this opened up opportunities for elites (though seldom for others) to make significant inputs into the policy process – counterbalancing somewhat the preoccupations of sub-district chairmen with the link to Ershad and Dhaka.

Canny sub-district chairmen also manipulated divisions among civil servants to strengthen their hand. Some of these divisions were based on personality clashes, but in most sub-districts, there was significant tension both between (i) generalist UNOs and specialists in health care, agriculture, etc., and between (ii) specialists in service provision on the

---

[28] Ahmad and Alam (1991), p. 142.
[29] This quotation came from a senior bureaucrat in that district. The comments which precede it are based on a large number of interviews with bureaucrats and politicians, mainly in Bogra and Manikganj Districts and in Dhaka, January–February, 1993.

one hand and, on the other, engineers and others dealing with construction projects.

By these varied means, adroit sub-district chairmen made themselves into potent figures. They had enough backing – most crucially from Ershad – to survive exceedingly serious trouble. We discovered a few examples of chairmen whose ties to the president kept them in office after sub-District councillors had passed no-confidence votes (which, in law, should have ousted them).[30] Others had such strong links to Ershad that discontented councillors never attempted such votes.

For the same reasons, many chairmen also survived scandals. In several parts of the country, brave reporters – despite threats of arrest and even torture from the military – exposed murky doings by chairmen. Criminal investigations were also undertaken by the police against some chairmen. And yet scarcely any chairmen were disciplined as a result. One chairman in Manikganj District was formally charged with corruption by the Ershad government itself, but eluded judgement by restoring good relations with Dhaka. In the same district, a newspaper printed over a dozen detailed revelations against another chairman, and the police developed evidence to support over 100 corruption charges against him, but he survived thanks to connections in the capital.[31]

This created major difficulties for the sub-District Council's senior civil servants, the UNOs. Most of them were faced with fulfilling the formal requirement to make dyarchy work when political informalities gave chairmen so much power that it could not work. Their troubles were compounded by the fact that all of the chairmen and councillors and many of the civil servants in the hastily expanded sub-district bureaucracy were inexperienced.[32] The UNOs were, as one of them in Bogra District put it, 'used to command'.[33] One study of eight sub-districts found that in three cases relations with chairmen were 'extremely bitter'. This occurred because chairmen found UNOs slow to execute council decisions and, in some cases, inclined to seek to dominate the sub-district and to make illicit profits. UNOs countered with charges against chairmen of corruption, and two allegations of attempted assault.[34] Our

---

[30] Our interviews yielded information on four such cases in and near just two districts. A further case, in the literature, involved a sub-District Council chairman who came into conflict with his councillors and stopped holding council meetings for nearly a year. Despite action against him by the chief bureaucrat up at the district level and a vote of no confidence by the councillors, his links to Dhaka enabled him to get away with all of this! (Ahman and Alam (1991), p. 200.)

[31] Interview with three knowledgeable informants (including an investigative reporter) in a sub-district in Manikganj District, 17 January 1993.

[32] I am grateful to Mohammed Mohabbat Khan for stressing this point to me.

[33] Interview, Bogra, 27 January 1993.

[34] Ahmad and Alam (1991), pp. 32–4.

investigation found a lower incidence of 'bitter' relations, but tensions were apparent none the less.

The transition to a system in which they had to leave most decisions to the sub-district chairmen was painful. Many of them spoke of their particular frustration at being made accountable to the chairmen and (to a lesser extent) the councillors, while the chairmen were not held adequately accountable to anyone – not even to Ershad, given the disinclination of the national leaders to engage in close monitoring.[35] Despite this, most UNOs coped tolerably well. They usually had had enough experience at adjusting to political realities which contradicted formal regulations and laws to do the same once again. For most of them, the hardest thing to accept was their loss of power. But they tended to possess the social skills and sufficient self-confidence to weather these troubles. Very few developed the enthusiasm for democratic decentralisation which was common among their counterparts in Karnataka (India), but very few were outright failures.

There were, for the UNOs, certain compensations. The new system placed them at the head of a much larger, better-resourced team of development specialists than had previously been available to persons of their rank. Many discovered that far more could be accomplished through co-ordinating the actions of different government departments than they had expected. For those who were interested in enriching themselves – and many were – the new system also offered major new opportunities, not least because the flow of funds from Dhaka had increased substantially. The new system was thus not entirely disagreeable.

Chairmen and less senior bureaucrats

Decentralisation posed greater difficulties for other bureaucrats working in the sub-districts. Different groups experienced the change in different ways. We need to consider two such groups: (i) the Project Implementation Officer, the Engineering Officer and their subordinates; and (ii) bureaucrats who worked for other line ministries.

The first group were pleased with the marked increase in funds available for their work, with the growth of their staffs, and with their enhanced importance thanks to councillors' bias towards constructing physical assets. Most of them also enjoyed their new autonomy from officials at higher levels, and the increased co-ordination between themselves and personnel from other line ministries (see part three of this

---

[35] This is based on numerous interviews with UNOs in Bogra and Manikganj Districts and in Dhaka, January–February 1993.

chapter) – especially since those personnel largely operated as advisers of lesser importance.

The second and much larger set of bureaucrats worked for other line ministries – education, health, fisheries, agriculture, etc. – and had more difficulty. They also welcomed improved co-ordination and the increased funds for development. They also tended to welcome the expansion in staff numbers, even if it was less marked for them than, for example, in engineering.[36] Many found that their chairmen welcomed discussions of their department's problems, a pleasant change from the days before decentralisation when they were often unable to exchange views with any senior bureaucrat.

But the problems that they faced far outweighed these advantages. Those who had worked at this level before decentralisation had been free to take many key decisions about where and how to apply their efforts. Now those choices were made by elected politicians who lacked specialised knowledge. The new system gave the UNO much greater power over them than any generalist bureaucrat had previously exercised. When they had trouble with their chairman or UNO, they got little support from line ministry superiors up at the district level.

Much of the annual report on each of these bureaucrats, a crucial document that went into their permanent file, was usually written or strongly influenced by the sub-district chairman. Some chairmen wrote glowing reports on everyone, while some others were uniformly negative, so there was a random, capricious element in this which unnerved many civil servants. Many chairmen based their reports on their personal relationship with an official (which often depended on whether the latter had done a chairman's bidding in dubious areas) rather than on his or her work. Another portion of the report was usually written by a civil servant in the line ministry up at the district level. This was sometimes reassuring, but these people also tended to inject personal considerations into the report, so that this was often of little help.

Some of these less senior officials, especially those in education and health, were further dismayed to see subordinates face far more transfers than ever before. This was often the result of politicians' and senior bureaucrats' efforts to extort bribes from those subordinates. Bribes could facilitate a favourable transfer. A failure to pay could result in an undesirable posting. This caused resentment among civil servants.

---

[36] In Saturia sub-district of Manikganj District, for example, the total number of employees under the sub-District Council grew to 276, more than two and a half times the number employed prior to decentralisation. Interview with a sub-District Council chairman, Saturia, 17 January 1993.

Attempts by politicians and senior bureaucrats to force junior civil servants to commit illegalities had a similar effect.

This is not to say that less senior bureaucrats were above corruption. Indeed, many of them were intensely frustrated because their illicit profits were so limited. Decentralisation and the government's increased spending on development greatly enhanced the opportunities for malfeasance, but these people knew that politicians and bureaucrats at the sub-district level were making far more than they could, and that rankled. Many councils also shifted money earmarked for services, which these less senior officials were meant to deliver, towards construction projects. This left many with little work.

Decentralisation necessitated the creation of a large number of new posts, especially in departments concerned with the construction of physical assets, but also for those delivering services. For some bureaucrats, this meant that they found employment for the first time. For others, it meant promotion or transfer from less responsible, less interesting posts, with improved provisions for pay, housing and office facilities. This naturally pleased them, but it also produced serious exasperation. Many of them lacked the technical training (usually after a three-month crash course) to fulfil their tasks. This laid them open to complaints about the quality of their work. More seriously, most of them had to pay sizeable bribes to obtain appointments and/or attractive postings. They usually had to borrow heavily to make these payments, on the assumption that they could recoup these outlays by acquiring bribes from those to whom they provided services. This seldom proved difficult for bureaucrats working in departments concerned with creating physical assets, but in the under-funded departments involved in service delivery, this was often impossible because they had too few services to sell.

Their problem was not that they would be caught. Citizens were far less inclined and able to make effective protests than in, for example, Karnataka (where the overall level of corruption declined). Elected officials in Bangladesh seldom took action on allegations of corruption, as their Indian counterparts did. But their inability to generate illicit income left them embarrassed before relatives who had advanced them money to purchase their posts or, worse still, exposed to the tender mercies of moneylenders. Both of these things generated extreme anxiety among many.

Decentralised planning

Decentralisation is intended to enable citizens to participate in or to influence the formulation of plans by elected authorities. How much was achieved in Bangladesh on this front?

One careful study of two sub-District Councils and two Union Councils found that in the first two years of their existence, they had not prepared either annual or five-year plans as they were supposed to do. The government failed even to provide them with any guidelines or booklets on planning design. Such materials were eventually supplied, but even then, it was impossible to achieve much because the bureaucrats who worked for councils lacked the essential skills. This is not surprising, since our study of Karnataka (India) revealed a similar incapacity among bureaucrats there – even though decentralised planning had theoretically been practised there for many years.

Councils evolved a rudimentary system that entailed making yearly lists of some, but not all, of their intended undertakings. These included estimates of the costs of projects. But since they did not conform even to the simplistic format set out by the Planning Commission's 'Proforma' and since all spending on service delivery and some on the construction projects was omitted from the format, this was hardly a serious exercise in 'planning'.

Both sub-District and Union Councils often failed even to prepare satisfactory annual budgets. A few produced nothing at all, while others generated documents which excluded expenditures and receipts for the previous year. One investigator described their doings as 'often ritualistic ... whimsical and erroneous'.[37] Our off-the-record conversations with junior bureaucrats indicated that this occurred not because the councils were unable to prepare such materials, but because by avoiding this, they remained free to do what they liked with funds.

Many sub-District Councils also neglected to constitute sub-committees to devise plans (and to perform various other functions) – even when their official records indicated that this was done.[38] Such 'planning' as occurred – usually last-minute, ad hoc decisions – tended instead to involve the sub-district chairman and his clique of allies, meeting informally. Our overall verdict is echoed by a further study of sub-District Councils' financial management and development planning. It concluded that 'In neither respect is the Upazila [sub-district] living up to even modest quality standards.'[39]

Officials at the district level, who were supposed to monitor plans and budgets by councils, often remained inert so that these problems

---

[37] Faizullah (1989a), p. 4.
[38] Similar tendencies were discovered in a separate investigation by Minhaj Uddin Ahmad. Interview, Bogra, 26 January 1993. See also Faizullah (1989a), p. 3.
[39] Holtsberg (1990), p. 17. It was his study which first drew our attention to an official report with findings in this vein: Faizullah (1989b).

Bangladesh 111

frequently went unnoticed.[40] The non-existence of adequate planning and budgetary documents also undermined hopes that the decentralised system might be more transparent and that councils might be made substantially accountable to their constituents. It made it impossible for citizens and groups at the grassroots to participate in any formal way in the planning process.

These are severe criticisms. But these failures did not prevent councils from achieving anything useful. It was plainly unrealistic to expect council staff who were experienced only in implementation and who were wholly unused to planning to accomplish much in this vein. They obviously accomplished much less than they might have done. But it is apparent from much else in this chapter that significant benefits on many fronts still flowed from the decentralised system. Powerful people and groups in the villages still influenced the decisions of elected representatives about the type and location of projects to be implemented. Participation – albeit mainly by elites – clearly increased as a result of decentralisation. Here and in our chapter on Karnataka, we see that much can be achieved by elected councils even though they are bound to fall short of unrealistic expectations on the planning side.

INSTITUTIONAL PERFORMANCE

Effectiveness

The autonomy, powers and resources of the councils
It is already apparent that sub-district chairmen and their councils had substantial autonomy and powers. They enjoyed great independence in deciding how to spend their considerable funds, and where to implement these decisions. In all of this, they paid scant attention to government guidelines.[41] This was partly because the government formally devolved significant powers upon the councils, but its informal willingness to let the chairmen do as they pleased was more important.[42] Here, as in our

---

[40] These comments are based on our discussions with numerous bureaucrats, councillors and others in Manikganj and Bogra Districts, January–February 1993; and on the findings in Saqui and Mukabber (1988), pp. 1–2. Another useful source is Khan (1988). Two further studies found councils to be very inadequate in these areas. One stated that 'Financial management is of a depressing state of affairs. The local level planning mechanism is non-existent . . . At most a few Upazila (Sub-District) plans have been prepared'. (Holtsberg (1990), p. 15). He was drawing on Faizullah (1989b).
[41] See, in addition to evidence provided in the second part of this chapter Saqui and Mukabber (1988), especially pp. 7–8. That document is littered with references to things done by councils 'contrary to government instruction' and 'contrary to rules'.
[42] The government in Dhaka and its agents at the district level (one level up from the sub-districts), for example, did not intervene in the 'planning' exercises (such as they were)

discussion of Karnataka in the previous chapter, we see that the dependence of councils on higher levels of government for resources did not necessarily imply that they were controlled from above or that they lacked freedom of action, as some have concluded.

The lower-level Union Councils had less power and autonomy, since they were dependent upon the sub-District Councils for both resources and bureaucratic support to implement projects and deliver services. But since the Union chairmen sat on the higher council and usually extracted abundant assistance from it, this was not a serious problem.

We have said far less, however, about the resources available to the councils. The Ershad regime increased development spending markedly and channelled most of this money through the sub-District Councils. This was extremely important, for three reasons. First, heavy expenditures were required to initiate decentralisation – to construct council offices, to hire bureaucrats to serve councils and to provide them with equipment, transport and accommodation. Second, the regime's permissive attitude to council chairmen meant that corruption assumed major proportions, so that the councils would need to receive huge injections of funds if significant amounts were to be left over for development after profiteering. Finally, since chairmen used their freedom to shift money earmarked for services to the construction of physical assets, huge injections would be needed if funds were to be left over after that for services. The Ershad government apparently did not consider these last two things when calculating spending, but they were still important.

The increase in spending was great enough to ensure a significant growth in the number of development projects undertaken and completed (as our discussion of 'Outputs' below indicates) and – despite the council's bias towards construction projects – some enhancement of services. Elected chairmen often said that they felt frustrated that they did not have more funds to respond to still more requests for projects, but they all acknowledged that they had far more to deploy than ever before. Indeed, councils occasionally found it difficult to spend all of the funds provided.[43]

Politicians and bureaucrats consistently estimated that each sub-District Council received around ten million takas in the first year after

which the Sub-District and Union Councils did. (See, for instance, in that connection Saqui and Mukabber (1988), p. 2.) Nor, except in a limited number of cases, did they make much effort to monitor the councils' spending patterns or their activities more generally.

[43] I am grateful to Minhaj Uddin Ahmad for stressing this point. He discovered this in his investigation of eight sub-District Councils.

decentralisation – when starting up costs were heaviest – and between five and six million in each year thereafter, awarded to sub-districts according to a complex formula.[44] They also received substantial further resources – the exact amount is a matter of dispute – mainly in the form of grain to pay labourers engaged on public works. This was, as one leading commentator has said, 'a lot of money',[45] an allocation greatly in excess of any previous or subsequent commitment to development since the end of British rule. This caused dismay among activists in political parties opposed to Ershad. One told us ruefully that this experiment in decentralisation 'was designed by a very clever brain'.[46]

The impressive scale of the Ershad government's financial commitment to the councils is apparent from the universally acknowledged fact that far more funds were available for development before decentralisation than after. It is further apparent from the contrast with the period immediately after the abolition of sub-District Councils in 1991. Bureaucrats providing services in sub-districts repeatedly told us that after 1991, once their salaries were paid, there was no money. This extreme statement appeared not to be an exaggeration in certain fields – particularly health and animal husbandry. In most sub-districts, only 4–10 per cent (or, in a single case, 16 per cent) of the total development funds which had previously been available to the councils was provided after their demise. This represents a drastic curtailment of spending and an indication of the lavish outlays by the Ershad regime.[47]

Mobilising local resources

One alleged advantage of democratic decentralisation is that it facilitates the mobilisation of untapped local resources. If government is brought closer to the grassroots and elected representatives are empowered, citizens will (it is argued) feel that they have a greater say and stake in the political process. They will therefore become more willing to pay taxes, to face tax increases imposed by elected councils and perhaps to make voluntary contributions to local projects.

In Bangladesh, this did not happen. Councils more or less completely

---

[44] Each sub-district received an award based as follows: 50 per cent on population, 10 per cent on area, 20 per cent on backwardness and 20 per cent on 'performance' (Bangladesh, n.d.). Sources consistently indicated that there was very little discrimination between councils on the basis of 'performance'.
[45] Blair (1989).
[46] Interview with Awami League leader, Manikganj, 12 January 1993.
[47] These comments are based on interviews with a large, diverse array of civil servants and others in Bogra and Manikganj Districts, and with central government officials in Dhaka, January–February 1993.

disregarded government encouragements and requirements in this vein.[48] The problem was not a severe shortage of mobilisable local resources amid extreme poverty. A sophisticated study has shown that some resources exist.[49] The problem was the disinclination of councillors to impose fresh taxes or to increase existing ones.

Their thinking on this needs to be understood. The prosperous people who occupied most of the seats on Union Councils, which had the main opportunity to enhance taxes, did not hold back out of humanitarian concern for poorer constituents. They presumed – usually rightly – that the poor would be able to pay hardly any new taxes and that, therefore, the burden would fall on prosperous groups. This is the nub of the matter. Councillors believed that their political futures and social standing depended on the good will of the village elites from which they came. To secure these things, they declined to mobilise fresh local resources.

Union Councils and their chairmen

Most of the sub-District Councils' powers and resources were devolved down to them from the national and district levels. But some were also transferred upward from the pre-existing Union Councils, near the grass-roots.[50] Union Councils had always been 'grossly understaffed'[51] and under-resourced,[52] and this change further undermined their capacity to undertake independent development projects. However, this was compensated for by the fact that the elected members of the sub-District Councils were the chairmen of the Union Councils. As a result, these people wielded greater influence over higher-level bureaucrats and obtained greater funds than had previously been available, even if most important decisions on spending were taken at the sub-district level. This meant that decentralisation enhanced Union chairmen's already substantial influence within their localities.

Relations between Sub-District and Union Councils

When decentralisers decide to create a system with more than one tier, as they did in our two South Asian cases, they need to devise ways of

---

[48] Saqui and Mukabber (1988), especially pp. 1–2 and 7–10. They found, for example, that Union Councils refused to meet the government's requirement that they levy taxes on street lighting, other utilities, births, marriages and feasts, as well as a community tax and certain tolls.

[49] Blair (1989). See also in this connection Holtsberg (1990), p. 16.

[50] In 1988, formal institutional changes supposedly made the Union Councils more independent of the sub-District Councils. But both this and the resuscitation of District Councils in that year (Faizullah (1989a), pp. 1–2) made little difference because the informalities remained unchanged.

[51] Ibid., p. 3. [52] Ahmad (1988).

integrating the levels in the system. We saw, in the chapter on Karnataka (India), that little integration occurred there for two main reasons. First, there was an enormous distance between the two tiers – the localised Mandal Councils and the District Councils which were pitched at a 'high intermediate' level. Second, elected members of the lower councils had no organic link to or representation on the higher councils.

This had certain virtues. It meant that both sets of councils were directly accountable to the electorate. But it produced a poorly integrated system in which the local-level councils, which are always short of staff to implement decisions, often had trouble obtaining adequate bureaucratic support.

In Bangladesh both of these problems were minimised. First, by locating the upper tier (the sub-District Councils) at a 'lower intermediate' level, they left less distance between the two tiers. The average population of a sub-district in Bangladesh was 225,000 as opposed to an average of 2.25 million in the districts of Karnataka. Second, by having the chairmen of the localised Union Councils sit as voting members on the higher sub-District Councils, they created a much tighter link between the two.

This had two disadvantages. First, it undermined somewhat the direct accountability of the higher councils to voters, although the direct election of the chairmen of those councils eased this difficulty. Second, it meant that the chairmen of the Bangladeshi sub-District Councils were less accountable to the members, since the former had an independent mandate. (In Karnataka, there was much more of that kind of accountability, since the chairmen of the higher councils were elected by the members thereof. It is no accident that chairmen in Karnataka were ousted by members on several occasions – even though that required a two-thirds vote – whereas in Bangladesh where a simple majority would suffice, this hardly ever happened.) Despite these problems, however, the advantages associated with the system in Bangladesh were substantial enough to enable it to work more effectively in this particular sense than its counterpart in Karnataka.

The immense freedom of action which most sub-district chairmen enjoyed in Bangladesh had ambiguous implications. It meant, as we have noted, that there was great variation in their behaviour since there was enormous scope for the free play of their individual eccentricities. In some sub-districts, it meant that chairmen heavily favoured those Union Councils that were led by close allies. The various localised councils here thus received less equitable treatment than their counterparts in Karnataka which were less dependent on higher-level councils for resources.

This sometimes caused problems for Bangladeshi Union Councils, but our investigations suggest that in most places this was not a serious difficulty, for several reasons. Sub-district chairmen tended to recognise that it made good sense to be relatively even-handed with council members since this assured them of a broad political base. They had been reminded of this during training courses that they all attended soon after their election. Those whom we interviewed usually said that the point had got home. The chairmen also knew that decisions on the distribution of resources within the sub-district had to be formally made at a full and very public meeting of the council – even if it had been privately sorted out beforehand. The possibility of protests by excluded councillors weighed against extreme bias.

There was little that Union Council chairmen who lost out could do about this. The substantial powers wielded by sub-district chairmen, and their ties to Ershad and his circle in Dhaka, prevented their being ousted even when votes of no confidence were passed. But Union Council leaders usually avoided severe discrimination by ingratiating themselves with the chairmen.

Improved administrative co-ordination

Our informants were virtually unanimous in believing that there was far more horizontal co-ordination among the various government departments working in rural areas than before decentralisation or after the sub-District Councils' abolition in 1991.[53] The steep decline since then indicates that UNOs (chief civil servants in the sub-districts) who resumed command regarded co-ordination as inconvenient. They were reluctant to state this openly, since to do so would have contradicted the official view. But their patent lack of interest in it since 1991 makes this clear.

How much developmental benefit did enhanced co-operation yield? Clear gains often resulted from monthly council meetings which all line ministry officials in the sub-district attended. A fisheries officer who had never previously been privy to discussions of minor irrigation works could make useful suggestions about how modifications might assist people who wished to stock ponds with fish. An agricultural officer could offer helpful comments on soil erosion while an irrigation project was being devised, and so it went on.

Once officers had showed how they could contribute, many sub-district councillors recognised the advantages of inter-departmental exchanges

---

[53] Faizullah (1989a), p. 5, found that in the planning process, there was 'no sectoral integration'. He is correct, but when we look beyond planning (an empty exercise, as we saw earlier), there was far more such integration than at any other time in recent history.

Bangladesh 117

and began to demand them at times other than monthly meetings. As a result, many micro-level projects were designed in ways that were of greater help to villagers. Many development bureaucrats began to see that they had new opportunities to make creative contributions. They could also explain problems which might otherwise have gone unattended and demonstrate their skills to councillors and senior bureaucrats. As one put it, 'it took time to get used to this new way of doing things, but a new, healthier administrative culture soon began to develop'.[54]

Absenteeism

We saw in the previous chapter how decentralisation in Karnataka reduced absenteeism among public employees. Their work rate on the job also increased. These changes occurred because elected councillors were in a position to monitor their doings, to receive complaints about poor performance, and to arrange for punitive action where necessary. This enhanced the effectiveness of public services at no extra cost to the state.

Only a very minimal improvement occurred in Bangladesh, even though absenteeism was a serious problem. The explanation for this failure is complex. It owes much to timidity among citizens who are aware of the problem but suffer in silence. The psychological gulf between them and professionals in education or health is often far greater than in Karnataka. This is true partly because education levels and living standards are lower in Bangladesh, and partly because the absence there of sustained democratic practice has made it more difficult for citizens to develop the conviction that the government and its employees have obligations to serve them. That idea has taken firm root among even poor people in most parts of India, and it was vividly apparent in the Karnataka districts which we studied.

Another important factor was the limited view which elected councillors in Bangladesh took of their role. If action was to be taken against public employees, it had to come from the sub-district level, since those employees were answerable to department heads in the sub-district offices. The members of the sub-District Council – that is, the elected chairman of lower-level Union Councils – might have pressed for such action, but we found that this possibility had not occurred to them. Most had served on Union Councils for long periods prior to decentralisation when the absence of the elected officials at higher levels made it virtually

---

[54] These comments are based on a large number of interviews with UNOs and more junior civil servants in Manikganj and Bogra Districts, January–February 1993.

impossible to persuade bureaucrats at those levels to tackle this problem.[55] They failed to see the opportunity offered by the new system.

They remained preoccupied with what had long been their main activity – obtaining and distributing resources from higher levels. This was in part understandable since the increased government spending that attended decentralisation in Bangladesh, and their inclusion on the sub-District Council, gave them much easier access to greater resources. But they had not fully grasped the principles which underpinned democratic decentralisation. These were, first, that government institutions should be responsible and obligated to ordinary people and, second, that elected representatives should serve as conduits through which popular discontents could be conveyed to higher authority.

The perceptions (or misperceptions) which most Union Council chairmen had of their role are not surprising. They follow logically from the comparatively high levels of inequality and destitution that exist in rural Bangladesh, from the privileged socio-economic positions which most of them occupied, from their preoccupation with distributing resources mainly among other privileged groups and skimming substantial private profits from the flow of resources from higher up. The high levels of profiteering in which sub-district chairmen were engaged (see immediately below) concentrated their attention even more firmly on this last activity. Their failure to internalise the principles that lay behind democratic decentralisation plainly undermined the promise of the Bangladesh experiment.

Corruption and its impact on effectiveness

We should begin this discussion by saying what, in our view, 'corruption' is not. Some commentators on decentralisation in Bangladesh tend to equate corruption with politicians' efforts to build networks of supporters by distributing political patronage. In our view, most such activities do not qualify as 'corruption', but as normal and often creative political action. If a politician has received support from a particular group, or seeks future support, and therefore responds assiduously to its needs, we regard this as understandable. It may be unfair to those who lose out, but it has the virtue of teaching the excluded that the way to obtain responses from the government is to back someone else at the next election – an important lesson in the workings of open politics.

'Corrupt' acts are those which enable a person with political influence

---

[55] It should be noted, with regard to school teachers, that there is a strong teachers' union whose leader had close ties to Ershad at the apex of the political system. But this consideration did not register with most of the Union Council chairmen with whom we spoke.

to enrich himself or friends by diverting resources from legitimate purposes or by demanding bribes for services. Patronage distribution only qualifies as corruption when it entails such actions. It is sometimes difficult to draw the line between patronage distribution and 'corruption' defined in this way, but it is a mistake to view the patronage game as wholly corrupt.

The story of corruption in Bangladeshi councils is complex. A large proportion of the considerable funds provided to elected councils was misappropriated. Estimates by well-informed, reasonably objective observers such as journalists, lawyers and school teachers at district and sub-district levels are remarkably consistent. They reckon that roughly 40 per cent of development funds were stolen. Most of this money went to sub-district chairmen and councillors, but some went to their clients and friends, to contractors on public-works projects and to bureaucrats at the district and sub-district levels, among whom corruption was widespread. In some areas, military officers also demanded and received sizeable amounts.

Forty per cent is probably a modest overestimate. Our studies of corruption elsewhere in South Asia suggest that it is logistically difficult to divert such large amounts in institutions near the local level (although not at higher levels in more centralised systems). But even if the figure is closer to 30 per cent, this is a serious problem.

Certain features of the decentralised system left two groups within it feeling the need to obtain funds by corrupt means. First, virtually all sub-district chairmen had spent heavily on election campaigns. Large expenditures were not sufficient to ensure election, but modest outlays meant certain defeat. Once elected, most of them stole funds to recoup their campaign 'investment'. Most also felt that they had to provide bribes to powerful figures in the district offices, one level up in the system, to prevent them from exercising their legal rights to intrude into the doings of sub-District Councils. A somewhat smaller number of chairmen also provided payments to members of parliament and other people of influence at the national level – again to ensure themselves a free hand.

Second, many junior-level bureaucrats who joined sub-District Council staffs when these were greatly enlarged had had to make an 'investment' of another kind. These jobs, like most others in the public service in Bangladesh, could only be obtained if a substantial bribe of many thousands of takas was paid to recruiters at the national level. Candidates had to borrow huge sums to make these payments, and they then felt driven to recover them by taking bribes.

Profiteering under this decentralised system assumed many forms. Sub-district chairmen and councillors often quietly skimmed percentages off budgetary provisions for development before specific projects were decided upon. Greater amounts were then allocated to projects than were actually spent. When the labourers engaged in construction were remunerated in kind – usually wheat – chairmen frequently demanded bribes before signing orders to release the grain. Portions of wheat deliveries were then diverted by lesser politicians and officials. These practices were so widespread that villagers commonly referred to elected politicians as 'gom chor' (wheat thief).

The main device used to extract further profits from construction projects was to claim that more labourers had been employed than were actually hired. It was more difficult for council chairmen and members and contractors to pay labourers less than the justified rate, because international agencies that supply grain have procedures to thwart this and because labourers were kept informed about the correct rates. This was, nevertheless, sometimes attempted and in a minority of cases, monitoring by agency representatives was inadequate and the labourers were sufficiently intimidated to permit it.

Banks linked to sub-District Councils required kickbacks from the mainly prosperous people to whom loans were advanced. Illicit payments were sometimes required to obtain supplies of scarce material and medicines. Contracts for construction projects were awarded to people without the legally required amount of capital because that meant that they were willing to offer bribes to acquire the necessary capital. And so it went on.

District-level officials had the power to audit construction projects, but knowledgeable observers argued that threats to do so were usually issued in order to elicit a share of the profits.[56] Other checks which, in Karnataka, reduced corruption were missing. Bangladesh lacked India's aggressively investigative press, although numerous brave reporters risked retribution by publishing exposés. These had little effect, mainly because the national leaders ignored them and protected sub-district chairmen. Opposition parties in Bangladesh (unlike Karnataka) played little role within elected councils. The high level of corruption did not cripple the councils' developmental capacity because of the lavish funding which the Ershad regime provided. But corruption was a severe problem none the less.

Are democratically decentralised systems such as this capable, over time, of curtailing such corruption? Our evidence suggests that the answer is a guarded 'yes', although this is not apparent in most of the literature on Bangladesh.

---

[56] For a rare exception, see Ahmad and Alam (1991), p. 200.

Most analysts of this system have been trained in public administration rather than in the study of politics more generally. Their training is in many ways valuable, but it instils a prim abhorrence of even modest levels of corruption which are inevitable in any democratic system. They therefore tend to react to it with despair and denunciations which are not entirely warranted.

They also tend to seek administrative solutions to the problem – more watertight systems of auditing, closer bureaucratic supervision of councils, etc. – which are unlikely to work. In Bangladesh, their prescriptions face two serious impediments. Politicians will probably have enough power and guile to get round the rules. And bureaucrats are – on our evidence – almost as inclined towards corruption as elected representatives.

The only effective counterweight to corruption in such circumstances is not administrative but political. It will only be curtailed when elected politicians realise that they will pay a heavy price for malfeasance. Did such a counterweight exist in the Bangladesh system? Did many of these politicians pay such a price? The answer is a resounding 'yes'.

We asked how many of the chairmen of sub-District Councils were re-elected to office in 1990, after their first five-year term. No reliable nationwide figures on this are available, but we gathered data on more than thirty councils in and around our two districts. Only two chairmen gained re-election. All of the others were either defeated or chose not to seek re-election since they knew that voters were aware of their corrupt activities and were eager to punish them. One chairman stated that he had become so unpopular that he felt it wise to retire from politics for several years to let people forget. Our enquiries about districts further afield indicated that the pattern was similar elsewhere.

Two things beyond the chairmen's control also contributed to their defeats in 1990. First, voters often opposed them to express unhappiness with the Ershad regime. Second, the regime had provided sub-District Councils with more resources and political backing in their first two to three years after than in their last two. This caused the chairmen to assume, early on, that they would be able to accomplish much more than turned out to be possible. Many therefore made promises and raised expectations which were unrealistic.[57] Despite this, however, our interviews consistently indicate that the over-riding reason for their unpopularity in 1990 was their tendency to abuse their powers and indulge in corruption.

The new chairmen elected in 1990 understood this and had two

---

[57] This emerges from our own interviews and from research undertaken by A. J. Minjag Uddin Ahmad, who helpfully stressed these points to me.

different reactions to it. Some, who sought office mainly to enrich themselves, concluded that since they were likely to be rejected after their five-year term, they had better steal as much as possible. In those cases, the threat of voter disfavour clearly did not curtail misappropriation. But many chairmen concluded that they should restrain themselves somewhat, in the interests of re-election and of their reputations. The pursuit of a high reputation apparently counted less to most chairmen than did profiteering, but it came a close enough second to have a significant effect.[58]

Research on India indicates that if representative institutions such as decentralised councils exist for more than a few years, ordinary people will grasp the implications of electoral politics and begin punishing errant politicians at the polls.[59] It is clear from the results of the 1990 election of sub-district chairmen that Bangladeshi voters had begun to do just that. Given similar opportunities in the future, the same outcome can be expected.

When this democratic, decentralised system existed, it gave citizens the ability to see and punish corruption and misgovernment which they have not possessed at other times. In the absence of this system, citizens have had no means of disciplining bureaucrats who have often handled development funds dishonestly. After the 1991 abolition of sub-District Councils, farmers seeking pump sets and other benefits from government had to pay substantial bribes, whereas before, councillors would provide them free or for smaller payoffs. One journalist in Manikganj District provided figures showing that the theft of wheat in his sub-district increased sharply after the councils had been wound up. So in the absence of elected councils, some forms of corruption increase.

It is also more difficult for citizens to discern corruption when ministers, members of parliament or senior officials are involved far away in the national capital, than when this occurs in decentralised councils.

So the evidence from Bangladesh indicates three things. First, when resources are devolved on to democratically elected councils, a permanent increase in the number of people involved in corruption is almost inevitable. Second, however, decentralisation – which makes government more transparent and accountable to voters – also enhances the likelihood that corruption at intermediate and local levels will be curtailed

[58] This long discussion of corruption is based on several dozen interviews with lawyers, journalists, non-governmental organisation activists, school teachers, bureaucrats and councillors in Bogra and Manikganj Districts, and with academic analysts in Dhaka and Bogra, January–February 1993. See also Ahmad and Alam (1991), pp. 35 and 41–2.
[59] Blair (1988) and Manor (1994).

after a time, in ways that are impossible when decisions about resource allocation are centralised. This means, finally, that democratic decentralisation holds considerable promise for eventually reducing the overall amount of political corruption – even though there will be more hands in the till.

Outputs – the bias towards infrastructure

Councillors in Bangladesh, like their counterparts in the other three countries, committed a large proportion of their resources to infrastructure, the building of physical assets.[60] Far more funds went to such projects than to service delivery in fields such as health, education, fisheries or agriculture. We asked a representative cross-section of villagers to identify projects in their localities in recent years, and 79.8 per cent of projects mentioned fall under the heading of infrastructure. A further 8.2 per cent of responses were vague or ambiguous, and some of those would also fall within this category. These figures exaggerate the bias somewhat, since the same project was sometimes mentioned by more than one villager. But the strong trend is clear. Table 3.11 lists the types of projects most frequently mentioned.

Most, perhaps all sub-District Councils went to the extent of violating guidelines from the central government for spending on services by transferring funds earmarked for them into building projects. (We exclude here the construction of council offices and housing for their personnel.[61]) The government increased spending on development at the time of decentralisation by enough to leave most (not all[62]) services with modest increases in resources, despite the diversion of funds to infrastructure, but the diversion was none the less substantial.

We saw earlier how the elected chairmen and members of sub-District Councils got away with these violations of the rules, despite some resistance from bureaucrats. Let us now consider the reasons for their enthusiasm for infrastructure.

Evidence from India, West Africa and elsewhere indicates that this is a well-nigh universal bias among elected members of decentralised coun-

---

[60] This intensity of councillors' preference for such projects comes across vividly in Saqui and Mukabber (1988), especially pp. 7–9 and tables 2 and 4 on pp. 17–20. See also Faizullah (1989a), p. 4.
[61] This added to the cost of decentralisation and, in the Bangladesh case, it was probably carried to excess. But a good deal of this is necessary if councils are to function adequately, and if key civil servants are not to be absent frequently on visits to their families elsewhere.
[62] Fisheries offices in Sherpur sub-district of Bogra District said, for example, that the diversion of funds to infrastructure cripples their department. They were able to develop a fish culture project in only one of the sub-districts.

Table 3.11 *Types of projects identified*

	percentage of responses
Road building and repair	16.7
School building and repair	15.0
Tubewells sunk	14.5
Sanitation facilities	8.0
Electrification	7.5

cils. The most common explanation is that councillors and their clients find it easier to pilfer money from construction than from service delivery. Interviews with numerous informed observers indicate that this was an important consideration among Bangladeshi councillors – and bureaucrats. There was, for example, a strong preference not just for construction but, specifically, for projects requiring earthworks because payment for that was rendered in wheat and it was easier to make money from that than from payments in cash.[63] Nevertheless, the explanation is more complicated than that.

First, huge proportions of the resources coming to the Bangladeshi sub-districts were in the form of grain which could only be used in construction projects – and the amounts increased over time. In 1984–5, the year in which councils were created, 50 per cent of resources took this form. In 1987–8, it amounted to roughly 70 per cent, and in 1988–9, to about 90 per cent.[64]

Second, council chairmen and members were neophytes when it came to making decisions on spending such large amounts. To such people, projects involving construction seemed (and often were) far less complex and far easier to comprehend than programmes that provided services. Government regulations on the delivery of services were also more complicated than those dealing with construction projects.[65]

They also thought that if they constructed a road, a warehouse or an extension to a school, they would have a tangible achievement to point to at the end of their time in office. They reckoned that this would help them gain re-election. But many of them also regarded it as a source of personal satisfaction and, not incidentally, as something that would live on after them and perpetuate their memory. The bias towards infrastructure was also reinforced by strong pressure from powerful bureau-

---

[63] I am grateful to a perceptive investigative journalist in Manikganj District (who deserves anonymity) for this point.
[64] Holtsberg (1990), pp. 13–14.
[65] I am grateful to Kazi Afsanul Saqui for stressing this point.

crats in the engineering and other departments whose importance would grow as a result.[66]

Finally, there was a strong popular desire for building works. This is not invariably true. We found several examples of unwanted construction projects which have gone largely unused. But most were of genuine use to villagers. Anyone who has spent time in rural Bangladesh cannot but notice that there is an enormous need there for basic infrastructure. The popular appetite for it is thus far from irrational.

Most construction projects were designed by Union Council chairmen who served as members of sub-District Councils, in response to appeals from their key supporters. Most of these projects were welcome to villagers – especially to more prosperous groups who benefited most from them, but also to some poorer folk who sometimes made use of them and who found employment as labourers doing the building. (Labour was nearly always hired locally, not imported from elsewhere.)

It is worth recalling here that one well-informed Indian observer sees improvements in infrastructure as more likely to assist the poor than many service delivery programmes, since the prosperous groups often take most of the benefits (even where this is illegal) from the latter.[67] One knowledgeable journalist in Manikganj District argued forcefully that the inequity which arose from construction projects there was geographical (with certain areas favoured over others) rather than along class lines.[68] Against this must be set evidence that when councils shifted funds from services to infrastructure, they tended to raid funds for those services that would have benefited the poor – funds for primary school teaching rather than secondary schools, for example.[69]

Responsiveness

The speed of responses

Nearly everyone who was familiar with the decentralised system in Bangladesh, including people who heartily disliked it, agreed that it provided much more rapid responses when problems arose or when

---

[66] In Saturia sub-district of Manikganj District, for example, the Engineering Department staff grew from seven to twenty after decentralisation. This made it the third largest department after Health and Agriculture which had been much bigger prior to decentralisation. Interview with officers of the Engineering Department, Saturia, 14 January 1993.

[67] Interview with T. R. Satish Chandran, former Chief Secretary to the government of Karnataka, Bangalore, 1990.

[68] Interview with the correspondent of *Dainik Bangla*, Manikganj, 11 January 1993.

[69] This emerged from discussions with sub-district education officers in Manikganj and Bogra Districts, January–February 1993.

influential groups sought action than previously. Before decentralisation, every request had to go up to the district level or higher. It was often necessary for rural leaders to undertake long journeys over wretched roads to the district headquarters to plead in person. This often meant that requests never got submitted, and those that evoked a response consistently took much longer.

It was also easier and quicker to get elected politicians to put pressure on bureaucrats who were slow to implement projects or to release loans or grants. An aggrieved citizen or group could go to their (local) Union Council chairman who had long been on hand locally, but who now sat on the sub-District Council with direct leverage over civil servants. When he or the sub-district chairman went directly to a bureaucrat and demanded an early response – as often happened – they usually had the influence to produce results. Many Union and sub-district chairmen took greater pleasure from their ability to act with alacrity than from anything else.

One aspect of the new system caused occasional delays. Cheques issued by a sub-District Council had to be signed by both the chairman and the UNO (the chief civil servant). If the two were at loggerheads or the chairman was away – as he sometimes was – it could take time to obtain both signatures. But this appears to have delayed civil servants' pay cheques more often than disbursements for government projects.[70]

The quantity and quality of responses

Elite informants also agreed that the overall number of responses grew markedly after decentralisation. Their views are supported by data from our survey of a representative sample of villagers. Of the 959 recent development projects which they identified, 66.2 per cent were funded wholly or partially by sub-District and/or Union Councils. By contrast, only 0.2 per cent had been funded by the government prior to decentralisation in 1985. Respondents had more vivid memories of the more recent period, but the difference between these two figures is so radical that the increase in projects is plain to see.

The main explanation for this was probably not the restructuring of institutions which decentralisation entailed, but the increase in government spending on development that accompanied decentralisation. The empowerment of locally elected representatives nevertheless had an

---

[70] These comments are based on numerous interviews with councillors, chairmen and bureaucrats in Bogra and Manikganj Districts, January–February 1993.

This section is again based on several dozen interviews with leaders of social groups, politicians and bureaucrats in the two districts, January–February 1993.

impact on the quantity of responses from government – the ambiguities of which need to be spelled out.

On the one hand, the rise in corruption that attended decentralisation in Bangladesh (discussed above) diverted a sizeable proportion of development funds. The sum total of responses still grew markedly, because so much extra money was pumped down through the system, but malfeasance curtailed that growth. It also undermined the quality of many construction projects, although this was compensated for somewhat by the improved inter-departmental co-ordination which decentralisation produced.

On the other hand, we should recall that the elected councillors who decided what sort of projects to fund strongly favoured small-scale schemes to construct physical assets. We have seen that they had mixed motives for this. But their taste for such projects was also in part a response to a strong preference for them among their constituents. As a consequence, the empowerment of the councils made a clear contribution to a significant – and for villagers, a very welcome – increase in the number of small-scale outputs.

Of the projects identified in our survey of villagers 85.7 per cent had been completed, as against 2.4 per cent which had been abandoned and 11.9 per cent in progress. This exaggerates the completion rate somewhat, since individual projects were mentioned by more than one interviewee, but the Councils clearly tended to see things through.

We can gain insight into the quality of responses by comparing the types of council projects mentioned by survey respondents with the things which they identified as community needs. For complicated methodological reasons, this comparison must be regarded as rather crude, but it is still worth making. Table 3.12 shows the type of projects and/or needs which were mentioned on more than thirty-five occasions. (Respondents were encouraged to mention multiple projects and needs.) The figures on the provision of food require comment. In mentioning it, people were sometimes referring to a mode of payment for labour which is partly covered by the projects provided under 'employment' in the list. There were no projects the sole purpose of which was to make food available. At the same time, this clearly indicates that food shortages were acutely felt by many villagers.

The overall pattern in this table is variable. The bias towards infrastructure went beyond villagers' desire for water works (mainly wells), roads and educational facilities (which mainly entailed the repair, extension or construction of buildings). There is, however, rough congruence on many items.

Our survey revealed high levels of satisfaction among respondents with

Table 3.12. *Projects and needs identified by respondents*

	Projects	Needs
Employment, provision of	129	138
Food, provision of	0	121
Houses, sites for houses	0	82
Road, building and repair	169	74
Electricity	76	66
Sanitation (drains, latrines, etc.)	81	65
Education facilities/programmes	153	54
Health facilities/programmes	59	51

Table 3.13. *Levels of satisfaction with projects (%)*

Very satisfied	68.0
Somewhat satisfied	26.7
Dissatisfied for unspecified reasons	3.9
Dissatisfied, project poor quality	0.4
Dissatisfied, project not usable	0.1
Dissatisfied, project unfinished	0.7
Dissatisfied, badly equipped	0.1
Dissatisfied, too expensive	0.1
Total dissatisfied	5.3

the quality of projects (see Table 3.13). We heard repeatedly that citizens found it easier to ask assistance from elected representatives than from the civil servants who had held sway at supra-local levels before decentralisation and with whom many ordinary people had a 'servant/master relationship'.[71] Since responses scarcely occurred before the creation of sub-District Councils (because the pre-existing, localised Union Councils had little leverage over bureaucrats at higher levels) the Ershad regime's decentralisation initiative had a significant impact here.

We saw in the earlier discussion of participation that a sizeable minority of respondents (23.8 per cent) had contacted councillors about a matter of personal concern, and that decentralisation had encouraged them to contact bureaucrats as well. We then asked whether they found councillors and bureaucrats 'honest and fair' and 'helpful'. The answers from those who made such contacts, are set out in Table 3.14.

In assessing these figures, we need to remember that most of the

---

[71] This section is again based on several dozen interviews with leaders of social groups, politicians and bureaucrats in the two districts, January–February 1993.

Table 3.14. *The nature of responses to contacts*

	Councillors (%)	Bureaucrats (%)
Honest, fair	66.2	66.7
Dishonest, unfair	33.8	33.3
Helpful	69.4	68.9
Unhelpful	31.6	31.1

Table 3.15. *Levels of satisfaction with elected councils*

	Union Councils (%)	Sub-District Councils (%)
Very satisfied	0.9	0.9
Satisfied to some extent	36.2	34.5
Not at all satisfied	62.9	64.6

respondents counted here were from the more prosperous sections of society. It was mainly such people who engaged in the contacting of people in authority. Had our entire sample engaged in contacting, it is likely that the satisfaction rate would have been lower since the elites who dominated the councils tended to favour elite petitioners.

This is strongly suggested by the answers that we obtained from our entire representative sample when we asked how satisfied they were in general with the councils. Three in ten declined to answer, but the views of the rest are set out in Table 3.15. These figures show that many interviewees who voiced their appreciation for the 'outputs' or development projects of the councils had serious reservations about the councils on other grounds. Further discussions with many of them indicated that the destructively cavalier behaviour of many sub-district chairmen, high levels of corruption, elite dominance of the councils and other problems eroded the popularity and perhaps the legitimacy of the councils.

Responsiveness to whom?

We need to ask which groups gained most from responses. As the section on participation by vulnerable groups in the first part of this chapter suggested, poor people and women received only minimal benefits. Elites (mainly prosperous males) received such a disproportionate share of the spoils that decentralisation intensified the marked inequalities which existed.

Both the sub-district chairmen and councillors came, almost entirely, from a small prosperous elite. These men (almost none were women) had networks of clients to whom they channelled resources, but our investigations found that the vast majority of clients were also from the wealthiest decile of the population.[72]

It might have been politically prudent for the chairmen of localised Union Councils to ensure that poor people in their communities received a modest share of benefits from the system, since the poor had plentiful votes to cast at the next election. But this notion occurred to very few of the chairmen whom we met. Indeed, they were much more preoccupied with delivering a portion of the benefits that they controlled to elite members of rival factions than to poorer groups.

By rewarding their elite adversaries, they were (as one put it) taking out an insurance policy against the day when rivals might win control of the council. Some also hoped that this largess would seduce some prosperous adversaries away from other factions. They reckoned, however, that it was unnecessary to assist poorer voters, since they would fall in with whatever faction was carrying the day in the future conflicts. In other words, politics at the Union level was seen, almost entirely, as an elite activity.

It is not possible to say of Bangladesh, as we did of Karnataka in the previous chapter, that decentralisation transferred resources from higher levels where vulnerable groups enjoyed some influence to lower levels where they did not. In Bangladesh national politics are as thoroughly dominated by elite interests as are sub-district and local politics.[73] So at whatever level, enhanced expenditures on development such as occurred with decentralisation in Bangladesh were bound to go mainly to elites and to exacerbate existing inequalities.[74]

Poor people clearly benefited by finding work as labourers on construction projects, but this did not adequately compensate for the disproportionate share of council resources going to prosperous groups. Labourers sometimes received less remuneration than they deserved or, more often, contractors skimmed off profits from projects by hiring fewer workers than they budgeted for – thereby denying employment opportunities to the poor.

How did the policies and machinations of councils and their chairmen affect women's interests? A study from the Philippines has shown that decentralisation there undermined women's influence in two ways. First, councils' hiring and firing policies reduced the number of women employees, especially in the health sector where they played an important

---

[72] See also in this connection Rahman (1988).
[73] Alam (1993) and Maniruzzaman (1992), pp. 203–24.
[74] See for example in this connection Kramsjo and Wood (1992), especially Wood's introduction BRAC (Bangladesh Rural Advancement Committee (1983a)) BRAC (1983b) and Holtsberg (1990), p. 1.

role. This did not occur in Bangladesh because councils did little hiring and firing, but our enquiries strongly suggest that only a tiny proportion of the new posts which were filled by the central government at the sub-district level went to women. Second, the Filipino councils diverted resources away from health services towards public works and infrastructure. This caused a net reduction in resources for that sector where women had influence and were benefited.[75]

We have noted elsewhere that councils in Bangladesh also did this. That implies that policies there also undermined women's influence and interests. It should be stressed, however, that despite this, the creation of sub-District Councils in Bangladesh also entailed a net increase in funds for health programmes, since comparatively little had been spent for this purpose at the sub-district level prior to decentralisation.

Finally, many of the labourers who gained employment on public works projects in Bangladesh were women. They were poorly paid, but given their desperate situation, this still constituted a modest benefit. On balance, however, women's interests were poorly served by decentralisation in Bangladesh.

Process

How did democratic decentralisation affect the political process – that is, the ways in which state institutions and society interacted? How did it influence popular perceptions of these processes and of government institutions? The answers are complex and ambiguous.

The significant, if scattered abuses which occurred during three of the four council elections, and the grotesque abuses during the 1988 Union Council elections caused a substantial minority of respondents to our surveys to express doubts about the fairness of the electoral process.

On the other hand, decentralisation created a system which could respond more quickly to grassroots requests for assistance, and which in many (though not all) respects delivered development projects which conformed to villagers' perceptions of their needs. This is explained both by changes in institutional structures and by the increased spending on development that attended decentralisation.

Corruption was a very serious problem here, as was the tendency of the rural elites who dominated councils to pass the lion's share of resources to elite recipients. These things and electoral abuses tempered somewhat people's enthusiasm for a system which was so much more responsive than its predecessors. They did not, however, inspire wide-

[75] De Guzman (1992).

spread dissatisfaction with the councils or serious popular scepticism about the legitimacy of the decentralised system. Ershad, who created it, hoped that it would lend legitimacy to his regime at the national level, but this did not happen. People distinguished quite clearly between the councils and the Dhaka government which was eventually brought down by mass agitation.

One test of changes in public perceptions of the government which receives emphasis in studies of Africa – the question of citizens' greater willingness to pay taxes and make voluntary contributions to community projects – cannot be applied in Bangladesh. This is because councils there were so generously funded from the above that they did not seek to raise much in taxes, and because the African tradition of voluntary donations is largely absent in South Asia.

We found that Bangladeshi councils (unlike their counterparts in Karnataka) made next to no impact on absenteeism among public employees, for reasons that yield important insights about the relative lack of change on the 'process' side. First, councillors were so preoccupied with distributing patronage among their clients that they took little notice of complaints about absenteeism. Second, few such complaints reached them, mainly because ordinary folk tend to have a 'master/servant' relationship both with elected politicians and with public employees. Both of these things suggest that politicians and citizens tend to be insufficiently conscious of the obligations which elected leaders and the state more generally have towards ordinary people. The contrast with Karnataka on this point is striking. We have not found evidence to indicate that this experiment in decentralisation had much impact on this set of attitudes.

CONCLUDING REMARKS

Decentralisation and the demobilisation of civil society

We have argued here that the Ershad regime failed to exercise 'control' over decentralised institutions, and that it is more accurate to say that it gained the 'acquiescence' of councillors. The regime's attempt to build a political party which would earn it loyal support from influential groups in the hinterland also failed. What they achieved was, again, 'acquiescence' more than outright 'loyalty'.

But let us first consider another aim of the regime, which was closely linked to its unsuccessful – if rather inept and half-hearted – quest for 'control' and 'loyalty'. This was its effort to demobilise civil society (organised interests with some autonomy from the state). It pursued this by various means including the close bureaucratic scrutiny and sometimes the harassment of non-governmental organisations indigenous to Bangladesh, and the intimidation and sometimes the forcible suppression of interests that the regime found inconvenient.[76]

An experiment in democratic decentralisation might seem to sit oddly alongside such doings, since it entails an opening up of opportunities for citizens, groups and their elected representatives to influence government institutions. Nevertheless, that is what the government undertook, and we need to examine the somewhat incongruous relationship between decentralisation and the attempt at demobilisation.

Ershad and his circle did not see a contradiction between these two things. Decentralisation was supposed to channel the political energies of citizens and groups into institutions which were spatially dispersed, localised and therefore non-threatening. The accomplishments of these institutions would, it was thought, enhance the legitimacy of the regime that had created them. The government hoped to control them, but although it failed, it still gained the acquiescence of most power-holders within them – no small benefit. So decentralisation did not entirely contradict the effort to demobilise civil society – indeed, to a degree, it complemented it.

At the same time, however, the elected councils acquired a life of their own which did not wholly suit the regime's plans. When elites diverted state resources to purposes of their own choosing, they sometimes did so in ways that ran counter to the regime's aspirations to smother organised interests. More crucially, many groups became exasperated with the disappointing performance of councils whose promise had been unwisely exaggerated by the regime. This had the effect of crystallising and mobilising discontented interests and of undermining the government's legitimacy. These were the opposite of the results which the regime had desired when it decentralised. So in different ways, decentralisation both bolstered and subverted the regime.

Building a party to back the regime

Similar ambiguities attended the government's attempt to use the Councils to develop Ershad's Jatiyo Party. This strongly influenced the way that decentralisation was managed and, sometimes, abused. Most (though not all[77]) analyses of this system by specialists in public administration, who dominate the literature, overlook these potent political concerns.

---

[76] I am grateful to Hussain Zillur Rahman for stressing this point to me.
[77] Kamal Siddiqui, Kirsten Westergaard and Mohammad Mohabbat Khan are exceptions, though Khan is excessively critical of the experiment.

The regime's political agenda enabled sub-district chairmen to exceed their authority so greatly and so often. In doing so, they did not always undermine the higher purposes of democratic decentralisation. Forceful action to cut through bureaucratic delays often produced quick and effective responses by government institutions to the felt needs of elite interests in rural areas. Their efforts to cultivate personal patronage networks often had the same effect, and enhanced participation by drawing local elites into transactional relationships with elected politicians on a scale seldom seen before.

But in the main, the cavalier doings of chairmen proved damaging both to the aims of decentralisation and to the political interests of the chairmen, the Jatiyo Party and the Ershad regime. This was vividly apparent at the second set of elections of sub-district chairmen in 1990, when only a tiny number were re-elected. This happened partly because they had become discredited and partly because wealthy rivals spent heavily on campaigns to capture these offices. How did the Jatiyo Party fit into this picture?

It tended to provide informal, vague endorsements both to incumbents and to their challengers at the same time! That way it would have links to the new chairmen, whoever won. When people without party ties won, the Jatiyo Party promptly warmed to them, and they to it. Some chairmen who suddenly announced their association with the party had changed allegiances before – several were described as having completed 'hat-tricks and even double hat-tricks' in the defection game. This enabled the party to maintain its connections with most chairmen, but it also meant that those connections were too loose to earn the party and the regime much commitment or loyalty.

Voters understood what was happening – indeed, decentralisation made these dubious practices more transparent than they otherwise would have been. This fuelled people's already well-developed cynicism about the chairmen, the party and the regime. So the 1990 elections and the subsequent deals with new chairmen intensified popular resentment at a time when it was reaching dangerous levels. Partly as a result, the regime collapsed in face of widespread protests a few months later. Once it fell, very few of the nominal Jatiyo supporters in the sub-districts retained their ties to the party, which largely evaporated.

Bangladeshi decentralisation – a study in ambiguity

This experiment in decentralisation had a very mixed record. Ambiguities crop up at nearly every turn. Most elections were largely (though not wholly) fair, while one was an outrageous charade. Within those limits, genuine democratisation and devolution to sub-district and local levels occurred, but this was the work of a military dictatorship which also sought to demobilise civil society. The most powerful figures in the system (sub-District Council chairmen) were directly elected by universal adult franchise, but the extravagant support that most of them received from the regime undermined their accountability to voters.

The decentralised system was far more responsive and transparent than the pre-existing order, and yet corruption soared. Despite that, however, the regime channelled enough extra money through the system to enable councils to deliver a sizeable increase in the number of micro-level development projects. This was very welcome to people at the grassroots, who were also reasonably satisfied with the quality of most projects. But the high level of corruption and other negative features of the system caused most villagers to express substantial reservations about it when they were asked for an overall judgement. Most knowledgeable observers believed that the system had achieved enough to justify its continuance – with certain reforms – but the regime which was elected to power after the fall of Ershad felt such resentment against his rule that it decided to scrap the experiment and start afresh.

We could go on with this litany, but the basic point is clear. Our studies suggest that most exercises in decentralisation in Africa and Asia are more likely to be marked by the kinds of ambiguities that we found in Bangladesh than by the creativity which was achieved in most (though not all) fronts in Karnataka.

4 Côte d'Ivoire

THE BACKGROUND

The socio-economic and political context

Côte d'Ivoire is one of the few sub-Saharan African states to have enjoyed a post-independence history of political stability and economic growth. Both characteristics have come under challenge more recently, with the commodity price slump of the 1980s, the subsequent squeeze on public finances and the move to multi-partyism in 1990. But decentralisation is still taking place within a context of dominant party rule and a legacy of effective but highly centralised administration. The stability and power of the ruling party, the Parti Démocratique de la Côte d'Ivoire (PDCI) survived the death in December 1993 of President Félix Houphouët-Boigny, following which Henri Konan Bédié, Speaker of the National Assembly, succeeded to the office of President in accordance with the Constitution. Bédié and the PDCI went on to win an overwhelming victory in the 1995 general elections, in the face of a violent opposition boycott of the presidential contest.

In spite of rapid urbanisation the economy of Côte d'Ivoire is still predominantly based on primary agricultural exports (coffee and cocoa). Commercialised agriculture developed much later and in a more restricted way in Côte d'Ivoire than in Ghana, and when it did it was associated with enormous waves of migration during the 1950s and 1960s from within the country or from the neighbouring West African states. Initially the majority of foreign migrants were employed as sharecroppers or labourers, but in the 1970s with the 'cocoa rush' in the far west of Côte d'Ivoire, many became farmers in their own right. By 1980 foreigners formed 41 per cent of the labour force.[1] The average cocoa smallholding in Côte d'Ivoire is now around 6 hectares, but in the west migrants developed farms of between 9 and 14 hectares[2] and there is also

---

[1] Crook (1991a) and (1991b).   [2] Ruf (1985); Lesourd (1988).

thought to be a small class of very large farmers, many from the upper urban elite of civil servants, business men and politicians – including the former President himself.[3] But at the level of the small towns of the interior, social inequalities present the same kind of picture as in Ghana, except that the poorest groups of farmers and labourers are likely to be foreign migrants.

Côte d'Ivoire has been ruled not just by the same regime but by the same small leadership group associated with President Houphouët-Boigny since 1952, when the French colonial administration decided to co-opt Houphouët-Boigny's party (the PDCI) as their local successors. Although the accession of Bédié represented a shift to a slightly younger generation (Bédié was born in 1934), the core of the elite, recruited over the decades through intermarriage and political and economic accumulation, has remained remarkable stable. This elite itself recruited heavily from the civil service, and it is now probably one of the most technocratic (as well as the oldest in generational terms) in Africa.[4] The creation of a large, well-financed and effective state machine was financed out of an economic growth based predominantly on foreign factors of production – foreign African labour for the cocoa farms, foreign capital, expatriate managerial manpower and Lebanese traders – and a policy of unrestrained expansion of export crops.[5] By 1980 Côte d'Ivoire was the world's largest cocoa producer.

Although the strategy adopted by the Ivorian regime produced a strong and effective state, the longer-term political results were not entirely healthy. Once in power the political elite presided over a process of departicipation that lasted for almost thirty years, until the democratisation policies of 1980 and after. The state overpowered or was out of all proportion to what had always been a weakly developed civil society. Between 1949 and 1959 no PDCI congress was held. After 1960 deputies to the National Assembly were 'elected' on a single national list drawn up centrally, and elections for local office bearers were never held. At the local level the party became moribund. Such limited local government as existed in Côte d'Ivoire – seventeen municipal councils (urban communes) at the time of independence in 1960 – was also allowed to decay; elected councillors died in office and were not renewed.[6] At the same time the colonial Prefectoral system of territorial administration was expanded and strengthened, building on the legacy of a ruthlessly centralised, highly policed French local administation. In Côte d'Ivoire's poor and sparsely populated rural interior, the development of community-

---

[3] Gastellu and Affou (1982).   [4] Bakary (1984); Crook (1989); Crook (1991a).
[5] Crook (1989).   [6] Tay (1974); Cohen (1980).

based politics or of a civil society based on local elites was snuffed out virtually before it had begun. Hence the almost unnatural quiescence and political apathy of the Ivorian countryside noted by many observers, and the under-development of small-town life in comparison with the burgeoning Abidjan metropolis.[7]

It was not until 1980 that a process of political reform began which was partly linked to the developing economic pressures coming from falling commodity prices and indebtedness which in turn gave leverage to the World Bank and other international agencies funding Structural Adjustment Programmes (SAPs). But there were also political motives which were in fact served quite conveniently by the thrust of the SAPs of the 1980s.

The President wished to reduce the power of the 'old guard' or 'barons' of the regime, whose increasing autonomy was based on their control of the burgeoning parastatal sector. In response to criticisms of over-centralisation and excessive state dominance of the economy, the President brought in a series of measures which were widely interpreted as clever ways of using a purge of the parastatal sector, combined with democratisation, in order to reassert his control and re-establish the legitimacy of the regime.[8] Competitive elections within the one-party framework were introduced for party, National Assembly and local government posts. Loss of office or failure to achieve entry to the political elite could then be blamed on the electorate rather than on the President himself. At the same time, the public were given an opportunity to punish political leaders (except the President) for the economic crisis, a process highlighted by the well-publicised official attacks on the corruption and incompetence of the parastatal organisations.[9]

Publicly, the President hoped to give opportunities to a younger generation of political aspirants to hold office, to root out corruption and lethargy, and to renew the democratic credentials of political officeholders. By showing that he could still command a following and renew the system using younger generations whom he judged to be more loyal, Houphouët-Boigny also hoped to head off pressures for him to step aside.

Decentralisation was an integral part of the democratisation process begun in 1980, and involved the creation of large numbers of new, elected local government authorities – the communes. One purpose of the *communalisation* policy was, therefore, its hoped-for link with political renewal of the ruling party, under the control of the President. The new

---

[7] Crook (1991a).   [8] Fauré (1989).   [9] Ibid.

communes were in particular intended to address the problem of public apathy and lack of trust or communication between government, party and the people. This meant, according to Léon Konan Koffi, Minister of the Interior, not only allowing people to elect their own councillors and mayors, but also enabling citizens to participate at a level of government 'which directly concerns them and which, therefore, is capable of being understood by everybody'. Furthermore, the official hope was that the communes would represent 'an institutional answer to the fundamental problem of encouraging popular participation'.[10]

The purposes of the new communes also related to the problems posed by the dual economic and political crisis in more subtle ways. Communalisation created new groups of office-holders and elected representatives who were institutionally separate from the party, locally based and also formally charged with responsibility for the development of their area or community. In the context of a squeeze on public expenditure, the government clearly hoped that new authorities would be able to improve the mobilisation of fiscal resources at the local level, and thus in the longer term enable central government to divest itself of some of its developmental responsibilities.[11]

This hope was based upon a sound political and social logic. In Côte d'Ivoire, as in other African societies, the successful sons and daughters of a particular community – those who had entered the modern urban elite and who had therefore almost certainly moved to Abidjan – had long been expected to take an interest in helping the development of their home town or village.[12] In many respects this was a social expectation which had become for many *Abidjanais* a burden honoured only through pious lip-service; but in some communities with particularly powerful or successful patrons it had become a reality, the national models being Yamoussoukro (the President's 'village') and Jacqueville.[13] Communalisation was a way of formally associating local elites or elites of local origin with the work of local development, a connection put very cogently by M. Harding, the head of the Local Government Department at the Ministry of the Interior in 1988. On being asked if it made sense to create large numbers of small communes which lacked the economic base to be financially viable, he replied: 'It's for that reason that I have emphasized the participation of "cadres" in the life of the commune . . .

---

[10] Côte d'Ivoire (1991a), author's translation.   [11] Attahi (1989a), p. 39.
[12] See Delpech (1983); Dubresson and Vidal (1991).
[13] Dubresson and Jaglin (1993); the mayor of Jacqueville is Philippe Yacé, former PDCI Secretary-General and President of the State Economic and Social Council (*Le Conseil Économique et Sociale*).

the people should be able to look to the ruling group for imaginative ideas'.[14]

It was the democratisation process nationally, however, which gave a real incentive for the 'cadres' to take up this challenge, either by becoming commune office-holders or by patronising the new communes. In order to join the political elite and thus gain access to the channels of patronage, it was necessary to get elected. The move to multi-party elections in 1990 added to this pressure. Getting elected required, at the very least, some kind of local power base as well as resources and popularity.[15] And one of the best ways of obtaining such local credibility was to be publicly associated with some visible evidence of development in the community.

In hoping that elite patronage of the communes would help to fulfil the goal of building local self-reliance, the government was perhaps guilty of a certain naivety in relation to the realities of Ivorian political culture. When the new communes were lauched in 1980, the financial structure of the decentralised system suggested a partnership between central and local government. It is incorrect, as some cynics would maintain, that the government's sole intention at the commencement of the reform was simply to force all local communities into financing their own development. On the contrary, the government seemed prepared to commit substantial resources both to setting up and sustaining the decentralisation experiment, with greater local self-reliance only a long-term goal for the majority.

By 1985, therefore, when the ninety-eight communes of the interior were created, the familiar logic of Ivorian politics had reasserted itself: the belief that 'decentralisation' was in fact a way of increasing the flow of *central* government sources for local development had clearly taken hold of the newly activated local elites, even in the face of the continuing economic crisis. This, at least, is the only way to interpret the evidence of the 8th Congress of the PDCI in 1985, and the subsequent National Assembly meeting at which party officials and deputies vied with each other to put intense pressure on the government to increase the number of new communes. In responding to this campaign, the government abandoned all considerations of potential financial viability in favour of giving a political token to the maximum number of local representatives. The idea that being 'granted a commune' was a form of central patronage continued into the 1990s (despite the severe cuts) with the creation of an extra sixty-one communes in the rural areas.

---

[14] *Fraternité Matin* (1988).   [15] Cf. Bakary (1986).

The structure of decentralisation

In a comparative context, the Ivorian communes form a particularly important and unusual case of democratic decentralisation. Instead of decentralising to administrative or traditional subdivisions of the national territory, the Côte d'Ivoire has adopted a Francophone perspective according to which local government is set within an 'urban' problematic. That is, local government is seen as appropriate only if based upon particular communities or urban settlements and charged with addressing problems of 'urban' management and development.

The decision to upgrade and increase the number of communes was taken in principle as far back as 1978, and in 1980 a modest beginning was made with the creation of thirty-seven fully democratised local authorities in the large and medium-sized urban centres, including the sub-division of the city of Abidjan into ten communes. But the major change came in 1985 when ninety-eight of the small 'towns of the interior' were also given commune status bringing the total to 135 and the City of Abidjan authority. By 1996, the extension of *communalisation* to all the main settlements in the rural areas had brought the total up to 196.

In spite of the 'urban language' of the legislation (the communes are called municipalities in French), 1985 in fact marked a significant change in that the majority of the new ninety-eight communes (73.5 per cent) had populations of less than 20,000 and the largest group (thirty-eight) had populations of less than 10,000.[16] Although classified as 'urban' by the demographers and by the legislators, in sociological and economic terms they are in fact – particularly since the creation of the sixty-one 'rural' communes between 1993 and 1996 – little more than large villages or small market and administrative towns in a rural setting. The territorial area of authority of the commune is confined to the immediate hinterland of the town with a few satellite villages – normally a radius of around 8 kilometres.[17] Although the Ivorian commune is, like the other countries, an elected authority based on the principle of representative democracy it therefore corresponds most closely to the ideal of decentralisation to the community level of politics.

In formal terms, the communes are devolved local governments.[18]

---

[16] Côte d'Ivoire DCGTx (1992a).
[17] Except for sixteen communes which had their boundaries extended in 1990 to a radius of 11 km in order to include larger numbers of villages. In 1990, the 135 communes covered only 6 per cent of the land surface of the country and around 50 per cent of the population (Côte d'Ivoire, DCGTx (1992a), Introduction).
[18] See Chapter 1.

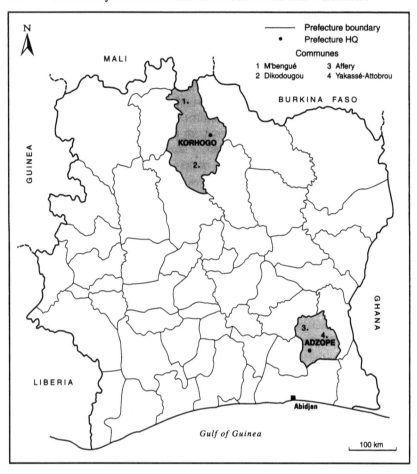

Map 3 Côte d'Ivoire: the Prefectures, showing location of case-study communes

Each commune is an authority with legal personality and 'financial autonomy', the latter phrase meaning not independence but the right to create and manage its own budget and its own property or resources.[19] Legal accountability to democratically elected officials is firmly based at the local level. The mayor and his assistants who form the Executive (*la Municipalité*) are elected councillors, elected to office by the commune council at its first meeting, not appointed by government as in the pre-

---

[19] In French legal terminology, an entity with *personnalité morale* can be the subject of legal action, hence in English it has 'legal personality'.

1980 system. The mayor can appoint and dismiss commune staff (except the seconded civil servants) but all the employees including civil servants are accountable to the mayor. The day-to-day administration of the commune is in fact the responsibility of an official called the secretary-general who in most cases is a seconded civil servant – as are the heads of the statutory Departments of Administration, Finance, Technical Services and Archives. The mayor can also appoint his own Head of Private Office, a power which only the mayors of the larger communes can afford to use.

Once elected the mayor has the character of an independent executive in that he can only be removed by the state authorities, and he becomes an official of the state, charged with responsibility for the maintenance of civil order and the *état civil* (registration of population).

The Executive is formally accountable to the Council, a wholly elected body which is elected as a single list in a first-past-the-post ballot. This has the unfortunate consequence that the winner literally takes all: the winning list forms the Council and the losers are totally excluded. There is therefore no opposition on the commune councils even after the advent of multi-party competition. The Council approves the budget and the mayor must give an account of his execution of the budget at each Council meeting during the year.

Unlike many other countries with 'mixed' forms of devolution/deconcentration, communal administration is not simply a regrouping of deconcentrated central ministries under the nominal control of an elected council. A transfer or devolution from the state to the communes of legal competence to perform a wide range of specified functions was set out in the law of 1985[20]: these include the provision of educational buildings and equipment; cultural and social facilities; public health and sanitary services; maintenance of local roads; markets, bus stations etc.; and administrative services such as the census, and the certification of births, deaths and marriage (*état civil*). Urban land use and planning remains for the most part under the control of central ministries, although the communes play an important political role in local 'mixed commissions' for the allocation of plots, particularly in the smaller rural communes, and have to bear many of the costs of plot development.

Although the communes share many of these functions with technical ministries and in practice are dependent on them in areas such as health or education for staffing and technical approval, the commune administration thus forms a separate, locally recruited and semi-autonomous agency of government with general authority over its specified territory.

---

[20] Law no. 85–582 of 29 July 1985.

Nevertheless, whilst the communes reflect one set of political goals as devolved local governments, another and older set of political and administrative imperatives is embodied in the structures of control within which the communes must operate. Throughout the democratisation process, the PDCI government has always acted cautiously, never relinquishing its determination to maintain stability and the continuation of PDCI control.

In the first place, the government's willingness to create large numbers of very small communes was perfectly consistent with its historic reluctance to contemplate any form of territorial devolution to larger areas of a regional or sub-regional kind. This reluctance is based on a fear of the potential dangers (to the PDCI regime – or 'national unity') which might spring from the creation of politically validated regional institutions. Even in 1991, when the government accepted the need for ten administrative regions to be run by 'super prefects', it was careful to emphasize that their purpose was purely to co-ordinate regional development funds and to bring the prefectoral administration more into line with the regional directorates of various deconcentrated technical ministries.[21]

Secondly, the communes are subject to the *tutelle* of the Ministry of the Interior, which is exercised locally by the prefectoral service. There are fifty-six Prefectures subdivided into 227 sub-Prefectures, which provide a parallel deconcentrated territorial administration.[22] The communes are, in effect, 'islands' of democratic local government set within the sub-Prefect's territory and thus provide for their inhabitants a daily contrast between the two kinds of administration. The French concept of *tutelle* means that the communes are monitored and supervised by a central ministry, which approves their executive actions where required and provides advice and support. There is no evidence that this power has been used in a partisan way since 1990, although the opportunity to do so has, admittedly, been limited: between 1990 and 1995, the opposition controlled only six out of the 135 communes, a total which increased to thirty-three after the 1996 elections.

---

[21] *Fraternité Hebdo*, 4 January 1991. The number of regions was increased to sixteen in 1997 and the President announced an intention to create advisory Regional Councils, each of which would elect representatives to the national Senate (*Fraternité Matin*, 15 March 1997). The fact that many of them were centred on traditional opposition areas such as Agboville in the south-east suggested that the old fear of regionalism was giving way to the idea that some limited degree of regional representation might help to overcome the alienation of these areas from the PDCI regime.

[22] Until 1997, there were 183 sub-Prefectures and it will be some time before the extra forty-four created in that year become fully operational (*Fraternité Matin*, 15 March 1997).

Until 1986, all the budgets and most of the decisions of municipal councils and mayors had to be approved by the Department of Local Government in Abidjan. In addition, under the 1985 law, eighteen subjects are listed covering virtually all matters of any significance in respect of which decisions of the Council cannot be executed until approved by the tutelary authority. Since 1986, power to approve commune budgets and decisions has been gradually deconcentrated to the Prefects; as of 1992, the Prefect acting through a *commission départementale* (inter-departmental committee at Prefectoral level) has the power to approve budgets of less than 100 million francs, which in effect covers 80 per cent of all communes.

The Ministry of Interior's *tutelle* is no mere formality. The actions of the mayors and councils are carefully monitored and frequently rejected or modified, usually for technical or legalistic reasons. The most common error is failure to make an action the subject of a formal resolution of the Council; but other problems relate to the functioning of commune democracy, such as mayors failing to obtain the approval of the Council for expenditure, councils failing to meet regularly, and attempts to engage expenditure not provided for in the estimates, or in the Three Year Plan.[23]

The closeness of central control can also be seen in the operation of the communes' fiscal and financial systems. As well as ceding a proportion of the proceeds of certain state taxes (on land and business) and giving the communes local tax-raising powers, the state was also prepared to give direct subsidies in the form of a general grant-in-aid and the secondment of centrally paid civil servants to staff the key administrative posts in each commune. The state grant was allocated according to a dual formula based on population and need, the latter element being intended to help poorer, less viable communes. The ninety-eight new communes received 68 per cent on average of their revenues from central government in 1987, a proportion which did not fall significantly (to 58 per cent) until the early 1990s.[24] (Abidjan and the larger cities were largely self-financing by the early 1980s.)[25]

The financial life of a commune begins – and ends – with the budget and its associated Three Year Plan which has to be updated each

---

[23] *La Voix des Communes* (1988), p. 21. In the first two years of the new 135 commune system, for instance, the Ministry of Interior disallowed 26 per cent of all Council acts submitted for approval and declared void 15.6 per cent of all the *arretés* and *décisions* promulgated by mayors (Côte d'Ivoire (1988a), p. 22). The government also used its power to remove six mayors during the first mandate of the new communes, 1985–90, and two Councils were wholly dissolved (Attahi (1992), p. 63); *Fraternité Matin*, 14 August 1987.
[24] Côte d'Ivoire (1988a) and (1993a).   [25] Attahi (1989b).

financial year. One important restraint on the freedom of local officials to allocate budget expenditures has been the insistence of the tutelary authority – laudable in itself – that at least 30 per cent of the total budget be devoted to investment (capital and development projects). Budgets which fall far short of this level are unlikely to be approved.

It is, however, in the execution of the budget that the inherently centralised nature of the existing financial administrative system is most clearly revealed. Unlike a devolved local government authority in the British or American tradition, the communes in Côte d'Ivoire do not have their own treasury or bank account. The system is based on two deeply entrenched principles of French administrative law which have been incorporated into the Ivorian system: the principle of the unity of the state treasury (*unicité de caisse*) and the strict institutional separation of the power to authorise expenditure (*l'ordonnateur*) from the power to actually pay creditors (*le payeur*). All commune taxes and other revenues are paid into the state Tax Office at Prefectoral level, where they are handled by a state official, the *Receveur Municipal*, who is accountable only to the Treasury. Once paid in, commune funds are not earmarked. When a commune bill has to be paid, the mayor authorises payment which can only be done under the approved budget heading, and the creditor goes to the office of the *Receveur Municipal* to collect his cash. The power which this practice has put into the hands of the *Receveurs* has only recently been revealed by the financial squeeze on state funds generally (see below); the communes are in effect totally dependent on the local offices of the state Treasury for the management of their cash flow, both as regards revenue transfers and expenditure.

The communes are equally constrained in fiscal matters. The majority of taxes available to the communes are neither assessed nor collected by the communes themselves. The majority of tax collectors are employees of the state Treasury and thus not answerable to the commune. Only the local fees and licence charges on such activities as markets and entertainments are collected by the commune employees; even here, however, the rates and incidence of taxation are set nationally.[26] The communes have very little control, therefore, over either the rates of taxation or the rates of collection, and little capacity – or incentive – to increase their revenues from local sources. In the case of smaller communes, which see little prospect of ever being financially viable, this once again reinforces the logic of dependence on state patronage.

As with most programmes of decentralisation the Ivorian communes thus embody a number of different and to some extent contradictory

---

[26] Attahi (1989b); Gbaka (1992).

purposes, deriving from conflicting political pressures and long-established institutional vested interests. The democratic potential of community-based devolved local authorities has been counterbalanced by an administrative and financial framework which retains tight central control over communal actions and programmes. Although formally devolved, the structure of decentralisation in fact reflects a determination to maintain central power.

The choice of case studies for field research

In selecting case studies for analysis and collection of data in the field, an attempt was made to choose communes which were typical of the majority of communes created in 1985 – that is, a commune territory consisting of a small town or large village, predominantly rural in character, together with a few surrounding satellite villages. The average new commune in Côte d'Ivoire has a population of 16,309 and the vast majority (73 per cent) have less than 20,000 inhabitants. The modal category (39 per cent) has less than 10,000 inhabitants. The domination of the main commune town or administrative centre is shown by the fact that the percentage of a commune population living outside the central settlement is, on average, 37 per cent. In fact, in 66 per cent of all the new communes, over 50 per cent of the population live in the main town.[27]

A further criterion was to represent the major cultural and economic regions of the country, whilst avoiding areas too close to Abidjan. Notorious special cases with regard either to their political or economic characteristics were also screened out of the list.

Finally, in view of the smallness of the communes, two 'pairs' were sought, each pair located in the same Prefecture in order both to facilitate the fieldwork and provide a common framework for longitudinal study.

Thus, following these critieria, the four communes selected were typical according to their size and structure and taken from the southern cocoa/coffee growing zone and the northern savannah zone respectively. The two northern communes chosen were located in the Prefecture of Korhogo, both being part of the Senoufo cultural area. Mbengué, to the north of Korhogo, is on the road to the border with Mali and has a population of 7,490. Its economic mainstay is cotton and rice together with some cattle herding, but it is a dry and poor area, hoping to benefit from increased trade if the road to Mali is ever improved. Dikodougou to the south has a population of 10,413 and is located in a more fertile area for growing foodstuffs as well as rice and cotton.

[27] Data calculated from Côte d'Ivoire, DCGTx (1992a).

The southern pair, Yakassé Attobrou and Affery, are both located in the Prefecture of Adzopé, the heart of the Attié-speaking cultural area (they have some affinities with the major Akan groups of southern Ghana and south-eastern Côte d'Ivoire but claim an older ancestry). The whole area was once prosperous from cocoa growing but the plantations are now old and farmers have shifted to food crops. The population of Yakassé is 14,559 and of Affery, 21,202.[28] By chance, however, Yakassé turned out to be one of the communes with an opposition (FPI) administration, elected in the first multi-party elections of 1990, which provided a very interesting case from the point of view of the politics of decentralisation.

PARTICIPATION

Popular participation

Electoral participation
The first councils of the new communes were elected in 1985 within a 'competitive single party' context, according to which only candidates approved by the PDCI could stand. The 1990 elections were, therefore, the first fully democratic contests in the sense that they were open to a multiplicity of political parties (Table 4.1). The overall 1985 participation rate in the municipal elections of 35 per cent of the registered electorate did not improve in 1990, when it in fact deteriorated very slightly to 34.5 per cent.[29] The impact of multi-party politics was perhaps less than might have been expected, but the degree of competition and participation which emerged in the small rural communes was in fact higher than these national aggregate figures would suggest. There were very significant differences between Abidjan and the large towns on the one hand and the smaller towns and rural communes on the other. Thus the participation rate in the ten Abidjan communes in 1990 was only 21.6 per cent, and in Abidjan plus the three largest cities of the interior, 25.4 per cent. This compared with 51.3 per cent for all other communes, and 46.2 per cent for all other communes with contested elections, a participation rate not significantly different from many local elections in Britain.[30]

[28] Demographic data taken from Côte d'Ivoire, DCGTx (1992a).
[29] Bakary (1986) and Côte d'Ivoire (1991b). The participation rate in the presidential contest between Houphouët-Boigny and Gbagbo was 69 per cent.
[30] Author's calculations, based on figures in Côte d'Ivoire (1991b). Participation rates in uncontested communes were in the 90–100 per cent range. The three largest cities are Bouaké, Gagnoa and Daloa, all with populations in excess of 100,000. See Crook (1995) for a full analysis of the 1990 elections. Average turnouts in British local elections have been around 40 per cent since the 1950s – better than the 25 per cent typical of the USA,

Table 4.1. *Côte d'Ivoire, commune elections, 1990 and 1996*

	1990	1996
Registered voters	2,364,484	1,658,876
Valid vote	806,561	726,713
Turnout (%)	34	44
Number of communes won by		
PDCI	126	157[1]
FPI	6	13
RDR	N/A	19
UND	N/A	1
Independents	3	3
Percentage of vote obtained by opposition + independents	4	11

[1] Three contests suspended.
Source: Crook (1997)

Competition itself did not, as some commentators have argued, reduce participation, in so far as the number of lists in communes outside the four main cities made virtually no difference to turnout.[31]

In the four case-study communes turnout in 1985 was as low or lower than the national average; but the 1990 elections saw a marked improvement with levels of participation ranging from 47 per cent to 70 per cent of the registered electorate – better than the 40 per cent national average for the legislative elections (Table 4.2).

The pattern set in 1990 was to a large extent repeated in 1996, except that participation was unfortunately affected not just by the continued weakness of the opposition challenge, but also by a violent opposition boycott of the earlier presidential elections. An apparent increase in turnout to 44 per cent in fact masked a 10 per cent drop in the total vote, and a 30 per cent drop in the number of registered voters (Table 4.1). The fact that turnout in the local elections was lower than in the presidential contests is explicable mainly by the bandwagon effect of the ruling Presidents' victories. Given the power of the presidency in the political system it is quite understandable that voters attributed less significance to the subsequent legislative and municipal elections.

Participation rates based on the registered electorate should, of course,

---

but much lower than the 70–90 per cent figures for France and Sweden; see Miller (1988), p. 59; Widdecombe (1986), p. 38.

[31] Turnout was 43 per cent in those with three or more lists, compared to 46 per cent in those with two. See Fauré (1991), p. 147 and Bakary (1991), p. 183 for the argument on the negative effects of competition.

Table 4.2. *Electoral turnout in the four case-study communes*

Commune	1985	1990	1996
Affery			
No. of lists	3	2	2
Total vote	3,313	4,866	4,362
Registered voters (%)	30.6	46.8	N/A
Yakassé			
No. of lists	2	2	3
Total vote	2,094	3,856	3,575
Registered voters (%)	24.5	70	N/A
Dikodougou			
No. of lists	1	2	1
Total vote	2,137	2,937	3,080
Registered voters (%)	56	60	N/A
Mbengué			
No. of lists	2	1	2
Total vote	871	1,865	1,701
Registered voters (%)	27	57	N/A

be treated with some caution in the Ivorian context. Both the official media and most of the politicians, bureaucrats and local opinion leaders interviewed acknowledged that the registers were inaccurate and often cobbled together on the eve of polling day. Generally, however, the 1990 registers were inflated, with many exceeding the total estimated adult population in certain constituencies.[32]

The opposition alleged that the 1990 election results did not reflect reality and were the product of widespread malpractice. In practice, it would seem that, outside the large cities, the inaccuracies of the registers did not prevent people from voting; what mattered was the success of the candidates in getting their supporters to turn out, an exercise which could be greatly affected by the efforts of the Prefects and PDCI officials who simple gave out polling cards (in lieu of identity cards) to those who wanted to vote. The opposition were particularly indignant about this practice in relation to immigrants or non-Ivorians who, it is alleged, were rounded up and brought in to vote for the PDCI; the exclusion of non-Ivorians in the 1996 elections did not, however, seem to have made any significant difference. In fact, since the majority of competing candidates in 1990 were from within the PDCI (each list using a local name), the

[32] Nationally, the total vote in the commune elections was the equivalent of around 30 per cent of the adult population of all the communes (figures calculated from Côte d'Ivoire (1991b) and Saint-Vil (1991)).

opposition was not really affected by any alleged unfair practices. In 1990 the FPI put up only thirty lists as against the PDCI's 299 and independents' twenty-nine. As only twenty-five (18.5 per cent) of the communes were uncontested, the real competition continued to be within the ruling party, a phenomenon confirmed by the fact that 50 per cent of incumbent mayors lost their positions. In 1996, in spite of the rise of a more serious challenge to the PDCI from the northern-based *Rassemblement des républicains* (RDR), the commune elections actually declined in competitiveness in the sense that the PDCI managed to impose a more strict discipline on itself by restricting the number of lists to 194. The new opposition party put up only forty-nine lists, and the FPI, fifty-eight. The result was that the PDCI won sixty-seven (34 per cent) of the communes with 100 per cent votes, and of the sixty-five incumbent mayors who stood again, forty-one (63 per cent) were re-elected.[33]

The four case studies were typical of this national picture, in that in 1990 the incumbent administration lost in two (Affery and Yakassé) whilst in a third, Dikodougou, the incumbent mayor won with an almost totally new list of councillors. In Mbengué the politically powerful Deputy for Mbengué-Niofoin was re-elected with his list unopposed. In 1996, however, all four sitting mayors were re-elected, including the FPI Mayor of Yakassé.

The local political conflicts unleashed by competitive elections were not, of course, confined to the commune arenas. The positions of deputy, mayor, assistant mayor and councillor formed a focus for interconnected struggles between the ambitious leaders of rival families and communities. In Dikodougou, for instance, intra-party competition was extremely fierce. Here, although there were no opposition parties, there were five candidates for the deputy's job in 1985 and six in 1990 together with two lists for the municipality. The losing candidate for the mayor's job was Nanga Ouattara, the former deputy for the 1980–5 period, who had acted as the political 'godfather' of the incumbent mayor in 1985. The former client (and member of the same family) was now a fierce rival. Two of the six candidates for deputy in 1990 became the first and second assistant mayors in the 1990 successful list. The fact that they were all 'PDCI' merely reflected the dominant political culture of the north, in which political elites calculated that the interests of both their communities and of their careers were best served by working through the ruling party.

Clearly, the politics of such electoral contests can best be understood

---

[33] Statistics calculated from results published in *Fraternité Matin*, 13 February 1996; see Crook (1997) for a full analysis of the 1995–6 elections.

in terms of predominantly local-level factors: the history of particular families, clans and communities, the personalities of the contestants and their links with chiefs or with grand patrons. Can such elections, with electorates of a few thousand voters – canvassed to support the rivalries of personally known elite politicians or 'cadres' of the town – in any sense be seen as a judgement on the record of the commune administration, and thus a fulfilment of the policy of creating more accountable local government? Or can they be dismissed as simply 'bought' elections? Many local informants, both politicians and electors, tended to explain electoral outcomes in somewhat cynical terms as the result either of 'incentives' paid to farmers to go and vote (the going rate was said to be 1000 CFA francs) or of *la technologie électorale* – an ability to manipulate the electoral machinery through control of ID cards and registers. (The high turnouts in uncontested elections can certainly be attributed to the efficacy of such techniques.) These attitudes are often linked with the perception that, because of the legacy of one-party rule in Ivorian politics, abstention is the main way of expressing opposition or disillusionment, and is treated as such by politicians.

Nevertheless there is evidence which suggests that the cynical interpretation should not be accepted at face value. Whilst the seriously disillusioned – or those who supported a faction not running in the contest – obviously did stay away, the most powerful of the local patrons mobilised the vote with the active participation of their supporters. According to the evidence of the mass survey, 27 per cent of respondents said that they had been involved in supporting candidates in 1990, the highest being in Affery (48 per cent) a town which had been deeply polarised by the elections, followed by Yakassé at 28 per cent.[34] In the northern communes, participation in the campaigns was much lower, at 23 per cent of respondents in Mbengué and 7 per cent in Dikodougou. In addition, local grievances over the corruption or ineffectiveness of the 1985–90 administrations were widely cited as reasons for the overthrow of incumbent mayors in Affery and Yakassé; in other words, voting was seen as an activity with a meaningful purpose and outcome. Participants did not, in any case, see anything very wrong with providing 'help' for poor farmers to come and vote. In such a society, rural dwellers do have to be persuaded that it is worthwhile to leave their farms for a day, and to spend time and money which they can ill afford. Overall, therefore, it would be wrong to explain the commune elections purely in terms of bought or manipulated votes. The voting turnout in the smaller communes was actually quite impressive when compared to its disastrous

---

[34] See Methodological Appendix for details of the survey.

Table 4.3. *Direct participation by citizens, group and individual activities, by commune (N = 500) (%)*

Measure	All	Affery	Yakassé	Mbengué	Dikodougou
Group activities					
attended neighbourhood meeting	17.7	27.0	28.2	7.1	7.6
attended and spoke	7.6	7.4	20.6	0.8	0.8
attended public meeting to discuss political/social issue	10.0	19.7	9.7	8.7	1.7
joined protest/ demonstration	4.2	9.8	6.1	0.0	0.8
members of farmers' co-operative	6.2	6.6	3.8	10.9	3.4
members of youth association	9.2	14.8	9.1	4.7	8.4
members of ethnic association	10.4	5.7	12.1	8.6	15.1
Individual activities					
signed a letter or petition	8.2	8.2	7.6	16.5	0.0
contacted councillor or mayor	9.6	13.9	15.2	6.3	2.5
contacted officials at commune office	4.6	6.6	12.9	2.4	0.0
contacted officials at other government offices	4.6	9.0	6.9	2.4	0.0

level in the big cities, where the economic and political crisis had clearly bitten more deeply. And it must also be recognised that the habits of thirty years of one-partyism cannot be overthrown during the course of one or even two elections.

Direct participation in commune affairs

Outside the electoral realm, participation generally was fairly low, as was knowledge of and participation in the affairs of the commune, even in a small town of 6,000–7,000 people. Evidence from the survey of ordinary citizens shows that engaging in 'group' activities such as 'neighbourhood committees', public meetings and associations attracted larger proportions of the electorate than individual activities such as contacting councillors or officials (Table 4.3). Surprisingly few citizens were members of associations, the most significant numbers being those who said they were members of farmers' co-operatives, youth associations or ethnic associations. The latter are of particular significance in Côte d'Ivoire's multi-ethnic society, with its large foreign migrant labour force.

The commonest form of participation was the neighbourhood committee (*comité de quartier*) which is essentially a traditional meeting run by family elders or notables and the chief. 17.7 per cent of respondents said that they had attended such a meeting, of whom half said they had spoken in the discussion. The status and indeed existence of these committees is, however, very ambiguous. Many respondents did not distinguish between them and the old PDCI neighbourhood committees (PDCI *comités de base*) whose decay in the 1980s had so worried the President. Many people, particularly officials and councillors denied that they existed saying that they were the same as the PDCI organs. The truth is probably that the old PDCI committees were in practice indistinguishable anyway from such informal meetings of local notables and they continue to function as such in the northern communes. What is certain is that they had no official status or function with respect to the commune's institutions.

Participation in activities whose purpose is to discuss and then raise issues with the local authorities involved smaller numbers of respondents. The most frequent activities were participating in a local (unofficial) meeting (10 per cent of respondents), followed by signing a letter or petition (8.2 per cent). 'Contacting' activities were equally rare, in that only 9.6 per cent overall had ever contacted a councillor or the mayor/assistant mayor to raise a social problem, and the proportion who had ever gone to the commune offices or any other government office in the vicinity to discuss a social or political problem was even smaller. There were, however, important differences between the communes in that in Yakassé 15.2 per cent had contacted a councillor, whereas virtually no one had in Dikodougou.

These relatively low levels of contacting and participation are somewhat surprising for such small rural communities, especially when compared with the levels found in formal local government in industrial societies such as Britain.[35] One explanation lies in the problematic nature of the relationship between elected members and the electorate in the Ivorian system, which is discussed below. Another reason can be found in more general attitudes towards the commune, which continued to be regarded as an agency of the 'all-providing' state (*l'état providence*) and its activities as the concern of the particular group of individuals who ran it – the mayor and his supporters and the commune's employees, rather than ordinary citizens. Reluctance to participate can also be attributed to particular local factors such as disappointment with the record of the

---

[35] Parry's survey of six British localities found that 24.4 per cent of respondents had contacted a councillor and 20.3 per cent had contacted officials at their council offices. Miller's 1986 survey found higher levels for the same activities in the English shire counties (29 per cent and 61 per cent) and in Scotland (30 per cent and 43 per cent). The greater contact with officers is comprehensible, given the nature of the services provided by British local government, but the more intensive interaction with councillors is more surprising given the generally apathetic attitude to local government found in Britain; see Parry, Moyser and Day (1992), p. 319; Miller (1988), p. 177.

commune, and local factionalism. Individuals or communities who did not support the incumbent mayor usually refused to contribute to 'his' projects or indeed to see the commune as acting for the collective good of 'their' town.[36]

Participation by disadvantaged groups

In the West African context, disadvantage is associated with a combination of overlapping socio-economic characteristics: poverty, illiteracy, low status, youth and gender. Thus the uneducated (except for the few who derive wealth and status from business or traditional family sources), small or middle peasant farmers, young people particularly those without waged jobs and women are on the whole excluded from power and from political participation.

As might have been expected, the mass survey shows that participation in selected activities such as contacting and attending neighbourhood or public meetings was dominated by men across all four communes (Table 4.4). More unexpectedly, however, participation in these activities was not excessively dominated by older age groups, the better educated or those with wealth or high status occupations (Tables 4.4–4.6). If the educational and occupational characteristics of participators are analysed by northern and southern regions (necessary because of their significantly different population profiles), then in the two southern communes the breakdown of participators by education mirrors that of the total male population quite closely. In the northern communes, the very small numbers of primary and secondary educated respondents were over-represented at the neighbourhood committees and public meetings, although still much less than might have been expected.[37] In occupational terms, the only groups which stood out as disproportionately represented amongst the participators were the larger, wealthier farmers, and, to a lesser extent, traders, small business people and artisans.[38]

Analysis of participation by age across all four communes shows that the relatively youthful 30–44 years old age group were slightly over-represented amongst those who had contacted their mayor or councillor, whilst the oldest age groups – all those over 45 – accounted for nearly 50 per cent of those who had spoken at a neighbourhood meeting (Table 4.4).

---

[36] The problems identified in the four cases echo the findings of a survey of the communes carried out by *Fraternité Matin* journalists in the late 1980s – see *Fraternité Matin* (1988).

[37] One explanation could be that, as the commune elections showed, the few educated cadres of these towns were unlikely to live locally unless they had a position which made them a member of the local elite anyway, and therefore less likely to attend popular meetings in an 'ordinary' capacity.

[38] The under-representation of the 'unemployed/ homemaker' group is mainly a function of the gender bias (predominantly female) of this category as used in the Ivorian census.

Table 4.4. *Sex and age group of participators, by selected activities, compared with profile of total population (four communes) (%)*

	Contacted mayor/councillor (N = 48)	Attended neighbourhood meeting (N = 88)		Attended unofficial public meeting (N = 50)	Total population of four communes
		all attenders	attended and spoke		
Sex					
Men	73.0	77.3	92.1	72	50
Women	27.0	22.7	7.9	28	50
Age					
18–29	25.0	37.5	36.8	34.0	43
30–44	41.7	25.0	15.8	36.0	30
45–64	22.9	29.5	39.5	22.0	22
65+	10.4	8.0	7.9	8.0	6

Table 4.5. *Educational and occupational characteristics of participators, by selected activities, compared with profile of population of southern communes (Affery and Yakassé) (%)*

	Contacted mayor/ councillor (N = 37)	Attended neighbourhood meeting (N = 70)		Attended unofficial public meeting (N = 37)	Total population of Affery and Yakassé (South)	
		all attenders	attended and spoke		M	F
Education						
None	59.5	70.0	75.0	56.8	61	81
Primary	24.3	20.0	13.9	29.7	24	15
Secondary/Tech/post-secondary	16.2	10.0	11.1	13.5	13	3
Occupation						
Farmer[1]	56.8	57.1	55.6	51.4	71	76
Farmer with employees	18.9	17.1	22.2	21.6	6	–
Trader/business	16.2	11.1	8.3	5.4	{	
Driver/artisan	5.4	7.1	8.3	8.1	{12	8
Teacher/admin/ professional	0.0	1.4	0	2.7	3	0.5
Student/unemployed/ homemaker	2.7	5.7	5.6	10.8	8	16

[1] includes sharecroppers and farm labourers

Table 4.6. *Educational and occupational characteristics of participators, by selected activities, compared with profile of population of northern communes (Mbengué and Dikodougou) (%)*

	Contacted mayor/ councillor (N = 11)	Attended neighbourhood meeting (N = 18)		Attended unofficial public meeting (N = 13)	Total population of Mbengué and Dikodougou (North)	
		all attenders	attended and spoke		M	F
Education						
None	90.1	83.3	100.0	61.5	87	96
Primary	9.9	11.1	0.0	23.1	6	3
Secondary/Tech/post-secondary	0.0	5.6	0.0	15.4	4	0.25
Occupation						
Farmer[1]	54.5	66.7	50.0	53.8	84	62
Farmer with employees	9.1	0.0	0.0	0.0	–	–
Trader/business	18.2	11.1	0.0	7.7}		
Driver/artisan	9.1	5.6	0.0	15.4}	9	5
Teacher/admin/professional	0.0	5.6	0.0	15.4	3	0.3
Student/unemployed/homemaker	9.1	11.1	50.0	7.7	5	33

[1] includes sharecroppers and farm labourers

Given the continuing respect for age found in West African rural societies, such a result is surprising only to the extent that the most youthful were not more generally excluded.

Overall, therefore, the expected higher *rates* of participation by older people, the better educated and large farmers (Tables 4.7–4.10) do not indicate a swamping or domination of participatory activities by these groups. On the contrary, disadvantaged groups, particularly the uneducated, were not excluded from what, it must be remembered, was in itself a very limited degree of participation. The failure of women to participate is more obviously explained by general cultural factors than by any specific bias in the commune structures.

The role of elected representatives

The difficulties faced by the communes in mobilising and involving the population can to some extent be linked to the electoral system itself, particularly the device of electing the council as a single list in a

Table 4.7. *Participation rates in selected activities, by sex (%)*

Measure	All	Women	Men
Contacted mayor or councillor	9.6	5.1	14.3
Attended neighbourhood meeting	17.7	8.0	27.5
Attended and spoke	7.4	1.2	13.9
Attended public meeting	10.0	5.5	14.7

Table 4.8. *Participation rates in selected activities, by age group (%)*

Measure	18–29	30–44	45–64	65+
Contacted mayor or councillor	5.6	13.6	10.3	17.2
Attended neighbourhood meeting	15.4	14.9	24.3	24.1
Attended and spoke	6.5	4.1	14.0	10.3
Attended public meeting	7.9	12.2	10.3	13.8

Table 4.9. *Participation rates in selected activities, by education (%)*

Measure	None	Primary	Secondary/Technical/post-sec.
Contacted mayor or councillor	8.0	13.7	24.0
Attended neighbourhood meeting	16.0	22.5	32.0
Attended and spoke	7.3	7.0	16.0
Attended public meeting	7.3	19.2	26.9

Table 4.10. *Participation rates in selected activities, by occupational group (%)*

Measure	Farmer/farm worker	Farmer with employees	Trader/sales service	Driver/artisan	Teacher/Clerk/Profess.	Student Unemployed/home maker
Contacted mayor or councillor	8.5	17.4	21.6	11.1	0.0	2.6
Attended neighbourhood meeting	17.1	26.1	27.0	22.2	33.3	7.9
Attended and spoke	6.9	17.4	10.8	11.1	0.0	2.6
Attended public meeting	8.5	17.4	8.1	18.5	42.9	6.6

'first-past-the-post' ballot. The effect of this system is totally to exclude the losers in an electoral contest from representation on the council; and, as is well known, where there are more than two lists the winners may not represent even a majority of those voting. The list system also creates two very particular kinds of problem in relationships between elected members and the electorate. First, is the issue of how the list is put together, which is related to how representative it is of the electorate and to how politically rooted its individual members are. Second, is the problem of establishing the individual accountability of list members to the electorate.

The representativeness of elected councillors
The council is, in effect, a team put together by a powerful political entrepreneur and his faction and embodies two quite distinct political purposes: the desire of the leader of the list and his supporters to become the Executive (mayor and assistant mayors) and the need for councillors – that is, those members of the list who remain ordinary councillors once the Executive has been elected – to represent the people. Although it may be politically prudent for the aspirant mayor to attempt to make his list 'representative' of particular groups or interests and of the various quarters and villages making up the commune, this is not built into the structure and is determined purely by political considerations. On being asked how the 1985 list for the Dikodougou commune had been put together, a leading councillor replied: 'that's easy; the former Deputy made the list, including the mayor (who is from the same family) as he did not want to be mayor himself'.[39]

The dangers of cronyism or even of capture by a particular clan or family are evident and were recognised in two new laws governing municipal elections introduced for 1990. One provides that relatives or members of the same family cannot be elected together onto the same council, and the other that at least 75 per cent of all elected councillors must reside within the commune.[40]

In looking at the way in which the lists were constructed in the four cases, it would seem that these laws had had some impact in so far as the majority of councillors elected in 1990 were, unlike the mayors, indeed local residents, particularly in the north. The change was most dramatic in Dikodougou, where the first Council of 1985 (the deputy's list) had virtually ceased to function because of persistent absenteeism on the part of the Abidjan or Bouaké-dwelling elite councillors. Of the 1990 Council

---

[39] Interview, Chairman of the Economic Affairs Committee, Dikodougou, 31 May 1993.
[40] *Fraternité Matin*, 20 December 1990.

only six of the twenty-seven members lived outside the commune, four of them in the relatively close (48 km) Prefectoral capital of Korhogo although the mayor himself was locally resident. In the other three communes between 33 per cent and 36 per cent of councillors were non-residents including all three mayors who were Abidjan-based. In Mbengué, however, most of the non-residents were to be found in Korhogo (80 km), whilst in the southern communes, as might have been expected, twelve of the sixteen were in Abidjan.

Excluding people who are related is very difficult in African rural communities, although the most blatant forms of nepotism seem to have been avoided. And it should also be remembered that members of the same 'family' often become political rivals. Mayors and assistant mayors claimed that in constructing their 1990 lists they tried to represent different quarters of the town and the outlying villages in their selections, and there is some evidence that this occurred.

In Yakassé, for instance, which is unusual in that there are six villages outside the municipal centre accounting for two-thirds of the total population, there was clearly a determined effort to make sure that every outlying village had at least one 'representative'. According to one informant the villagers themselves, through their chiefs and elders, were asked to nominate candidates. But that was not the end of the story. As this was the first election which the FPI had ever contested, very large numbers of meetings followed in which the local party committee tried to agree a list. The mayor himself was very clear that ultimately the determining criterion was 'FPI militancy'.[41]

In Dikodougou there was also some evidence of a geographical spread on the list, but again this was not the dominant criterion, especially in view of the fact that communities which supported the rival candidate for mayor were totally excluded. In Affery on the other hand it was clear that the list represented the old PDCI establishment loyal to the mayor, himself a very important member at the national level of the PDCI 'old guard'.

As well as the criteria of geographical representation and party loyalty, notions of interest group representation and social status were evidently also at work. Thus mayors sought to include important or respected 'community leaders' such as the chairman of the Farmers Co-operative or the Parent-Teacher Association, transport owners (particularly in the north), PDCI office-holders, important family elders and chiefs of quarters. There were also conscious attempts to represent religious groups such as Muslims, and migrant communities; the new 1990 list in

[41] Interview, mayor of Yakassé-Attobrou, 20 May 1993.

Dikodougou included for instance the leader of the Malian women, and the leader of migrants from Boundiali (a town some 100 km to the east).

In addition, as the government hoped and expected, there was great pressure to include (within the restrictions of the residence rule) the town's 'cadres' – the well-educated and successful scions of the community who, almost by definition, lived and worked in Abidjan or the big cities. As many informants emphasised, this is something which the electors themselves expect and want, on the grounds that an influential and well-educated person is more likely to be able to 'do something' for the community and of course has a social obligation to help those from whom he or she sprang. Social and political attitudes are not entirely consistent in this respect, since the same electors also complain about councillors and mayors who do not live in the commune and thus do not understand what is really needed.

To what extent were the council lists constructed in this way also representative of the general population in socio-economic terms? As might be expected, an analysis of the social composition of the four case-study councils reveals that 33.3 per cent of the total of 108 councillors were from the 'elite' occupational groups: administrators, professionals, business managers in the modern sector and teachers. Male, highly educated, elite occupational groups were clearly 'over-represented' in relation to their incidence in the total local populations (see Table 4.11).

In age terms, too, older people were to some extent 'over-represented' in that 63 per cent of the councillors were over 41 years of age in 1990, whilst the average age was 45.4.[42] But in the context of the social traditions of these communities this can be seen as a surprisingly young average. There were also significant differences amongst the four cases: the Affery Council had the highest average age at 51.6, reflecting perhaps the mayor's political generation, whilst the most youthful council was the Dikodougou 'new list' of 1990, with an average age of 38.6. In this council, none of the councillors was over 61, and 18.5 per cent were under 30. This relative youthfulness reflected the markedly less elite social character of the Dikodougou Council.

Nevertheless, the statistical over-representation of elite groups on the four councils did not mean that the disadvantaged were excluded. On the contrary, the most striking feature of the councils was their extreme social dualism. On the one hand was a small group of highly educated professionals, civil servants, engineers and teachers. On the other, forming the numerical majority, were illiterate farmers, artisans such as tailors, masons, or mechanics and small traders, people who could be

---

[42] This age group accounted for 32 per cent of all adult men.

Table 4.11. *Social composition of the four commune councils*

	Affery	Yakassé	Dikodougou	Mbengué	total	%
Occupational group						
Profess./ admin.	7	6	–	3	16	14.8
Teacher						
primary	1	3	7	3	14	
second.	3	2	–	1	6	18.5
Techn./ medic./ clerical	2	3	2	1	8	7.4
Small business/trade	5	2	2	6	15	13.8
Artisan/ services	1	–	7	3	11	10.2
Farmers	10	11	9	8	38	35.2
TOTAL	29	27	27	25	108	
Education group						
Grads.	7	6	–	4	17	15.7
Illits.	10	7	16	14	47	43.5
Gender						
Women	2	–	2	–	4	3.7

said to be genuinely representative of the ordinary citizens of the locality. Many of these were acknowledged community leaders. The election of the commune councils had, therefore, brought into public life significant numbers of uneducated or poorly educated, low status, younger people, the kinds of citizens who had been virtually totally excluded from Ivorian politics and from local decision-making in the previous thirty years.

Overall, the council lists in the four communes reflected the employment of a multiplicity of social and political criteria in their selection: the representation of geographical quarters; the incorporation of interest groups, community leaders and certain political office-holders; the need to involve the town's cadres and people perceived as 'competent'; loyalty to the mayor and his party or faction. In practice, such lists were probably no less representative of, or more remote from, the electorate than a council chosen through a party system or, as in Ghana, through a constituency-based, 'no-party' system. The main problem which still faced some of them was that council meetings were conducted in French, with breaks for translation. Given the multi-ethnic character of most Ivorian communities and the fact that the commune administrators were likely to be 'strangers' this was to some extent unavoidable. But it did not encourage spontaneous contributions from less well-educated councillors.

Relationships between councillors and the population

The second issue raised by the list system, however, goes beyond the question of the representativeness of the council – and indeed calls into question whether the social character of the councillors is the most important determinant of access for ordinary citizens to local political institutions. The evidence suggests that the lack of institutionalised constituency relationships and the lack of formal accountability mechanisms had a more serious impact on the accessibility of councillors than their degree of social closeness, place of residence or 'representativeness'.

Because of the list system, Ivorian councillors do not have to report to or through formal consultative mechanisms such as local committees or meetings of constituents. As indicated earlier, neither the local party committees nor the neighbourhood notables form part of the commune machinery and are not recognised as such, except as informal channels through which the authorities – and councillors – may choose to work. It might be thought that the communes under discussion were such local level institutions anyway, with a very close representative ratio of one councillor to 300/400 electors,[43] that formal mechanisms were irrelevant. Such, indeed, was the argument of many councillors who claimed that everbody knew them and that they engaged in 'informal' soundings of popular opinion.

According to the councillors interviewed, if they needed to consult the population, they spoke to the village or quarter (neighbourhood) chief and if necessary organised a meeting. Both commune documents and survey data indicate, however, that most 'consultations' went no further than the elders and notables, except for major exercises involving formal public meetings. The data on consultation in respect of particular projects show, for instance, that for the majority of projects mentioned (except in Dikodougou), the form of consultation (if any) was a 'public meeting'.[44] Most significantly, virtually nobody reported any consultation with councillors (Table 4.12).

The fact that 58.3 per cent of respondents could not name a councillor (either alone or in conjunction with the name of their mayor) also rather belied the idea that councillors were well-known figures who engaged in informal consultations. By contrast, only 10 per cent could not name the mayor, confirming popular perceptions of the nature of the list system. Virtually no respondents could name just a councillor without the mayor (Table 4.13). In addition, 75 per cent of respondents, when asked how

---

[43] The national average is one to 1000, according the Minister for the Interior, Léon K. Koffi (Côte d'Ivoire (1991a)).

[44] In Dikodougou 45 per cent of projects mentioned had not been the subject of any form of consultation.

Table 4.12. *Type of consultation reported by respondents for main projects mentioned, by commune (N = 1,187)*

	Percentage of projects:						
	Don't know	Not consulted	Public meeting	With councillor	With aid agency	'Top down'	Unspecified
Affery	10.2	19.7	54.2	–	2.8	–	13.0
Yakassé	18.6	10.2	48.7	0.7	1.9	5.3	14.6
Mbengué	30.0	6.3	50.6	–	–	0.6	12.5
Dikodougou	3.5	45.5	2.2	–	1.3	2.6	44.9
Total	14.2	21.2	38.1	0.25	1.7	2.7	21.9

Table 4.13. *Political knowledge: % respondents who can name elected councillor and/or the mayor, by commune (N = 501)*

	Cannot give any name	Names both mayor and councillor	Names only councillor	Names only mayor
Yakassé	23.5	53.0	1.5	21.2
Affery	2.5	45.9	2.4	48.4
Mbengué	7.8	36.7	0	55.5
Dikodougou	2.5	26.1	0	68.1
All	9.4	40.7	1.0	47.7

frequently councillors organised meetings with them, answered 'never', although they were contradicted by a small group (13 per cent) saying 'once per month' (Table 4.14). (Even in Yakassé a majority of respondents (56 per cent) agreed that councillors never held a meeting.)

All the evidence, together with the finding that 17.7 per cent of respondents had attended a 'neighbourhood committee' points to the groupings of neighbourhood notables as the main channels of communication for councillors who did involve themselves in any consultation at all. This impression is reinforced by the results of the elite survey of community leaders, half of whom claimed to have contacted a councillor or the mayor about a social or political issue (Table 4.15). A large proportion had also attended a neighbourhood committee meeting at which nearly all of them had spoken. And when questioned about the frequency with which councillors held meetings, a much larger proportion of community leaders than ordinary citizens felt that councillors had organised at least some consultation meetings.

Another crucial factor in explaining councillors' poor record of

Table 4.14. *Frequency with which councillors hold meetings with their constituents, by commune (N = 470)*

	Say never (%)	Say once per month (%)	Say once per 3–6 months (%)	Say once per 7–12 months (%)	Say less than once per year (%)
Yakassé	67.9	17.6	5.3	1.5	2.3
Affery	78.0	3.0	2.0	3.0	3.0
Mbengué	62.3	16.4	9.0	2.5	0.0
Dikodougou	91.5	4.3	1.7	0.0	0.9
All	74.5	10.9	4.7	1.7	1.5

Table 4.15. *Community leaders: participation and relationships with commune councillors (N = 67)*

	Percentage
Contacted mayor or councillor	49
Attended neighbourhood meeting	38
Attended and spoke	24
Say councillors never held a meeting	42
Say councillors held meetings more than twice per annum	40
Say councillors held meetings less than twice per annum	18

contacts with the electorate is their very limited and ill-defined role in the operations of the commune. Many councillors themselves expressed a low opinion of the value of their own role. This was a fairly realistic reflection of the council's lack of formal power and its remoteness from the work of the Executive (see below). In some of the communes, councillors' apathy also reflected the demoralisation caused by the financial crisis. In others, it was a sign of the dictatorial stance adopted by the mayor, or councillors' feelings of exclusion.

Consultation procedures and the problem of popular support for development

The weakness of relationships between councillors, mayors and the local electorate, and the ineffectiveness of consultation procedures were vividly demonstrated in the difficulties which each commune experienced in persuading the population to contribute towards the funding of major commune projects such as secondary schools.

In all four communes, the mayor and Council of the 1985–90 administration had agreed to make a secondary school one of their major investment projects. A new secondary school required the permission of the Ministry of Education which would have to post and pay for teachers and allocate pupils; even so, the building and equipment costs were considerable in relation to the very limited resources of these small communes and it was recognised that popular contributions, not just from the commune but from the whole sub-Prefecture, would have to be sought to supplement the municipal budget. In spite of central government grants, by 1993 secondary school projects in Yakassé, Affery and Dikodougou remained half-completed and effectively stalled because of the inadequacy or even collapse of voluntary public funding schemes. Only in Mbengué was a ten-class school successfully up and running by 1992. The main reason was the method of funding adopted: deductions on local Farmers Marketing Co-operative sales receipts, a device well known in Ghana, but little used in Côte d'Ivoire. The commune had not, therefore, been dependent on collection of cash from individuals and households. Even the Co-operative levy was not without its problems, however, in so far as certain branches in communities hostile to the mayor had refused to pay up, a matter which formed the subject of fierce discussions at virtually every council meeting from 1989 onwards.

In Yakassé, on the other hand, mismanagement and suspected embezzlement of the fund during the 1985–90 period had led to the withdrawal of the contractors and the disillusionment of the population. Here, and in the other two communes, the granting of further state funds had only made the situation worse, in so far as citizens now felt that the state would complete the project anyway; the popular attitude was (according to some elected members): 'if the state and the commune had started the school, it was up to them to finish it'.[45]

The underlying problem, in fact, was that in each case the project had been started without adequate consultation and the campaign to raise additional funds through public subscription had only been launched *after* work had commenced – even though it had been foreseen that commune and government funds alone would never be sufficient. Councillors tended to justify the collection of contributions after the project had come to a halt through lack of funds as a form of incentive to pay; starting a project, they argued, was a way of encouraging the population, of showing them that something concrete was being done. Citizens were, in fact, suspicious of why it had been impossible to complete it, and did not understand the role of government funding or the sheer scale of the funds required. To them it looked like bad planning or worse. Most

---

[45] Interviews with the Chairman of the Economic Affairs Committee, the Second Assistant mayor and Third Assistant mayor, Dikodougou.

councillors were also convinced that a secondary school was a popular and worthwhile project, which would be fully supported by their electorates. As many councillors admitted, however, the general public meeting is not an ideal way of gaining real consent, because the ordinary citizen does not like to seem to disagree publicly with something proposed by the community leaders and officials. It is easier simply to put up one's hand. It is only afterwards when the levy collectors come round, that any hidden reluctance becomes apparent, and excluded factions can gain their revenge by organising a refusal to pay.

A further problem was the extension of the levy to the whole sub-Prefecture, on the quite legitimate grounds that the school would serve a wider population than that of the commune. This had led commune politicians to involve the Prefect in approval and 'announcement' of the levy in the old style. In Affery, for instance, the Prefect had been enlisted to support sanctions on those who failed to pay the levy – including denial of administrative and medical services.[46] Whatever consultations there might have been, such actions harmed the political legitimacy of the commune by making the Prefectoral service appear responsible for the decision, and undermined the idea that the communes represented a new, more democratic way of doing things.

No doubt popular reluctance to contribute to development projects was also a product of the economic crisis. It is clear, however, that the communes were still struggling with the legacy of thirty years of PDCI rule, during which the main contribution demanded had been enforced purchase of party cards. Participation and consultation had always been seen as 'top-down' devices. The communes' difficulties simply replicated those which the sub-Prefects had long experienced with FRAR projects.[47] Under this scheme, introduced in 1973 as a way of encouraging self-help and of giving the Prefects access to direct funding of development projects in their areas, matching grants were given for projects 'chosen' by communities after a consultation process initiated by the sub-Prefect. The relative proportion of the government's contribution was determined by poverty of the area. The record of FRAR in completing projects had, however, been poor, mainly because of a failure to collect the local population's share of the overall cost.[48]

Under the commune administration the situation had, if anything, got worse, in so far as the communes were allowed to bid for FRAR projects,

---

[46] Minutes of the Affery Executive Committee (*la Municipalité*), meeting of 23 January 1993; *arrête municipal no. 93 du 13 mai 1993*.

[47] *Fonds régionaux d'aménagement rurale*.

[48] See Dutheil de la Rochère (1976) and *Fraternité Matin*, 'An 28: spéciale indépendance', 7 December 1988.

on the basis that the 'popular contribution' was paid out of the commune budget as a lump sum. This device improved development performance in so far as it enabled communes to complete projects which had been threatened with cancellation because of non-payment of the popular contribution (e.g. a post and telephone office in Yakassé, a primary school in Dikodougou) or to begin new ones in the 1990s (e.g. a primary school in Affery). But it made the connection between popular participation (in the form of being consulted about and agreeing to contributions) and development expenditure even more remote.

Some councillors in fact cited the 'free' character of FRAR development projects as one of the features of the communes which made them more popular with ordinary citizens – an attitude which the *Fraternité Matin* survey found to be widespread throughout the country.[49] By paying the FRAR contributions without involving the population the communes were in fact making it harder to develop popular acceptance of the idea that local taxation, even project-specific levies, could contribute to a collective or community good.

In the final analysis, however, the difficulties experienced by the communes in collecting contributions for development projects were a symptom of a more fundamental problem: because the relationship between the communes and the electorate was so weak, citizens were unwilling to trust their money in the hands of local elected officials. So long as Ivorian citizens continued to see mayors as agents of the government disposing of central government patronage, and councillors as simply the mayor's hand-picked 'stage army', developing a genuine local democracy was an uphill task. The list system had produced councillors who, however representative they might have been in socio-economic terms, had only weak links with the electorate, and, as the history of the secondary school projects demonstrates, were relatively ineffective in either consulting with electors or in persuading them to be involved in commune affairs. The only element of accountability in the system came from competitive elections for what was accurately seen as the mayor's rather than the council's administration.

Apart from electoral participation, the level of popular involvement through consultation and contacts with representatives of the commune and through contributing to commune projects was, therefore, relatively limited. But this does not mean that it was non-existent. Compared to the sub-Prefectoral administration, the commune did represent an advance. There was now a highly localised elected body with its own budget and resources and the capacity to represent popular issues. Given

---

[49] Interview, Second Assistant mayor, Dikodougou, 2 June 1993; *Fraternité Matin* (1988).

the way in which councillors and mayors had been selected, they were undeniably a product of the local political scene which linked them to certain elite factions. Councillors certainly *thought of themselves* as understanding and representing popular local feelings, and the mayors' own political careers were inextricably linked with their successful self-projection as fighters for the development of the community. Whether these self-images were justified can only be tested by looking at the extent to which popular issues and demands were represented and transformed into policies and outputs at the institutional level.

Representation and institutional accountability

Whatever their levels, the impact of new forms of democratic participation is, in a representative democratic system, necessarily mediated through institutional processes. Elected councillors can only transmit popular demands or 'represent' the public according to their own judgements if the institutions of local government allow them to participate in policy formulation and the budgetary process. Equally as important, they must be able to establish the accountability of officials for the implementation of policy and the execution of the budget. Much of this depends upon the operation of formal institutions such as council meetings and committees, and the legal structures of control over council employees, as well as on more informal political and administrative relationships.

The role of mayors and their assistants
In assessing the role of elected members in the Ivorian communes, the distinction between those councillors who become the Executive (*la Municipalité* – mayors and their assistants) and those who remain ordinary councillors must once again be stressed. For both structural and sociological reasons, the Executive has a clear and authoritative control over the administration of the commune. In all four cases the Executive, chaired by the mayor, met regularly each month with the chief officers – usually the Secretary-General and the Director of Finance – to review the execution of the budget and to approve expenditures. Records of their decisions were complete and well kept. There is little doubt that it was this group which drew up the Three Year Development Plan with its development priorities, and proposed the budget estimates. In two of the communes where the mayor was not resident, whichever assistant mayor lived closest came into the office virtually every day to sign papers or letters, issue documents and generally to check on any problems. In any case, the mayors tended to come at the weekends as often as possible

(thus provoking grumbles from officials and the assistants about Saturday meetings). The Executive therefore not only set policy within the limits permitted by the *tutelle*; it also had a 'hands-on' management role in the execution of the budget. The mayor himself has the legal status of an accounting officer; he authorises payments under the budget, makes contracts and represents the commune at law.

The mayor has complete control over locally employed commune employees, except for an accounts officer paid for by the commune but seconded to the office of the state *Receveur Municipal* as a 'go-between'. There is as yet no local government service with legally established terms of employment, and commune employees are supposed to be employed under the terms of the general Labour Code. Most of the communes experienced some friction between the Executive and employees when, as a result of the financial crisis of the 1990s, savings had to be made either through redundancies or, in the case of Yakassé, an attempt to 'restructure' (i.e. reduce) salaries according to qualifications. There were also indications that the FPI mayor of Yakassé had to deal with a certain amount of hostility and non-co-operation from existing employees taken on by the previous PDCI mayor. But in general the mayors did have an effective power to discipline or sack staff as they saw fit.

Although the chief officers of the commune are civil servants seconded to work in the communes and therefore work under civil service conditions, they are responsible to the commune Executive for the execution of their duties. The influence of the mayors is such that they can, and frequently do, discipline the seconded civil servants by reporting them to the ministry, either because they have complaints about their work or simply because they are not co-operating well. If a mayor does not want a particular officer, he can usually have that officer transferred. Except for the Secretary-General of Mbengué, who had, very unusually, been in his post since 1986, the senior officers in the case-study communes had all moved quite frequently, either at their own request because of a difficult situation or at the instigation of a mayor.

The legal powers of the mayors and their Executives are strongly reinforced in practice by informal relationships deriving from the elevated social and political status of most mayors. Socially, the majority of all Ivorian mayors are from the upper elite stratum of professionals, managers and civil servants. Of the group elected in 1985, 44 per cent were civil servants or professional engineers, 15 per cent were modern sector businessmen or bankers and 18 per cent were teachers or professors.[50] The political status of at least 40 per cent of the mayors reflected

---

[50] *Fraternité Hebdo* (1987).

precisely the political logic or intention of the commune reforms discussed earlier, reinforced by the government's encouragement of the practice of *cumul des mandats*. Thirty-nine mayors (29 per cent) were simultaneously *députés* in the National Assembly, and at least eleven were ministers and holders of high state offices.[51] As might have been expected, eighty of the 125 mayors of communes outside Abidjan did not reside in their commune town; seventy-four of them lived in Abidjan itself.

The current mayors of the four case-study communes are typical of this national image; one of the northern mayors is a former sub-Prefect, now a *député* and businessman holding an important office in the National Assembly, whilst the other is of more modest status, a school teacher and PDCI activist who is now virtually a full-time politician and lives locally. In the south, one of the mayors is a wealthy professor of medicine in Abidjan, a member of the Bureau Politique of the PDCI and a member of the national State Economic and Social Council since 1971. His power and status in a small town like Affery are symbolised both by the large and opulent mansion he has constructed there and by his role as a patron of public works. Since his election in 1991 he has personally financed a maternity unit building and a primary school, made well-publicised and generous donations to the secondary school fund and given the commune expensive office equipment. He is the African equivalent of an English 'lord of the manor' (without, of course, the power associated with land ownership). The FPI opposition mayor of Yakassé is, of course, in a very different position politically, but lives in Abidjan like two of the others, where he works as a senior technical civil servant at the Ministry of Agriculture.

The high status of the mayors reflects their particular role as political entrepreneurs within the Ivorian democratisation process, and in this respect they can be distinguished even from their assistants on the Executive. Seven of the twelve assistant mayors of the four communes were school teachers and two were retired Agriculture Department Field Assistants; only two had high-status jobs, one as an engineer with SODESUCRE, the other as a pharmaceutical representative for a European company. Nevertheless the majority of the assistants, like the mayors, did not live locally. These problems of residence were an inevitable consequence of their occupations and the need to find educated people to deputise for the mayor.

The mayors, and to a lesser extent their assistants, were therefore socially distinct and often spatially separated from the rest of the

[51] Côte d'Ivoire (1988a).

Council. But it was the mayors alone who disposed of sufficient political status and resources to enable them to reinforce their legal position and to dominate both the Executive, the Council and the commune employees. The assistants acted merely as the delegates of the mayor and there was evidence of friction and resentment in some of the communes caused partly by the simple fact of the mayor's absence, and partly – perhaps as a consequence of fear of losing control during their absence – by the tendency of mayors to try to make decisions themselves without fully informing their assistants. The feeling expressed by some assistant mayors that they were landed with most of the work without receiving the due credit and status was understandable enough – especially where the assistants had political ambitions of their own. These resentments usually surfaced as complaints that the mayor had engaged contractors without consulting his colleagues, or that the mayor's transport and petrol expenses were too high.

The problems caused by the non-residence of mayors were also referred to by other ordinary councillors, some of whom agreed with the assistants that the mayor really ought to be someone who lived locally and experienced the everyday problems of the community and the commune administration. In effect, mayors were on the receiving end of a resentment directed against the 'big man' who, according to the popular image, descends on the town once a month in his Mercedes Benz, gives out the orders to his civil servants and assistants and then disappears back to Abidjan. But whilst the mayors are often criticised in the press and by the Ministry of the Interior for being merely 'weekend' leaders, remote from their councils and electors,[52] it should be recognised that they are operating according to the sociological and political realities of Ivorian society. The domination of Abidjan and of the central government is still such that little can be achieved unless one has access to Abidjan-based networks. And most educated people have to leave these small country towns and rural areas to find employment. In seeking office at the commune level, the elites are simply following the logic of the local democracy reforms.

The Council and ordinary councillors

The Executive of the commune is to a large extent dominant over the Council, by virtue both of its legal powers and the socio-political status of the mayors. In law, the Council is the legislative body of the commune which gives legal force through its resolutions to all the policies and actions of the commune. In practice its main function is to approve the

[52] see *Fraternité Matin* (1988).

budget and the rolling Three Year Development Plans submitted to it, and to approve the mayor's interim and annual reports on his execution of budget expenditures. In the four cases, the Councils also debated policies on taxation, allocation of urban plots, the local security situation and many other issues requiring local regulation.

Given both the power of the mayor and the fact that there is by definition no opposition on the Council it would not be realistic to expect any serious questioning of the Executive to emerge from the Council. On the whole, if the mayor wishes to change the priorities in the Development Plan, or to stick by his budget proposals, he can usually persuade the Council to follow his advice.

Nevertheless, in terms of their representative role the four Councils were not wholly formal in their proceedings. On many occasions there were genuine debates on development plans and priorities, and the Councils did act as sounding boards for local issues such as the location of markets and other projects, encroachments on ancestral 'sacred areas' and public concern about violent crime. In Dikodougou, councillors were given an opportunity to vote on the ranking of priorities, which has to be done in order to allocate available funds in any one year and in Yakassé, in particular, considerable efforts were made to consult councillors during the planning process. As noted earlier, there were even outright confrontations with the 1985–90 mayors of Yakassé, Affery and Dikodougou over the funding and management of the secondary school projects. It was only after 1990 that the Dikodougou Council, having been purged of most its educated absentees, became more co-operative with the mayor. In Mbengué, which on the whole was a docile Council, issues which were of real concern to the population such as harassment by gendarmes on the highways, the depredations of the Peul cattle herders, the state of the road to Korhogo and the inability of ordinary peasant farmers to afford the costs of developing controlled building plots were all raised by councillors over the 1986–93 period.

After 1990, these publicly debated confrontations diminished, in Yakassé perhaps because of the awareness of both councillors and public that they had to demonstrate support for one of the few FPI administrations in existence, and in Affery because of the overwhelming dominance of the new mayor. No councillors in Affery dared to suggest that the punitive measures proposed for non-payment of the secondary school and gendarmerie levy were perhaps politically ill-judged.

The main limitation on the ability of councillors to play a more significant role in policy-making and in monitoring the Executive was in fact the shortness and infrequency of Council meetings – at most half a day, three or four times per year. Even when they did meet, councillors rarely had sufficient detailed information in advance of the meeting to make informed or critical comment. Because of the lack of photocopying or duplicating facilities, for instance, minutes of previous meetings were not usually available. More importantly, financial information on the trial balances and even the annual accounts of the execution of the budget were simply read out to the meetings by one of the officers or an assistant mayor.[53]

Councillors frequently complained about the lack of consultation or the lack of time to read available papers, but to little avail. Because the tutelary authority was very strict in its insistence that budgets, accounts and other commune actions go through all the necessary stages of approval, meetings would sometimes be adjourned for these purposes. But only once amongst the four cases did a Council refuse to confirm the accounts because they had not had time to study them.[54]

In any conciliar system the task of detailed scrutiny of policy and of executive actions is in fact usually delegated to sub-committees. The Ivorian Councils were by law obliged to form at least two permanent sub-committees, one for Finance and Economic Affairs and another for Social and Cultural Affairs. The budget estimates and the development plans had to be certified as approved by these committees before going to full Council. But in none of the four cases did these sub-committees work very effectively. It proved very difficult to find councillors capable of or willing to serve on them and they tended to meet even less frequently than the full Council. In Dikodougou for instance, instead of meeting in between one Council meeting and another, Council meetings were often suspended for half an hour when the agenda required a sub-committee report, in order to allow the designated members of the sub-committee to meet. With a few exceptions, sub-committee reports were generally formal confirmations of items proposed by the chairman – usually one of the assistant mayors.

Some councillors referred to the absence of allowances for attending meetings as an explanation of the difficulties of the sub-committee system. But compared to the difficulty and expense of attending meetings in the large rural districts of Ghana or Bangladesh, the councillors of these small Ivorian towns did not seem to have a valid complaint. The non-functioning of the sub-committee system seemed rather to reflect the generally restricted role of ordinary councillors in the Ivorian commune.

It was principally, therefore, through election to the Executive that a

[53] The mayors justified this on the grounds that the majority of councillors are illiterate, but this is not the case in the southern communes (see above) whilst in the two northern communes, between 50 and 55 per cent were illiterate.
[54] Minutes of the Affery Municipal Council, meeting of 8 October 1988.

small group of elected councillors was able to exercise real power and influence over commune policies and expenditures. The extent to which popular wishes were translated into government outputs was in practice dependent on the representative character, political sensitivity and responsiveness of the elite elements who, in the vast majority of cases, became mayors or assistant mayors.

Central control: the role of the tutelary authorities

Whilst the mayors were very powerful at the local level, it should be remembered that they acted under the supervision of the Ministry of the Interior, within the administrative framework of the Prefectoral service. As indicated earlier, the actions of the tutelary authorities were close and rigorous, and only the most politically powerful mayors could short-circuit these controls. None of the case-study communes had in any way managed to step outside the constraints of the centralised financial and fiscal systems, and all complained bitterly about the control of the state Treasury over the communes' cash flow.

Officials of the communes confirmed that the ministry played an active role, not just in approving budgets, but in giving technical advice on proposed projects, pointing out when actions or expenditures were *ultra vires*, ensuring that the public accounting rules were followed and even correcting the figures in accounts. Often resolutions in Council minutes or budget proposals were referred back because they did not follow the correct legal form, and the ministry was constantly vigilant to ensure that the investment budget came close to the recommended 30 per cent of total expenditure.

The ministry also tried to implement national guidelines on the proportion of expenditure to be allocated to staffing (a maximum of 50 per cent) and after the 1990 financial crisis all communes were forced to reduce their establishment. Even the mayor of Yakassé's unpopular decision to harmonise the salary scales of local employees in accordance with standard civil service qualification levels was in fact a national policy recommended by the ministry and was equally unpopular in the loyal PDCI commune of Mbengué.[55] The mayor of Yakassé was especially sensitive about the subject of ministry supervision, in so far as his predecessor had been summoned to Abidjan to have his knuckles rapped over the problems created by the commune's maladministration of the secondary school project. He was insistent that the minutes of a Council meeting which described him as having been 'ordered' to Abidjan in 1992

---

[55] Minutes of Mbengué Municipal Council, meeting of 26 December 1992; interview, mayor of Yakassé-Attobrou, 20 May 1993.

to discuss the contract for the commune's FRAR-funded post office project should be amended to read 'invited to attend'.[56]

The extent to which the communes had any budgetary and executive autonomy was in fact a real issue for many mayors and officials. It was, after all, quite common for the mayors of much larger city communes to be called to Abidjan to 'discuss' and defend their budget estimates before they were approved. Particularly irksome was the length of time taken by the ministry to approve budgets, which in the 1985–90 period often stretched many months into the relevant financial year. After the devolution of this function to the Prefects for the large majority of communes, the situation did, however, improve.

Did the tutelary role of the Ministry of the Interior in fact prevent the communes from fulfilling their democratic functions? On balance, this would not be a fair assessment. In many respects, the role of the ministry can be justified as a genuine attempt to protect local electorates against corrupt or illegal administration and wasteful expenditures, particularly when comparing the Ivorian situation with that in Ghana or Bangladesh. Within the very strict accounting rules and the increasingly crippling financial constraints, communes were free to choose their development priorities and budget patterns. How else can one explain the large number of town hall and secondary school projects approved by the ministry, proposals which any interventionist central government might well have vetoed on grounds both of uneconomic use of resources and lack of responsiveness to local wishes? (It was in the end the Ministry of Education which had to intervene, first of all to protect pupils from attending schools which were not up to standard and later to help with costs.)

Another, more positive result of the strict *tutelle* was to be seen in the relative administrative efficiency of the communes; the accounts and the files were accurate and well managed, even in a situation of extreme scarcity of resources. The continuing presence of well-trained civil servants at this very local level means that the potential for development of the communes' range of activity in the future remains strong.

INSTITUTIONAL PERFORMANCE

Effectiveness

The output effectiveness of the communes, as narrowly defined in this study (see Chapter 1) was assessed using three main sets of measures. First, the actual pattern of official expenditures over the period 1987 (the

---

[56] Minutes of the Yakassé-Attobrou Municipal Council, 22 February 1993.

Côte d'Ivoire 177

first full year of operation) to 1992 was established, focusing on resources, and trends in the proportionate size and type of development expenditure. These patterns were compared with official objectives, both national and local. The trends were also examined to see whether the 1990 shift from single-party to multi-party electoral competition made any difference. Secondly, although the preceding sub-Prefectoral administration which the communes replaced could not (because of differences in resources and area) provide a clear base-line for comparison, the extent to which the communes represented an improvement on the sub-Prefectoral administration was measured using elite and popular perceptions of the communes' record, as related to specific projects. This provided a useful supplement to the government's national-level data. Thirdly, survey data was used to measure general levels of satisfaction with the outputs of the communes.

The record since 1986

Under Ministry of Interior guidelines, a commune's development or investment budget was supposed to account for 30 per cent of annual budgeted expenditure. In addition, local priorities had to be agreed and ranked in a rolling Three Year Plan, which in turn determined the structure of the annual budget estimates. As Tables 4.16–4.20 show, during the period of their first administration, 1986–90, the four case-study communes were reaching government targets for development expenditure and quite a wide range of projects was commenced, albeit concentrated in two main areas: basic municipal and public health infrastructures, and social needs, particularly schools, youth and community centres. By 1989–90, however, both total and development expenditures began to fall (except in Yakassé) and by the beginning of their second administration the four communes (in common with the rest of the country) had entered a grave financial crisis which severely limited their ability both to fulfil government targets and to implement their own planned expenditures. This crisis was a direct result of the severe economic slump and consequent reduction in central government expenditure which hit Côte d'Ivoire at the end of the 1980s, and from which the country only began to emerge in the latter half of the 1990s.

By 1991/2 actual expenditures were falling way below the officially agreed budget estimates. In Affery, for instance, out of a total investment budget of 13.8 million francs for 1992, only 5.8 million was authorised to be spent, and in Yakassé, only 3.5 million out of a budget of 16.8 million. In fact from 1990 onwards, partly because of the ambitious nature of the projects started in the 1980s, between 70 per cent and 100 per cent of their shrivelled investment budgets were being swallowed up by one or

Table 4.16. *Development expenditure as a proportion of total expenditure (actual or* ordonnancées) *in the four case-study communes (millions of current CFA francs)*

		1987	1988	1989	1990	1991	1992
Affery	dev. expend	24.3	23.3	30.8	14.9	13.0	5.8
	total expend	72.4	73.5	73.1	54.8	44.6	33.4
	% de/te	*33.6*	*31.7*	*42.0*	*27.2*	*29.0*	*17.4*
Yakassé	dev. expend	19.1	18.4	14.6	27.7	8.43	3.5
	total expd.	58.3	56.3	51.3	62.0	29.6	30.5
	% de/te	*32.8*	*32.7*	*28.5*	*44.7*	*28.5*	*11.5*
Dikodougou	dev. expend	24.4	14.5	20.6	18.8	10.3	11.4
	total expd.	49.9	53.8	48.1	42.5	33.3	38.0
	% de/te	*48.9*	*27.0*	*42.8*	*44.2*	*30.9*	*30.0*
Mbengué	dev.	28.9	14.2	18.4	9.6	15.3	8.0
	total expd.	53.9	40.9	43.8	33.9	37.9	27.6
	% de/te	*53.6*	*34.7*	*42.0*	*28.3*	*40.4*	*29.0*

two projects such as half-finished secondary schools or municipal offices ('town halls') – projects which for the most part remained uncompleted. Total actual spending on development projects in the four communes fell by *70 per cent in current cash terms* between 1987 and 1992. The severity of these cuts was caused partly by successive falls in the absolute levels of central government grants – upon which the the smaller communes were still highly dependent – and partly by the 'liquidity crisis' in the unified state payments system.

Whilst government grants to the four communes over the period 1987–92 remained fairly constant as a proportion of total revenues (around 70 per cent), in absolute (current cash) terms they fell by 28 per cent over this same period (Table 4.21).[57] The case studies, therefore, did better than the ninety-eight new communes generally, which saw government grants fall from 68 per cent to 58 per cent of budgeted revenue, and fall by 30 per cent overall in absolute terms.[58]

[57] The figure would have been higher had not Mbengué received an especially generous settlement in 1992.
[58] The difference between the small rural communes and the big cities is vividly illustrated by the comparable figures for all communes, which show that the state grant was reduced from an average of 30.5 per cent of all budgets in 1987 to 16 per cent in 1992, and the total grant fell in absolute terms by 42 per cent. (Figures recalculated from Côte d'Ivoire (1993a); Côte d'Ivoire (1992b); Côte d'Ivoire (1988a).)

Table 4.17. Commune of Mbengué: breakdown of actual development expenditure (réalisations) by kind of project, 1986–92 (millions of CFA francs)

	1986	1987	1988	1989	1990	1991	1992	Cum.T	%	Rank
Hospital ward	3.32	12.10	9.31	0	0	0	0	24.73	20.2	2
Social centre(youth)	5.22	8.84	0	0	0	0	0	14.06	11.5	3
Main street improvement	0.85	3.76	0	0	0	0	0	4.61	3.8	
Wells/boreholes	0	0	0.13	0	0	0	0	0.13		
Secondary school	0	0	0	15.71	9.58	15.26	8.00	48.55	39.6	1
Repair of primary school	0	0.45	0.99	0	0	0	0	1.44	2.9	
Commune offices	8.41	0	0	0	0	0	0	8.41	6.9	4
Enclosure main square	2.50	0	0	0	0	0	0	2.50		
Mosque	0	1.28	0	0	0	0	0	1.28		
Market kiosks	0	0	0	1.20	0	0	0	1.20		
Building plots	0	1.75	0	0	0	0	0	1.75		
Office equipment	7.55	0.27	0	0	0	0	0	7.82	6.4	
Official vehicles	0	0	0	0	0	0	0	0.00		
Official housing	0.46	0	0	0	0	0	0	0.46		
Social centre equipment	0	0	3.40	1.45	0	0	0	4.85	4.0	
Health equipment	0	0.50	0	0	0	0	0	0.50		
Planning study	0	0	0.38	0	0	0	0	0.38		
Total	28.31	28.95	14.21	18.36	9.58	15.26	8.00	122.67		

Table 4.18. Commune of Affery: breakdown of actual development expenditure (réalisations) by kind of project, 1986–92 (millions of CFA francs)

	1986	1987	1988	1989	1990	1991	1992	Cum.T	%	Rank
Secondary school	0	0	6.80	20.0	10.44	3.66	4.00	44.90	31.6	1
Building/repair primary schools	5.50	5.39	1.90	0	0	0	0	12.79	9.0	}1
Town Hall	0	0	0	0	0	7.92	0	7.92	5.6	
Commune Offices	5.30	0	0	0	0	0	0	5.30	3.7	}3
Street maintenance/culverts	5.40	6.47	0.37	0	0	0	0	12.24	8.6	5
Hospital/clinic/morgue	1.50	2.24	2.50	5.60	1.99	0	1.85	15.68	11.0	2
Social centre(youth)	0	0.57	0	0	0	0	0	0.57		
Sports facilities	0	0.95	0.32	0	0	0	0	1027		
Cemetery	0.17	0.57	0	0	0	0	0	0.74		
Police station	0	0.87	1.20	1.70	1.16	0	0	4.93		
Agricultural project	0	0.32	0	1.20	0	0	0	1.52		
Abattoir	0	0	1.10	0	0.27	0	0	1.37		
Market	2.90	1.42	3.70	1.00	0	0	0	9.02	7.3	
Building plots	0	2.48	3.20	1.30	0	0	0	6.98	5.2	
Telephone	0	0	0	0	0	1.40	0	1.40		
Office equipment	8.93	1.69	2.05	0	0	0	0	12.67	8.9	4
Planning study	0.60	1.35	0	0	1.00	0	0	2.95	2.7	
Total	30.30	24.32	23.14	30.80	14.86	12.98	5.85	142.25		

Table 4.19. *Commune of Yakassé: breakdown of actual development expenditure (réalisations) by kind of project, 1986–92 (millions of CFA francs)*

	1986	1987	1988	1989	1990	1991	1992	cum. T	%	Rank
Secondary school	0	0	0	6.00	21.00	4.13	2.39	33.52	}29.3	1
Building/repair primary schools	0	0	0	1.04	0	0	0	1.04		
Town hall	0	0	5.00	6.72	5.00	0.90	0	17.62	}19.7	2
Commune offices	5.60	0	0	0	0	0	0	5.60		
Street maintenance/culverts	1.70	0	0	0	0	0	0	3.60		
Hospital/clinic/morgue	2.30	1.00	0	0	0	1.90	0	3.30		
Doctor's house	0	0	6.59	0	0	0	0	6.59		
Social centre(youth)	0.40	0	0	0	0	0	0	0.40		
Sports facilities	0	0	0.49	0.26	0	0	0	0.75		
Lorry park	0	0	2.68	0	0	0	0	2.68		
Rubbish skip	1.30	0	0	0.42	0	0	0	1.72		
Police station	0	0	0	0	1.80	0	0	1.80		
Agricultural project	0	3.70	0	0	0	0	0	3.70		
Markets	6.70	6.75	0	0	0	0	0	13.45	11.4	4
Building plots	0	1.50	2.27	0	0	0	0	3.77		
Telephone	0	0	0	0	0	1.50	1.12	2.62		
Office equipment	8.33	6.01	0	0	0	0	0	14.34	12.1	3
Official vehicles	0	0	1.40	0	0	0	0	1.40		
Total	26.33	18.96	18.43	14.44	27.80	8.43	3.51	117.90		

Table 4.20. *Commune of Dikodougou: breakdown of actual development expenditure (réalisations) by kind of project, 1986–92 (millions of CFA francs)*

	1986	1987	1988	1989	1990	1991	1992	Cum. T	%	Rank
Secondary school	0	0	0	0	0	0	9.90	9.90	} 21.0	} 1
Building/repair primary schools	0	6.49	0	0	0	0	0	15.49		
Teachers' housing	0	4.49	5.88	2.31	0.20	0	0	12.88		
Town hall	1.86	0	0	10.35	9.26	0	0	21.47	17.8	2
Roads/repairs	0.26	4.52	1.57	0	0	1.99	0	8.34		
Hospital/clinic/morgue	1.00	0	3.00	3.30	0	0	0	7.30		
Doctor's house	0	0	0	2.98	4.51	1.00	0	8.49		
Social centre(youth)	0	0	1.00	0.27	0	0	0	1.27		
Markets	1.55	0.72	0	0	0	0	0	2.27		
Building plots	1.00	0	0	0	4.80	7.28	1.50	14.58	12.1	4
Wells/boreholes	0	0	0.44	0	0	0	0	0.44		
Office equipment/vehicles	6.33	8.16	2.56	1.36	0	0	0	18.41	15.2	3
Total	21.00	24.38	14.45	20.57	18.77	10.27	11.40	120.84		

Côte d'Ivoire

Table 4.21. *State grant (*dotation globale de fonctionnement*) as a proportion of total actual revenue (*recettes émises*) in the four case-study communes (millions of current CFA francs)*

		1987	1988	1989	1990	1991	1992
Affery	state grant	52.5	49.4	49.4	37.0	33.3	33.2
	total rev.	77.8	76.3	73.2	51.1	47.5	50.1
	% grant/rev	*67.5*	*64.7*	*67.5*	*72.4*	*70.1*	*66.3*
Yakassé	state grant	45.0	42.3	42.3	51.7	28.6	28.6
	total rev.	66.2	59.5	55.6	62.5	35.7	44.8
	% grant/rev	*68.0*	*71.1*	*76.1*	*82.7*	*80.1*	*63.8*
Dikodougou	state grant	40.0	37.6	37.6	33.2	25.4	25.4
	total rev.	66.0.	61.0	52.9	45.6	37.8	38.1
	% grant/rev	*60.6*	*61.6*	*71.1*	*72.8*	*67.2*	*66.6*
Mbengué	state grant	37.0	34.8	34.8	26.1	23.5	38.5
	total rev.	55.5	44.9	46.8	37.4	32.3	44.2
	% grant/rev	*66.6*	*77.5*	*74.4*	*69.8*	*72.8*	*87.1*

The situation caused by the government cuts was made worse by communes' inability to improve their mobilisation of tax revenues as a way of compensating for the loss of central government subsidy. Between 1987 and 1992 the total budgets of the ninety-eight communes also fell by 23.5 per cent, and those of the four communes by 33 per cent. As noted above, the communes have little control over either the levels or the rates of collection of some taxes, and little incentive, because of the centralised financial system, to improve local revenue mobilisation.[59] It is true that the crisis in export and commercial agriculture had produced a general drop in economic activity and hence reduced the already restricted revenue potential of these small towns. It was also evident, however, from discussions with commune officials and politicians that, in general, little thought had been given to the possibility of finding new revenue sources. The favoured solution was normally that of hoping that the state would improve its level of aid, or that the commune would have the luck to attract DCGTx projects funded by overseas donors.[60]

The 'liquidity' crisis
Even the absolute falls in total revenue cannot, however, account for all of the 70 per cent drop in investment expenditure. This can only be

---

[59] See Gbaka (1992).
[60] *Direction et Contrôle des Grands Travaux* – the all-powerful public works and urban planning agency directly responsible to the President, staffed by foreign and Ivorian technocrats and channel for much overseas project aid.

explained by the impact of the 'liquidity crisis' which meant that the communes found it difficult to actually pay their debts *even when in principle the money was available in the budget*. This problem arose directly from the unified state Treasury account, described above. In the early 1990s the local *Receveur Municipal* began to delay payments to commune creditors on the grounds that there was no cash available to pay their duly authorised invoices. Commune revenues had, in effect, been swallowed up into the unified state account, and whatever cash was available to Treasury offices at the Prefectoral level was being used to pay more 'pressing' state obligations, such as the salaries of civil servants (one of the primary features of the country's political stability).

From a local perspective, it looked as though commune funds were subsidising other areas of the state machinery; indeed, some officials suggested that the central government was a net beneficiary even after its payment of grants-in-aid and salary subsidies to the communes. Whilst the figures to prove this are hard to come by, it is certainly the case that the state was delaying the transfer of tax credits to the communes, as well as permitting the local Treasury offices to use commune funds for more general purposes. The only other explanation of the constant delays and difficulties lies in the possibility of a massive abuse of power by the *Receveurs Municipals*, although it is more likely that the *Receveurs* were simply using the possibilities created by the shortages.[61]

Whatever the explanation, the practical effect of the liquidity crisis was to delay or even bring to a halt what remained of the investment programmes of the communes, as well as to make routine maintenance jobs difficult to carry out – i.e. repairs to vehicles and equipment. As of 1993, none of the four communes had had an operational rubbish collection lorry for two years. Other budgeted expenditures were simply not engaged out of fear that the suppliers could not be paid, or because of a general refusal of suppliers to accept commune contracts. In the two northern communes, the response was to adjust estimates to more 'realistic' levels, although Mbengué also received special help. By the mid-1990s, therefore, the communes were clearly failing to meet either local or national objectives.

Comparisons with the sub-Prefectures

In spite of the post-1990 crisis, it should be recognised that, in objective terms, *communalisation* represented a real shift in government investment and expenditure towards locally determined projects and services, by

[61] One mayor went so far as to publicly accuse the local Treasury office of collecting 10 per cent kickbacks from creditors wanting to be paid – Minutes of the Affery Municipal Council, meeting of 1 September 1990.

comparison with the almost total neglect of their needs in the previous period under Prefectoral administration.[62] The communes automatically benefited from the government grant and tax revenues allocated to each authority, which, even after 1990, provided net new local employment, services and development projects. The setting up of the ninety-eight new communes in 1985 created 3,604 new salaried jobs and, according to the calculations of the Ministry of the Interior, a further 1,500 jobs were created from the indirect benefits of commune expenditure. In 1987 the total labour force employed by all the communes including Abidjan was 13,065, and another 8,365 jobs were estimated by the Ministry to have been created indirectly.[63]

For a small town like Affery or Dikodougou to change from being under direct Prefectoral administration to having its own commune authority was, therefore, to move from a situation of little or no development spending to at least some. The effect was an almost automatic consequence of the allocation of government resources to the new authorities. Thus in 1987, the total investment budgets of all communes *including Abidjan* were the equivalent of 2,000 CFA francs per capita (US$6.66 at 1987 exchange rates), whereas the total cumulative investment spending of the four case-study communes over the four years 1987–90, before the financial crisis hit, was 6,009 CFA francs per capita (US$20, or an average of US$5 per annum) – still a very modest amount, but not insignificant when compared to the earlier figure almost entirely dominated by Abidjan expenditures.[64] Unfortunately, as noted above, development output was to remain highly dependent on continued high levels of central government funding, and therefore collapsed after the 1990 cuts.

As might be expected, virtually all of the officials, councillors and mayors interviewed saw the commune as an improvement on the sub-Prefectoral administration, both in terms of quantity of projects and effectiveness of completion. Most referred to the poor record of FRAR projects, which had been on the point of abandonment until the commune took them over, and to the fact that these projects were now seen as 'free' by the population. In Yakassé, the sub-Prefecture had a slightly better record in that a clinic and community centre had been built and a new market nearly completed before 1985. Unfortunately the

---

[62] See the report of the Ministry of Public Works on the record of public investment in the towns of the interior, prepared for the World Bank's urban aid programme (Côte d'Ivoire (1985)).
[63] Côte d'Ivoire (1988a), pp. 121–4.
[64] Dubresson (1990). The per capita spending of the Ivorian communes was nevertheless substantially higher than that of the Ghanaian District Assemblies in the same period, which only managed between US$0.18 and 0.45 per capita (see Chapter 5).

new market proved to be a white elephant in that it was situated on the outskirts of the town in an area where neither traders nor shoppers wished to go – a classic case of inadequate consultation by the bureaucracy. By 1993 the new market had been effectively abandoned after a series of conflicts between the commune authorities and the local population. Even the community centre was very little used.

Community leaders interviewed in the elite survey tended to agree with commune officials in that 70 per cent of the sample said they positively preferred the commune to the administration of the sub-Prefect. Ordinary citizens, however, were less clear about the difference, understandable perhaps in view of the continued presence of the sub-Prefectoral administration in the area, and the financial crisis of the 1990s. When asked whether they preferred their town to be administered by the sub-Prefecture or the commune, just over half of respondents positively preferred the commune, whilst the other half preferred the sub-Prefecture or said that 'both were necessary' (see Table 4.23). Nevertheless, when asked more specific questions about who originated and funded local projects ordinary citizens clearly did not see the former sub-Prefectoral administration as a source of development. Only 6 per cent of projects mentioned by respondents were identified as having been funded through or by the sub-Prefecture, whilst 37 per cent were identified as commune projects, and most of the rest as 'government' (usually FRAR or parastatal agencies) or local self-help (Table 4.22).

Popular perceptions of the output record in the four communes

Given the almost total paralysis which hit both the investment and service programmes of the four communes after 1990, it is not surprising to find a high level of disillusion amongst the population with regard to their development record. Overall, only 36 per cent of respondents in the mass survey gave a positive response when asked whether they felt that the commune was in a position to 'satisfy the needs of their area' (as they perceived them); 42 per cent gave a definitely negative response ('No, not at all'), whilst 21 per cent were unable (or unwilling) to venture any opinion (Table 4.23). In only one of the four communes was there a bare majority prepared to say that the commune was able to satisfy the needs of the area.

Such popular scepticism was not inconsistent with a more general willingness to recognise that the sub-Prefectures had not done very much before 1986, and that in principle being part of a commune was preferable to being administered by the sub-Prefecture. Respondents understood the difference between the general political desirability and

Côte d'Ivoire

Table 4.22. *Respondents' perceptions of funding of main projects mentioned, by commune (N = 1,252)*

	% of projects:					
	Don't know	Sub-prefect	Contributions from population	Aid agency	Govt. (FRAR, SODECI)	Commune
Affery	9.5	0.3	6.5	–	2.4	81.3
Yakassé	17.8	11.4	33.8	–	22.1	14.9
Mbengué	11.1	1.1	25.0	2.2	16.7	43.9
Dikodougou	1.3	7.1	33.4	–	35.1	23.2
All	10.8	6.2	26.0	0.3	19.9	36.7

Table 4.23. *Popular perceptions of commune and sub-prefecture performance (N = 500)*

	% prefer commune to S/P	% prefer S/P or see no difference	% say commune can satisfy needs (definitely/ somewhat)	% say commune cannot satisfy needs	% unable or unwilling to give opinion
All	51.8	46.6	35.8	41.5	21.0
Affery	71.3	23.8	27.1	53.3	18.0
Yakassé	47.7	52.3	28.0	43.2	28.8
Mbengué	26.6	70.3	37.5	31.3	27.3
Dikodougou	63.6	35.6	51.3	38.7	8.4

potential of their commune and the objective situation of the four communes as experienced by local residents in 1993. By that date, per capita development spending had dropped from an average of 1500 CFA francs (US$5) per annum over the period 1987–90 to 700 CFA francs (US$2.33) per annum during 1991 and 1992, and development programmes in all four communes had ground to a halt (see Tables 4.17–4.20).

Citizens' responses were also undoubtedly affected by local political factors. In Affery, the conflict over the secondary school levy had soured relationships between the mayor and the population after 1990, whilst in Yakassé voting for the opposition had released a willingness to openly blame government for the failings of what was perceived as a PDCI-inspired reform. There were real frustrations facing an FPI administration which had taken office promising to improve things, only to be faced with two years of financial paralysis. In the northern communes, by contrast, the grip of the PDCI and a traditional unwillingness to challenge government were reflected in the reluctance of respondents to criticise.

Responsiveness

Congruence between policies and popular preferences

During the period when they had some resources at their disposal, the communes did manage to build or commence building some projects and provide certain services. A judgement can, therefore, be made as to whether the policy choices made by the new Councils – in practice, as we have seen, choices made by the mayors and assistants – did or did not correspond more closely to the wishes of the local electorate, and in particular to the needs of peasant farmers, the uneducated, women and other disadvantaged groups in the population.

Respondents in the mass survey were asked an open-ended question: 'What in your opinion are the most important needs of the people in this area?' From the responses a rank-ordered list of the most popular needs was constructed, grouped into types (see Tables 4.24–4.26). These popular preferences were then compared with official priorities as ranked in the communes' rolling Three Year Plans, and with actual expenditure realisations over the years 1987–92 (Tables 4.28–4.29).

The survey results reveal an overwhelming popular concern with the issue of travel and communication between their local communities and the rest of the country. Not only were 'better roads' the most frequently mentioned need overall; they also featured as the first or second preference in all four communes. Respondents were mainly concerned with the state of the main road linking the town to the nearest big centre (Korhogo in the north) or to the Abidjan trunk road in the south. They were also concerned with the local roads linking the commune centre to its surrounding villages.

The other two most popular needs, 'social' and 'markets', ranked amongst the top three in three out of the four communes. The 'social' category grouped together various kinds of preferences for social facilities such as youth, cultural and community centres, sports and entertainments including TV reception (particularly mentioned by younger people) and housing. It also included the small number of respondents (4.5 per cent) who talked of a general need for 'more money' or 'more cash' to buy the things that people want, which is an Ivorian (and West African) way of referring to the general existence of poverty and the need to raise the standard of living of rural folk. Electrification and water supplies were also of some significance, coming closely after social

Table 4.24. *Rank order of most frequently mentioned popular needs* by commune (N = 501)*

Rank	All / %	Affry / %	Yakssé / %	Mbgé / %	Diko / %
1	roads 58	social 70	roads 70	roads 50	electr 61
2	social 37	roads 54	educ 54	social 46	roads 59
3	mkts 29	mkts 52	mkts 44	agric 44	water 57
4	electr 28	electr 26	health 38	water 38	empl 20
5	water 25	agric 18	social 16	electr 20	educ 16
6	educ 24	health 18	electr 6	empl 20	social 14
7	agric 18	educ 16	water 4	mkts 12	health 8
8	health 18	water 2	agric 4	educ. 10	agric 6
9	empl 12	empl 2	empl 4	health 6	mkts 6

* The figures after each need indicate the percentage of respondents mentioning that need

Table 4.25. *Rank order of most frequently mentioned popular needs, by sex (N = 501)*

Rank	All / %	Men / %	Women / %
1	roads 58	roads 73	roads 45
2	social 37	social 36	mkts 42
3	mkts 29	electr 35	social 37
4	electr 28	agric 28	water 29
5	water 25	educ 26	health 22
6	educ 24	water 21	electr 20
7	agric 18	empl 19	agric 8
8	health 18	mkts 16	sanit 6
9	empl 12	health 13	nursry 5

Table 4.26. *Rank order of most frequently mentioned needs, respondents with no education (N = 400)*

Rank	%
1	roads 57
2 }	electricity 34
	water 34
3	social 28
4	agriculture 22
5	market 21
6	education 18
7	health 17
8	employment 10

Table 4.27. *Elite survey: rank order of most frequently mentioned needs, by commune (N = 67)*

Rank	All / %	Affry / %	Ykssé / %	Mbgé / %	Diko / %
1	roads 56	social 92	roads 66	water 53	roads 75
2	social 46	mkts 58	health 63	social 31	water 69
3	water 39	roads 50	ed/mkts 50	agric 40	electr 56
4	mkts 36	ed/water 17	social 31	roads 33	social 25

facilities and markets in three of the communes and in the top three for Dikodougou.[65]

Differences of emphasis between men and women were not as great as might have been expected (Table 4.25). Roads and social still emerged as two of the three most frequently mentioned needs by both sexes. But men were much more strongly concerned about roads (70 per cent of all male respondents) whereas women's second most popular choice was markets, and more of them (although still only a minority) mentioned health needs than men. Even breaking down preferences by educational level revealed no substantial differences between educated and uneducated respondents; roads remained the top priority of the latter group, the main difference being that more of them were concerned about water and electrification than about social facilities or markets (Table 4.26). In fact, as the results of the elite survey show, there seemed to be general agreement amongst all strata of local society – educated and uneducated, farmers and professionals, elites and ordinary citizens – that the main priority was improving the roads, except for the greater emphasis laid by community leaders in the north on water supplies (Table 4.27).

The analysis presented in Tables 4.17–4.20 and 4.28–4.29 shows quite clearly the glaring contrast between the policy priorities and actual expenditures of the four communes, on the one hand, and popular preferences on the other. None of the communes committed any significant resources to roads, social facilities or water supplies. With a few exceptions in the earlier, pre-1990 period, the main priorities of the communes were the building of new 'town halls' or commune offices and secondary schools. Cumulative actual expenditure patterns reflected these priorities in that, over the whole period 1986–92, education

---

[65] Compare the random sample survey of villagers carried out by the Ministry of Economy and Finance in 1980 which found that the great majority (70 per cent) of respondents saw building physical infrastructure as the first priority for the 'development of their village', followed by health facilities. Education came third, with 44 per cent (Côte d'Ivoire (1980)).

Table 4.28. Top three development priorities of the four communes in Three Year Plans, 1986/7–1994/5

		Plan 1986–88	Plan 1988–90	Plan 1989–91	Plan 1990–92	Plan 1991–93	Plan 1992–94	Plan 1993–95
Yakassé	1.	Town hall	Town hall	Town hall	Secondary school	Town hall	Secondary school	Secondary school
	2.	Markets	Secondary school	Secondary school	Town hall	Secondary school	School furniture	Telephone office
	3.	Building plots	Doctor's house	Rubbish skip	Gendarmerie	Telephone office	Roads	
Affery	1.	Markets	Secondary school	Secondary school	N/A	Town hall	Secondary school	Town hall
	2.	Social centre	Sports facilities	Gendarmerie		Secondary school	Town hall	Secondary school
	3.	Sports facilities	Markets	Morgue		Hospital extension	Hospital repairs	Hospital repairs
Dikodougou	1.	Building plots	Town hall	Town hall	Town Hall	N/A	N/A	Secondary school
	2.	Primary school		Doctor's house	Doctor's house			Town hall
	3.	Health centre		Enclosure of health centre	Enclosure of health centre			Building plots
Mbengué	1.	Hospital extension	Hospital	Secondary school	N/A	Secondary school (3rd phase)	Secondary school	Secondary school
	2.	Social centre[a]	Social centre[a]	Social centre[a]		Abattoir	Abattoir	Abattoir
	3.	Lights for main street	Boreholes	Markets		Markets	Markets	Primary school

[a] variously described as 'cultural', 'youth' and 'women's' centre

Table 4.29. *Four main areas of cumulative expenditure, 1986–92, by commune*

Affery	% total	Yakassé	% total	Mbengué	% total	Dikodougou	% total
Education buildings	40.6	Education buildings	29.3	Education buildings	42.5	Education buildings	21.0
Public health	11.0	Town hall/offices	19.7	Health	20.2	Town hall/offices	17.8
Town hall/offices	9.3	Office equipment	12.1	Social centre	11.3	Office equipment	15.2
Office equipment	8.9	Markets	11.4	Town hall/offices	6.9	Urban plot layout	12.1

received the largest percentage of total development expenditure in every commune, closely followed by town halls, except in Mbengué. In so far as town halls were not mentioned by any respondents in either the mass or elite surveys, it may be concluded that the citizens of the communes did not share the desire of their respective mayors for more suitable offices, 'worthy of the dignity of the town' as one mayor put it, however justified they may have been in administrative terms.

The high priority given by all the commune administrations to their local secondary school project was not supported by popular opinion either, except in Yakassé, although even here it was a poor second to the roads issue. Although this may seem a surprising result, it could be explained by the fact that secondary education, particularly in the northern communes where illiteracy rates are very high, is such a remote possibility for most poor people that it is not considered to be a realistic goal or priority. The argument that the low scores for education simply reflected the communes' existing commitment to school projects can be rejected on the grounds that, if secondary education had been a strong preference, the failure (except in Mbengué) to bring these projects to fruition would have evoked an even more definite desire for them to be completed. Even in Yakassé, expressions of popular preference for educational development were not matched by a willingness to make any contribution to the secondary school fund!

The congruence between policies, outputs and popular perceptions of need in each of the four communes and for each period, 1986–90 and 1991–3 can be rated using a simple three-point scale (Table 4.30). In so far as the financial crisis after 1989 was a factor common to all four, the variations in responsiveness amongst the cases may be attributed both to political factors and to the interaction between local demands and institutional or legal limitations on the capacity of the communes themselves.

In the early years of two of the communes, Affery and Mbengué, official policies tended to incorporate more of the projects – such as markets, local road maintenance and social facilities – found to be most popular in the survey. This was most pronounced in Affery, a fact which was reflected in the higher proportion of respondents preferring the commune to the sub-Prefecture, and identifying projects as commune-funded. Affery was therefore rated as highly responsive in this first period. After 1989/90, however, the responsiveness of commune policy deteriorated in both cases. The financial crisis alone cannot explain this change, since although it forced the communes into making harder choices with reduced resources, it did not necessarily force them to be less responsive. Given the weak links between elected councillors and the

Table 4.30. *Responsiveness ratings of the four communes*

Commune	Responsiveness (86–90)	Responsiveness (91–93)
Yakassé	low	high
Mbengué	medium	low
Affery	high	low
Dikodougou	low	low

population, it is more likely that the 'pet projects' of mayors and influential councillors, particularly projects which would enhance the public profile of the commune, gradually took over as priorities.

In Affery the changes were undoubtedly associated in the public mind with the new administration which took office at the end of 1990. This may well have been hindsight, with respondents blaming the new administration for cut-backs over which they had no control and looking back on the 1986–90 administration as a time of plenty. But there is evidence that the new administration's authoritarian methods made it unpopular, as the story of the secondary school levy demonstrates. It may also explain why projects such as the town hall, telephone office and police station should have assumed such importance. In the case of the secondary school, there was at least an argument (from the administrative point of view) that having started down that road and enrolled pupils, the commune was virtually obliged to do everthing possible to finish it even though it meant sacrificing everything else. In Mbengué, on the other hand, there was no change of administration – just a decision to concentrate what remained of the investment budget on the one project. Here it is clear that the mayor was and always had been the decisive influence.

The character of the administration had an equally important effect in Yakassé, but in a reverse direction. Here, formal policies became more responsive after the new FPI administration took office in 1991, in so far as the popular preference for roads appeared in the top priorities of the Three Year Plans for the first time, as well as markets and health as fourth and fifth priorities. It is clear that the FPI was under enormous pressure to prove its credentials as a more 'democratic' party than the PDCI, and therefore probably did make more efforts to consult and to represent the population through the commune Council. Hence its responsiveness for 1991–3 can be rated as 'high'. Unfortunately its efforts bore little fruit in terms of public support, in so far as its failures on the output performance front caused the public to lose faith in the commune as an institution capable of achieving anything, no matter how responsive it tried to be.

Dikodougou's policy record throughout both periods was, perhaps, the least responsive of all and again political factors are important in explaining the difference. As in Mbengué, there was no change of administration in 1991 except that a new list of councillors more willing to support the mayor unquestioningly was elected. The mayor's influence was decisive, in that the main priorities over the 1987–95 plan periods remained the town hall and what might be called indirect health expenditures – building a house for a doctor and enclosing the health centre. The appearance of 'urban planning' as a priority on a number of occasions reflected the mayor's success in persuading the DCGTx to support Dikodougou for an Integrated Development Programme with a projected cost of 255 million CFA, funded by the World Bank Municipal Development Project. In order to obtain approval for such a plan, documentation on urban lay-out and provision of services was required although the planners at the DCGTx commented that no further designated building areas were necessary until beyond 2001, and advised the commune to stop extending these areas without proper provision for water, electricity and sanitary services.[66] No doubt the mayor calculated that obtaining development funding from the World Bank would do more good for both Dikodougou and for his political future than any amount of consultation with his councillors or the population. Ironically enough, the concerns of the DCGTx planners were more in tune with those of respondents in the Dikodougou survey than the commune itself, which had spent virtually nothing since 1986 on water, electrification, sanitation and roads.

In the Ivorian situation, therefore, the responsiveness of actual policy outputs was crucially affected by political and institutional factors such as the character of the mayor, his political standing within the national elite, relationships between the mayor and the Council and his degree of sensitivity to councillors' opinions. It was these which determined the extent to which public preferences were likely to be transmitted via elected members (whatever their degree of representativeness) into the policy and implementation processes.

Factors beyond the control of the communes also help to explain the generally low levels of responsiveness found in the Ivorian cases. Many of the needs cited by respondents were not really within the competence of the communes, for instance TV reception, a cotton ginnery or major roads. The same was true for some of the basic economic issues which

[66] Côte d'Ivoire DCGTx (1992c).

were occasionally raised by councillors at Council meetings, or mentioned in in-depth interviews and were clearly of deep concern amongst the electorate. Most of the farmers in the southern communes, for instance, were mainly worried about the breakdown of the formerly efficient marketing system for cocoa and coffee (at the time of the fieldwork, the mid-season campaign had been totally cancelled). Northern farmers were concerned with the encroachment of Peul pastoralists from the Sahel on to their fields and the delays and low prices in the cotton purchasing system. In Dikodougou, in particular, there had been violent confrontations with the Peuls (in the village which had voted against the mayor) and many local people arrested. Many other respondents wanted wage employment opportunities for the youth of the area. The communes did not have the resources or the powers to address these issues.

Speed of administrative response

Another measure of responsiveness may be derived from the relative speed with which the new democratic authorities handled administrative services for the public, dealt with requests and implemented repair or other development works. The main administrative services offered by the Ivorian communes concern the *état civil* (births, deaths and marriage registrations and certification of legal documents) formerly handled by the sub-Prefect. For the many migrants working in the rural areas of Côte d'Ivoire these services can be of critical importance and assume political significance at election times. Most citizens do not otherwise have much need for the services of the commune and, as the survey shows, do not have very much contact with the commune authorities.. There was some evidence from the survey, however, of complaints that the issue of documents by the commune took longer, mainly because they often had to wait for the mayor or the assistant mayor delegated with the requisite powers to be in town to sign the paper. This was a problem which flowed from the non-residence of commune officials. In addition, some respondents who were not indigenes of the area complained of 'ethnic bias' in the processing of documents, comparing the local employees of the commune unfavourably with the more disinterested administration of the Prefects. (Of course it should also be remembered that the PDCI regime had political reasons for being kind to foreign migrants.)

With regard to procedures for making decisions and for authorising executive actions, for instance to repair a school roof or to unblock drains, there is little doubt that the communes were slower as a consequence of restraints imposed by the need to ensure the legal accountability of the mayor and commune officers to the Executive and to the Council, and by the constant need to obtain the approval of tutelary authorities. One of the penalties of democratisation in such a system is the increased elaboration and complexity of decision-making procedures, particularly those involved in spending money. With the onset of the financial squeeze and the liquidity crisis, the capacity of the communes for efficient executive actions was reduced even further. By 1992 most suppliers and contractors were refusing to accept commune work and the communes lacked the manpower to carry out their own works.

Process

The process element of performance concerns the extent to which the procedures by which a government authority deals with members of the public are perceived as fair, legal and transparent. It is also concerned with the procedures by which decisions to collect and allocate resources are made; do the public accept the decision to site a project in one place rather than another, or the imposition of a particular tax or levy as legitimately reached, from the point of view of their particular interests?

In respect of the procedures for dealing with the public there is little evidence available for the Ivorian communes in so far as so few citizens have much contact with the officers or representatives of the commune. Taxes are very limited in their incidence, falling mainly on the few local businessmen, market traders and transporters and property owners. Only the small market and other fees are physically collected by agents of the commune. Those going to the commune for legal documents and births/ deaths registration have direct contact with the administrative services; other citizens may have a specific issue or dispute to be settled. Of the very small number of respondents in the mass survey who said they had been to the commune offices to ask for a service or to raise a problem (4.6 per cent), the majority felt that the officers who dealt with them had been helpful and fair – which may be a reflection of the high calibre of the civil servants employed by the communes. On the other hand, as they were more likely to have been seen by local employees, the reliability of such a general assessment has to be judged against the more specific complaints raised by respondents about local commune employees (see above).[67]

---

[67] The disjunction between what people will say as a matter of general opinion and what they feel when specifically affected by a government policy or action is a familiar feature of opinion surveys.

With regard to the fairness of the electoral process, important in establishing the initial legitimacy of the communes, the survey results provide some insights of a negative kind. Whilst 64.8 per cent of respondents were prepared positively to accept the elections as 'fair', a very large 31 per cent would only reply 'don't know' or refused to answer. Informal investigation and 'off-stage' comments by respondents to interviewers revealed the sensitivity of the subject and the rich folklore of election-rigging stories popular with the electorate. Again, this popular cynicism was perhaps a legacy of the era of one-party rule. But such attitudes have to be balanced against the quite healthy voting participation rates in the four communes and the characteristics of these very localised and small-scale electoral contests discussed earlier. The elections can be regarded as at least a basis for legitimation. The non-acceptance of the victory of the winners by the losers is an attitude which requires more than one electoral cycle to be modified.

Whether the public accepted the legitimacy of commune decisions on taxation and the allocation of resources can be more easily inferred from political behaviour. As indicated earlier, the citizens of the Ivorian communes were not used to the idea of local taxation and did not easily accept it, even in the form of a specific levy for a named project. In so far as the mayor and the commune were seen as agencies of the state, they were also seen as the responsibility of the state. But it was essentially the failure of consultation procedures in most of the communes which exacerbated a general reluctance to accept that funds were legitimately collected by the commune because they were for a common purpose or benefit.

The faults of the usual procedures for consultation outside the Council itself, such as the public meeting or consultation through traditional community leaders such as chiefs or elders have already been discussed. Official domination of meetings and the particular interests of chiefs both reinforced the authoritarian or 'top-down' character of the consultation. Decisions taken by the Council itself were accurately viewed by most citizens as for the most part the decisions of the mayor and his assistants or leading councillors. The infrequent general meetings of councillors who rarely met with their electorate canot be seen as effective ways of taking decisions acceptable to the largest number of citizens, as the responsiveness data show. Inevitably, in any competitive democratic system not everybody accepts the correctness of a particular decison. But acceptance that the decision was reached by fair or due process is essential.

CONCLUDING REMARKS

There is much popular suspicion and ignorance to overcome before the Ivorian communes can begin to fulfil the political purposes envisaged by the reforms of the mid-1980s. The first and most intractable problem which they face is that, in spite of the potential of a system so close to the grassroots, there has been a failure to develop strong links between the population and the elected authority. Projects such as new town halls, secondary schools, visible spending on official cars, administrative expenses and accommodation all aroused popular suspicions that commune resources were being allocated for the benefit of mayors and their elite supporters or for commune employees, whilst opponents of the mayor (excluded from the Council by the first-past-the-post single list system) found pleasure in accusing the commune of simply serving the interests of the particular faction or community which had captured it. Such popular perceptions of the way commune decisions were taken were manifested in a reluctance to contribute to public projects, although a lack of trust in the honesty of those handling the funds, as in Yakassé in 1988–9, is another equally plausible explanation.

The general lack of trust can be attributed, in part, to the lack of structured forms of consultation and interaction between representatives and electors, and to the failure of councillors to represent popular opinion more effectively within the decision-making process. The periodic election of a mayor from a fixed list of councillors is clearly insufficient to establish genuinely responsive and accountable local government. At the institutional level, there need to be mechanisms for the continuous monitoring and discussion of both policy-making and policy implementation, with the power to correct executive behaviour if necessary. The influence of ordinary citizens could be enhanced by the creation of consultation and report-back procedures for elected representatives and by a modification of the single list system in order to end the exclusion of opposition elements from the Council. The more general problems of lack of public debate and lack of mass media capable of playing a 'watchdog' role cannot, of course, be tackled at the local level, in so far as they are the product of a deeply rooted pattern of centralised, patronage-based politics which is only likely to change as a result of more general political and societal reforms.

Another major problem for the communes lies in the division of responsibilities and financial resources between central and local authorities. Even if the financial crisis of the 1990s had not occurred, the majority of both existing and planned communes – i.e. those outside the big cities – are so limited in their capacities that for most important services such as secondary education, main roads, urban planning/ development and agricultural development services or projects, they have to rely on securing the co-operation of central ministries and agencies, some but not all of which may have field offices in the prefecture. Only these ministries have the expertise and the resources to implement many of the communes' planned developments. The four case-study communes were by no means unusual in their attempts to set up full secondary school provision for their areas, provision which depended upon the ministry agreeing to staff and supply the school once it had been built. In the case of piped water and electricity, the communes have to deal with powerful parastatal companies, recently privatised.

Popular involvement and interest might well be enhanced if the communes had the resources to do more for their citizens, but this is an unrealistic prospect unless the govenment is willing to cede them a greater share of the available revenue sources, or to increase the incentives to collect local taxes. Even these resources, however, given the population base of the majority of communes, would be unlikely to make a significant difference and it would probably make more sense to reduce the range of functions of the smaller communes, in order to confine them to more realistic and locally based forms of service provision. Unfortunately, the government's plans to increase the number of communes from 196 authorities to a total of around 365 represent a move in the opposite direction. The intention is to move away from the 'urban' or community focus of local government by creating 'rural communes' which will cover the whole of the remaining national territory, thus giving every area its own 'Anglo-Saxon-style' local council. These rural communes will have fewer powers and less generous funding than the urban authorities, however, even though they will have responsibility for larger numbers of villages and settlements.[68] Such a scheme will create more under-resourced local governments whilst reducing the potential for community involvement and increasing the likelihood of inter-communal conflict, political apathy and refusal to contribute.

The Ivorian communes created by the 1985 reforms are a genuine attempt to give limited power to democratically accountable local authorities at the level of individual communities; it must be recognised, nevertheless, that they have yet to emerge from a context of single-party dominance and a political economy in which the state was the all-powerful provider. Popular attitudes are simply a mirror image of the behaviour expected of a town's rich and successful 'cadres' – those who

---

[68] Côte d'Ivoire (1993b); see also speech by President Bédié at Agboville (*Fraternité Matin*, 15 March 1997).

live and work in Abidjan or the nearest big city. The communes are, in many senses, a formalisation of the patronage or *noblesse oblige* expected of the local elite, who are celebrated in public life according to their efforts to help their home town. These deeply rooted attitudes, together with the government's own intention that local democratisation should reinforce the connections between access to a political career and elite involvement in local politics, tend to conflict with the other policy aim of increasing local self-reliance. The logic of dependence on the state has also been reinforced by fiscal and financial structures and by the fragmentary and territorially restricted nature of the decentralised authorities.

5 Ghana

THE BACKGROUND

The socio-economic and political context

Ghana has experienced considerable political instability and economic decay since independence in 1957. Its deepest crisis occurred during the economic recession of the late 1970s and early 1980s, when the public services disintegrated and government lost much of its authority. One of the causes of this instability lies in the relationship between state and society which emerged during the late colonial period.

Unlike its neighbour, Côte d'Ivoire, the earlier development of cash crops, the greater density of population and colonial 'indirect rule' policies all combined to produce a well-developed, rich peasant/small town society, particularly in southern Ghana. The rural economy of the south became highly marketised, being dominated by smallholder production of export (mainly cocoa) and food crops.

Ghana has never known landlord, or plantation systems of agriculture on any significant scale, although recent trends have encouraged agribusiness investment in rice and palm oil. Of course there are inequalites in the smallholder sector, although by Asian standards a Ghanaian 'rich farmer' who employs small amounts of contract labour might be termed a 'middle peasant'. In the cocoa industry, as in rice, there is thought to be a very small class of large-scale farmers, but the average cocoa smallholding is 2.6 hectares.[1] Landlessness is not a major issue, most employed rural labour being traditionally migrant. The dominant elites of Ghanaian rural and small-town life are thus agro-commercial rather than landlord-based, being composed of the bigger farmers, traders and transporters together with government employees, teachers and professionals in the service sectors.[2]

This society or rather group of societies is rooted in local communities

---

[1] Jacobeit (1991), p. 225. [2] Crook (1991a).

with highly elaborated political, moral and legal institutions and identities. In the 1950s and 1960s these identities were mobilised through vigorous political competition and participation, and the overlay of party, class and associational groupings. The resulting conflicts gave a political structuring to society which has determined all subsequent conflict within the realm of the state.

The first indigenous group to take power in the 1950s, the Convention People's Party (CPP), was not an unchallenged elite; it was opposed or at least rivalled by communal and neo-traditional elites, and the forces of regionalism and localism; there was a well-established business class and farmers' and trade union associations. Even more important, there was by the time of independence a large indigenous civil service established independently of the CPP, and an articulate, educated middle and professional class. Successive political elites have failed to control or integrate the permanent contestation which developed, either within the state or from social challenges to its very legitimacy and identity. After the overthrow of Nkrumah and the CPP in 1966 Ghana experienced a series of military regimes, interrupted by brief interludes of weak civilian government which culminated in violent, revolutionary upheavals within the armed forces and the installation of Jerry Rawlings' soldiers and junior officers regime, the Provisional National Defence Council (PNDC), in 1982. Because of their impact on the state's effectiveness, these political failures led in turn to an inability to maintain the conditions for continued extraction from the peasant and mercantile economies. The radical decline in cocoa production in the late 1970s at a time when other producers were taking advantage of the boom in world prices, led to the collapse of the state's revenue base in the late 1970s and early 1980s.[3]

Ghana's turbulent political history and the strength and articulation of its civil society do not, however, present a wholly negative aspect, especially with regard to the democratisation and decentralisation reforms planned and implemented by the PNDC between 1982 and 1992. Rawlings ruled (and still rules) a country not just with a strongly developed sense of party politics but also a tradition of community politics, and a history of local government experiments going back to the colonial reforms of 1951.

The 'Rawlings Revolution' of 31 December 1981 initially stressed the need for genuine accountability and popular participation in public life. Coming seven years after the revolution the Local Government Law of

---

[3] See: Chazan (1983); Crook (1991a); Herbst (1993); Jeffries (1989); Kraus (1991); Rimmer (1992).

1988 in fact embodied – or was intended to satisfy – at least three distinct policy aims of government, which were in some respects not entirely consistent with each other.

First was civil service reform, a policy dating from the first Economic Recovery Plan of 1983, in which decentralisation was simply one element in a continuing process of rationalisation, retrenchment and 'divestiture' by government of its responsibilities. Deconcentration of large numbers of government ministries to district level, was intended to improve the efficiency and effectiveness of administration through the transfer of both planning and executive resources to the rural areas. The powerful committee in charge of this process – PARDIC – clearly saw the new District Assemblies as a way of rationalising responsibilities and costs whilst the aspirations for greater developmental efficiency were embodied in another new institution, the National Development Planning Commission.[4]

Second was Rawlings' long-standing commitment to 'popular democracy' which in its initial populist form meant direct democracy and the encouragement of community-based, self-reliant development. This ideology was associated with the leftist attack on the corruption and oppression of Ghanaian political, legal and military elites. After the purge of the left in 1983, and the transformation of the 'class-based' (unelected) People's Defence Committees into government-controlled Committees for the Defence of the Revolution (CDRs), Rawlings continued to stress the need for developing new forms of accountability and participation in public life which would avoid the errors and shortcomings of multi-party representative or parliamentary democracy. Elements of the District Assembly reform, such as the 'no-party' rule or the Unit Committee system for each local area, therefore reflected this continuing strand in the thinking of certain factions within the regime.

Third was the contribution of the Assemblies to the PNDC's quest for a 'Ghanaian' form of national democratic constitution. The Assemblies were the first fruit of the work of the National Commission for Democracy (NCD) set up in 1982 to consult and devise a new system of 'true' democracy which would embody the PNDC's particular vision. It is clear from the 'regional seminars' launched by the NCD in 1990 on the theme of 'The District Assemblies and the Evolving Democratic Process', that the PNDC's original aim was to use the Assemblies as the basis for a national system of representation, built up through indirect elections to regional and finally national levels, with other organisational representations added at each level. After Rawlings' belated (and reluctant)

[4] Public Administration Restructuring and Decentralisation Implementation Committee, formed in 1983, which spawned the Decentralisation Oversight and the Civil Service Reform Committees of the PNDC (Ahwoi (1992); Ghana (1991)).

acceptance of the need to move to civil rule through a multi-party liberal democratic system many aspects of the District Assemblies appeared as hang-overs from this flirtation with a Ghanaian version of 'democratic centralism'. The Assembly system in fact incorporated an array of competing principles – representative democracy, grassroots populism, CDR-managed 'non-party' democratic centralism and deconcentrated national development planning – which were unlikely to be resolved without a decisive shift in the character of the regime. (Whether this has happened with the election in November 1992 of Rawlings as a civilian President supported by a party, the National Democratic Congress (NDC), remains to be seen.)[5]

By mid-1992, the Assemblies first elected in 1988 had had their life extended for a further year so as not to distract attention from the transition to civil rule elections scheduled for the end of the year.They had therefore been in operation for four full years up to the end of the PNDC period. This offered an ideal opportunity for assessing the Assembly experience.

The structure of decentralisation

The 107 District and Municipal Assemblies and three Metropolitan Assemblies were created in Ghana at the beginning of 1989, after elections held at the end of 1988.[6] They directly succeeded, after the subdivision of many of the larger districts to create forty-five new authorities, the sixty-five administratively run District Councils which had been in operation since the mid-1970s. The rural districts are relatively large authorities with populations of between 150,000 and 240,000.[7]

The Assemblies are, in structural terms, a 'mixed' or 'fused' type of decentralised authority: that is, they form part of a single integrated hierarchy of government administration from local to national levels. Each District Assembly is meant to incorporate under one authority the twenty-two line departments and agencies deconcentrated by the new law to district level. The Assemblies thus combine the prefectoral-style rule of

---

[5] See Nugent (1995), chapter 5, and Jeffries and Thomas (1993) for accounts of the transition to civilian rule. Nugent (p. 205) interprets the decentralisation reforms as a convenient compromise between 'technocrats' and 'traditionalists', with the latter seeking to mobilise rural elites as part of the regime's search for a popular political base.

[6] See *Local Government Law, 1988* (PNDCL 207). This law was consolidated, with minor amendments, in the *Local Government Act, 1993* (Act 4); four of the District Assemblies became Municipal Assemblies, which must have a minimum population of 95,000.

[7] All population figures are estimates, as the most recent census was in 1984. The minimum population for a District Assembly is now 75,000 (*Local Government Act, 1993*, s.1 (4)).

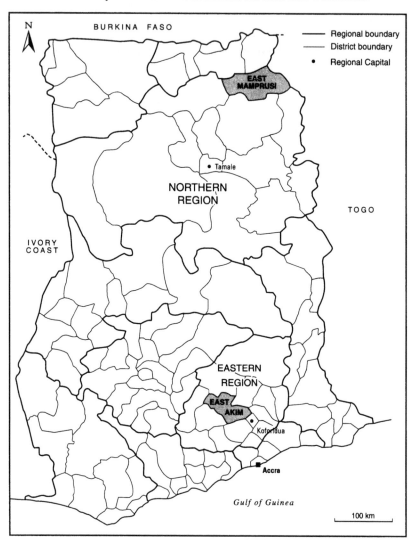

Map 4 Ghana: the District Assemblies, showing location of case studies

traditional district administration, responsible to central government, with the democratic control, service provision and tax-raising powers of devolved local government.

The administration of the district was, under the PNDC regime, headed by a government-appointed, politically loyal official called the District Secretary (DS), normally from outside the civil service. He or she was not elected and could not be removed by the District Assembly.[8] Under the District Secretary was the District Administrative Officer (DAO) – now District Co-ordinating Officer (DCO) – a career civil servant who in practice carries out the day-to-day work of the administration and acts as Secretary to the Assembly.[9] The Assembly also elects from amongst its members at its first session a Presiding Member who chairs the general meetings of the Assembly and has a rather ambiguous role as both a kind of 'Speaker' of the Assembly and respected district leader.

Two thirds of the Assembly members are elected by universal suffrage on the basis of one member per ward in a first-past-the-post election. Parties, however, are not allowed in the district elections, candidates standing on the basis of their respect in the local community and commitment to local development. In 1988, government funded the campaigns of all 12,482 candidates (see below, 'Popular participation'). The Assemblies are quite large bodies with numbers ranging from thirty-five to eighty elected members, depending upon population and the numbers of wards created. The other one-third of the Assembly is appointed by government on the basis of lists compiled by the District Secretary/DCE after consultation with the traditional authorities (chiefs) and other local interest groups (including, before 1993, the PNDC's 'revolutionary organs'). In 1989, these lists were then passed through the National Commission for Democracy. The majority of these appointed members are educated professionals and other representatives of local elites.

The Assembly, with the District Secretary/DCE as Chairperson of its Executive Committee, is the overall governmental district authority with responsibility for development planning and a very wide range of government services including security and public safety, health, education, agriculture, public works, communications and social services.

---

[8] Under the *Local Government Act, 1993*, this official has been renamed District Chief Executive (DCE), and although he/she is still politically linked to the ruling party, the National Democratic Congress (the PNDC's civilian metamorphosis), the appointment has now to be approved by the Assembly, and can be terminated after a motion of no-confidence passed by two-thirds of the Assembly.

[9] See *Civil Service Law, 1993* (PNDCL 327); the DCO's role as professional administrative assistant to the DCE remains unchanged.

There is supposed to be a District Planning and Budgeting Unit in each district, whose work feeds into a regional and national planning system headed by the National Development Planning Commission.

A District Treasury combining the district financial staff and staff of the decentralised Controller and Accountant General's Department is intended eventually to manage and control the budgets of all deconcentrated departments and ministries. The finances of the District Assemblies themselves are based on a mixture of central government grants, assigned taxes and locally collected taxes. Government currently funds the recurrent and development budgets of the deconcentrated departments, and pays 100 per cent of the salaries of the principal administrative staff of the Assembly. It also pays 50 per cent of the wages of all manual and other locally recruited staff such as revenue collectors. Other sources of finance fall into six categories: local taxes such as rates, fees and charges; internal borrowing and investment income; ceded revenues collected by the Inland Revenue Service such as taxes on entertainment and betting, advertisments, transport taxes and a small business income tax; 'shared revenues' collected by the Lands Commission for Stool lands;[10] special central government grants; and, since 1993, a share of the 5 per cent of total government revenues allocated to the District Assemblies Common Fund.[11] A revenue sharing formula was finally agreed in 1992, based on three elements: an equal or minimum base line allocation to each authority; a population factor; and a development status factor based on the concept of access to services in the district capital town.[12] Central government grants have also been supplemented since 1988 by special funds under the Programme of Action to Mitigate the Social Cost of Adjustment (PAMSCAD) which has enabled each district to bid for funds for Community Initiated Projects (CIPs).[13]

Below the districts are two further tiers, Urban, Town or Area Councils and Unit Committees, which were not legally defined and established until 1991. The Town and Area Councils are not directly elected but are essentially consultative bodies to whom certain administrative tasks may be delegated by the Assembly, for instance helping to

---

[10] Stool lands are lands claimed under traditional land tenure by the chieftaincy on behalf of their communities. Revenues such as rents and royalties are collected and then distributed on a derivation basis. These benefit mainly the southern areas where there have long been commercial export crops and mineral workings. The income from these sources was integrated into the local government system in the late 1950s.

[11] See *Constitution of Ghana, 1992*, and *District Assemblies Common Fund Act, 1993* (Act 455).

[12] See below, p. 211.

[13] PAMSCAD was an attempt to alleviate the poverty and unemployment (and deflect the political odium) allegedly caused by Ghana's SAP in the 1980s (Herbst (1993)).

enumerate taxpayers and collect taxes, or organising local self-help projects. In the latter connection they are frequently assigned funds by the districts (rebates on tax collected) in order to distribute to local projects. Their membership during the PNDC period consisted of up to five elected Assembly members for the area, ten representatives of the Unit Comittees, five appointees of the District Secretary and the Organising Assistant of the PNDC's Committee for the Defence of the Revolution (CDR). They were not, therefore, fully elected bodies and in practice could easily be dominated by government loyalists and administrative nominees. But even under the post-1994 system (which omits all reference to the CDR) their importance is limited as they have no funds of their own and no permanent staff except a Secretary.[14]

At the grassroots are the Unit Committees, which finally replaced the well-established Town/Village Development Committees which had survived under the law of 1967.[15] Before 1991, Unit Committees were the basic organisational unit of the government's main 'revolutionary organ', the CDRs. The idea was that of a revolutionary cell for each neighbourhood or work group of 500 people. They existed next to (and often in rivalry with) the unelected Town/Village Development Committees which generally combined the traditional leadership of chiefs and elders with the 'educated youth' and other respected elements in the community. According to the 1991 law, the Unit Committee replaced the Town /Village Development Committee and was responsible to the Assembly for all local government matters and to the CDR Zonal Secretary for all other matters. It consisted of fifteen members, ten elected at a public meeting organised by the Zonal CDR, and five appointed by the District Secretary 'with the concurrence of the Presiding Member of the District Assembly and the District Organising Assistant of the CDR'. In the view of the PNDC Secretary for Local Government this meant that there was no longer any distinction between the CDRs and the grassroots bodies of the Assemblies.[16]

The Unit Committee reform therefore represented a rather cumbersome compromise between the demands of the 'revolutionary peoples' democracy' faction in government and those who wanted to boost the democratic credentials of the Assemblies. As with the Town and Area Councils, a legally prescribed role for the PNDC's revolutionary organs formally disappeared in the 1994 legislation, which provided that the

---

[14] See *Local Government Urban, Zonal, and Town Councils and Unit Committees (Establishment) Instrument, 1994*, L.I. 1589.
[15] See *Legislative Instrument (L.I.) 540* of 1967 and *L.I. 1514* of 1991.
[16] Ghana National Commission for Democracy (1991).

DCE's appointments must be made in consultation with the Presiding Member, the traditional authorities and 'organised productive groupings'. In practice, where they function at all the significance of the Unit Committees is limited and depends very much upon the local political situation.

There is no tier of local government above the district level; but the ten administrative regions of Ghana still form a powerful focus of administrative deconcentration, supervising district-level offices of the various departments and ministries and co-ordinating the work of the District Assemblies. There is a Regional Co-ordinating Council consisting of the political supremo of the region, the Regional Secretary (now Regional Minister), together with all the District Secretaries/DCEs and the elected Presiding Members.[17] This body supervises the distribution of grants-in-aid and other public funds, a task formerly carried out by the Local Government Grants Commission, as well as 'harmonising' district plans through a Regional Planning Co-ordinating Unit. The government claims nevertheless to have reduced the 'bureaucratic bottleneck' at the regional level, by reducing its role to that of co-ordination, and by removing the region's power to approve bye-laws, which now become valid unless objected to by the central government.[18]

The choice of case studies for field research

The case-study method required the selection of two District Assemblies in Ghana, both for detailed analysis of the relationships between participation and institutional performance and as sites for the popular surveys. The following criteria were used in the selection.

First, in order to facilitate comparison both cross-nationally and within Ghana, it was considered desirable to avoid extreme differences in levels of development between one case and another.

Secondly, whilst holding levels of development as constant as possible, there was an attempt to represent major differences in culture and ecological zone within the country, on the assumption that these differences would provide the bases for differing levels and styles of participation.

Thirdly, it was decided to avoid the forty-five newly created districts in order to minimise the impact of difficulties created purely by 'newness' – in this case, lack of office and staff accommodation, severe shortage of

---

[17] Since 1993, two chiefs from the Regional House of Chiefs have been added, and regional heads of deconcentrated ministries attend as non-voting members.
[18] Ghana National Commission for Democracy (1991).

staff, remoteness (most new districts were created *because* they were the remoter and less favoured areas of existing districts) and lack of political identity. In addition, choosing a district with a pre-1989 history as an administrative entity greatly facilitated comparison of the performance of district government before and after democratisation.

With regard to levels of development, the choice was largely determined by the Ministry of Local Government's own classification scheme, developed in 1991 for the purposes of operating a revenue distribution formula for ceded or assigned taxes. The assessment of development status is derived from the concept of 'access to services' in the district capital town, on the assumption that the town is a 'central place' which reflects generally the level of services in the district. Points are allocated for the presence of different levels and numbers of government agencies, health and educational institutions, water, electricity and banking services, and the level of urbanisation of the capital town itself. With each district scored in this way, a four fold classification was adopted: 'most deprived' (less than 20 points); 'deprived' (20–39); 'moderately developed' (40–59); and 'developed' (60+). The latter category covers only seven authorities – the three Metropolitan Assemblies and four regional capitals – and was thus excluded from consideration. The 'deprived' category in fact accounts for 65 DAs or 59 per cent of all districts ; the average score of this group is 29.8, as compared to the average for all districts – excluding the 7 most developed – of 28.7.[19]

Given the above distribution of districts according to officially defined levels of development, it was decided to take two 'average' districts from the middle – and modal – category. Combining this with the other criteria of 'old district' and 'different cultural zones' led to the choice of the following two districts: from the Northern Region, East Mamprusi District (capital, Gambaga) with a score of 29, and, from the Eastern Region (southern forest zone) East Akim District (capital, Kibi), with a score of 30.

East Mamprusi District is located in the north-eastern corner of the Northern Region, bordering Togo to the east, and had an estimated population in 1992 of approximately 183,839.[20] The main agricultural

---

[19] *Local Government Information Digest*, 5, 3, 1992; DA scores from Research Branch of MLG, Accra.
[20] Projected from a 1984 census total of 141,742 (Nalerigu Local Council), assuming the standard annual population growth rate for Ghana of 3.3 per cent given by the World Bank (Ghana (1985); World Bank (1995)). This is probably an over-estimate, given the disturbed conditions and drought in the district over this period. The district administration declined to give any population estimate at all in its general report on the district.

activities are cattle herding and cereal crops such as millet and maize; the soil is poor and the whole area prone to drought. The district is coincident with the core of the historic Mamprusi kingdom whose paramount chief, the Nayiri, lives at Nalerigu near the district capital. The Mamprusi were the traditional overlords of other ethnic groups in the area, two of whom, the Bimoba and Konkomba, have recently come into open armed conflict over (amongst other things) land and the role of the Mamprusi sub-chiefs; armed police and troops had to be used in 1985 and again in 1989. When the District Assembly was created in 1989, the western part of the then Mamprusi District Council was carved out to create the new DA of West Mamprusi. The East Mamprusi District Assembly has fifty-four elected members and twenty-seven appointed members.[21]

East Akim District is located in the centre of the Eastern Region, straddling the main Accra–Kumasi road. It had an estimated population in 1992 of 209,710.[22] As one of the original cocoa-growing areas of southern Ghana, much of the forest has been cleared and cocoa has given way in many places to oil-palm and local food crop cultivation. The majority of the working population (70 per cent) is still engaged in agriculture. Rich gold deposits also permit small-scale mining activities as well as attracting a few big industrial companies. Its bauxite reserves have long been the subject of hopes for industrial development which no Ghanaian government has ever brought to fruition. As with East Mamprusi, the district has a historic political identity, being the seat of the Akim Abuakwa State. During colonial times the chiefly family of this Akan kingdom was one of the wealthiest and most influential members of the 'neo-traditional' elite created by the British policy of indirect rule. Since independence, however, the leadership of the Akims has tended to be on the 'wrong' side politically, and the area has remained surprisingly undeveloped considering its resources and its proximity to Accra. When the East Akim District Assembly was created in 1989, the Begoro area of the then East Akim District Council was hived-off to form the Fanteakwa District Assembly. The East Akim District Assembly has fifty-four elected members and twenty-seven appointed members.[23]

---

[21] See *L.I. 909*, 1974 and *L.I. 1456*, 1988.
[22] Projected from the 1984 census figure of 166,191 (Abuakwa and Kwaben Local Councils), provided by the District Planning Officer assuming an annual population growth rate of 2.95 per cent for the Eastern Region as a whole. If the World Bank 3.3 per cent growth rate were used, there would have been a population of 215,549 (see note 20).
[23] See *L.I.937*, 1974 and *L.I.1420*, 1988.

Ghana 213

PARTICIPATION

Popular participation

One of the major claims made by the PNDC for the Assembly system was that it represented a significant contribution to the development of popular (non-party) democracy at the local level. It is true that it contained novel features, both in the system for electing Assembly representatives and in the mechanisms for encouraging popular participation. The policy seemed to herald both a boost in resources and in government attention to the problems of the rural areas, albeit that it was linked by the government to the policy of encouraging self-help and community initiative. The electorate were, naturally enough, more inclined to listen to the former message whilst ignoring the implications of the latter. Nevertheless, expectations were high and this was as true of the newly elected Assembly men and women as it was of the public.

Electoral participation

The Assembly elections at the end of 1988 and beginning of 1989 demonstrated that initial popular enthusiasm for the new District Assemblies was remarkably high. After registering an estimated 89 per cent of the population there was a high overall turnout of 59 per cent, ranging from 67 per cent in the Upper West to a low of 44 per cent in Greater Accra. 12,842 candidates stood for the estimated 7,260 seats, of whom only 532 were unopposed.[24] The turnout in East Akim was an especially high 71.6 per cent, whilst in East Mamprusi it was slightly below average at 53.5 per cent. As in Côte d'Ivoire there is some evidence that participation rates were generally lower in the big cities, reflecting perhaps greater hostility to government initiatives amongst the urban population together with the lack of interest in local government and political apathy characteristic of the more cosmopolitan and shifting urban electorates.

The government mounted an intensive and well-funded registration camapign which, in the absence of party activity, was seen by local officials and the CDRs as linked to the credibility of the PNDC's democratisation programme. The fact that registration officials went to people's homes and offices registering names provoked some accusations of PNDC 'rigging', although it can also be seen as an effective way of overcoming the immense problems faced by any African country attempting to register a largely illiterate, rural electorate. Given that

[24] Ayee (1990a); Ninsin (1991).

these were local, non-party elections, however, there is nothing to suggest that inaccuracies in the register affected the fairness of the electoral process.[25] The more important achievement was in generating a healthy participation rate by comparison with the previous local government elections, also held under military rule, which had attracted only 18.4 per cent of registered electors.[26] Unfortunately, this initial enthusiasm waned significantly during the Assemblies' first electoral mandate, such that in the 1994 elections the turnout dropped to 29 per cent of registered voters. Even with the enlarged electoral register drawn up for the 1992 'transition' elections, this represented an absolute as well as a proportionate drop in the numbers participating, from 3.4 million to 2.4 million citizens actually voting.[27]

The method of selecting and electing candidates was certainly an innovation in Ghanaian politics. The ban on parties, although reminiscent of the Acheampong 'Union Government' elections of 1978,[28] was in fact, as indicated, linked to Rawlings' desire at that time to use the Assemblies as the basis for a national, non-party form of 'people's democracy'. The provision for popular election of only two-thirds of the Assembly members harked back to colonial local government of the 1950s and probably had a similar purpose which was to enable the government to balance the Assemblies with what it saw as 'suitable' people if popular choices proved to be lacking in competence or representativeness (e.g. not enough women). It also guaranteed government supporters and leaders of the 'revolutionary organs' a place on their local Assembly.

The main innovations lay in the provisions designed to encourage ordinary citizens from the locality to put themselves forward as representatives. The level of representation was close; the number of wards in East Mamprusi provided an average ratio of one member to about 2,200 electors and one to about 1,800 in East Akim. Five candidates were permitted for each seat, who had to stand on their personal merit, integrity and 'proven participation in community development'.[29] No deposit was required and the government funded all campaign literature and publicity, in order, it was said, to ensure equality of all candidates.

---

[25] In the 1992 presidential and parliamentary elections there were allegations by the opposition parties that the register based on the 1988 exercise was inaccurate and partial.
[26] Ayee (1990a).
[27] The 1988 electoral register listed 5,895,098 voters; the number increased to 8,255,056 in the 1992 (corrected) register. For the 1996 elections a new register of 9,185,660 voters was constructed (Nugent (1995), p. 236; Ayee (1997)).
[28] The ill-fated Union Government referendum aimed to legitimise a permanent, mixed civil-military form of government; see: Jeffries (1989), p. 82.
[29] Ankomah (1988); Gyimah-Boadi (1990); Ayee (1990a); *West Africa*, 9 November 1987.

The form of the campaign was also novel; each candidate had to submit a photo and a 'life history' which was publicised. Candidates were then exposed to questions from the public at government-organised hustings over a period of three weeks, at which the candidates presented their manifestos.[30] In many respects the system was an attempt to formalise what had always been one of the realities of Ghanaian electoral behaviour – namely the emphasis put by voters on finding trustworthy communal representatives.

The PNDC's carefully crafted scheme for non-party election of respected local individuals seemed to have worked remarkably well, in spite of evidence that the government-nominated District Election Committees did not have sufficient time to vet the candidates thoroughly after they had been nominated. The National Commission for Democracy also admitted that the three-week campaigning period was not always sufficient for candidates, particularly in difficult rural areas, to present their manifestos or to be disqualified after popular challenge.[31] Nevertheless the results in the two case-study districts were quite positive.

Of respondents in the mass survey 19 per cent said that they had been involved in the campaign of their local Assembly candidate, which is evidence of a high level of interest in and knowledge of the candidates.[32] In each district, only a handful out of the fifty or so elected members did not live in the wards which they represented. Of the seventeen Assembly members who gave in-depth interviews, five of the eight in East Akim and all nine in East Mamprusi were indigenes of the same ward.[33] Over half (nine) claimed to have had no political experience at all, either in a political party or in local government.

Overall, therefore, Assembly members for both districts were locally rooted, community leaders and community activists, for the most part politically uncommitted except for the small core of well-known regime sympathisers on each Assembly. Although relatively well educated (see below), it could not be said that they were from the 'absentee' urban elite so typical of previous party regimes in Ghana or of local politics in countries like Côte d'Ivoire. The legacy of political mobilisation and local community consciousness in Ghana had therefore had positive

---

[30] Ayee (1990a, 1991); *Africa Report*, July 1989; Woode (1989).
[31] Ayee (1990a).
[32] See Methodological Appendix for a full description of the questionnaire survey. 'Participating in a campaign' means, for Ghanaian respondents, a much wider and more informal range of activities than in the British context, where it refers to formal party activities such as canvassing.
[33] The interviewees represented the villages chosen according to criteria of remoteness from main roads and the district capital.

effects at the beginning of the district government experiment. Where the government had perhaps miscalculated was in assuming that participation in non-party elections for community representatives would somehow produce a consensual form of district government.

Participation in District Assembly affairs

Direct participation by citizens in political activities

Evidence from the survey of ordinary citizens in both districts shows that, in general, larger numbers were likely to have participated in village-level group activities of an official or semi-official kind, such as attending public meetings called by the Assembly member, the Village Development Committee/Unit Committee, or the CDR, than to have engaged in unofficial pressuring activities such as an issue-specific meeting or making individual contacts with their councillor or with officials at government offices (see Table 5.1). This is hardly surprising given the nature of rural society, fear of attracting the attention of the authorities in what was still a military, self-proclaimed revolutionary regime (what Rawlings himself has castigated as the 'culture of silence'), and the sheer practical difficulties of making such contacts. Within the category of individual contacting, small numbers of individuals with particular personal or family grievances, or representatives of particular groups, still benefited from the colonial-era tradition of administrative dispute-settling by sending petitions or making personal visits. The survey nevertheless shows the significant impact of the Assembly system in so far as more than four times as many respondents had contacted an Assembly member than had used the 'colonial'-style tactic of approaching the district or other government offices.

The more frequent form of participation, attending public meetings, is not necessarily evidence of 'popular empowerment' in the sense that such village meetings are frequently dominated by local leaders and government supporters, seeking 'approval' for their plans. But few observers of Ghanaian local politics would accept that they can be characterised by passivity or lack of debate, particularly in the Akan cultures of the south – a point confirmed by the survey evidence. In Akim, not only had remarkably high numbers attended an Assembly member's meeting, but 38 per cent of attenders said that they had been able to make a contribution. Of the smaller numbers who had attended the Unit Committee or CDR meetings, 45 per cent had spoken. Even in Mamprusi, 33 per cent of the 14 per cent who had attended an Assembly member's meeting said they had spoken.

Table 5.1. *Direct participation by citizens, group and individual activities (N = 623) (%)*

Measure	E. Akim DA	E. Mamprusi DA	All
Group activities			
Attended meeting called by councillor	43	15	32
Attended and spoke	15	5	11
Attended Unit Committee meeting	16	7	12
Attended and spoke	7	4	6
Attended CDR meeting	11	2	7
Attended and spoke	5	0	5
Attended public meeting to discuss political/social issue	6	4	5
Joined protest/ demonstration	3	3	3
Individual activities			
Signed a letter or petition	6	2	4
Contacted their councillor	14	10	12
Contacted officials at DA office	3	2	3
Contacted officials at other government offices	3	3	3

Relations between the public and Assembly representatives

Once elected, Assembly members were under an official injunction to be responsible for the development of their areas, and were to be judged by their success or failure in encouraging development. (The duties of a councillor include taking part personally in 'communal and development activities', i.e. encouraging 'self-help' projects.[34]) They were also to be judged by how closely they maintained contact with their electors, a task facilitated both by their local residence and the closeness of representation built into the system. They must hold regular clinics and under an amendment to the Local Government Law are supposed to hold meetings with their constituents at which they report on their work and ask for advice at least twice before each quarterly full Assembly meeting.

Assembly members are also subject in law to novel forms of monitoring. Elected members can be recalled after a complaint by 25 per cent of voters and a 60 per cent vote in a recall referendum. In the case of a nominated member, either a single voter or 75 per cent of the Assembly can complain to the government via the District Election Committee. (The decision to sack the councillor is taken by central government.) The CDRs, as the 'eyes and ears' of the PNDC government, were also supposed to monitor the conduct of councillors.

[34] *Local Government Law 1988* (PNDCL 207), s.17 (1) (j).

In so far as Assembly members lived up to the high expectations created by their legally defined duties, they had in effect dual or even triple roles: they were delegates for their communities, sent to fight for a share of the Assembly's resources for their area, governors of the district administration and, in their capacity as community leaders, animators of local self-help efforts. In one official policy statement one of the functions of the District Assembly in relation to self-help projects was described in glowing terms as being: 'to help the communities to make the effort which would lift them out of apathy or lethargy and out of a practice of leaving community development decision to central government'.[35] All three roles obviously depended upon maintaining good contacts with their electorates.

Generally, the level of collective contact between Assembly members and citizens at the local level was quite good compared with the situation in Côte d'Ivoire and, in the case of East Akim, better than the Indian or Bangladeshi authorities (see Chapter 6). The formal requirement to hold regular meetings with their constituents was interpreted by Assembly members in a variety of ways. In both districts, 55 per cent of the Assembly members interviewed said that they consulted the chief and elders and organised public meetings through these traditional authorities. The others said that they used the CDR/Unit Committee structure; in East Akim all but one mentioned the chief as well, but in East Mamprusi those using the CDRs did not link the process with the chieftaincy. In East Akim there was evidence that many of the Assembly members had poor relations with the CDRs, a reflection of the situation in the Assembly as a whole where there was clear polarisation and rivalry between the activists of the revolutionary organs and some of the members. Whichever channel was used, a common feature was that, at the local level, Assembly representatives had to work through whatever groups were most dominant or effective, or with whom they had the best relationships. In a sense the Assembly representative system was superimposed upon the existing informal and formal power structures in each village, and it was very difficult (and probably undesirable) for an Assembly representative to either by-pass or transform those structures, e.g. by establishing direct links with the population.

In both districts, as judged by the percentage of respondents who could name their representative, Assembly members were clearly well

---

[35] *Local Government Information Digest*, 5, 1, 1992. The PNDC Secretary for Local Government has also described the policy in less soothing terms: '"Power to the people" means the people pulling themselves up by their own bootstraps... central government will assist, but only after the chief and the people have shown a willingness to help themselves.' (Ghana (1991), p. 13).

Table 5.2. *Relationships between elected councillors and their constituents (N = 622) (%)*

Measure	E. Akim DA	E. Mamprusi DA	All
Knowledge			
Can name councillor	83	83	83
Frequency of meetings			
Said councillor held meetings:			
never	30	62	43
once per month	28	15	23
2–4 times per year	18	8	14
once per year	11	6	9
once in 2 years	10	1	6
other	3	8	5
total agreeing at least once since elected	70	38	57
Attendance at meetings			
Said had attended meeting called by councillor	43	15	32

known in the local community (Table 5.2) Only a minority of respondents agreed (or were aware), however, that their Assembly member held as many meetings as he or she claimed.[36] Nevertheless, as the survey data shows, contacts between the public and Assembly members did take place mainly through these organised report-back meetings; the high scores in East Akim are evidence of really quite impressive levels of community activity on the part of Akim representatives.

Public participation in District Assembly affairs through contacts and consultation with Assembly representatives was therefore relatively high, particularly in East Akim, as judged by public knowledge of their representatives and participation in collective consultations such as local meetings and the organs of village government. The 'elite' survey demonstrates, however, that the main avenue for Assembly members' contacts with constituent communities was through the mediation of power brokers and community leaders, both official and unofficial (see Table 5.3). The intensity of these contacts also reveals the extent to which many Assembly members – again mainly in Akim – had actively developed their role as local development animators through collaboration with village leaders.

---

[36] In East Akim, 62 per cent of members interviewed claimed to hold meetings eight times per year (before and after each general Assembly meeting).

Table 5.3. *Direct participation by community leaders (N=56) (%)*

Measure	E. Akim DA	E. Mamprusi DA	all
Group activities			
Attended meeting called by councillor	68	33	49
Attended and spoke	48	7	27
Attended Unit Committee meeting	24	30	27
Attended and spoke	20	7	13
Attended CDR meeting	28	20	24
Attended and spoke	28	7	
Attended public meeting to discuss political/social issue	40	10	23
Joined protest/ demonstration	4	7	6
Individual activities			
Signed a letter or petition	36	13	23
Contacted their councillor	56	27	40
Contacted officials at DA office	40	17	28
Contacted officials at other government offices	24	7	15

The role conflict between self-help animator and tax collector

There was undoubtedly a growth in self-help (locally funded and organised) development projects between 1989 and 1992, both in the case-study districts and more generally throughout Ghana.[37] But this was symptomatic of a real difficulty facing Assembly members in their relations with constituents, deriving from an unacknowledged contradiction between their official duty to encourage self-help projects, and their duty to mobilise resources for Assembly-led development.

As members of the overall authority responsible for the government of the district, Assembly representatives were under constant pressure to help improve revenue collection, both through the basic rate or poll-tax, and through the payment of market, lorry park and trading licence fees. Whenever members questioned the expenditure priorities of the administration, they were told that the remedy lay in their own hands. As community leaders, they had to persuade their constituents to pay their taxes, and to explain the connection between taxpaying and the ability of the Assembly to provide the facilities which people demanded. Within one or two years of the inauguration of the Assemblies, elected representatives were therefore being urged to 'get involved' in helping the CDRs in 'pay-your-tax' campaigns and to help supervise and check the work of

[37] Cf. Oquaye (1995), p. 220; Ayee (1996), pp. 37, 44.

local revenue collectors.[38] The administration and the CDR organisation even began to blame Assembly members for the low rates of taxpaying, accusing them at best of a 'lackadaisical attitude', and at worst, of sympathising with non-payment of taxes or even of interfering with the work of revenue collectors. It was implied that elected members were simply looking to their political popularity instead of working for the good of the Assembly as a whole. In East Akim the CDR leaders more or less accused some of the members of being 'saboteurs' of government policy. Many members therefore lent their support to task force strategies which were little more than reinventions of the old colonial punitive tax expeditions, using the untrained cadres of the CDRs and the CDO militia.[39]

The problem for Assembly members who went along with this strategy was that their success depended crucially upon their ability, as delegates of their community, to persuade the Assembly to deliver on its promises. For most, this was an unrealistic hope. The expectations aroused by a campaign based on the promise of a tangible return for taxes paid could not by definition be fulfilled except in a tiny minority of communities, given the limited resources and the large number of 'represented' communities in each district. Only a few of the Assembly members representing the larger towns or those with special political influence were able to succeed in 'bringing development' to their constituents. The government was not unaware of the problem, and most districts, including the two cases here, were encouraged by the government to try to make the link between taxpaying and development resources more transparent by using 'local rebate' schemes, which returned a proportion of locally collected taxes to the Area Councils on a pro rata basis. Most of these schemes collapsed because of corruption, or inability to generate meaningful resources.[40]

Many Assembly representatives and their constituents therefore turned to self-help as an alternative to waiting for Assembly-managed development. They received official encouragement for this. Whenever their

---

[38] Inevitably, in spite of official government warnings against members actually collecting taxes, many crossed the fine line between being involved in 'checking' and 'encouraging' and handling funds themselves. The worst case was that of Yilo Krobo, the first District Assembly in Ghana to be totally suspended by central government because of the extent of corrupt involvement by Assembly members in tax collection. *Local Government Information Digest*, 5, 6, 1992.

[39] In East Mamprusi the CDR organisation caused considerable trouble and resentment with its heavy-handed methods in markets in various towns in the District, according at least to complaints raised in the Assembly.

[40] In East Mamprusi, the administration decided that the results were too embarrassing for the scheme to be continued.

constituents asked for a new school roof, a bridge to be repaired or their feeder road to be resurfaced, Assembly members had to encourage them to show evidence of self-help, through levying local contributions and organising local communal labour. The crux of the problem, in a political sense, was that self-help came to be seen as a response to the *shortcomings* of the Assembly, not as a triumph of the decentralisation policy as such. The fact that respondents in the mass survey identified the majority of projects started in their village in the previous six years as wholly or mainly self-help-funded was more a cause for complaint than celebration as most respondents wanted the Assembly to step in to finish projects which lay incompleted (see below).

Where there were favourable circumstances, the encouragement by the Assemblies of self-help was building upon a well-established feature of Ghanaian rural life, which has been termed the 'politics of communal aggrandisement'.[41] But the logic of the self-help movement contradicted the idea of district government as a collective good (except in cases of a real partnership between the Assembly and village self-help projects). The more that villagers successfully funded their own projects, the less likely they were to want to pay Assembly taxes. In fact every half-completed 'self-help' primary school or latrine block represented another demand for Assembly expenditure, usually for roofing sheets to finish the project. Villagers could not see the purpose of Assembly taxation – or indeed of the Assembly itself – when the only projects or services they obtained were through their own local efforts. And the more successful Assembly members were at developing self-help projects, the more they undermined the legitimacy of Assembly taxes, and their own role as representatives of a District-level institution.

It is not surprising, therefore, that by 1992 many Assembly members felt betrayed and demoralised. The pressure to become over-involved in tax-collecting had had a profoundly destructive effect on their efforts to be at the same time popular community leaders in close contact with their constituents, and animators of local voluntary initiatives. The more closely identified a member was with his or her electorate, the more keenly he/she felt the pressure of disappointed expectations. Over half of the members interviewed did not want to stand again, and twelve out of the seventeen had what could be described as a poor or very poor level of morale, derived from their feeling that the Assembly did not have the means to help them to help their constituents. These feelings were undoubtedly reflected in the small proportion of members who stood and

---

[41] Dunn and Robertson (1973), p. 310.

were re-elected in the 1994 elections: 24 per cent in East Mamprusi, and only 17 per cent in East Akim.[42]

Paradoxically it was, therefore, the success of one aspect of democratisation, namely the election of representatives who were close to their electors and maintained good contacts with the community, which led to severe pressures on the popularity of the Assemblies themselves. The levels of popular participation which had emerged at the village level had aroused popular expectations, all of which fell upon the Assembly member as delegate of the community to fulfil. When these proved impossible to fulfil except through self-help, a few active members lucky enough to represent prosperous towns with effective institutions of community politics were able to achieve something. Many others, particularly in East Mamprusi, lapsed into resentment, gave up attending meetings and were embarrassed to meet their constituents. The disappointed expectations of the electorate also, no doubt, played a part in the fall in the 1994 electoral participation rate.

Participation by disadvantaged groups

The District Assembly reform was seen by the PNDC as one of, if not the most important of its policy initiatives for fulfilling the fundamental aims of the 31st December Revolution: to ensure that 'power is exercised by the people organised from the grassroots'.[43] Indeed it was described by the Secretary for Local Government in 1989 as a 'test case' of whether 'people's power' was mere rhetoric or practical reality. In particular he described the Assembly electoral system as a 'major democratic departure from past practice whereby the poor, the unschooled in English and public officers were discriminated against'.[44] Certainly, the first two groups mentioned by the Secretary could be described as historically disadvantaged groups in terms of their access to political power, to which one might add women and younger age groups. Given what had happened with the People's Defence Committees in the early years of the PNDC, the hopes of the PNDC revolutionaries for Assemblies of unschooled 'peasants and workers' were probably unrealistic. Nevertheless it is still worth considering whether the Assemblies did offer a greater chance to disadvantaged groups of actually participating in political institutions, not just at the village level but also as elected representatives.

---

[42] Calculations based on information in the *Local Government Information Digest*, 7, 3, 1994 and 8, 1, 1995. This reluctance to stand for a second term was widespread; according to Ayee, only around one-third of members across the whole of Ghana stood for re-election in 1994 (Ayee (1996), p. 44).

[43] Ghana (1991), p. 2.   [44] Ibid., pp. 54 and 79.

Table 5.4. *Occupational groups of Assembly members elected in 1989, Ghana*

Occupational group	%
Agricultural	33.2
Medical/paramedical	2.4
Teaching	32.3
Accounting/banking	1.7
Development	1.2
Civil/public service	12.7
Self-employed	9.5
Religious leader	0.9
Legal practitioner	0.6
Others	1.9

Source: *Local Government Information Digest*, 7, 1989

The representativeness of Assembly members

The figures produced by the government on the socio-economic background of all elected Assembly members, covering gender and occupation, show that nationally a reasonably broad cross-section of the population had in fact come forward and been elected (Table 5.4). Although farmers or 'agricultural occupations' were under-represented and teachers massively over-represented, this might have been expected given the character of Ghanaian rural society and the voters' expectations of representation. Nor can local school teachers be portrayed as necessarily a privileged elite; primary-school teachers would earn less than local traders or cocoa farmers. The most that could be said with regard to access to political participation by 'the poor and the unschooled' on the basis of these figures, however, was that it was probably an improvement on the past; a small proportion of the elected representatives were illiterate farmers, artisans, traders and clerks who would not have gained access before. But the educated and the professional classes were still over-represented.

The government's hopes of encouraging women to take part in larger numbers were not, however, fulfilled – only 112 (1.6 per cent) out of over 7,000 elected councillors were female.[45]

In the two case-study districts, the over-representation of better educated and professional groups was much more apparent but coexisted particularly in East Mamprusi with a sharp duality in the composition of the Assembly between a block of poorly or uneducated people and the

[45] Ayee (1990a).

Table 5.5. *Educational level of Assembly members in East Akim and East Mamprusi*

Educational level (%)	East Akim		East Mamprusi	
	Elected	Appointed	Elected	Appointed
None	–	–	31	–
Muslim school	–	8	–	4
Primary/middle	26	12	10	13
Secondary/technical/commercial	46	44	10	22
Teacher training (Cert.A.)	15	12	44	52
Teacher training degree level	7	–	–	–
University	6	24	2	9
Unknown	–	–	3	–

rest (see Tables 5.5 and 5.6). In East Mamprusi, 56 per cent of the elected members had a post-middle school education – the overwhelming majority of those being school teachers with a teacher training college background – compared to 5 per cent of the adult male population.[46] On the other hand, 31 per cent of the members were uneducated, forming the next largest group on the Assembly. The occupational profile of East Mamprusi was close to the national average, although farmers (who formed 80 per cent of the local adult male population) were more underrepresented than nationally.

In East Akim, a southern district with a long history of Western education and cradle of the commercial cocoa-growing industry, a very different profile was to be expected. Even so, the domination of the East Akim Assembly by highly educated people was quite striking and out of all proportion to the local population profile. In occupational terms the East Akim elected members had a more varied background than the Mamprusi Assemblymen and women. The largest single group was in fact full-time officials of the CDR, National Mobilisation or 31 December Women's Movement organisations, followed by the teachers.

In both cases, however, the presence of the government-appointed members brought in people with more professional backgrounds, and experience in positions of responsibility. In East Akim these included an accountant, a university lecturer, business managers, civil service and retired Ghana Education Service administrators, retired high-ranking police and army officers and four well-educated chiefs. Mamprusi's appointed members were mainly medical and educational professionals

---

[46] See quota tables in Methodological Appendix.

Table 5.6. *Occupational characteristics of Assembly members in East Akim and East Mamprusi*

Occupation (%)	East Akim		East Mamprusi	
	Elected	Appointed	Elected	Appointed
Professional/administrative	–	20	–	13
Teaching/educational Administration	18	16	42	13
Technical (Agricultural/medical)	7	8	6	13
White-collar/clerical	9[a]	–	10	–
Owner/manager private business /commerce	2	12	4	4
Retired army/police	9	8	–	–
Officer of revolutionary organisation	28	4	–	18
Farmer/forester	17	4	33	4
Chief	2	16[b]	–	4(13)[c]
Skilled worker	2	4	–	–
Religious leader	2	8	–	4
Homemaker	2	–	–	–
Unemployed	2	–	2	–

Notes: [a] mainly retired
[b] all well educated, including a graduate of Nkrumah's Winneba Ideological Institute
[c] 13 per cent if two professionals – a vet and an Assistant Director of Education – are included

including two secondary school heads, and an Assistant Director of Education who was also a chief.

Although the government had frequently justified the nomination of one-third of the members on the grounds that the electoral process might put off well-respected community leaders who had a valuable contribution to make, the 'top elite' profile of the nominated members did not, therefore, sit very easily with the 'revolutionary' rhetoric of the reform. On the contrary, it confirmed another and rather different policy aim which was to associate the successful sons and daughters of the rural areas with the development of their home towns. Other observers have seen a political motive, namely to build a locally-based 'political class' in advance of the national democratisation process planned by the PNDC.[47]

As regards the gender and age balance, the situation was not encouraging for those who had hoped to encourage women's participation: in

---
[47] Gyimah-Boadi (1990); *Africa Confidential*, 14 April 1989. Like most political schemes, however, the PNDC could not control the consequences of its experiment in the 1992 multi-party elections, when many Assembly members (e.g in East Akim) helped to form the local organisations of opposition parties.

East Akim, only three of the fifty-four elected members were women (5 per cent) and four of the twenty-five appointed members. East Mamprusi was little different with only one elected woman member, but eight women amongst the twenty-three appointed members. The larger percentage amongst the appointed members reflected government attempts to restore the balance. The average age of elected members in East Akim was 45.3, and of appointed members, 48, relatively young for such a body although not in relation to the general age structure.[48]

Overall, therefore, the representation of disadvantaged occupational groups on the two District Assemblies was even lower than the national figures would suggest, particularly in East Akim. In East Mamprusi, however, the substantial number of uneducated members gave the rural population a much greater degree of formal representation than it had ever experienced before. In this respect, however, a further point should be made about the language of discussion at Assembly meetings. The PNDC quite rightly regarded it as crucial that Ghanaians unable to speak English should not be excluded from full participation in the Assemblies. In East Akim (where there were no completely uneducated people), all the meetings including those of the Executive Committee were conducted in Twi, the language of the area and indeed the most widely spoken language in Ghana, although the minutes were written up in English. In East Mamprusi, however, where large numbers of members could not speak English, the general meetings of the Assembly were mainly in English, with those who could not speak English or preferred their own language allowed to speak in that language followed by translation into English. The reason for this was the multi-linguistic character of the area, as well as the fact that not all of the administrative officers could understand Mampruli (the locally dominant language). This system did not seem to inhibit the uneducated from making their contributions, but it clearly did prevent them from taking a full part in discussions, although no easy solution to the problem could be suggested.

Direct participation

Although it was to be expected that the participation of disadvantaged groups as members of the Assemblies would be limited, it does not necessarily follow that the elite character of many representatives would inhibit poorer people, illiterates or women from participating through consulting or contacting Assembly representatives. Even less should it have affected direct participation in grassroots institutions such as

---

[48] Data on the age of members is incomplete. Of the adult population (both districts) 72 per cent is under 44 years of age.

Table 5.7. *East Akim DA: socio-economic characteristics of participators, by selected activities, compared with the profile of the total population of the district (%)*

	Contacted councillor (N=54)	Attended councillor's meeting (N=162)		Attended Unit Committee (N=59)		Proportion of total population of district		
		All attenders	Attended and spoke	All attenders	Attended and spoke	All	M.	F.
Sex								
Men	81	58	62	39	63	50		
Women	19	42	38	61	37	50		
Age								
18–29	30	37	25	29	19	41		
30–44	42	39	45	41	51	31		
45–64	24	18	21	19	19	20		
65+	4	6	9	12	11	8		
Education								
None	33	38	46	39	41	50	42	57
Primary/middle	56	46	50	51	56	45	50	40
Secondary/tech	6	7	2	9	4	4	6	2
TTC/university	6	3	2	2	0	2	2	1
Occupation								
Farmer	48	48	41	48	48	57	60	54
Farmer with employees	7	8	12	5	7	7	10	4
Trader/business	11	17	20	17	19	9	3	14
Driver/artisan	19	12	16	10	15	10	10	10
Teacher/admin/ professional	4	4	4	7	4	7	9	4
Student	0	1	0	3	0	12	14	10
Unemployed/homemaker	6	7	5	10	7	6	4	8
Other	6	3	2	0	0			

Village Development Committee or Unit Committee meetings, traditional meetings or report-back meetings with the Assembly member.

Analysis of selected forms of participation by their rates in each social group and by the extent to which participators were representative of the population as a whole yields both expected and unexpected results (see Tables 5.7–5.12).[49] Looking first at contacting a councillor, it is clear

---

[49] Because the educational and occupational profiles of the two districts differ quite significantly, the data showing the representativeness of participators is presented by district.

Table 5.8. *East Mamprusi DA: socio-economic characteristics of participators, by selected activities, compared with the profile of the total population of the district (%)*

	Contacted councillor (N=24)	Attended councillor's meeting (N=36)		Attended Unit Committee (N=18)		Proportion of total population of district		
		All attenders	Attended and spoke	All attenders	Attended and spoke	All	M	F
Sex								
Men	79	50	83	67	80	50		
Women	21	50	17	33	20	50		
Age								
18–29	46	47	42	61	60	41		
30–44	42	45	50	28	30	31		
45–64	12	8	8	11	10	20		
65+	0	0	0	0	0	8		
Education								
None	54	75	75	67	60	88	82	93
Primary/middle	33	14	8	17	20	9	12	6
Secondary/tech	0	6	8	11	10	3	4	1
TTC/university	13	6	8	6	10	0.75	1	0.5
Occupation								
Farmer	67	42	75	61	80	55	80	29
Farmer with employees	0	3	8	6	10	0	0	0
Trader/business	13	19	0	0	0	8	2	13
Driver/artisan	0	8	0	0	0	9	3	14
Teacher/admin/ professional	21	17	17	17	10	3	5	1
Student	0	0	0	0	0	3	5	1
Unemployed/homemaker	0	8	0	11	0	22	5	41
Other	0	3	0	6	0			

that participation in this activity – the most proactive and 'difficult' of those surveyed – was strongly differentiated by gender. Men's participation rate was more than three times that of the women; in representative terms, men predominated, in that between 79 per cent and 81 per cent of those respondents who had ever contacted their Assembly representative were men. Clearly, as might have been predicted, women were discouraged both by general social expectations and by the structure of the Assembly system from engaging in this kind of direct political pressuring.

Table 5.9. *Participation rates in selected activities, by sex (%)*

Measure	All	Men	Women
Attended meeting called by councillor	32	36	28
East Akim DA	43	50	37
East Mamprusi DA	15	14	15
Attended Unit Committee meeting	12	11	14
East Akim DA	16	12	20
East Mamprusi DA	7	10	5
Contacted their councillor	12	20	6
East Akim DA	14	23	5
East Mamprusi DA	10	15	4

Table 5.10. *Participation rates in selected activities, by age group (%)*

Measure	All	18–29	30–44	45–64	65+
Attended meeting called by councillor	32	29	38	28	29
Attended Unit Committee meeting	12	10	14	11	21
Contacted their councillor	12	10	16	14	6

Table 5.11. *Participation rates in selected activities, by education (%)*

Measure	All	None	Primary/ middle	Secondary/ technical	TTC/ univ.
Attended meeting called by councillor	32	26	41	35	35
Attended Unit Committee meeting	12	10	15	19	10
Contacted their councillor	12	9	17	8	30

Table 5.12. *Participation rates in selected activities, by occupational group (%)*

Measure	All	Farmer/ farm worker	Farmer with employees	Trader/ sales service	Driver/ artisan	Teacher/ clerk/ profess.	Student	Unemployed/ homemaker
Attended meeting called by councillor	32	29	67	36	45	33	5	23
Attended Unit Committee meeting	12	7	19	14	12	18	10	12
Contacted their councillor	12	13	19	11	20	18	0	5

On the other hand, neither age, education nor occupation seemed to have as much of a differentiating effect on contacting (see Tables 5.10–5.12). Although young people's participation rate was slightly below average, and that of the 30–44 age group slightly above, the youth were by no means excluded or significantly under-represented amongst the 'contactors'; on the contrary, it was the older generation (over 65s) who were less likely to have contacted a councillor, although they were not totally excluded.

The figures for education and occupation suggest that wealth, local social status and political salience or activism were more important in determining people's propensity to contact elected Assembly councillors than formal levels of education or occupation as such. The highest rates of participation were in fact associated with being a large farmer, driver, artisan or teacher; but ordinary farmers nevertheless participated at rates around or not far below the average. (The prominent role of drivers in rural society had, of course, been much enhanced by the political links which existed in 1992 between the Rawlings regime and the road transporters' union, GPRTU.) It was only students (although highly educated) and 'unemployed/homemakers' (a predominantly female category) who recorded significantly lower rates of contacting – a characteristic best explained by their position at the bottom of the social status hierarchy.[50] Those with the highest levels of education (a very small group) did display a much higher propensity to participate in contacting, as did all the educated generally, but this did not mean that the uneducated or the mass of ordinary farmers were excluded, or that participation was straightforwardly a function of increasing levels of education.

In East Akim, the more educated and commercialised district, the educational profile of contactors did not deviate markedly from that of the total population (particularly the adult male population), with one-third being uneducated and another 56 per cent having only an elementary education. The occupational profile of the contactors also more or less reflected that of the population, with ordinary farmers accounting for 48 per cent of the total, although the drivers and artisans were slightly over-represented. It was only in East Mamprusi, the less developed district, where there was a greater polarisation between the 'schooled and the unschooled'; the former group accounted for nearly half of all contactors whilst forming only 12 per cent of the population, and teachers, clerical workers and traders accounted for 34 per cent of the contactors, as against 11 per cent of the population.

---

[50] In fact, if the unemployed are separated from homemakers, they show a low contacting rate of 7 per cent, whilst the 'homemakers' drop to zero.

Participation in 'collective' activities such as local-level public meetings or committees, on the other hand, was not only much more frequent than contacting amongst the population generally, it was also much less differentiated by gender. Even in the more traditional society of East Mamprusi, where the overall rate of participation in this activity was low, women were equally willing and able to attend public meetings of this kind. (Men, however, still formed a large majority of those who said they had spoken at such meetings in both districts.) The higher levels of participation by both men and women in this activity may be attributed to its more socially acceptable (even socially expected) and 'everyday' character, and the ease with which it could be undertaken. The same considerations also, perhaps, explain why the age factor had so little impact on the propensity to attend councillors' meetings.

The other expected social barriers to participation such as poverty and lack of education showed patterns similar to those associated with contacting: the uneducated and the broad mass of farmers were *not* excluded to any great extent. The profile of those who attended the meetings was in fact broadly representative of the general population except for an over-representation of teachers and clerical staff in East Mamprusi, and of traders and businesspeople in both districts. The uneducated were also less likely than those with any level of education to have attended, but it is noteworthy that those with secondary or higher education had a *lower* participation rate than the primary educated. One explanation of this pattern is that the more highly educated individuals had less interest in, or even contempt for, involvement in village meetings of this kind, regarding them as activities more specifically aimed at the 'masses' and local political leaders.

A more interesting contrast emerges from an analysis of participation in Unit Committee meetings. It should be recalled that before the 1991 merger of Unit and Village Development Committees, Unit Committees were linked to the CDR structure and were thus composed of Rawlings loyalists. Where there was local factional conflict they therefore formed a potential base for opponents of the more traditional and well-established Town or Village Development Committees. In other cases, however, the 'revolution' was absorbed, as on many past occasions, into the structures of village life and the same group (including the elders) which had run the Development Committee continued to run the Unit Committee. The particular political history of the Unit Committees is reflected in the unusual features found by the survey for this activity, which show very clearly the differential impact of the 'Rawlings revolution' on the kinds of societies represented by the two districts.

In the southern, more commercialised Akan cultural area the power and influence of the 31 December Women's Movement undoubtedly accounts for the unusually high female participation, whilst the ability of the more traditional, elder-dominated village committees to survive and adapt to the 'revolution' explains the participation of the older respondents.[51] In both districts, there is evidence of the attraction of the CDRs and Unit Committees to younger, lower-status groups such as students and unemployed school-leavers. The starkest social division, however, is revealed by the Mamprusi figures which show how, in the context of a poor, highly traditional, elder-dominated rural society, the Unit Committees *were* revolutionary in that they attracted a small group of predominantly young people (the largest group in the population), but disproportionately drawn from the ranks of teachers and clerks.

Overall, it may be concluded that, whilst the Assemblies themselves were disproportionately composed, as might have been expected, of the better educated and elite members of society, the young, the uneducated and ordinary farmers were not at all excluded from participation in activities such as village-level meetings and institutions and contacts between representatives and citizens. Only in East Mamprusi did the educated play a significantly disproportionate role in the Unit Committees and in contacting, although given the fact that nearly 90 per cent of the population was recorded as uneducated, it was still remarkable that they formed a majority of participants in all activities. The main differentiating factor in participation was gender, in that women continued to form a minority – albeit a substantial minority – of participants in all activities, except for the Unit Committees in East Akim and attending councillors' meetings in East Mamprusi.

Representation and institutional accountability

Regardless of the levels of popular participation, or the degree to which elected representatives genuinely consult with and 'represent' their constituents, the impact of enhanced participation can only be felt through the work of elected representatives at the institutional level. They must not only transmit the wishes of their constituents but also devise appropriate policies and oversee their implementation. The most important mechanisms in this institutional process, as in the relations between elected members and their constituents, are the structures of accountability.

The most crucial issue in the Ghanaian case concerned the relation-

---

[51] Although in Kibi (the district capital and town of the paramount chief of Akyem Abuakwa) the Town Development Committee dominated by the powerful chiefly elite refused to hand over to the Unit Committee after the 1991 reform, and the District Secretary had to intervene to force a handover of the files (and funds!).

ships between Assembly members and bureaucrats, both centrally appointed and local. When bureaucratically run local administrations such as the Ghana District Councils are taken over by an elected authority, the first and most important change to be felt is in the formal structures of accountability. Officers now have to report to and be guided by the decisions of elected members. In Ghana this involved not just officers of the former District Administration but also, according to the Local Government Law, officers of all the deconcentrated line ministries and agencies at the district level who were supposed, once the transition had been completed, to work to the District Assembly. This meant working closely with elected members in sub-committees and reporting personally when required to the Executive Committee of the Assembly.

Structural factors impeding accountability to the Assembly

During the final years of the PNDC regime elected members in Ghana were still struggling to achieve control over policy-making, policy implementation and the execution of the budget. Problems in the formal structure of the decentralisation reform were partly to blame: the position of the District Secretary, the continuing role of the CDRs and the revolutionary organs, and the failure of the government to establish a legal basis for a genuinely decentralised civil service.

Executive power and the District Secretary

In Ghana, the Local Government Law of 1988 gave what at first sight seemed quite an extensive role to Assembly members in the administration of the Assembly. An elected Executive Committee, with a maximum membership of no more than one-third of the total Assembly, was charged with the 'executive and co-ordinating functions of the District Assembly', including oversight of the 'day-to-day administration of the district'. The Executive was to co-ordinate the detailed planning and policy work of its five subject sub-committees which reported to the Assembly through the Executive: Economic Development, Social Services, Technical Infrastructure, Justice and Security and Finance and Administration. The law stated that officers of the relevant departments and decentralised ministries 'shall attend' meetings of the sub-committees as non-voting members in order to give professional advice.

The model was that of a parliamentary system, with an Executive drawn from the elected legislative body, with one crucial difference: the chief executive and chair of the Executive Committee was, by law, a central government political appointee, the District Secretary. The District Secretaries were regime loyalists, many of them former armed forces personnel or activists of the parties and revolutionary organs from the early days of the 31 December revolution. As a direct representative of the PNDC, the District Secretary was charged with ensuring conformity to the framework of national policy and strengthening the 'National Democratic Revolution'.

The Assembly was also obliged to elect annually from amongst its number a Presiding Member, and there was much comment in Ghana on the supposed conflict inherent in having a dual 'headship' of the Assembly. But neither in law nor in practice did the Presiding Member ever represent a real threat to the dominance of the District Secretary, however much he may have criticised him. As the PNDC and the Ministry of Local Government explained many times, the Presiding Member was, continuing the parliamentary analogy, intended to be like a Speaker of the Assembly.[52] For this reason he was specifically *excluded* from membership of the Executive Committee, on the assumption that this would provide a check or balance when the District Secretary made his report on the activities of the Executive to the full Assembly. As Ayee has also pointed out, 62 per cent of all Presiding Members of District Assemblies were nominated members, thus further weakening the link between the electorate and control over the Assembly by elected representatives.[53]

In spite, therefore, of the active role given to elected members in the all-powerful Executive, and the election of a Presiding Member, the ability of elected members to take full charge of the district administration was *structurally* limited by the position of the District Secretary. As the law stated, the work of the Executive Committee had to be carried out 'in collaboration with the office of the District Secretary'. For this official, political and administrative functions were truly merged.

As somebody who owed his appointment to his political connections or acceptability to high-ups in the PNDC, his position was virtually unassailable and the government had occasion to remind the Assemblies more than once that they had no power whatsoever to remove a District Secretary. This is not to say that District Secretaries were never removed or transferred by the PNDC itself if they behaved especially badly or caused trouble at the local level; on the contrary, these officials seem to have been constantly on the move. But their postings were a matter of high policy and personal intrigue.

---

[52] See *Local Government Information Digest*, 5, 3, 1992.
[53] Ayee (1990b). It should not be concluded from this that Presiding Members were merely government stooges, however. As with the other nominated members in the two districts studied they were often people with sufficient local status and prestige to act as effective critics of the district administration. Not having any political base they were both free to criticise but also powerless when it came to the District Secretary.

No matter how well-educated and active the elected members of the Executive Committee might be, therefore, they stood little chance of pushing through a policy or of monitoring the work of the administration unless they had the backing of the District Secretary. If the District Secretary and the elected members co-operated together, much could be achieved; if not, the structure of the situation suggested that elected members would find it very difficult to achieve the upper hand. The fundamental problem remained the apparent inability of successive Ghanaian governments to abandon the colonial-style district administration system.[54]

The role of the revolutionary organs

The central government power wielded by the District Secretary was reinforced by the continuing role of the PNDC's 'revolutionary organs', of which the DS was expected to act as leader. In this capacity he had to pay as much attention to the District Organiser of the CDRs and the 31st December Women's Movement as he had to the Assembly, particularly in matters of civic action, taxpaying campaigns and political security. The institutional rivalry between the CDRs and the Assembly was often acute. Some of the more ideologically committed officers of the CDR organisation viewed the Assemblies as a betrayal of the direct 'people's democracy' policies of the PNDC; others, even though the government was careful to include them on the Assemblies if they were not elected, simply feared that they were being sidelined as a prelude to their abolition.

It was probably in order to assuage the fears of these local regime supporters that the government brought in its 1991 law replacing the old Town and Village Development Committees with the Unit Committees, a change which actually strengthened the position of the CDRs at the grassroots level.[55] The position of the CDR personnel was finally secured in 1992 when the organisation became the *de facto* local organisation of the National Democratic Congress, the party formed by the PNDC to fight the multi-party transition to civil rule elections at the end of that year.

The failure to decentralise the civil service

The other structural impediment to the achievement of full control by elected Assembly members was the government's slowness in imple-

---

[54] The involvement of the Assemblies since 1993 in approving the appointment of the district head has only marginally reduced the power inherent in a post which is essentially a political appointment made from the centre.

[55] See above, 'The structure of decentralisation'.

menting administrative and financial decentralisation. Even four years *after* the District Assemblies had been set up, a legal basis for the decentralisation of the twenty-two department agencies and central ministries had not been enacted. Indeed an operational plan encompassing all the detailed legal, administrative and financial measures necessary to decentralise all the different agencies had never been drawn up and as of 1991 the Ministry of Local Government was still commissioning studies on the problem.[56] Under the transitional provisions of the Local Government Law, staff in the 'decentralised' departments at district level were still appointed by and responsible to their parent ministries through the civil service system.[57] It was not until 1993 that the legal position of the civil service departments was amended, making civil servants responsible to the district and regional political heads (District Chief Executives and Regional Ministers).[58] Even this reform, however, did not give the DAs responsibility for recruitment and payment of staff, and structural conflict is likely to remain a continuing feature of the system.[59]

Some of the most important and powerful ministries already had well-established field administrative systems at the district level such as the Ghana Education Service, the Ministry of Agriculture Extension Services and the Ministry of Health; others such as the Ghana Highways Authority operated mainly at a regional level or with districts which did not correspond to the new District Assemblies. For the civil servants working in these agencies little had changed; indeed the Ghana Education Service had openly flouted the government's intentions in 1989 with a decision to *centralise* the administration of teachers' postings.[60] District Directors of Education were not legally responsible to the District Assemblies even in 1992, although this does not mean there was no informal co-operation. District Administrative Officers had always had a co-ordinating role and the routine courtesies of governmental work in a rural district no doubt continued, often dependent upon the personal relations between the officers concerned. In the two case-study districts, officers of the education, agricultural and medical services did report to and give advice to the Assembly and its Committees as required, and in East Mamprusi relations between the Education Service and the district administration were quite close and cordial. In East Akim the difficulty

---

[56] Ghana (1991), p. 139.   [57] PNDCL 207, s.133(2).
[58] *Civil Service Law, 1993* (PNDCL 327).
[59] Ayee (1994), p. 162. One can only agree with Ayee's comment that the PNDC's attempt to blame the civil service for obstructing decentralisation was simply 'passing the buck' for the government's failure to take appropriate action earlier.
[60] Ghana (1991), p. 113.

with the Agricultural services was that they were based in a different town (New Tafo) some 30km away and the staff clearly regarded the Assembly as an irrelevant nuisance – just an extra meeting to attend. The Ghana Highways Authority, the Department of Feeder Roads and the Public Works Department continued to be a law unto themselves, and were very unwilling to co-operate. Indeed there was no financial or administrative structure within which it made any sense to co-operate.[61]

The problem was in fact not *just* a legal one. Many of the twenty-two departments and agencies scheduled to come under the control of the Assemblies had not established a 'physical presence', i.e. had not been able to open or staff offices in every district.[62] Some simply did not have the resources, e.g. 'cinderella' Departments like the Ghana Library Board, Rural Housing and Cottage Industries, Parks and Gardens or the Fire Service. Others, e.g. Fisheries, could not see the relevance of an office in every district whilst powerful agencies such as Highways or Feeder Roads were simply unwilling to change their mode of operation. Even where district offices had nominally been established many were barely operational. East Akim reported eighteen of the twenty-two established by the end of 1992, but in some cases, e.g. Feeder Roads, the officer had simply not turned up.[63] In East Mamprusi, seventeen offices were reported established but again in some cases, e.g. the recently established Statistical Service Office, it was difficult to see what the one or two staff posted were doing, or could do, with the meagre resources at their disposal.[64]

The staff of the former district administration had, obviously, been taken over by the Assemblies with the District Administrative Officer (DAO) becoming Secretary to the Assembly and handling all the day-to-day administration for the District Secretary (in effect the DAOs were still doing most of the work). And by 1992 a District Treasury had been formed in most districts, merging the former central government Controller and Accountant General's staff with the former District Council Treasury. This new Treasury handled all the funds coming down to the district decentralised departments and agencies. The chief officers of the

[61] In East Mamprusi, the District Engineer of the Department of Feeder Roads wrote to the Assembly in June 1991 saying that he had been told by his regional boss not to attend any Assembly meeting as their district office was not yet fully established. Any invitation from the District Assembly to the District Engineer should therefore be 'routed through the Regional Engineer in Tamale'. Minutes of the East Mamprusi District Assembly, 14 June 1991.
[62] Ghana (1991), p. 139.
[63] East Akim still lacked an office of: Ghana Library Board, Ghana Highways Authority, Department of Fisheries, and Department of Agricultural Engineering.
[64] East Mamprusi lacked an office of: the Department of Town and Country Planning, Parks and Gardens, Fisheries, Agricultural Engineering, and the Fire Service.

Treasury, the District Administrative Officer and his executive officers remained, however, civil servants whose salaries were paid 100 per cent by the government. And the DAO's position as a career civil servant was specifically safeguarded with the provision that he (unlike the staff of the yet-to-be-decentralised departments) was not legally regarded as a member of the Assembly's staff.[65]

Perhaps even more importantly, the Assembly's subordinate staff including all the revenue collectors were not fully at the disposal of the Assembly. The districts had been given strict instructions on manning levels by the Office of the Head of Civil Service (OHCS) and districts were not permitted to recruit without permission from OHCS and the Ministry of Finance. Even the transfer of a Grade 1 typist had to be done through the civil service machinery.

The provisions for financial decentralisation were no further forward. The purpose of an integrated District Treasury was to draw up a composite budget for all the decentralised departments and agencies under the Assembly. But as of 1992, very few if any districts were near achieving this goal, partly because of the legal and administrative impediments already described. But it was clear that the idea of a district composite budget would remain a fiction so long as the Ministry of Finance and Economic Planning refused to relinquish control to the new district system and continued to keep control over the budgets of the ministries. The district offices of the various ministries and departments were unlikely to submit to a district budgeting process when their funding was still controlled and allocated by negotiation with the Ministry of Finance in Accra. In East Akim, the District Budget Officer was a young (and very competent) graduate doing his National Service who confessed that the composite budget exercise had been abandoned as he simply did not have the authority or the information to implement it. In East Mamprusi there was no Budget Officer, but the Treasury staff had at least made an effort to draw up the Assembly's budget using the new headings and definitions recommended by the Ministry of Local Government as suitable for composite budgeting.

There is considerable informal evidence that the Ministry of Finance was hostile to the decentralisation project; one of its particular dislikes was the idea that the districts would be the focus for a new national Development Planning System, based on 'bottom-up' plans coming from the democratised districts. A new agency, the National Development Planning Commission (NDPC) was set up in 1989/90 with funding and support from UNDP. It was this body which was given the responsibility

---

[65] PNDCL 207, s.30(2).

for training and appointing the District Planning and Budgeting Units (DPBUs) provided for by law, together with Regional Planning and Co-ordinating Units. As a separate and potentially powerful agency with a mission to draw up and implement national Five Year Plans including public investment it was immediately seen by the Ministry of Finance as a rival empire. More importantly, from the point of view of the districts, the composite budgeting and planning processes were clearly linked, as the DPBU idea implied. But if the composite budgets were proving difficult to implement, the associated district planning exercise was even less far advanced in 1992. Few districts had permanent Planning Officers in post, partly because the civil service was dragging its feet on agreeing the conditions of service for these officers recruited by the NDPC.[66] As with the Budget Officers, districts were using National Service personnel where they could. In East Akim, a Planning Officer had been appointed but the unfortunate man had not been paid for six months because of the bureaucratic wrangles. He was thoroughly demoralised and in any case could achieve very little without any administrative support whatsoever. His first basic task, to draw up a roll of taxpayers, had made no progress. East Mamprusi had no Planning Officer at all. Yet the original grandiose intention of the NDPC was to have had DPBU teams of ten people appointed to each of the 110 districts. In the context of the difficulties already being experienced with staffing the district offices of the key functional ministries, this was clearly a totally unrealistic aspiration – as were the planning circulars being sent out to the districts by the NDPC, written in the language of an academic postgraduate planning seminar. In effect the Ministry of Finance's lack of enthusiasm for the new district-based planning system simply reinforced its reluctance to decentralise the financial and budgeting procedures with which the DPBUs had been linked.

The Assemblies and their sub-committees at work: the struggle to establish accountability

In both case-study districts, Assembly members often made quite strenuous and conscientious efforts to participate in policy-making and in the monitoring of policy implementation and expenditure control. This was most evident in the proceedings of some of the East Akim sub-committees with active chairmen, and in the Executive Committees of both districts. But the full Assemblies themselves often generated lively exchanges as well, even in Mamprusi where the level of members' participation was generally much lower. But the end results in both

[66] Faber (1991).

districts were not dissimilar: frustration and an inability on the part of members to follow up the decisions of the Assembly. An explanation of why this was so must take into account both the common structural problems outlined above and the particular features of each district.

Policy-making, planning and budgeting

Because of the failure of the new NDPC and of the DBPUs at district level, few of the Assemblies in Ghana developed 'plans' as such. The formulation of the annual budget estimates was the nearest they approached to a detailed allocation of expected resources to both capital projects and current costs. Longer-term priorities and plans did, however, emerge during the discussions of the various sub-committees and the debates of the general Assembly meetings.

In the case of East Akim, the main outlines of development policy were set early on with the full participation of members: the commitment to major new market projects, the search for revenue-generating enterprises such as transport services, and the new senior secondary school building programme. Thereafter, members spent most of their time trying to control and monitor expenditure decisions and to make sense of the often chaotic state of the Assembly's budgeting and accounting procedures.

The major problem confronting any attempt at rational management of the budget derived from the character of the budget estimates themselves. If the link between budget expenditure estimates and actual expenditure was often tenuous, that between revenue estimates and actual revenue was pure fiction. Every year officers submitted revenue estimates which were so over-optimistic as to be incapable of fulfilment, particularly as regards basic rates (poll-tax) and property rates. With shortfalls of between 200 and 400 per cent it was hardly surprising that attempts to establish a coherent relationship between estimated and actual expenditure were difficult; in practice, because of the erratic nature of the revenue flow, expenditure decisions were always having to be made on an *ad hoc* basis. The lack of revenue meant that the affairs of the Assembly were conducted in an atmosphere of permanent crisis. Assembly members spent most of their time reviewing schemes for (a) persuading the public to pay their taxes and (b) how to make the revenue collectors more accountable for what they had collected. In the process, longer-term policy considerations tended to get pushed out as the revenue issue seemed always to take precedence.

In East Mamprusi, members also showed, at least initially, a capacity and willingness to participate, but did not succeed in getting very far beyond first base: convincing the administration to give members access to decision-making, and to improve on what members felt to be token forms of consultation.

The tone of the East Mamprusi DA was set early on by the District Secretary and the DAO who insisted, against the publicly expressed doubts of members, that the initial priorities of the Assembly should be: (a) to reduce its staff in line with government policy; and (b) to purchase a tractor and a pick-up truck for commercial operations.[67]

The priorities set in this first year were to persist throughout the life of the Assembly, even after the appointment of a new District Secretary in mid-1992. At his first Executive meeting the latter announced the release of 12 million cedis of ceded revenue by the government and proposed a 'shopping list' of expenditure items covering over half the available funds. The major part of the money was to go on repairs to the Assembly's vehicles, furniture for the District Secretary's bungalow and for Assembly meetings, and the building of guest accommodation in the district. There was no resistance.[68]

The major concerns of Assembly members, on the other hand, as expressed at the first few meetings of the authority, focused on the appalling state both of the main roads traversing the district and of rural feeder roads, the crisis in the schools in the aftermath of the Bimoba-Konkomba conflicts, the lack of health facilities apart from those provided by foreign missions, the water shortage and the threat of famine caused by the continuing drought.

It would be unfair, however, to say that the administration totally failed to respond to the concerns of members. The DAO did acknowledge in his internal reports that the main problems facing the district were the roads, the very high illiteracy rates and low school enrolments and the low levels of 'community development' such as water supplies and health facilities. The first District Secretary spent much time in Accra lobbying on behalf of the district and after three years was able to point to some improvement in the condition of the road linking the district to the Tamale–Bolgatanga trunk road. But the road to Bunkpurugu on the eastern border of Ghana – passable only by the most rugged FWD vehicles – was still unrepaired at the end of 1992. The issue of the Bunkpurugu road fuelled the secessionist tendencies which had always been present in the eastern half of the district, and which, after the ethnic conflict of 1989, had resulted in a virtual complete halt to taxpaying in the area.

The administration was also successful in obtaining funds for the

[67] Minutes of the East Mamprusi District Assembly, meeting of 28/29 March 1989.
[68] Minutes of the Executive Committee of East Mamprusi District Assembly, meeting of 18 June 1992.

junior secondary school and senior secondary school programme – mainly committed to the eastern sub-district – as well as PAMSCAD aid for the Gambaga dam and a special famine relief programme. Unfortunately, however, failure actually to implement these projects meant that relations between Assembly members and the administration did not enjoy much improvement. Even the famine relief loan fund proved to be a source of discord when Assembly members discovered that the committee to handle the loans had been formed without reference to the Assembly, although the Presiding Member had been included.[69]

The main concern of Assembly members in Mamprusi – as in East Akim – was in practice not with policy setting in the broad sense, but with the struggle to participate in management decisions concerning the way money was spent or a service handled, and with budgetary control.

Monitoring execution of the budget

In both districts there was a lack of well-understood (or well-observed) day-to-day controls and procedures for incurring and authorising expenditure. It was not democratisation itself which brought about increased allegations of corruption; it was rather the accountability requirements imposed by democratic institutions which brought into the open the long-entrenched practices of government officials and local government employees.

The financial affairs of the East Akim District Assembly were overshadowed for the first one and a half years of its life by a major payroll fraud carried out by some of the Executive Officers. In July 1990 the Executive Committee was unable to discover what had happened to central government grants spent on the purchase of building materials on the authority of the previous District Secretary. Throughout 1989, 1990 and 1991 the Finance Committee made regular reports on over-expenditures or unauthorised expenditures on such items as: entertainment, travel, office expenses, the DAO's bungalow and furniture for the District Secretary's house.[70] The Committee recommended the adoption of reformed procedures including such obvious necessities as obtaining an invoice, and clearing with the Finance Officer that funds were available in the budget!

In the case of the Assembly's commercial transport, day-to-day management had been delegated to the local Ghana Private Road Transport Union (GPRTU) – a political power in the land equal to if not

[69] Minutes of the East Mamprusi District Assembly, Meeting of 14 May 1991.
[70] He occupied the imposing former residence of the colonial DC on a hill overlooking Kibi.

greater than that of the CDRs.[71] Members therefore spent most of their time discussing the revenue returns, and the costs of repairs. It is doubtful, given the power of the GPRTU and its close integration locally with the CDR organisation, whether they could have successfully challenged the continuation of the policy itself, although some did publicly question its advisability. The education building programme also threw up constant problems of contract procedure and building delays, concerning which members were vigilant even to the extent of challenging the advice and the behaviour of officers. But ultimately it was no more than a retrospective control, a case of trying to call officers to account after expenditures had been incurred.

In East Mamprusi, the most persistent complaint of both the Finance Committee and the full Assembly also concerned the management of the Assembly's vehicles. By 1992 expenditure on administrative travel and transport had reached nearly 40 per cent of the total budget. The principal cause was the heavy maintenance and running costs of the new truck and tractor which the Assembly had been persuaded to buy in 1989/90. The other was the travel claims, fuel and maintenance costs of the vehicles used by the District Secretary and the administration. There was little, it seemed, that members could do about the latter.

Members developed, therefore, a deepening sense of grievance that they were being excluded from budgetary management. Every year from 1990 on there were complaints that the Treasurer's financial report was either read out directly to the Assembly without prior circulation or, on other occasions, had not even been considered by the Finance Sub-Committee before going to the full house. This is not to imply that the district was badly or improperly administered. On the contrary, the administration in East Mamprusi was well-ordered and efficient, and the accounts up-to-date; they revealed only too clearly the financial results of a policy and expenditure process dominated by successive District Secretaries.

Relations with bureaucrats and control over staff

The most fundamental problem facing the efforts of Assembly members to establish accountability was their lack of control over staff, due partially to the delays in implementing the decentralisation reforms. It was all very well to review the budget and call for better performance in the succeeding year, or to refuse to accept the Finance Officer's accounts.

---

[71] The GPRTU was one of the most important organisational auxiliaries of the PNDC, with its own fleets of vehicles and a large force of employees. The government had sub-contracted the collection of commercial vehicle taxation throughout the country to this organisation.

But such criticism amounted to little more than preaching in the light of the unresolved nature of the relationship between Assembly members and officers. It was only when Assembly members attempted to discipline or control Assembly personnel that the crucial significance of continued central control over staffing was revealed.

In East Akim, the DA was unable to control procedures for disciplining civil servants involved in the pay-roll fraud affair, or to force the sacking of domestic staff assigned to the District Secretary's bungalow, in spite of government policy on retrenchment.[72] In East Mamprusi, one of the main explanations of the poor relations between officers and Assembly members was the position adopted by successive District Secretaries and the DAO. The behaviour of these officials constituted an extreme example of the possibilities inherent in the structure of the DA system.

The administration blamed the elected members for many of the difficulties which had arisen with the committee system. In their view the members lacked public spirit and were only interested in attending meetings if they could claim their allowances. Even when they did attend, the contributions made by many members were (in the eyes of the administration) minimal and of little value. Given the financial position of the Assembly, the DAO had concluded that large numbers of sub-committee meetings were a luxury which could not be afforded, unless members were prepared to attend without claiming allowances. At one particularly heated Assembly meeting, the DAO defended himself by asking whether members were really prepared to work for nothing, and whether they were 'qualified' in any case to make a contribution.[73] The idea that there was no money for allowances was in effect a policy decision which had been taken unilaterally by the administration.

Underlying the failure of Mamprusi Assembly members to establish any real hold on the district's financial affairs was the delicate issue of the behaviour of successive District Secretaries. The first holder of the post made contracts without reference to a Tender Board, and came into bitter conflict with the CDR organisation over the handling of funds from an anti-smuggling campaign. The new District Secretary appointed in 1992 proceeded to demand unlimited funds from the near-empty Treasury to fuel his cars as the election campaign hotted up in September and October 1992. During this period the District Secretary of East Mamprusi had personal use of two of the DA's four FWD office vehicles

---

[72] The District Secretary, who was working virtually full-time for the Rawlings/NDC election campaign, claimed that the staff were needed because of the 'political situation' in the district. Minutes of the East Akim District Assembly, meeting of 1 October 1992.

[73] Minutes of the East Mamprusi District Assembly, meeting of 14 May 1991.

– a new Nissan Patrol, and a new Niva – as well as a Niva allocated directly by the PNDC, making a total of three new vehicles.

A second problem in East Mamprusi was a lack of control over DA subordinate personnel, in this case due not so much to civil service power as to the strength of local social and economic networks. The Assembly found it impossible, for instance, to sack the driver whose abuse of the Assembly truck and corrupt practices were the root cause of so many problems. The driver was protected by the GPRTU and the then Presiding Member, one of the largest transport owners in the district and District Chairman of the GPRTU. There were similar problems with attempts to discipline revenue collectors, and both the DAO *and* the Chairman of the Finance Committee (the local secondary school headmaster) shared a certain pessimistic fatalism about the prospects of ever running a local government enterprise efficiently. It was perhaps for this reason that Assembly members were curiously reluctant to take the issue of the Assembly workers' salary arrears seriously (see below).

Conclusion: the capacity of Assembly representatives to formulate and implement policy

Compared to East Akim the level of participation by East Mamprusi members in policy formulation and discussion was much less. But it was not from want of trying, and cannot be entirely attributed to the lesser levels of education amongst elected members. In Mamprusi it was simply that the District Secretaries and the DAO were more determined to use the powers inherent in their respective positions, both to keep control of the administration and to set policy and financial priorities. This meant that by 1992 the sub-committee system was virtually moribund, even the Executive Committee met only infrequently and full meetings of the Assembly were a ritual rehearsal of familiar demands and grievances, taking up only half a day each quarter. Members in East Mamprusi therefore felt more excluded and demoralised, whereas in Akim members were still prepared to get up and argue and discuss and the Executive Committee provided a venue for the most detailed discussion of policy.

The practical results in both authorities were not, however, very different. In both cases, members found great difficulty in monitoring expenditure patterns, and in ensuring budgetary compliance, even though in East Akim members had undoubtedly had a greater influence in setting the planned targets and priorities. And in both cases, members' capacity to force staff to rectify mistakes or to improve performance were inhibited by legal, political and social restraints of a quite fundamental kind.

The peculiarity of the Ghanaian situation was, therefore, that whilst elected members developed quite close links with the grassroots and were

Ghana 247

seen by the communities they represented as delegates for the purposes of community development, when they got to the Assembly level they met with severe frustrations. Their ability to establish the accountability of the bureaucracy to Assembly members turned out to be severely impeded, mainly because of structural flaws in the design and/or implementation of the decentralisation reforms.

INSTITUTIONAL PERFORMANCE

In spite of the difficulties experienced by Assembly members in holding bureaucrats accountable for their administration, the ultimate test of the new forms of representative local government in Ghana lies in whether they were able to improve the performance of local government institutions (see Chapter 1).

Effectiveness

Three interconnected measures were used to assess the effectiveness of the District Assemblies, as narrowly defined in this study. First, having established the resource base of the new authorities, the patterns of allocation of resources to development and services as provided by the District Assemblies were compared with those of the pre-1989 District Councils. For this purpose the years 1986 to 1991 were taken as the test period: three years before and after the reform.[74] Secondly, patterns and trends in the allocation of actual expenditures were compared with official objectives, as set both locally and nationally. Thirdly, outputs as described by these official expenditure statistics were compared with popular perceptions of what had actually been provided, and by whom, in selected villages.

Resources

The total output of development projects and services is ultimately, of course, determined by the objective limits set by the resources or revenue available to a local authority. As noted earlier, a large proportion of the DAs' financial resources came from central government, in the form of salary reimbursements, special grants and assigned and ceded taxes. It would be misleading, however, to see the output performance of a district Assembly as purely a function of a resource base over whose total size it had no control. The government was determined to reduce and phase out

---

[74] The areas of the District Assemblies corresponded to the core areas of the former District Councils, minus the new districts created in 1989. Comparison of absolute levels of expenditure has therefore been avoided.

Table 5.13. *Central government contribution to revenue: East Akim District Council and Assembly,1986–91 (000s current cedis)*

	East Akim District Council			East Akim District Assembly		
	1986	1987	1988	1989	1990	1991
1. Total revenue	26,012	33,584	41,685	59,005	80,680	92,549
2. Govt. grants[a]	15,698	19,810	27,555	30,491	31,014	42,200
2. as % 1.	60.3	58.9	66.1	51.7	38.4	45.6

Note: [a] Includes remimbursement of 50% contribution to salaries and special grants for capital projects

direct government grants, which even in the pre-1989 period accounted on average for an important but not majority share of local government income. The intention was to replace non-specific grants with earmarked funding either through specific grants for capital projects such as secondary schools (usually two-thirds of the capital cost), or through the PAMSCAD programme for rural development initiatives, entitled Community Initiative Projects (CIPs).[75] In the two case-study districts, grant revenue from central government did indeed decline from somewhat above-average levels to less than 50 per cent of their total revenues after 1989 (see Tables 5.13–5.14), but this decline was to some extent compensated for by increases in other revenues.[76] In this respect the DAs seem to have fulfilled an aim of government policy which was to become more independent of central government financing both through more effective mobilisation of the local tax base, and, at the village level, through self-help projects.[77]

The record: comparisons with the District Councils

The actual revenue and expenditure accounts of the two case-study districts reveal to some extent any changes in the pattern of official allocations of resources after 1989 (Tables 5.15–5.16). A crude com-

---

[75] In the period 1984 to 1988, government grants are estimated to have accounted for between 24 per cent and 43 per cent of average local government revenues. (These figures are only indicative, being based on a World Bank staff survey carried out in 1989 of the Greater Accra, Brong-Ahafo, Upper (East and West) and Western Regions for the period 1984–88.) See World Bank (n.d.); Address by Mr S. Y. M. Zanu in Ghana National Commission for Democracy (1991); Ayee (1990b).

[76] Financial data in the following tables is derived from monthly trial balances of the two District Assemblies, and summary accounts of annual revenue and expenditure, kindly provided by the District Finance Officers and the Ministry of Local Government.

[77] The District Assemblies Common Fund, set up in 1994, seems to have reversed this trend, at least in the short term, simply through the provision of significant amounts of extra finance tightly controlled by central government (Ayee (1995)).

Table 5.14. *Central government contribution to revenue: Mamprusi District Council and East Mamprusi District Assembly, 1986–91 (000s current cedis)*

	Mamprusi District Council			East Mamprusi District Assembly		
	1986	1987	1988	1989	1990	1991
1. Total revenue	12,362	12,471	17,606	23,569	31,591	39,509
2. Govt. grants[a]	5,158	3,962	8,888	8,730	11,028	16,938
2. As % 1.	41.7	31.7	50.5	37	35	42.9

Note: [a] Includes reimbursement of 50% contribution to salaries and special grants for capital projects

Table 5.15. *East Akim District Assembly and District Council compared: expenditure on development 1986–91 (000s current and real cedis, 1990=100)*

	East Akim District Council				East Akim District Assembly			
	1986	1987	1988	1986–88	1989	1990	1991	1989–91
Total expenditure:								
Current	26,532	33,686	40,749	100,967	57,897	77,176	91,589	226,662
Real	87,564	80,014	72,507	240,085	80,301	77,176	76,134	233,611
Development expenditure:								
Current	801	3,156	2,749	6,706	4,131	14,916[a]	12,485	31,532
Real	2,644	7,450	4,891	14,985	5,730	14,916	10,378	31,024
Development as % total	3	9.4	6.7	6.6	7.1	19.3[a]	13.6	13.9
Cumulative development, real cedis per capita[b]	–	–	–	62	–	–	–	148

Notes: [a] Includes purchase of a bus, put to Works and Communications recurrent expenditure in original accounts

[b] Based on 1988 and 1992 populations; the population of the former East Mamprusi District Council was 242,525 (Ghana 1985). For the population of East Akim DA, see note 22.

Table 5.16. *East Mamprusi District Assembly and Mamprusi District Council compared: expenditure on development, 1986–91 (000s current and real cedis, 1990=100)*[a]

	Mamprusi District Council				East Mamprusi District Assembly			
	1986	1987	1988	1986–88	1989	1990	1991	1989–91
Total expenditure:								
Current	12,127	12,484	17,617	42,228	23,567	32,529	36,743	92,839
Real	40,023	29,653	31,347	101,023	32,687	32,529	30,543	95,759
Development expenditure:								
Current	361	1,825	851	3,037	1,429[c]	4,800[c]	4,745[c]	10,974
Real	1,191	4,335	1,514	7,040	1,982	4,800	3,944	10,726
Development as % total	3	15	5	7.2	6	15	13	11.8
Cumulative development, real cedis per capita[b]				35				58

Notes: [a] Current cedis in Tables 5.15–5.16 deflated using GDP deflators – International Monetary Fund (1995)
[b] Based on 1988 and 1992 populations; the population of the former Mamprusi District Council was 200,897 – Ghana (1985); for the population of East Mamprusi DA, see note 20
[c] Includes purchase of a tractor, under new 'composite budget' accounting conventions adopted after 1989.
Under the old rules, East Mamprusi's development expenditures in the years 1989 to 1991 would have been 1.8%, 11.7% and 9.7% respectively

parison of overall 'development effort' can be obtained by measuring the cumulative, real per capita development spending of each authority during the 1986–8 and 1989–91 periods. This shows that in both districts the per capita development expenditures of the Assemblies were an improvement on those of the District Councils. There were also some rather erratic increases in the proportion of total expenditure allocated to the development budget, although these hardly constituted a clear break with previous patterns.

Unfortunately, these apparent improvements in the overall balance between development and recurrent spending were of limited significance. Recurrent expenditure continued to account for 85–87 per cent of District Assembly spending, and many of the improved figures were in fact functions of changes in accounting conventions, according to which the purchase of vehicles was put under the capital budget. Under the old conventions, East Akim's 19 per cent development budget would have dropped to 15 per cent, and East Mamprusi's to a much lower level for the whole 1989–91 period.[78] More importantly, the absolute amounts remained pathetically small in relation to the potential demand coming from these rural communities. East Mamprusi's cumulative development expenditure for the whole 1989–91 period was the equivalent of US$0.18 per capita at 1990 exchange rates, whilst East Akim's was US$ 0.45 per capita.[79] The most significant changes in the actual patterns of spending after 1989 were within the recurrent rather than the development budgets. The latter continued to focus mainly on social infrastructure such as schools and latrines (see below, Tables 5.25–5.26). On the recurrent side, however, wage costs fell sharply, both in absolute and proportionate terms (Tables 5.17–5.18). At the same time, in both districts, expenditure on 'travel and transport' allowances and the costs of running and maintaining vehicles rose significantly; East Mamprusi was the most extravagant in this respect, expenditure under this heading having risen to 36 per cent of total expenditure by 1992. Other administrative costs, including the costs of Assembly meetings, entertainment, and provision of offices, accommodation and furniture for officers also went up substantially. In East Akim there was a particular emphasis on shifting expenditure into 'trading services' such as local passenger transport and haulage, cement block manufacture, agricultural enterprises and markets. The dominant motive here was revenue mobilisation, in an attempt to fulfil the government's desire for districts to become more self reliant. By mid-1992, the East Akim DA was running two commercial passenger buses and a haulage truck on a hire basis. The buses were certainly generating considerable revenue, as might be expected in such an area, and were being run on a 'commission' basis by the local branch of the GPRTU. East Mamprusi had also invested in a truck and a tractor, with considerably less success.

The fall in wage costs was in fact a symptom of a real crisis in manpower and service provision, caused by government policy. Whilst central government continued to pay 100 per cent of the salaries of key administrative and financial staff, and 50 per cent of all other staff (including successive pay increases over the period), it attempted to pursue a national policy of public service retrenchment – an essential element in the Economic Recovery Plan approved by the World Bank. In 1992, the Office of the Head of the Civil Service (OHCS) set tough new guidelines for the total number of direct District Assembly staff permitted, and made it clear that all recruitments as well as transfers would

---

[78] East Mamprusi also benefited from a special government grant of 5.75 million cedis in 1991.
[79] 1 cedi = US$ 326 (International Monetary Fund (1995)).

Table 5.17. *East Akim District Council and Assembly: selected expenditure patterns 1986–91 (% of total expenditure)*

	East Akim District Council			East Akim District Assembly		
	1986	1987	1988	1989	1990	1991
Salaries[a]	84.8	77.8	79.0	65.8	48.2	47.2
Other admin. costs (excluding T & T)	6.9	7.7	7.8	16.5	19.5	20.4
T&T & maintenance of vehicles	4.4	4.6	6.2	10.2	11.2	11.8
Trading services	0.9	0.5	0.2	0.3	1.8	4.3
Grants to revolutionary organs	–	–	–	–	–	1.6
Development/capital projects	3.0	9.4	6.8	7.1	19.3	13.6

Note: [a] Does not include salaries of main administrative staff 100% paid directly by government

Table 5.18. *Mamprusi District Council and East Mamprusi District Assembly: selected expenditure patterns 1986–91 (% of total expenditure)*

	Mamprusi District Council			East Mamprusi District Assembly		
	1986	1987	1988	1989	1990	1991
Salaries[a]	64.8	54.5	67.8	54.3	41.2	32.2
Other admin. costs (excluding T & T)	13.3	12.6	11.6	17.6	16.0	12.0
T&T & maintenance of vehicles	16.6	17	13.3	17.3	25	36.3
Entertainments /funerals	2.1	1.3	2.0	4.8	3.3	5.9
Grants to revolutionary organs	–	–	–	–	–	0.8
Development/ capital projects	3.0	14.6	4.8	6.1	14.8	12.9

Note: [a] Does not include salaries of main administrative staff 100% paid directly by government

have to be cleared through OHCS and the Ministry of Finance. The government claimed that, prior to the 50 per cent policy, the District Councils were simply over-staffed by thousands of relatives and clients of bureaucrats and appointed councillors who were paid for doing nothing – or in many cases did not exist at all![80]

At the district level the impact was dramatic, reflecting the two main

---

[80] According to the OHCS, the overstaffing was at least 50 per cent.

responses of the districts: the sacking of many clerical, service and labouring personnel and the withholding by the districts of their 50 per cent share of employees' wages. The total staff complement of East and West Mamprusi District Assemblies, which together were the equivalent of the old Mamprusi District Council, fell from 308 to 210 between 1986 and 1992, a 32 per cent drop. In East Akim reliable figures were hard to obtain, such was the chaos in the Assembly's records caused by the investigation into the pay-roll fraud. The best estimate is that total staff numbers across the two districts which made up the old District Council (East Akim and Fanteakwa) also fell by around the same percentage.[81]

The effect of the failure to pay wages was even more serious. By 1992 most of the revenue collectors and labourers in East Mamprusi had been on half pay for almost two years. In spite of the government's view that the majority of district employees were paid for doing nothing, there was a real impact visible in the deterioration of public cleanliness, and the collapse in tax-collection rates. Sanitary services were virtually non-existent in many places, and attempts to organise sanitary labourers to make up their wages by collecting 'user charges' were largely unsuccessful. In Akim, government buildings were gradually disappearing under weeds and secondary bush, and the lorry formerly used as the Council's cess-pit emptier had been converted to commercial use after the failure of a 'user charges' initiative. Revenue collectors simply resorted to corruption to survive, leading some officials of the Assembly to joke that they probably made more from their corrupt practices than they were owed in wages!

The government was not entirely to blame, however, for the manpower crisis. Although central policy was forcing the Assembies to reduce staff numbers, the 50 per cent reimbursement of salaries for those on the roll was automatic. The districts themselves had allowed other items of expenditure to grow proportionately to the point where it could be said that a decision had been taken not to pay staff.

To what extent did post-1989 changes reflect the official and legal objectives of the District Assemblies? Unfortunately, the Ghanaian government never set minimum targets or even guidelines for the allocation of expenditure to particular purposes or for the ratio of development to total expenditure. Nevertheless, the legal duties of the Assemblies, as set out in the Local Government Law of 1988, do form a useful benchmark against which to judge their outputs. Their general objectives include responsibility for the 'overall development of the

---

[81] The fall was from 297 to 194; calculated from figures provided by the DAO and the Finance Officer.

district', the formulation of 'strategies for the effective mobilisation of human, physical, financial and other resources' and the provision of 'basic infrastructure and municipal works and services'.[82] Whilst success in achieving such goals is very difficult to measure, the Legislative Instruments setting up each Assembly provide a very specific list of up to eighty-six particular duties. In the case of East Akim these include, for instance, the duty to 'ensure the provision of adequate and wholesome supply of water throughout the entire district'; to 'provide or arrange for electric lighting in streets ... in consultation with the Electricity Corporation'; to 'construct, repair and maintain all public roads other than trunk roads'; to 'maintain ... all public buildings'; to 'build, equip and maintain all public primary, middle and special schools'; and to 'be responsible for the improvement of agriculture including extension services and allotments'.[83]

As the above analysis of actual expenditure patterns shows, although development expenditure did increase in real per capita terms after 1989, the totals remained meagre and the purposes to which the increased expenditures were allocated bore little relationship to the official developmental objectives of the reformed local authorities. This was even more the case with regard to recurrent spending, where the provision of services clearly deteriorated. These expenditure patterns reflected for the most part the priorities of the government-appointed political bosses of the districts, the District Secretaries, and, in spite of its slow pace, the administrative and capital costs of the decentralisation programme itself.[84]

Popular perceptions of effectiveness

The rather unimpressive picture which emerges from the official financial data is reflected in popular assessments of the performance of the District Assemblies after four years in operation (see Table 5.19). Overall only 22 per cent of respondents in the village-level mass survey were prepared positively to say that the District Assembly's performance was better than that of the former District Council. The objective differences between the capacities of the two Assembles were also reflected in the much stronger negative scores in East Mamprusi, where only 10 per cent thought the Assembly was better compared to 36 per cent in East Akim.

Another general indication is provided by the 70.2 per cent of

---

[82] PNDCL 207, s. 6.
[83] *Local Government East Akim District Assembly Establishment Instrument, 1988*, L.I. 1420. The list for East Mamprusi is identical.
[84] Cf. Ayee's findings for Krachi DA in the Volta Region, which revealed a similar pattern of excessive expenditure on the DS's transport (Ayee (1992)).

Table 5.19. *Popular perceptions of Assembly performance (N = 624)*

	Say DA is better than DC (%)	Say DA cannot satisfy needs (%)	Projects attributed to DA (%)	Projects attributed to DC (%)	Projects attributed to self-help (%)
E. Akim	36	55[b]	13.4	16	66.2
E. Mamp.	10	84	4	26	26
Both DAs	22.2[a]	70.2	7.9	27.8	40

Notes: [a] Dont know = 13.5%
[b] Dont know = 19%

respondents who replied with a definite negative to the question 'Is the DA able to satisfy any of these needs [i.e. those identified by the respondent in the previous open-ended question] with its projects or services?'

It is, of course, easy to make sweeping condemnations of this kind in response to a general opinion-seeking question. But when asked to discuss particular projects or services provided in their own village or town in the previous 5–10 years, respondents again tended to confirm the objective evidence. In East Mamprusi, respondents attributed only 4 per cent of all the projects they identified in their own locality as funded by the District Assembly, as compared to 26 per cent by the former District Council (see Table 5.19).

The growth of the self-help form of development as encouraged by the role of the Assembly members (see above) was even more strongly marked in East Akim, where 66.2 per cent of all projects identified by respondents were said to be 'self-help' of some kind. This did not mean that the projects were all wholly funded by local 'communal labour' and local contributions; many had been started in this way, but in the expectation of help from the Assembly to finish off – usually roofing sheets. It is interesting to note, however, that when asked about their level of satisfaction with particular named projects in their own village, 71 per cent of the projects with which respondents were 'very dissatisfied' were of the self-help type. The main reasons were that self-help projects were frequently unfinished for lack of funds or needed repairs for which help was not forthcoming.

That the general pattern of popular perceptions of performance was not unreliable is confirmed by the results of the survey of village community leaders (elite survey) who identified the funding of local projects in much the same kind of proportions (Table 5.20). In East

Table 5.20. *Elite survey: perceptions of project funding (N = 56)*

	Projects attributed to DA (%)	Projects attributed to DC (%)	Projects attributed to self-help (%)	Projects attributed to aid (%)	Projects attributed to central govt. (%)
Both DAs	7.1	12.9	67	8.6	4.3

Table 5.21. *Elite survey: perceptions of District Assembly performance (N = 56)*

	Say DA better than DC	Say DA cannot satisfy needs
E. Akim	53	47
E. Mamprusi	19	87
Both	35.5	68

Mamprusi, the elites also strongly agreed that the District Assembly had a worse record than the District Council; only in East Akim did a bare majority of elite respondents take a more favourable view of the Assembly's developmental capacity (Table 5.21), perhaps reflecting the greater involvement of this group in Assembly affairs.

Responsiveness

Responsivenesss to whom?

As the evidence on the functioning of Assembly institutions has already demonstrated, although Assembly members did make quite considerable contributions to the policy process, at least in East Akim, they were engaged in a constant struggle with officials and with the central government-appointed chief executive to establish control over both the budget-making and budget execution processes. These struggles were reflected in the patterns of actual expenditure, both capital and recurrent, in which both well-established conceptions of development need and new priorities connected with revenue-raising, administrative and political needs can be identified.

In assessing the performance of the District Assemblies it is not, however, sufficient to look just at outputs or patterns of allocation. One has to ask whether the products of these expenditures were valued by the electorate, that is, whether they were reasonably congruent with popular conceptions of development priorities. In particular, did the outputs

Table 5.22. *Rank order of most frequently mentioned popular needs, by district*

Rank	All (N=624) (%)		E. Akim (N=374) (%)		E. Mamp.(N=250) (%)	
1	roads[a]	54.5	roads	55.9	education	56.0
2	education	42.0	electricity	41.1	roads	52.4
3	water	39.0	sanitation	35.5	water	49.2
4	electricity	36.2	water	32.5	health	48.0
5	sanitation	33.7	education	32.3	agriculture	39.2
6	health	33.0	health	22.8	sanitation	31.2
7	agriculture	20.0	markets	17.0	electricity	29.2
8	markets	19.2	employment	14.2	markets	14.4
9	employment	9.9	agriculture	6.7	social	14.0
10	social	9.1	social	5.9	food	5.6
11	transport	4.3	transport	4.8	transport	5.2
12	shops	2.4	shops	3.2	employment	3.2
13	food	2.2	day nursery	2.7	shops	1.2
14	day nursery	1.8	P.O.	1.6	P.O.	0.8
15	P.O.	1.3	food	0.0	day nursery	0.4

Note: [a] 'roads' includes 'repairs to bridges'

respond more to the perceived needs of the disadvantaged groups which the government itself claimed to be championing – the poor (i.e. most rural dwellers but particularly smaller farmers in the less favoured rural areas), the unschooled, women and youth?

Whether the pattern of Assembly outputs did correspond to popular demands was measured first by asking respondents in the mass survey an open-ended question: 'In general, what do you think are the most important needs of the people in this area?' The needs spontaneously mentioned were then grouped into types and ranked according their popularity (Table 5.22).

The survey shows quite conclusively that a clear majority of respondents, of both sexes and in both districts, saw improving the roads as the main 'need' of their area. The majority of respondents in fact specified that by roads they meant either the opening up or improvement of feeder roads to their village. In East Mamprusi, broken-down bridges were also a major issue linked with roads – some of the villages surveyed were frequently cut off because rivers had to be forded, or the bridges were about to collapse. The next most frequently mentioned needs were educational (this included requests for more staff and equipment as well references to repairs or new buildings and the junior and senior secondary school programme), water supplies and electrification. It is also noteworthy that, if lack of education is taken as the most powerful indicator of disadvantage in Ghanaian rural society, the priorities of uneducated respondents differed hardly at all from the general rankings (Table 5.23). The survey can therefore be treated as giving a plausible indication of popular perceptions of need in these two rural areas.

There were, as might be expected, some differences of emphasis when comparing the two districts. Although water supplies and educational needs appeared in the top five in both districts, being mentioned by more than a third of respondents, these areas (together with health facilities) were clearly seen as a high priority by a larger number of respondents in East Mamprusi, and there was greater agreement in this district on what the leading priorities were. In East Akim, there was a wider spread of choices, with electrification being favoured to a much greater degree than in the north.[85] These differences are perfectly comprehensible given the different climatic, social and economic characteristics of the two areas. In the arid zones of the north, there is an obvious need to prepare against the constant and devastating threat of drought; in the forest zones of the south, when people say they need water, they mean it would be good to have clean and/or piped water supplies. Similarly, although the desire for educational opportunity for one's children is common throughout Ghana, the much higher levels of illiteracy in a district such as East Mamprusi undoubtedly produce a stronger awareness that the area requires drastic action to escape from its perceived backwardness and deprivation.

There were surprisingly few gender differences in perception of needs (Table 5.24), with the exception of health which was mentioned by 41 per cent of women, making it the second most popular, as compared to only 25 per cent of men (sixth ranking). Men mentioned sanitation more frequently, making it one of their four top choices. Apart from these two needs, three out of the five most popular needs were common to men and women. It is also of interest that only a small handful of women (2.6 per cent) spontaneously mentioned day nurseries, a programme much favoured by the 31 December Women's Movement and overseas aid agencies as catering to the needs of women.

In order to assess whether the outputs of the District Assemblies did respond more closely to popular demands, the needs as expressed in the survey were compared with the actual expenditure patterns of the two Assemblies. In the absence of planning documents, this was virtually the

---

[85] In the case of electricity, demand had been renewed and inspired by the PNDC's much publicised programme for the extension of the Volta Dam national grid. This was a national policy heavily funded by external donors, and for the first time made the dream of many rural communities for electricity seem a real possibility.

Table 5.23. *Rank order of most frequently mentioned needs, respondents with no formal education*

Rank	All (N=621) (%)		Respondents with no education (N=342) (%)	
1	roads[a]	54.5	roads	56.5
2	education	42.0	education	44.4
3	water	39.0	water	40.9
4	electricity	36.2	health	37.4
5	sanitation	33.7	electricity	34.8
6	health	33.0	sanitation	31.3
7	agriculture	20.0	agriculture	27.5
8	markets	19.2	markets	20.0
9	employment	9.9	social	10.0
10	social	9.1	employment	7.3
11	transport	4.3	food	3.8
12	shops	2.4	transport	3.8
13	food	2.2	shops	2.0
14	day nursery	1.8	day nursery	1.5
15	P.O.	1.3	P.O.	1.0

Note: [a] 'roads' includes 'repairs to bridges'

Table 5.24. *Rank order of most frequently mentioned needs, by sex*

Rank	All (N=621) (%)		Women (N=307) (%)		Men (N=314) (%)	
1	roads[a]	54.5	roads	52.5	roads	56.0
2	education	42.0	health	41.0	education	44.3
3	water	39.0	education	39.4	water	41.4
4	electricity	36.2	electricity	37.5	sanitation	39.2
5	sanitation	33.7	water	36.5	electricity	35.0
6	health	33.0	sanitation	28.3	health	25.2
7	agriculture	20.0	markets	22.5	agriculture	22.0
8	markets	19.2	agriculture	18.0	markets	16.2
9	employment	9.9	social	12.1	employment	8.0
10	social	9.1	employment	11.4	social	6.1
11	transport	4.3	shops	3.0	transport	5.7
12	shops	2.4	transport	3.0	food	2.0
13	food	2.2	food	2.6	shops	1.6
14	day nursery	1.8	day nursery	2.6	day nursery	1.0
15	P.O.	1.3	P.O.	2.0	P.O.	0.6

Note: [a] 'roads' includes 'repairs to bridges'

only way to establish the official priorities of the Assemblies as they worked out in practice.

In East Akim (Table 5.25), the small development budgets of the District Council between 1986 and 1988 were virtually all distributed to Area or Town Councils or used to finish off self-help projects. In this respect they were relatively responsive to locally defined needs, mainly materials for small-scale educational or sanitary projects. Unfortunately, this kind of allocation virtually disappeared from the development programme during the first three years of the District Assembly, although there is evidence that it was finding favour again during 1992.[86] The main problem with this form of spending, according to Assembly officials, was that it was extremely difficult to control the actual disbursement of the funds once they were released and there was considerable scepticism about its efficacy. In the first year of the District Assembly, however, virtually all of the development budget was allocated to a 'low-cost housing' project in the district capital (rented accommodation for civil servants, teachers and others working in the district), offices and new market projects. Cumulatively over the whole period 1989–91, education, with 34.3 per cent of total development expenditure, emerged as the largest single item, but was dwarfed overall by the Assembly's new commitment to its revenue generating projects – markets, the 'Assembly farm', the Assembly bus, the 'councillors' Football Club' – and administrative infrastructure. What the figures show most clearly, however, is that the areas of most concern to the ordinary citizens of East Akim – feeder roads, electrification, sanitary and water supply facilities – had virtually *no funds* allocated to them during the first three years of the Assembly.

In East Mamprusi (Table 5.26), the former District Council had allocated the majority of its derisory development budget to educational needs, with other smaller amounts going to health, water and sanitary projects. Under the District Assembly, although education continued to form an important part of the increased development budget it declined to only 24 per cent of cumulative development expenditure. This was due to the huge burden imposed on the Assembly's finances by the purchase of an Assembly tractor, and by the 1991 decision to make a one-off allocation to the different zones of the district for local self-help projects. The only popular area which experienced a significant rise in expenditure was water supply, although it only ranked fourth in overall terms.

Curiously enough, therefore, the little that the East Mamprusi Assembly spent on development did seem to be more responsive to

---

[86] By August 1992, 65 per cent of development spending for 1992 had been allocated to community self-help projects (Minutes of the General Meeting of the East Akim District Assembly, 6 August 1992).

Table 5.25. *East Akim District Council and Assembly: breakdown of development/capital expenditure 1986–1991*

	1986 % DE	1987 % DE	1988 % DE	1986–88 % DE	1989 % DE	1990 % DE	1991 % DE	1989–91 % DE
Education: school buildings/furniture	24.2	–	–	2.9	2.1	24.6	56.5	34.3
Aid to town/area/village community projects	49.6	30.5	22.7	29.6	–	2.3	1.9	1.8
Sanitation	–	1.0	0.4	0.6	0.5	0.2	4.7	2.0
Markets	6.6	0.4	2.4	1.9	31.8	4.8	3.5	7.8
Roads	0.6	9.5	–	4.5	–	–	–	–
Water supply	–	0.8	–	0.4	–	–	–	–
Unspecified projects	18.2	57.8	75.5	60.0	–	–	24.2	9.6
'Low cost' staff housing	–	–	–	–	45.6	6.41	6.7	11.7
DA commercial farm	–	–	–	–	–	34.7	1.4	17.0
DA offices/stores	–	–	–	–	20.0	0.1	0.5	2.8
Purchase passenger bus	–	–	–	–	–	22.1	–	10.5
31 Dec. Womens Movement	–	–	–	–	–	4.8	0.6	2.5
Day care centre	0.8	–	–	0.1	–	–	–	–

Note: DE = development expenditure

Table 5.26. *Mamprusi District Council / East Mamprusi District Assembly: breakdown of development/capital expenditure 1986–1991*

	1986 % DE	1987 % DE	1988 % DE	1986–88 % DE	1989 % DE	1990 % DE	1991 % DE	1989–91 % DE
Education: school buildings/furniture	88.0	81.3	49.0	72.5	8.8	32.0	21.1	24.1
Aid to town/area/village community projects	–	3.5	12.2	5.6	5.2	–	40.8	18.2
Sanitation	–	–	36.5	10.8	–	–	–	–
Health	12.0	10.4	–	7.4	8.0	9.2	2.1	6.0
Water supply	–	2.2	–	1.3	11.7	22.0	11.5	16.0
Community centres	–	2.6	2.3	2.3	–	–	–	–
Markets	–	–	–	–	–	16.2	–	7.1
Purchase of tractor	–	–	–	–	66.3	20.6	24.5	28.5

Note: DE = development expenditure

popular conceptions of need than in East Akim, in so far as education, water and community projects did continue to receive significant proportions of the development budget. Nevertheless they were hardly top priorities, and the areas of health and road repairs received little or nothing. And, as in East Akim, the development budget itself must be judged in relation to the overall pattern of Assembly spending. Decisions had been taken which had allowed spending on the purchase and running costs of vehicles both commercial and administrative to reach three times that of the *total* development budget, an amount still increasing in 1992, under pressure from the new District Secretary.

In both Districts, therefore, most of the leading popular development priorities as revealed in the mass survey – road repairs and improvements, sanitation and water supplies, health, electrification – had little or nothing spent on them after 1989. Education, perhaps, was the only popular need which received significant although erratic proportions of the development budget in both districts, either through direct allocations or through the help given to self-help projects for construction or repair of school buildings.

In the case of education, however, it should be noted that much of the education spending was driven, not by local demands but by a central government policy imposed upon the districts. During its 'revolutionary' phase, the PNDC (with strong donor support) had decided upon (and implemented without adequate resource planning) a radical restructuring of the education system.[87] Its main features were the upgrading of the old middle schools into junior secondary schools (JSS), which could offer a more 'practical' or vocational education and simultaneously broaden the base of entry into the reformed, 'non-elitist' senior secondary schools. To do this, they required new workshops and laboratories. The DAs and the Ghana Education Service (GES) were pressured to exhort town and village committees to build their own JSS facilities, with the DAs contributing either directly or with local tax rebates for purchase of materials. In East Akim, for instance, the plan for the district's eighty-nine junior secondary schools had been drawn up by the GES District Director of Education. The enormous costs of this programme had in effect been pushed down on to the DAs and village communities throughout the land, with some help from the PAMSCAD community development funds. The major emphasis of the local development effort in education had therefore been dictated by central government policy, and its congruence with local perceptions of educational need was more apparent than real.

[87] Cobbe (1991), pp. 105–6.

Apart from education, many of the other post-1989 expenditures of the Assemblies can be linked to central initiatives or pressures. The new emphases on revenue generation and user charges, for instance, were strongly pushed by the government and owed much to theories of decentralisation currently fashionable in Western countries. Within a different institutional and economic setting they may indeed have made good sense. In Ghana they led many DAs into expensive schemes few of which corresponded to any popular need, or offered much prospect of commercial viability. Charging for sanitary services achieved little except the destruction of those few that existed.

The costs of decentralisation itself, such as setting up or improving offices, providing accommodation and furniture for civil servants and officials, also took a signficant proportion of the Assembly's budgets, and were in many respects an automatic consequence of government policies. It would be unfair to blame the DAs for incurring such expenditures, which were clearly necessary at the outset to create a new or expanded district-level administration in the rural areas. In the case of the forty-five new districts, the government recognised the need and provided special setting-up grants, although visits to some of the new districts confirmed that their lack of basic facilities continued to be desperate, and the situation of the administrators working in them was unenviable. In short, the government had under-estimated, as with other aspects of the decentralisation reform, the real costs of decentralisation. Even in 'old' districts of the type considered in this study, it was not sensible that the districts themselves had to allocate large proportions of scarce resources to administrative setting-up costs. The Assemblies must, nevertheless, take some of the responsibility for a misallocation of resources, in so far as the District Secretaries forced through unnecessarily extravagant expenditures in this area.

An overall assessment of the responsiveness of the policies and institutional outputs of the two District Assemblies would not, therefore, rate them very highly. Any explanation of this rather disappointing outcome would seem to lie in the area of institutional relationships rather than in a failure of democratic representation as such. On the participation side of the equation, the Assemblies had been relatively successful in involving the mass of rural citizens, and elected Assembly members had emerged who were genuinely representative of their communities and on the whole worked hard and represented their constituents' needs as vociferously as they could. The major problem facing Assembly members was their relative inability to translate demands into institutional action – a problem with both external and internal dimensions.

On the one hand, the structure of decentralisation meant that the ability of the Assemblies to mobilise the actions or resources of other departments and agencies, nominally decentralised to the district level, was in practice severely limited. Such co-operation was particularly crucial in the areas which most concerned the rural population – roads, water, electricity – where the Assemblies did not have the resources or the expertise to achieve very much in isolation. In the case of major roads (which were a burning issue in East Mamprusi) it was a case of persuading the crisis- ridden Ghana Highways Authority to take action, something which only happened if enormous political pressure from the centre could be applied. Even feeder roads were the responsibility of another ministry, the Department of Feeder Roads, which demanded that they be paid cash for the costs of the fuel and wages of a grader machine sent to do a rough (and always inadequate and temporary) repair of local laterite roads. Similarly, electrification by its very nature required joint action between the national authority and local communities. In the case of water, much could have been done locally but in the Northern Region responsibility for a rural water supplies programme had been virtually handed over to an externally funded, integrated regional development agency with its own parallel administrative structure – the Northern Region Rural Integrated Prgramme (NORRIP). This agency was engaged in a massive borehole sinking programme, which required consultation with and minimum contributions from the communities it was servicing. Its work, although extremely effective, nevertheless by-passed the DA system totally and was a living contradiction of the decentralisation policy.

On the other hand, not all the blame can be put on the external agencies. In the cases of both feeder roads and electrification, action was conditional upon specific community contributions, in line with the new economic doctrines of 'cost recovery' from beneficiaries. Villages which wanted electricity had to pay for the poles and low-density transformers, just as they had to pay for their feeder roads to be repaired.[88] A District Assembly which really wanted to prioritise these areas could have helped to fund such projects, perhaps on a matching basis. Instead, villagers were told to rely on 'self-help', and it was little wonder, therefore, that such large proportions of the population were disillusioned with the record of the Assembly and sceptical of the purposes of local taxation. The root problem was the failure of elected representatives to establish

---

[88] In practice, this meant that larger towns near the main roads were the most likely to obtain electricity.

sufficient control over actual spending patterns and priorities. This also was a product of the structure of decentralisation itself, in so far as central government policies were still determining large areas of spending, which when combined with the unrestrained behaviour of the District Secretaries at local level, left little room for democratically responsive spending decisons.

Process

The process element of performance concerns the extent to which the procedures by which a government authority deals with members of the public are regarded as fair, legal and transparent. To some extent it is connected to the legitimacy of the process by which the government institutions themselves were created and defined (e.g. elections, boundaries). It is also concerned with the procedures by which decisons to collect and allocate resouces are made.

The elections for the new Assemblies followed novel procedures and attracted, as indicated earlier, high participation rates. In both districts the majority of respondents (74 per cent) felt that the elections had been fair, although 17.5 per cent gave a 'don't know' response to this question, indicating some degree of caution about expressing an opinion on the subject.

An assessment of how District Assembly officers and representatives dealt with the public is hampered by the very small numbers of respondents who had actually contacted a councillor or been to a district or other government office. Of the 12 per cent of respondents who had contacted their Assembly member, half were prepared to say that he or she had not been very helpful, which is not a very good performance rating, and probably reflects the generally perceived impotence of Assembly members when it came to actually providing answers to specific complaints. A much larger proportion of community leaders in the elite survey (40 per cent) had contacted a councillor, and of those only 21 per cent had found them unhelpful, confirming the more frequent and more intimate ties between elected members and community 'elites'. Of the 28 per cent of elite respondents who said they had visited the District Assembly offices to raise a community issue, the majority were satisfied. This was probably because any delegation of this sort would have been dealt with by the DAO and/or the District Secretary.

With regard to the question of public acceptance of the procedures by which 'resource decisions' on taxation or the allocation of Assembly spending were taken, the evidence from political behaviour is clearer. The hope that representative democracy would improve the performance of local government in 'process' terms was only partially fulfilled. The principle of community-based self-help did not fit easily with the institution of representative district government, in so far as it undermined the legitimacy of district taxation and raised irreconcilable differences in the procedures for allocating very limited resources. Rural communities within a district did not automatically accept as fair or 'rational' the procedures by which projects were allocated to one community rather than another, even after open discussion in the Assembly.

In the first place were the problems caused by the pressures on Assembly members to act as delegates for their communities. The principle of 'non-party' democracy, whilst defensible in terms of community politics, had a negative impact on the processes of democratic decision-making and scrutiny at the district level in so far as it reinforced the delegate character of elected members. It made it difficult for members to find a basis for allocating resources or criticising policy which could not be dismissed as 'special pleading'. The government was not unaware of this problem, since it frequently justified its appointment of one-third of Assembly members on the grounds that it was necessary to balance the pressures of special pleading from elected members with a 'rational' or 'district level' perspective, which was more likely to come from members who did not have an electorate to please.[89] (This did not, however, prevent some appointed members from being identified with their 'home towns' in the district.)

Secondly, as indicated earlier, elected members found it hard to justify the legitimacy of district taxation when their only argument was that the community would receive a direct return on its contributions. For most members, this implied link could never be demonstrated, and their constituents could then accuse them of breaking their promises. The problem with resorting to the 'general interest' argument lay in the scale or size of the districts; they were too big for community politics but too small to dispose of significant development capacity such as might have been located at the more remote (and hence less contested) regional level. From the point of view of individual communities, the district was just as much a remote and abstract interest as Accra or the national government. In 1991, the amounts collected in basic rates showed that in East Akim only around 12 per cent of adults had paid the tax, and in East Mamprusi only 14 per cent. Clearly the legitimacy of local taxation had not improved on that of colonial times.

---

[89] Ghana (1991), p. 15.

CONCLUDING REMARKS

When the elected District Assemblies took over from the District Councils in 1989, they were the beneficiaries of a much wider array of powers, including control over a radically deconcentrated civil service machine and increased tax resources, than any previous form of district government in Ghana. How did their performance compare overall with the previous institutions of local government?

In the two 'average' districts studied, spending on development or capital projects did increase, both in per capita terms and as a proportion of total expenditure, although recurrent expenditure still accounted at the end of 1991 for around 85 per cent of the Assemblies' actual outturn. But service provision clearly declined under the impact of a nationally imposed policy on staff retrenchments and the local crisis in salary payments. Although no comparable data is available for the country as a whole, case studies from other regions of Ghana suggest that these outcomes were not untypical.[90] Patterns of spending in the two districts also changed, much of the increase in the development budget going into either centrally determined policy areas or into projects and services with an expected revenue return. There is little evidence that these new policies either succeeded in creating real returns or responded more closely to popular demands.

The mechanisms of democratic accountability did have a significant impact at both the popular and institutional levels. The mass of ordinary rural dwellers – 'the poor and the unschooled' – were able to participate in many of the political activities linked to the Assembly system. Elected councillors for the most did try to represent their very small electorates, although they were often disproportionately from the better educated groups in society. But in so far as councillors fulfilled official injunctions to work actively with their communities, which was true of between a third and a half of the two Assemblies, there was a paradoxical outcome. The more councillors acted as community representatives, the greater were the difficulties experienced by the Assembly in its role as an

---

[90] A study of seven selected Assemblies in the Ashanti Region showed that there was no consistent pattern of increase in the percentage of expenditure allocated to development between 1989 and 1992, and the cumulative proportion over the four-year period ranged from 7 per cent to 20 per cent, with one special case of 28 per cent – the Obuasi District, home of Ashanti Goldfields, from whom it received substantial assistance (Acheampong (1995) p. 223). The Assemblies of Ho and Keta districts (Volta Region) showed little change in the proportionate size of their development expenditures, with averages of 14.8 per cent and 23 per cent respectively over the period 1986–92. Ayee argues, however, that the actual output of the Assemblies declined compared to the 1982–8 period (Ayee (1996), pp. 42–3).

institution for mobilisation and allocation of development resources. The acceptability or legitimacy of local taxation did not improve – indeed it may have deteriorated as a result of government pressure to intensify local revenue collection. It must be admitted, of course, that the long history of local government failure and corruption in Ghana presented the Assemblies with a Herculean task in attempting to restore public confidence. Many officials at both national and local levels privately accepted that the main local tax – the 'basic rate' or poll-tax – was both ineffective and counterproductive and should probably have been abandoned.

The impact of the Assemblies on the policy-making and administrative performance of district government was less positive. It was in the area of budgetary control and monitoring that democratic accountability faced its toughest challenge. The Assemblies were continuing to operate within a structure of central political, administrative and financial controls of a quite fundamental kind. It was not for want of trying that members were unable to challenge the power of District Secretaries or of the Ministry of Finance and the civil service hierarchies; or that they were unable to co-ordinate the work of other executive agencies at the district level, as the decentralisation reform had intended.

Democratisation of district government in Ghana between 1989 and 1992 did therefore achieve some success in political terms – as might have been predicted given the vigour of Ghanaian civil society. But the very success of this democratisation process produced deep frustrations at the institutional level, frustrations which were reflected in the only marginal improvements in development performance. These frustrations, as well as the lack of developmental output, in turn led to the apathy surrounding the second set of elections for the District Assemblies in April 1994.[91] As the government of Ghana was fully aware, lack of tangible development outputs in turn undermined the other mission of the Assemblies which was to create a more legitimate and responsive form of government at the local level. A common explanation of these difficulties, in Ghana as elsewhere, was to invoke the 'lack of resources'. Whilst it is true that the Assemblies did lack both the personnel and the financial resources adequately to fulfil all of their very broad functions, this was by no means the whole story. The Assemblies themselves failed to maximise the revenue sources available to them, and their actual

---

[91] Although it should also be acknowledged that the atmosphere in 1994 was still soured by the opposition boycott of the 1992 legislative elections, and their refusal to recognise the legitimacy of the presidential election. This stance was not moderated until after April 1994.

expenditure patterns frequently demonstrated a poor and erratic commitment to development and services.

An explanation of *why* the PNDC government failed to implement many of the legal and financial measures necessary for the success of the decentralisation reform must of course be sought at the level of national politics. First, the Ministry of Finance and the Office of the Head of the Civil Service were principally concerned to implement an Economic Recovery Programme most of whose requirements directly contradicted the provisions of the decentralisation programme. The Ministry of Local Government was not powerful enough to resist or change their failure to co-operate. The continuing role of the District Secretaries and the 'revolutionary organs' was linked to a political ambivalence within the PNDC itself. It would seem clear that once it had been decided that the Assemblies were no longer to be part of a new national system of PNDC-controlled 'people's democracy', certain elements in the PNDC lost interest in them. There was no longer a political pressure to bring the reform to fruition. There was also the uncomfortable fact that the Assemblies did come to represent a source of complaints, disgruntlement and criticism directed at the local agents of the regime.

The Assemblies continued therefore to be the subject of debate and conflict within the PNDC – a debate which obviously continued right through the drawing up of the 1992 Constitution and the transition to civil rule. Those fighting for the Assemblies managed to obtain a constitutional guarantee of their survival, a promise of greater resources through a District Assemblies Common Fund endowed with 5 per cent of national revenues, and a provision that the newly titled District Chief Executive should have to be approved by the Assembly. But the structural *role* of the government-appointed DCE continues unchanged, and the influence of the former 'people's democracy' faction within the NDC government is clearly visible in the continuing ban on party politics at District Assembly level.

The Ghanaian experience of decentralisation since 1989 highlights once again certain basic problems which have to be addressed in any decentralisation reform. First, accountability to locally elected officials cannot work properly unless the government is prepared to allow the decentralised authorities some genuine autonomy in the management of resources.

Secondly, the understandable fear of government that resources will be wasted or mismanaged (often coupled with the mistaken belief that decentralisation is a way of saving money when it in fact requires very considerable extra resources to set up properly) suggests very strongly that the functions and areas over which autonomy is to be granted should be realistically manageable. In other words, the problem in Ghana may have been the over-ambitious nature of the reform. The legal, financial and administrative implications of fully deconcentrating twenty-two line Ministries and agencies and putting them under the control of new and poorly staffed district authorities should have been considered long before the enactment of the Local Government Law of 1988, not five years afterwards.

In addition, the scope of the functions allocated to the Assemblies in relation to their size and resources almost guaranteed that large numbers of the electorate would be disappointed. Even if the Assemblies had made a better job of revenue collection, it was impossible that every community in the districts studied could have their demands for large-scale infrastructural and social development met. It is well known that the World Bank advised the Ghanaian government against creating larger numbers of smaller districts; but the view advanced here is the opposite, namely that autonomous local government is more likely to work at a very local and correspondingly modest level, concentrating on small-scale projects and services. The larger infrastructural developments (secondary schools, water, roads) would be better provided by well-funded regional authorities which in the Ghanaian context at least had always been the most effective levels of close administration until the District Assembly reform attempted to by-pass them.

On the evidence of this study, the potential for a vigorous local democracy exists in Ghana. But it is by no means clear that the districts as presently constituted can be a viable basis for both community-based politics *and* effective mobilisation and allocation of development resources. The ghost of district administration lives on.

6 Conclusions

The principal purpose of our investigations into democratic decentralisation in four different countries was to establish whether any relationship could be discerned between enhancements in popular participation, which occurred everywhere, and changes in the performance of governmental institutions. This naturally raises a larger question: if our data show differences in performance among different authorities in the same countries or among different forms of decentralised government in the four countries, how can they be explained? The differences among the decentralised authorities within each country have been discussed in Chapters 2, 3, 4 and 5. Here we summarise our findings on participation and performance for each country and then compare the patterns or configuration of factors associated with the various performance outcomes. With such a limited number of cases it is clearly not posssible to draw any statistical inferences. The purpose of the comparison is to establish whether there is any particular combination of variables associated with a particular outcome. We conclude by discussing the significance of these four experiences of democratic decentralisation for our understanding of the relationships between enhanced participation and decentralisation on the one hand, and institutional performance and good governance on the other.

ASSESSING PARTICIPATION

In all four countries popular participation was considerably enhanced. Table 6.1 summarises the data on electoral and non-electoral participation, using turnout figures and selected indicators from the mass surveys which were found to be most significant. Of particular interest are the levels of electoral participation which, compared to the turnout for local elections typical of Britain and the USA, were remarkably high.[1]

---

[1] Karnataka reached the higher levels more typical of Sweden or France; see Miller (1988) and Widdecombe (1986).

Even the rather low national figure of 35 per cent for Côte d'Ivoire concealed a very large difference between the big cities and the majority of rural communes in which the average turnout was 51.3 per cent, while in the four case studies the turnout in the 1990 multi-party elections ranged from 47 per cent to 70 per cent. Such rates of participation are strong evidence of the popular interest and enthusiasm which these reformed local government institutions aroused among local people, both when they were first inaugurated and in those circumstances when a second set of elections allowed the electorate to express their opinion of the first administration of elected politicians. In Côte d'Ivoire, for instance, 50 per cent of all incumbent mayors were replaced in 1990 and 37 per cent in 1996, whilst in Bangladesh around 90 per cent of all the directly elected sub-district chairmen lost their jobs in the 1990 elections.

The number of respondents in each country who claimed to have taken part in election campaigns was also remarkably high, but these figures probably reflect the rather broad understanding which people in both South Asia and West Africa had of the idea of 'participating in an election campaign'. In the Western world, campaigning usually means a rather formal set of activities organised by political parties such as canvassing or delivering leaflets. In both of the Asian cases respondents who had attended election meetings, become involved in processions or been touched by the election events in some way felt that they had 'participated' in the campaigns. In Côte d'Ivoire the impact of electoral conflict on small rural communities was to create factions based on personal or familial loyalties or competing sub-communities (such as quarters of the town). In such a context, to be identified or to identify oneself as the 'supporter' of a candidate was sufficient to make respondents feel that they had participated in the election, even without taking into the account the other activities and events of the election campaign itself. The same phenomenon occurred in Ghana where, although the District Assemblies were large authorities compared to the communes, no-party electoral competition was based at the ward level where up to five candidates could be competing for the votes of a village or group of villages. In the absence of the structuring which party organisation can provide (even when contests are mainly within the ruling party), and a very close level of representation – an average of 2,000 electors per representative – the Ghanaian local election campaigns were even more personalised than those in Côte d'Ivoire.

The numbers of people saying they had 'participated in election campaigns' in all four countries was therefore an indicator with very real local meanings; it showed the extent to which formal electoral competition had meshed with and even reinforced existing social conflicts and, in

Table 6.1. *Summary of measures of popular participation and relationships with elected councillors, by country.*[a]

Measure	Ghana	Côte d'Ivoire	Bangladesh Sub-District	Union	Karnataka District	Mandal
Electoral turnout (overall national %)	59	1990: 35	55	55	1987: 60	75
Turnout compared to previous elections?	Much better	Same overall, but better in case-studies	Little change	Little change	Better	Better
% participated in election campaign	19	26	31	38	25	23
Kind of competition	No-party, factional/ inter-personal	Multi-party but govt. dominated	Multi-party but govt. dominated		Strong two-party competitive system	
% contacted councillor	12	10	24[b]		6	16
% signed letter/petition	4	8	17[b]		20[b]	
% attended unofficial meeting	5	10	13[b]		14[b]	
% attended official meeting	32	18	24[b]		17[b]	
% can name councillor	83	42	91	90	55	75
% say councillor held at least 1 meeting	57	25	50	62	41	63

[a] The figures represent the aggregates of the case-studies for each country, or national level figures where relevant
[b] Only aggregate figures available for Sub-District/Union or District/Mandal

the process, involved the loyalty, interest and/or support of significant proportions of the electorate. There was no guarantee, unfortunately, that such enthusiasm would be translated into more accountable or better-performing local government.

Non-electoral forms of participation were organised for the purposes of analysis into two main categories: first, direct or proactive participation by individuals in the political process, and second, the quality of relationships between representatives and their constituents (Table 6.1). The first category – individual participation – is covered by the three indicators giving the percentage of respondents in the mass survey who had personally contacted their elected representative, signed a letter or petition or attended a political meeting (a meeting to discuss or pursue a collective issue of local interest). These scores give some indication of the extent to which people took advantage of the opportunities offered by the new forms of democratic decentralised government to interact with and make demands upon those institutions.

The second category is covered by indicators based on popular perceptions of elected representatives which measure the extent to which representatives were known by and had regular contacts with their constituents. The first indicator in this group shows how many people could recall going to an 'official' meeting – that is, a meeting which had been organised by an elected representative, either as a regular 'report back' session or as a public meeting to consult constituents. (It also served as an additional indicator of individual participation.) In some cases these meetings were an institutionalised part of the local government system, such as the Gram Sabhas in Karnataka, or the legally prescribed reports on the proceedings of the Assembly by Assembly members in Ghana. In Côte d'Ivoire, because councillors did not have a particular constituency as such, the question referred to meetings of notables and party leaders which had long operated as organs of deliberation and village governance, and through which councillors could have maintained their links with the community. The second indicator is a simple test of how well elected representatives were known by the population, and the third aggregates answers to the question of how frequently respondents thought their representative organised meetings with the population. The figure given is the combined percentage of respondents who gave frequencies ranging from at least one such meeting since the date of the election to as much as once per month. This figure also reveals the obverse, namely the proportion of respondents who simply said that their representative had *never* organised a meeting.

The indicators summarised in Table 6.1 do not, of course, tell the whole story of the impact of democratisation on popular participation in the four countries. As was shown in Chapters 2 to 5, the surveys covered many other questions, which were supplemented with a wide range of other material relating to levels of individual participation, the social character of participation and the role of elected representatives.

In Ghana, individual participation in activities aimed at contacting and pressuring the District Assembly was relatively limited. To some extent (given Ghana's political history) the surprisingly low percentages for attending meetings or signing petitions may have been the result of eleven years of military rule under the watchful eye of the regime's local 'revolutionary organs' – the Committees for the Defence of the Revolution. This experience could have induced what Jerry Rawlings himself had attacked as a 'culture of silence'. But such figures must also be seen in the context of the continuing vibrancy of village-level institutions, as demonstrated by the capacity of many local communities to organise 'self-help' projects. Most contacts with the District Assembly or its representatives were in fact mediated through village-level institutions, community leaders and collective events such as officially organised public meetings. This finding is confirmed by the indicators for the second category of participation which show that Assembly members were well known to their constituents, and their contacts with local communities, using these mediating mechanisms, were relatively intense particularly in the southern District Assembly.

The no-party, government-financed electoral system had on the whole been quite successful in ensuring the election of locally based, respected members of local communities as Assembly representatives with (as demonstrated by the electoral figures) widespread popular support. Many (although by no means all) of the Assembly members had also been quite successful in working with their communities to develop local self-help projects. But the very success of this aspect of the Ghanaian democratisation reforms led to popular frustration and disillusion with the Assemblies, in so far as it highlighted the contradiction between the member's role as community delegate/development animator and his or her loyalty to the District Assembly as an institution.

The official hope that the District Assemblies would fulfil the aims of the 'Rawlings revolution' – to bring 'power to the people' and incorporate hitherto excluded classes of the population into the political process – was only partially achieved. Elected representatives on the Assemblies still tended to come disproportionately from the male, educated and professional strata of society – although not as dramatically as might have been expected relative to both the known preference of Ghanaian rural voters for 'educated' representatives and the almost universal pattern established by comparative political study. The case-study Assemblies had a distinctly dualistic membership, in which whilst 56 per cent and 74 per cent respectively of the elected members had secondary or higher levels of education, the remainder tended to be uneducated or poorly educated farmers. But the elite character of the Assemblies was substantially boosted by the government nominees who formed one-third of the membership. The most that can be said is that the Assemblies did give access and representation to small numbers of locally based and uneducated farmers, traders and artisans who had previously been excluded from politics at the national level even in previous democratic interludes.

The Assembly system had a more positive effect on the character of individual participation in non-electoral, village-level and contacting activies. Those who had engaged in contacting their representative or had attended official and unofficial meetings were fairly typical of the general population in terms of their age, occupation and educational level. As regards the 'gender balance', men were strongly dominant in contacting but less so in the other activities. In this category of participation (as in the others) there were also important differences between the more developed, commercialised, Christian area of southern Ghana and the remoter, poorer and more Islamicised north. In the north, women participated hardly at all in any of the activities and even the men who participated were generally more educated. In the south, women did participate in meetings (particularly the Unit Committees) but very rarely engaged in contacting activities. It may be concluded that the formal representative democracy of the Assemblies militated against women engaging in contacting or pressuring activities, particularly where pre-existing social and political structures were strongly exclusionary. On the other hand, where women had begun to successfully participate it was through an aspect of the 'Rawlings revolution' which in effect undermined the popular democratic character of the Assembly reform. The strength of the revolutionary women's association was reflected in the dominance of the local Unit Committees by the younger and better educated elements in local society, including better educated women.

Individual participation in contacting and pressuring activities was similarly limited in Côte d'Ivoire although, as in Ghana, if the figures are interpreted in their local context there were some unexpected results. The communes in Côte d'Ivoire were small-scale authorities; three of the case studies were, in Ghanaian terms, little more than large villages. One might have expected, therefore, at least levels of knowledge of council affairs and perhaps contacts with council politicians more typical of a grassroots institution. In fact, contacting was restricted to the small minorities familiar to students of comparative local government, as was participation in both unofficial and official meetings.

Such levels of individual participation can be linked to the apparent failure of the communes' elected representatives to establish any meaningful role in or contact with their local communities. They did not hold meetings with the population and were not well known to the electorate. The figures for attendance at 'official' meetings in Côte d'Ivoire, as noted, relate to local forms of governance (*comités de quartier*) that predate the communes and were associated with traditional or former ruling party structures. In the southern communes a more significant number of respondents had had some involvement with these bodies, but

Conclusions 277

there is no evidence that councillors used them as consultative sounding boards as happened with the equivalent bodies in Ghana.

In so far as commune councils were the product of lists deliberately put together by the political entrepreneurs who hoped to become mayors, it would be unrealistic, if not inappropriate, to analyse them in terms of whether they succeeded in 'representing' externally defined disadvantaged or vulnerable groups. The lists were put together using a multiplicity of overlapping criteria – geographical or communal representation, interest groups, political loyalty, high social status – none of which placed any premium on social *dis*advantage. Surprisingly enough, then, the composition of the four case-study councils in terms of occupation, age and education was even more dualistic than that of the Ghana District Assemblies. Whilst elite occupations were very over-represented, the commune councils did bring into public life quite significant numbers of uneducated, low-status, younger people who had hitherto been completely excluded from politics. (Women, as in Ghana, were barely represented at 4 per cent of the membership.) At the same time the communes continued to embody a very strongly rooted social expectation that effective representation of a community's interests, and its ability to advance its development, were best assured by electing the town's 'cadres', i.e. its successful, well-educated sons and daughters.

Those few citizens (mainly men) who had engaged in contacting or pressuring activities were not significantly different in socio-economic terms from the general male population except that the primary educated were over-represented and the very youngest (under 30s) under-represented – as might be expected in a society where age is still respected and most people do not finish their schooling until well into their twenties. The local or neighbourhood committees and other bodies, in which more significant numbers of the population had participated, were much more effective in involving ordinary people in local governance. The differences between the northern and southern communes were, however, very marked, reflecting the same broad cultural and socio-economic differences as those found in Ghana: on the one hand, in the highly commercialised, older cocoa-growing communities with multi-ethnic populations, high levels of education and close links with regional urban agglomerations, wealthy farmers and businesspeople tended to participate disproportionately. In the poorer, more remote societies of the north, on the other hand, with much lower levels of Western education and a long history of outward migration, the very tiny numbers of primary educated people living and working in the locality were inevitably more active in participatory activities.

In spite of differences between north and south, however, it may be concluded, on the basis of both the survey data and the institutional case-history material, that generally the communes were effectively run by, and accurately perceived by the population as dominated by the mayor and his group of elite supporters. Virtually all respondents in the mass survey could name their mayor! Although direct popular participation and representation in official bodies had increased by comparison with its virtual absence under the previous, administratively dominated prefectoral system, it remained limited in both numbers and scope (apart from electoral participation) and showed a surprising lack of contact between citizens and bodies endowed with power at the level of single communities. In so far as the communes did not provide for any institutionalised form of report-back or consultation and councillors were not elected for a particular constituency, this was perhaps a function of the institutional structure itself. Another factor, however, was that the new communes were having to confront a legacy of elite dominance and public quiescence created by thirty years of single-party rule which the mayoral system reinforced rather than challenged.

The figures for Karnataka (India) show that non-electoral forms of participation were generally slightly below those for Bangladesh, although they were reasonably strong by comparison with many industrialised democracies. The difference with Bangladesh is partly explained by the greater appetite for democratic participation in the latter country, after years of military rule – in contrast to India, where opportunities for participation had always been substantial and 'normal'. But a smaller proportion of respondents in Karnataka were able to name their elected representatives than in Bangladesh or, indeed, Ghana.

This comparison should not, however, obscure the fact that a very substantial minority of Karnataka respondents had personally contacted councillors and (less often) bureaucrats. Smaller numbers were active in associations. Both types of activities increased as a result of decentralisation – in Karnataka as in our other three countries.

Members of Mandal Councils near the local level were legally required to hold mass meetings in every village in their constituencies twice per year – to discuss council policies and to consult villagers on which people deserved to receive benefits from anti-poverty programmes. Our surveys of villagers and numerous interviews with councillors indicated, however, that the latter soon found popular criticisms at such meetings unendurable because of the assertiveness of citizens, and they largely abandoned them after a year or two. Citizens also found councillors reluctant to consult them in other ways, although when the opportunity arose, the popular response was good.

We found high levels of participation by members of vulnerable groups in Karnataka. The Scheduled Castes (ex-untouchables) exhibited levels of political awareness and of electoral and other forms of participation that usually fell just short of those in a cross-section of society. This owed something to the fact that roughly 20 per cent of council seats were reserved for members of these groups. But it owed more to a political awakening that had occurred among them over many years of representative politics in India, and to efforts by political leaders in Karnataka to mobilise the lower castes in the period after 1972. However, Scheduled Caste councillors were able to make only a minimal impact on District Councils and virtually no impact on Mandal Councils near the local level where landowning castes still tend strongly to dominate social life, despite decades of power-sharing between dominant and low-status groups in state-level politics in Karnataka. Councils at both levels tended to be controlled by members of the landowning and slightly less prosperous castes.

Women there displayed reasonably high levels of political awareness, and engaged in moderate-to-high levels of participation; 25 per cent of council seats were reserved for them, but on the councils they participated and accomplished less than did Scheduled Castes councillors. What little they did accomplish tended to occur in the somewhat more cosmopolitan atmosphere on the District Councils, rather than lower down at the Mandal level. There were signs, however, that over the longer term they might exceed the Scheduled Castes in participation rates and effectiveness as councillors.

Bangladesh witnessed higher levels of participation in election campaigns, and in most other types of activities than the other three countries studied here. More respondents there were able to name their elected representatives than elsewhere, although that is partly explained by the fact that those who represented them on higher-level sub-District Councils were the (usually long-standing) heads of local Union Councils. But these findings indicate that even amid the extremes of poverty and illiteracy, substantial political participation and awareness can exist and grow in response to decentralisation.

Councillors tended strongly to be drawn from elite strata of society – indeed, they were usually the same people who had been in place for long periods, since the Union Councils predated the decentralisation of power to the sub-district level in 1985. There were no reservations, as in India, for people from poorer groups, since the military government's main aim in decentralising was to create a mechanism for cultivating support from powerful groups at lower levels, rather than to promote democracy.

This thrust towards the co-optation of elites undermined hopes that decentralisation might help to alleviate poverty – partly by ensuring elite dominance of the councils and partly by focusing councillors' attentions on the opportunities that close ties to central authorities offered, which weakened accountability to the mass of poorer voters. The weakness of such accountability mechanisms made decentralised institutions less responsive to the felt needs of ordinary folk than was seen in Karnataka. This caused citizens to conclude that their quite substantial and growing participation in the political process had produced only very modest gains. It reminds us again that participation alone, in the absence of accountability, can deliver relatively little.

Seats were reserved for women on the lower-level Union Councils, but they were filled by appointment at the chairman's discretion – in contrast to Karnataka where women were elected in their own right. This nullified any benefit that might have flowed from such reservations, since such women seldom even spoke in council meetings, and when they did they invariably backed the chairman. So while women in Bangladesh participated in decentralised politics more extensively than the poor, such participation yielded very few benefits.

In comparing the record of democratic decentralisation schemes in encouraging participation by hitherto excluded or marginalised groups, an important contrast must be drawn between the Asian and African countries. People in those countries have different perspectives on what constitutes success in this field. India, and to a lesser extent Bangladesh, have a long history of experimentation with affirmative action to incorporate the poor and the excluded into politics, and there is a political discourse on poverty and related issues. The success of democratic local government is therefore often measured by the extent to which local elite dominance has been challenged or mitigated by participation of the poor, lower castes or women; one report noted that the 'danger' of decentralisation was that power might 'fall into the hands of the wrong people'.[2] In Africa, on the other hand, such issues are not prominent in the political discourse. On the contrary, there is a general cultural expectation that elite groups – the 'successful sons and daughters' who have left to work in good jobs in the urban areas – have a duty to participate in and help with the development of their home towns or districts. Ghana and Côte d'Ivoire are typical of this in that the success of the new local governments is frequently discussed in terms of whether it has attracted 'high quality' candidates to be elected councillors or village committee members. To be dominated by poor people of no influence or standing would lead to such institutions being regarded as of

---

[2] CIRDAP (1992), p. 105. See also Webster's extensive work on this issue in West Bengal: Webster (1994).

little consequence, or as failures. Such attitudes are a practical acknowledgement of the realities of development politics in clientelistic political systems.

ASSESSING PERFORMANCE

In each country we assessed the performance of the decentralised system in very broad terms according to whether it represented an improvement on the previous system and scored positively on our performance measures, particularly responsiveness. This enabled us to 'rate' the outcome of each reform up to the given date (1992) as, on balance, either good, mixed or poor, or, in other terms, as successful, partially successful or unsuccessful.

The Karnataka District Councils emerged with the most clearly positive rating. The output of development projects at the local level improved considerably and the responsiveness of both the District and Mandal Councils to popular felt needs was high. Not were only projects implemented and services provided more expeditiously but the councils' priorities as reflected in expenditure allocations were largely congruent with the expressed needs of most villagers. Systems of early warning against natural disasters improved markedly, and absenteeism amongst employees decreased. The emphasis of development efforts shifted to infrastructural micro-projects such as wells, roads, clinics and school buildings. Only in the case of special programmes directed at identified social groups, such as the obligation to devote 18 per cent of the council's resources for the benefit of Scheduled Castes, was there a slippage in performance. Under the process dimension, greater transparency led to a popular belief that corruption had increased, although, according the evidence of institutional 'insiders', it had in fact decreased.

The outcome in Bangladesh was mixed. On the one hand, development outputs undoubtedly increased compared to the previous forms of administration. As in Karnataka, the major emphasis shifted to micro-level construction projects such as roads, schools and wells. On the other hand, however, whilst there was a reasonable but somewhat ambiguous correspondence between popular perceptions of need and outputs, responsiveness and process considerations were marred by elite bias, the domination of patronage considerations, extensive corruption and electoral manipulation. Vulnerable groups received few of the resources provided. Much of this was due to the efforts of the military regime to co-opt council leaders into its national party-building exercise.

Both of the African cases presented considerable ambiguities in terms of performance assessment. In Côte d'Ivoire two clear periods emerged in the record of the communes. During the initial phase (1985–9), outputs clearly improved compared to the previous sub-Prefectoral administration. But from 1989 onwards, outputs collapsed disastrously, and responsiveness can only be rated as generally poor throughout. The commune executives tended to favour infrastructural projects such as secondary schools or commune offices ('town halls') which were high-profile but not necessarily highly valued by ordinary farmers, the poor and younger age groups. In addition it was clear that the most strongly felt popular needs were often beyond the capacity or competence of the communes as authorities to provide. In process terms, the impact of *communalisation* was weak in so far as local citizens still tended to see local development policies as decided by an elite group led by the mayor. As in Bangladesh, this was linked to the national political role and status of the locally elected leaders.

In the case of Ghana, although development expenditures did increase slightly after democratisation both in absolute and proportionate terms, the overall performance rating was low, for several reasons. First, there was not a marked improvement compared to the previous form of administration; recurrent expenditure continued to account for the major part – around 85 per cent – of total District Assembly expenditures, and per capita development expenditure remained derisory. Much of the improvement at local level in fact came from voluntary or local initiatives.

Second, responsiveness levels were very poor. The increases in District Assembly-funded outputs were mainly in areas which bore little or no relation to popular preferences for road repairs, health facilities, water supplies and electricity. Instead, they tended to reflect either government pressure to mobilise local revenue sources, leading to expenditure on commercial transport services, farming or manufacturing enterprises and markets; or they reflected centrally determined programmes and priorities, the costs of which had been pushed down on to the districts. One of these was the government's national educational reform which required the construction of junior secondary schools throughout the country; another was the cost of office buildings and equipment, official housing and the like. Political corruption in the shape of excessive transport, travel and entertainment expenditures was again linked to the pressures on – and lack of local control over – the government-appointed District Assembly bosses, the District Secretaries.

These different performance assessments are confirmed quite clearly if we compare the responses to a common question asked in the mass survey in each country. After asking respondents to talk about what they saw as the 'most important needs of the people in their area' we asked:

Table 6.2. *Comparing popular performance assessments*

Country	Outputs better than previous form of govt.?	Responsiveness?	Authority	Say council can satisfy needs (positive responses) (%)
India (Karnataka)	yes	good	District	69 (N=384)
			Mandal	66 "
Bangladesh	yes	medium	Sub-District	36 (N=384)
			Union	37 "
Cote d'Ivoire	only until 1989	poor	Commune	36 (N=500)
Ghana	marginal improvement	poor	District Assembly	18 (N=624)

'In your view is the [name of council or councils] able to satisfy any of these needs?' This was intended to elicit a 'general feeling' about the performance of the relevant councils, to use alongside more specific topics. Table 6.2 shows the percentage of respondents who said that the council could satisfy their expressed needs either a lot or to some extent – i.e. all those who felt able to give a positive response.

Overall, it should also be noted that it was only in Karnataka that some modest success was recorded in redistributing development benefits to poorer or marginal social groups. In the other three, it could be argued that the allocation of central government funds to the new authorities did benefit remoter and rural areas, and that there was therefore some performance achievement in reducing spatial or inter-jurisdictional inequalities. In Ghana, however, the effect was almost entirely achieved through subdivision or fragmentation, in other words spreading more or less the same amount of jam more thinly. In this respect the cases confirm that decentralisation is likely to have only marginal impact on existing patterns of uneven development, unless substantial central resources are put into equalisation programmes (as in West Bengal).

EXPLAINING PERFORMANCE

As indicated in our analytical model in Chapter 1, we did not expect that differences in performance would be explicable solely in terms of participation levels. It is also necessary to consider the impact of other factors such as the socio-political context, resource constraints and the political and administrative features of decentralised structures themselves.

First, as the Ghana case shows, high levels of public interest in council affairs and relatively good levels of contacts between elected members and their constitutents are not necessarily translated into better performance. In Ghana, poor performance is most plausibly explained by the political context and by institutional factors. The military regime there was unwilling to relinquish political control of the districts, and at the outset of the reform clearly viewed the District Assemblies as a form of 'substitute' participation which would not threaten the central government's grip on power. This problem was compounded by the government's commitment to a Structural Adjustment Programme (SAP), the requirements of which meant that the Ministry of Finance and the head of the civil service were simply unprepared to devolve financial planning and control and manpower allocations to the districts.

The resulting inability of the Assemblies to participate fully in policy-making and control of implementation and to establish the accountability of government-appointed officials and civil servants to elected representatives produced low levels of responsiveness. The elected leader of the Assembly, the Presiding Member, had no executive powers and was indeed excluded from the Executive Committee. In addition, the Assemblies lacked both the political and the legal capacity to establish control over the field agencies of the supposedly deconcentrated ministries. This meant that whatever their level of awareness of popular demands, they often lacked the means to translate those demands into outputs in such areas as roads, water supplies or electricity. The government was to blame for much of this in so far as it failed fully to implement its own decentralisation programme and because it put an unaccountable official in charge of the overall administration of each district.

Resource constraints, however, were also partly to blame in so far as the government under-estimated the costs of decentralisation (or was not willing to fund them). It was perhaps over-ambitious to combine the setting up of the elected Assemblies with a radical programme of deconcentration which was not well established (in many cases, hardly begun) before the Assemblies took up their responsibilities. Sufficient qualified staff to fill the posts theoretically required were simply not available (or were unwilling to be transferred) in spite of the efforts of UNDP mobile training teams. On the contrary, the reform was implemented simultaneously with a centrally inspired attempt to impose policies of staff retrenchment on the new authorities (another feature of the SAP). In spite of some government programmes to compensate for these costs and to allocate additional ceded revenues, the Assemblies were therefore forced into: (a) increased spending in areas which were not congruent with popular needs and (b) local revenue-raising campaigns which further damaged responsiveness. Thus even though outputs increased slightly, they were not 'valued' by the electorate. The only area where more popular projects increased – the village self-help movement – did reflect the relative strength of democratisation measures at the ward and village levels. But these kinds of outputs were regarded by electors, with some justification, as not attributable to the performance of the Assemblies themselves. On the contrary, they were regarded as a measure of how much the Assemblies had let them down.

In Côte d'Ivoire, on the other hand, the legacy of single-party dominance and the repression of civil society made itself felt at the very first stage in the participation process: the relationship between elected representatives and the electorate. Here, as the figures show, the failure of elected representatives to establish close relationships of accountability between themselves and the electorate was one of the most distinctive features of the Ivorian system. Given the small-scale and community-based character of the communes, this was one of our more surprising results.

That this is the main explanation of poor performance on the responsiveness dimension is clearly demonstrated by the fact that at the institutional level elected officials did establish good control over the administration. The legal powers of the commune executives – the mayor and assistant mayors – were very much put into practice, as demonstrated by their 'hands on' management role in the execution of budgets, and the power of the mayor over commune staff, including the seconded civil servants. The formal power of mayors was often reinforced by their political and social status; nationally, around 40 per cent of all mayors also held office as parliamentary deputies or ministers, and seventy-four out of the 125 provincial mayors in 1988 resided in Abidjan.[3]

Nevertheless, because the mayors were elite politicians geared to working through national networks, and the structure of the commune system itself required them to report closely to supervisory bureaucracies and centralised accounting systems, their responsiveness to the electorate was bound to be weak. This was compounded by the weak role played by non-executive councillors on the commune Council, and by the impact of the single list electoral system.

The commune Council was simply the winning list, normally put together by the mayor and his supporters. With the opposition *excluded*

---

[3] See Chapter 4, p. 171.

from the Council by definition, the executive was in effect reporting to a body of supporters and clients who were unlikely to engage in serious questioning of their policies, unless factional rivalries emerged during the course of the mandate. The single list also meant that councillors did not have to report to a particular constituency, and the exclusion of losers reinforced an uncooperative attitude towards the commune on the part of those sections of the community who had not voted for the mayor's list. The responsiveness of commune policies therefore depended very much on the political sensitivity and the consensual or representative inclinations of the mayor and assistant mayors. Few of them performed impressively.

Another factor underlying lack of responsiveness and weak accountability was to be found in the formal structure of the decentralised system. As in Ghana (although for different reasons), the communes did not have the powers or the administrative capacity to take action in many of the policy areas such as road-building, agricultural marketing, employment opportunities or obtaining TV reception which most concerned local residents. These were matters which required action by central government or other agencies over which the communes had no call; but this was not always understood or appreciated by the public.

Poor performance on the output effectiveness dimension was also connected to resource constraints of the most severe kind, which were undeniably the cause of the near-total collapse of the communes' development output after 1990. These restraints were imposed by central government as the result of a national crisis in public finances; but their impact was made worse by (a) the still-centralised fiscal and financial systems and (b) the communes' lack of capacity or willingness to compensate by mobilising local resources. It should be noted, however, that even when resources were available in the 1985–9 period, the communes' responsiveness performance was not high. If they had had the same quality of local democratic/participatory traditions as those of Ghana, they might have managed to survive the crisis a little better – although given the extremely small scale and lack of autonomous viability of the rural communes, this argument should not be taken too far.

With the Bangladesh decentralised authorities, any explanation of their performance record must start with the objective fact that real resource allocations to the new authorities were substantially increased by central government.[4] This, together with the relatively healthy figures

---

[4] Blair (1989).

for political knowledge, levels of electoral and other participation and contacts between councillors and the electorate would suggest that performance should have been good.[5] But the intervening institutional factors once again demonstrate that neither plentiful resources alone nor high participation scores automatically translate into better performance. The responsiveness of the Bangladesh authorities was flawed in many respects and the popular assessment of their overall capacity to provide development was distinctly lukewarm.

One explanation at the institutional level concerns administrative capacity; as in Ghana, the sub-District Councils were created hastily at a level where deconcentrated offices of central departments had not previously been established. Large numbers of inexperienced or under-qualified staff were recruited, whilst others were transferred to postings which were suspected of being demotions.

The main explanation, however, is to be found in the failure of the legally constituted authorities – the Council representing the electorate and the administrators charged with upholding regulations – to hold the executive chairmen accountable for their actions. This was so even though the chairmen were popularly elected officials. The indirectly elected sub-District Councils consisted of the chairmen of the lower level Union Councils whose main motivation was to maintain a potentially advantageous relationship with the sub-district chairman. For, like the Ivorian mayors, the chairmen derived a lot of their power and patronage from their political relationships with the centre (President Ershad). Unlike the Ivorian mayors, however, there were fewer legal or administrative constraints on their behaviour. The civil service at the local level was not secure or well-established, and chief officials who did not fall into line with the chairman found themselves facing exclusion from the decision-making process.[6] The performance of the Bangladesh councils was therefore vitiated by corruption, patronage allocations to social and political supporters and domination by local elites. Channels of accountability to the electorate had to await the ultimate sanction of the electoral process, which did apparently work in that in the 1990 elections many chairmen were punished for their disregard of the requirements of public accountability.

Nevertheless the political and social context was generally unfavourable. The military regime was more concerned to throw resources into creating a network of clients loyal to itself, and social norms were such

---

[5] National turnout in a series of local elections was around 55 per cent; 90 per cent of respondents could name their local councillor and 24 per cent said they had contacted their councillor.

[6] Cf. similar findings by Khan (1996), p. 60 and McCarthy (1993), p. 121.

that most villagers had a 'servant–master' relationship with bureaucrats and council representatives which did not easily support the making of complaints about bad behaviour or lack of accountability.

The Karnataka experiment started from the same advantageous position as that of Bangladesh, namely a context of generous (but not increased) resource allocation. In addition, the Karnataka districts were already well established as sub-centres of large and sophisticated bureaucratic field administrations and thus had adequate administrative capacity. All that changed in 1987 was that these agencies were given greater control over their existing budgets, for which they were made accountable to the newly elected District Councils. Any extra costs created by the reform in terms of manpower needs and administrative infrastructure were also fully funded by the state government. At the grassroots level the Mandal Councils did even better after 1989 when they became the beneficiaries of greatly increased resources directly allocated from New Delhi under the auspices of the national rural employment fund (Jawahar Rozgar Yojana) – 80 per cent of which went to the Mandal Councils and only 20 per cent to the districts.

The impact of democratisation at the institutional level was also strong in that elected councillors and the elected council presidents – who had the status of junior minister in the state government – were endowed with more than adequate legal powers and political clout to establish strong control over these large and well-endowed bureaucracies. The council presidents were therefore able to hold their own in dealings with their senior civil servants, whilst at the same time the scale and resources of the councils enabled them to offer reasonable career rewards to bureaucrats who adapted well to the new system. Unlike Bangladesh, however, the elected executives were not out of control. They were held accountable to the councils through their sub-committees which met at least once a month. And they were also held accountable through the law, which senior civil servants such as the chief secretary or chief accounts officer had sufficient autonomy to invoke if presidents sought to exceed their powers.[7] Reinforcing these local accountabilities was the strong framework provided by the Karnataka state government and party system, which helped to guarantee developmental performance by setting targets for each sector.

The political and social context also had a positive and very important effect at both the institutional level and the level of relations between the councils and the public. First, Karnataka had a free and lively press, ever

---

[7] Other researchers confirm this view, suggesting that civil servants in India would normally resist implementing 'unsound' decisions – (CIRDAP (1992)).

ready to investigate and publish stories about political corruption or other council affairs. Second, it had a well-established competitive party system which loomed large in council chambers and generated constant pressure on a council's ruling party administration. (In the other three cases, party competition at the institutional level was absent.) Third, it had a bureaucracy which had long internalised the notions that elected politicians should determine policy, and that the law and formal rules should largely be obeyed. There was thus a 'culture of accountability', as demonstrated by a willingness on the part of both officials and the public to complain or to report illegal or dictatorial behaviour.

In spite of all this, however, it could not be argued that enhanced participation resulting from democratic decentralisation was an especially positive or high-profile factor in the Karnatakan case. Although electoral participation was high (between 60 per cent and 75 per cent turnouts), other forms of participation such as taking part in meetings or contacting councillors achieved levels very similar to those in Bangladesh, whilst the performance of councillors in reporting back to or meeting with their constitutents was marginally worse than their Bangladeshi counterparts. In the case of the Mandal (local level) Councils, the record of councillors in consulting with their constituents through report-back meetings was actually very poor, partly because the obligation to hold twice-yearly Gram Sabhas (village meetings) ceased to be observed after the first year or so.[8]

Thus the main factors which adversely affected performance in Côte d'Ivoire, Ghana and Bangladesh – resource constraints, including administrative capacity, and the failure of institutional or public accountability – were not major problems in Karnataka. But participation was not significantly stronger either. Together with the record of the other cases on participation, this indicates that participation alone cannot be a satisfactory explanation of performance. Comparative analysis of the patterns of explanation in each case can, however, help us to develop a more complex and realistic assessment of what were the most significant influences on performance.

COMPARING EXPLANATIONS OF PERFORMANCE: A CROSS-NATIONAL ANALYSIS

Our assessment of the different factors influencing performance in the four countries studied is summarised in Table 6.3, which is presented for heuristic purposes only. Comparing the various participation factors in

---

[8] One reason was the conflict they provoked and the embarrassment suffered by councillors called to account in public.

Table 6.3. *Factors explaining performance*

	Ghana	Côte d'Ivoire	Bangladesh	Karnataka
Performance: responsiveness rating	poor	poor	medium	good
Performance: outputs higher than previous form of government?	marginal improvement	only until 1989	yes	yes
Elect. participation	good	medium	good	good
Contacts reprs/public	medium/good	poor	good	medium/good
Public knowledge	good	poor	good	medium good
Institut. account. to elected reprs.	poor	good	poor	good
Resources/capacity	inadequate	v. inadequate after 89	plentiful, increased	plentiful, stable
Political context	not supportive	not supportive	not supportive	v. supportive
Social context	fairly supportive	not supportive	fairly supportive	v. supportive

each country reveals that there is no consistent pattern according to which enhanced participation is associated with better institutional performance. In all four countries, popular (especially electoral) participation was considerably enhanced by the democratic decentralisation reforms. Yet in so far as there were differences amongst the four countries in the relative successes and failures of participation and consultation, these were not reflected directly in performance outcomes. Thus the quite positive record of participation and consultation in Ghana did not prevent Ghanaian institutions from performing poorly, whilst the better participatory record of the Bangladeshi councils did not translate into a better performance outcome than their Karnatakan counterparts.

The provision of adequate resources to decentralised councils is clearly an essential prerequisite to improved performance, but again it does not suffice on its own to explain varying levels of achievement. The Ghanaian institutions foundered in part because they were starved of resources, and the performance of Ivorian institutions declined radically after 1989 when a national fiscal crisis caused a drastic reduction in the resources available to them. In the case of Bangladesh however, the government made substantially more resources available to decentralised councils than had been spent under the previous system, whereas the Karnataka councils were given the same amount of development funds as centralised institutions had dispensed earlier. Despite this, however, the Karnataka system achieved a substantially greater improvement in performance than the one in Bangladesh.[9]

If the emphasis of the analysis is shifted to looking for patterns or combinations of factors it it clear that the distinctive or 'deviant' case – Karnataka, the only country with an unambiguously positive performance outcome – is associated with a distinctive pattern of explanatory factors. Only in Karnataka was there a benign combination of adequate resources, a supportive political and social context, a well-established administration, at least adequate levels of participation, and publicly accountable elected representatives who were able to make the fruits of that participation effective at the institutional level. This in turn enabled institutions to produce more effective and responsive development outputs.

In so far as we emphasise responsiveness (i.e. the production of ouputs by government which are valued by the public) rather than mere quantity of ouputs as the most significant dimension of performance, the Karnataka case also exhibits a particularly distinctive feature, namely the combination of positive popular accountability with effective mechanisms of institutional accountability. We identify accountability (in these two forms) as crucial in so far as it enables the benefits which follow from enhanced participation and adequate resource provision to be transmitted through the representative system to the governmental institutions which manage resources and implement policy.

In conclusion, therefore, our model for explaining the differences in performance amongst the experiments in democratic decentralisation in India (Karnataka), Bangladesh, Ghana and Côte d'Ivoire compares the following combinations of factors: resources, levels of participation, accountability of representatives to the electorate, and accountability of bureaucrats and executive authorities both to elected representatives and to legal/administrative mechanisms. We suggest that for these mechanisms to be effective requires not just the appropriate form of decentralised structure to be successfully put in place by central government, but also a supportive social and political context. Only the optimum combination of these factors is likely to lead to better performance, as defined by improvements on the previous form of administration and a positive assessment by the population in our surveys. No one of these factors is

---

[9] The Bangladesh case is very similar to those of Nigeria after 1976, and Brazil in the 1980s. In Nigeria, the federal government generously funded local councils with guaranteed shares of a central fund. Unfortunately, poor accountability (and minimal participation) at the local level meant that most of the money disappeared into the patronage machines of state party bosses and elite politicians. See Graf (1988), p. 193; Gboyega (1994); Olowu (1994); Shah (1991).

sufficient on its own to guarantee a positive outcome; but the most crucial requirement is that there be effective systems of both popular and institutional accountability, combined with positive readings for the other factors.

DEMOCRATIC DECENTRALISATION IN COMPARATIVE PERSPECTIVE

Democratic decentralisation has been and continues to be advocated as an important component of policy packages to improve governance in developing countries. But the claim that it will lead to better governmental performance, particularly in the formulation and implementation of locally oriented development policies, has to be treated with some caution. If the experiences of the four countries which have been presented in this study are compared with those of a wider range of cases, a number of more general points can be made concerning the conditions under which democratic decentralisation can be successfully established and the kinds of systems which are more likely to produce performances in accordance with the expectations placed upon it.

Accountability systems

Comparative analysis of the structures through which accountability is established suggests that there are real differences in effectiveness between some kinds of decentralisation and others in this absolutely vital area. Democratic decentralisation involves, at the very least, the introduction of elections for local councils and/or for the chief political executives of local authorities, even within one-party or military regimes. It is clear, however, that elections alone are not sufficient to improve legitimacy and to guarantee public accountability. In fact there is a wide variety of methods for selecting councillors and office-holders, with differing effects on both public and institutional accountability.

Systems which undermine accountability

Some of the worst cases of corruption and ineffectiveness are associated with the direct popular election of mayors or chief executives and a 'separation of powers' between the elected chief executive and the representative council, as found in our Bangladesh case. In such systems the elected boss is armed with a popular mandate, but is not a member of the elected council which is supposed only to approve budgets and pass local laws, rather than to continuously involve itself in monitoring executive action. The main sanctions on executive behaviour are the verdict of the electorate at the next election (assuming that regular elections are held), or 'last resort' interim measures such as vetoes or impeachment by the elected council.

Compared to Bangladesh, Nigeria provides an even more extreme example of a 'presidential'-style chairman who, since the 1992 reforms, has been able to appoint his own team of 'supervisory councillors' (each with administrative portfolios) and the chief administrator of the council. Most observers agree that the Nigerian chairmen have acquired a reputation for behaviour which is corrupt, dictatorial and lacking even 'minimal' consultation with popular opinion.[10] Councils have been unable to exercise any restraining influence on them and as a consequence have begun to abuse the impeachment process, for instance in an effort to influence the allocation of resources.[11] These conflicts have led to the paralysis of many councils. And because of direct funding by the federal government, the chairmen have become independently powerful patrons whose main concern is to maintain their fruitful relationship with the federal authorities.

Most of Latin America also has a long-established tradition of elected executive mayors who are powerful political patrons in their own right, appointing both their team of (paid) elected office-holders and most of the municipal employees on a spoils basis. The lack of accountability of the Latin American mayors is, however, less a product of central government patronage (although this is also a factor) than of the weak political and legal status and restricted functions of the councils themselves.[12] (In Brazil and Colombia, the mayor can even veto opposing council resolutions.) The effect of spoils systems is deepened by the provision in some important countries (Brazil, Colombia, Ecuador, Mexico and Paraguay) banning mayors from holding more than one term of office.

One of the supposed benefits of the 'strong executive mayor' is that it enables an elected official to establish much stronger control over bureaucrats, and this is certainly true of the Nigerian, Latin American and Bangladeshi cases. Unless, however, this is tempered with the counterbalancing controls which derive from a well-established civil service, administrative law and effective financial control mechanisms, there is no restraint on excessive behaviour by the politicians, as the Bangladesh experience under Ershad clearly showed. In Nigeria, local government staff were so appalled at the prospect of being transformed into wholly locally employed staff, under the control of the executive

[10] Olowu (1994); Gboyega (1994); Awotukun (1995).   [11] Awotukun (1995).
[12] Nickson (1995).

chairman, that trade union action and other pressure persuaded the government to reverse its proposed abolition of the Local Government Service Commission.[13]

Cote d'Ivoire is a good example of the problems of lack of accountability which occur where the elected councillors are elected 'at large' on single lists. This is typical of Francophone and Latin American systems, the most extreme being Latin American 'closed and blocked' party lists – that is, lists where the candidates list is ranked and exactly matches the number of seats, and no cross-list voting for other candidates is permitted. In other words, the elector is faced with a choice between two or more complete sets of councillors, on a winner-takes-all basis.

The first problem here is that the accountability of councillors to the electorate is weak where there is no constituency relationship; councillors do not represent a particular ward but are part of the team selected by a party machine and/or the political entrepreneur who is running for mayor. In many Latin American countries local elections are deliberately held on the same day as national elections, and local party lists may be integrated with those for higher levels, so that electors have to vote the same slate for all offices, both local and above. This further reduces the political connection between representatives and the electorate. The situation in Côte d'Ivoire, where even in quite small rural communes only a small minority of citizens could name any elected councillors, has also been reported in Senegal.[14]

Secondly, the list system also produces elected councils which are weak in relation to the chief executive – even if, as in the Francophone system, the mayor is elected by the council from amongst its members, i.e. from the winning list. With the mayor entered as the head of the list, this is usually a formality. The council in effect is a group selected by a powerful political patron, whose influence, at least in the Francophone systems, is often boosted by the practice of *le cumul des mandats*. In Côte d'Ivoire, this practice was taken to extremes, producing a group of mayors who were predominantly members of the capital-city-based professional and political elite.

Thirdly, the winner-takes-all list system excludes opposition to the victorious mayor from the council altogether. The only possibility of challenge to the mayor at the institutional level comes from disgruntled factions which might develop amongst his selected clients on the winning list. A further deleterious consequence of this situation for public accountability is that, with the opposition and its supporters totally excluded from the local deliberative body, a spirit of non-co-operation

[13] Awotukun (1995).   [14] Vengroff and Johnston (1989).

and even refusal to accept the legitimacy of the local administration can easily develop. In effect, as with the direct election of chief executives, the only ways of holding the chief executive accountable are the judgement of the electorate, or mechanisms of legal and central administrative control which are (it is true) available more in the Francophone system than in most others.[15]

In countries under military or other authoritarian rule, as in Ghana in 1989, local 'no-party' elections are frequently held as a form of restricted democracy, in which the regime does not want to allow mobilisation of parties which might threaten its position. No-party elections have both good and bad consequences for the accountability of local authorities. On the one hand, as in Ghana, they can succeed in their specific aim of electing representatives who were genuinely locally based and respected members of their communities, with a good relationship with their constituents. Ghana is, however, unusual in that even after the transition to multi-party constitutional rule in 1992, the no-party provision for local elections was maintained and justified on these grounds. The Ghanaians argue that parties are too obsessed with creating patronage machines and gaining lucrative offices for their members, and lead too easily to dysfunctional intra-community conflicts which undermine the community agreement necessary for development. Whilst there is some force in this argument at the community level, there are three main problems with the refusal to permit party activity:

(a) Given that local politics is as much an arena for class or caste conflict as any other, an idealised representation of community interest can lead to exclusion of certain groups and/or a failure to develop mechanisms for channelling and resolving the plurality of interests. (Although in West Bengal, local party activity was actually directed at a transformation of social and economic structures.)

(b) In any representative local government council which aggregates a number of communities within its area, it is very difficult to resolve conflicts of interest when the council consists of community delegates whose sole purpose is to fight for the allocation of resources to their particular area. All arguments become special pleading, and in the absence of party resolution of such conflicts, the resources will be allocated on the basis of whoever has most favour with decision-makers. This can have deleterious consequences for the transparency

---

[15] Some Latin American countries have, however, recently reformed aspects of their electoral systems: Venezuela and Chile have moved to permit *panachage* or open, cross-list voting, and Venezuela has also adopted the German system of two-thirds of councillors elected on a ward basis, the other third on a party list – Nickson (1995).

and legitimacy of allocative decisions (as reported for Bangladesh and Nigeria, as well as Ghana).
(c) The lack of party competition on the council itself can, as with the single-list system, produce supine elected bodies with no interest in monitoring and challenging executive behaviour.

Single-party systems replicate some of the same problems as the single-list and no-party systems of election (see Zimbabwe, Uganda, Tanzania and countries such as Kenya, Sri Lanka or Singapore where the ruling party is so dominant that in practice most of the country is under single party rule). There is a denial of the plurality of interests within communities and the lack of competition at the institutional level reduces the accountability and transparency of local government decision-making. A well-organised and internally democratic party can, of course, be quite effective at mediating inter-communal and interest-group conflicts at local level, but over time most single parties suffer the same fate, as the lack of transparency and the need to justify decisions in public produce self-perpetuating and corrupt oligarchies taking decisons behind closed doors.

Ghana is also an important example of the practice by which the chief executives of local authorities are political appointees loyal to the national government; sometimes they are civil servants appointed by the President, in other cases party officials or politicians integrated into a national hierarchy. Other well-documented cases include Uganda, Kenya, Sri Lanka and Zimbabwe. Whilst it is unrealistic to expect that there will not be informal political relationships between centre and locality (especially when there are effective party systems), formal central appointment of local chief executives is undesirable if it cuts across administrative and legal mechanisms. In some cases this can render ineffective a formally devolved system, and undermine accountability to local citizens.

Uganda's system of Resistance Councils under a presidentially-appointed District Administrator provides a vivid example of the contradiction between a rhetoric of 'bottom-up', locally accountable institutions and a reality of dual national hierarchies of political control. The more 'radical' decentralisation set in motion by the 1993 reforms shifts more power to the District Resistance Councils whilst retaining a deconcentrated field administration for the line ministries. Whether the pyramidal RC structure is anything more than an organisation of government supporters and 'watchdogs', similar to Rawlings' Committees for the Defence of the Revolution in Ghana between 1984 and 1992, is a matter for dispute between researchers.[16] But it is clear that whatever

[16] Brett (1994); Omara-Otunnu (1992).

authenticity they might have as local representative bodies, their ability to hold government administration accountable at the local level is severely limited by the power of nationally appointed officials.

In other cases politically appointed executives can undermine the hierarchical/legal accountability of deconcentrated officials, as either patronage considerations or corrupt deals can override agreed planning decisions and expenditure allocations. In Kenya, for instance, the District Focus system is a tightly controlled deconcentration of central officials, intended to improve the co-ordination and rationality of local development efforts. Even the lower-tier local government councils, self-help organisations and NGOs have been incorporated into this all-powerful, district-level institutional direction. Yet researchers report that the local MPs in collaboration with presidentially-appointed District Commissioners make decisions on local development and resource allocations which are routinely determined by considerations of political patronage and access to centrally controlled networks. In the process, the rules set by Tender Boards, and the work of District Treasuries and Auditors and the District Development Committees count for little.[17]

Perhaps the most extreme case is Sri Lanka, where MPs of the ruling party officially have control of the development budget of the District Development Council, which is thus used to sustain political machines, whilst the work of locally elected councils is relegated to insignificance.[18]

The existence of such a system of central political appointment is usually associated with the political purposes of the decentralisation reform: either the government is wanting to reinforce the regime's control in the rural areas (Ghana, Sri Lanka, Kenya, Uganda, Zimbabwe), or actively to build support bases.

Systems which promote accountability
The Karnataka case suggests that executive authorities are best held accountable if they are elected indirectly from amongst the body of elected councillors, and are subject to continuous monitoring through committees or 'administrative commissions' of the council. The same kinds of relationship are reported for other Indian states such as West Bengal, Maharashtra and Bihar, and, in Africa, for the frequently cited 'successful' (but limited) Botswana local governments.[19] Apart from the Nigerian authorities, this was the also the case in the group of 'successful' African urban and small town councils examined by Smoke and Olowu, all of which were, as the writers put it, operating with structures

---

[17] Oyugi (1990); N'gethe (1994); Smoke (1993).
[18] Bastian (1994); Islam (1987); Leitan (1990).   [19] Gasper (1989).

'inherited from their colonial experience'.[20] In other words, they were (including the Nigerian councils) of the devolved type of local government recommended so strongly by Mawhood.[21] It must be remembered, however, that the Smoke and Olowu studies emphasise richness of resources as their main explanation of success.

What makes such a system effective is that: (a) the political power base of the executive authority is primarily the local council (modified of course by the effect of party systems); (b) the executive has to report in a detailed and regular way on the implementation of the approved budget expenditures, and on other managerial matters. This helps to ensure financial responsibility and accountability to local taxpayers and beneficiaries for the use of public funds.[22] As Day and Klein comment, 'It is day-to-day accountability, in which the rulers explain and justify their actions to the ruled, which distinguishes a democratic society from an elective tyranny.'[23] (c) A sub-committee system means that councillors develop detailed knowledge of particular areas, in contrast to the 'rubber stamp' character of full council meetings. A final, practical advantage of committee systems is that in the rural areas of LDCs, it is difficult and expensive to hold full council meetings very frequently; when they are (as is often the case) reduced to only two or three per annum they become very much 'set piece' occasions. In Karnataka, sub-committees met once a month.

Whilst executive authorities need to be held politically accountable, it is also important that there is a balance between political control and legal/administrative constraints. In Karnataka or West Bengal, elected politicians were/are definitely 'in control', in that they have the status and the capacity to deal with civil servants, discuss policies and if necessary push them through against a reluctant bureaucracy. Officials can therefore be held accountable. But, as noted, over-powerful political executives can cause problems too, and their actions need to be balanced by a well-established civil or public service which has sufficient autonomy and strength to prevent politicians from breaking the law or financial regulations. In some of the Indian states this fine balance has been achieved – partly because the decentralised authorities inherited well-established field administrations and partly because they were large enough to offer meaningful careers to good quality staff. Some degree of tension or conflict between bureaucrats and politicians is, of course, inevitable, especially in newly democratised authorities; and where there is a strong civil service the balance can change constantly. Other researchers on

---

[20] Smoke and Olowu (1992). [21] Mawhood (1983). [22] Bird (1994).
[23] Day and Klein (1987), as quoted in Foster (1996), p. 567.

India report that in Maharashtra, for instance, officials felt quite strongly that they had to be accountable to elected politicians, but that they should not implement 'unsound' decisions made by political bodies – a set of attitudes that can have both positive and negative effects.[24]

The Francophone system, as noted above, is well known for its ability to hold both officials and elected politicians accountable for financial and budgetary matters. But as this is achieved through rigorous centralisation of tax collection and expenditure disbursement, it can hardly be counted as a form of decentralised local accountability, except in so far as it helps to prevent misuse of funds allocated for the benefit of local people. The same might be said of recent reforms in Chile, which require municipal auditors to make monthly budget reports to the comptroller-general.[25]

As the Ghana case shows, in representative forms of local government (as opposed to direct community participation) it is best if representatives are elected for specific wards or areas, and the ratio of representation is as close as resources permit. In this way, other devices for ensuring a close relationship between representatives and their constituents, such as regular report-back meetings, 'surgeries', village development committees and so on, have a better chance of working. In Ghana such schemes were found to have worked well, in the context of a representative ratio of around 1:2,000 and a strong tradition of village government and self-help activities. The problem in Ghana was, as noted, that this kind of popular representation was undermined by a lack of accountability at the institutional level. In Latin America, by contrast, a major problem is the political under-representation in local governments, characterised by representative ratios of between 1:20,000 and 80,000 in the urban municipalities, and over 1:100,000 in some of the big cities.[26]

Finally, although it has been argued that elections alone are insufficient they nevertheless do form an irreplaceable element in any system of public accountability. It is, therefore, an obvious requirement that whatever the system of representation, elections should be regular and fair if they are to function effectively. This has been shown in India over many years, and even in unpromising conditions such as Bangladesh, Côte d'Ivoire or Nigeria, they have been important in showing that local people can sanction local administrations which have become unpopular.

One conclusion which might be drawn from such a comparative analysis of how to make representative local government accountable is that the macro-context of decentralisation is somewhat unpromising, and that in many LDCs representative government is fraught with too many

[24] CIRDAP (1992). [25] Nickson (1995). [26] Nickson (1995).

problems for it to work effectively above the village or community level. Is it, therefore, better to argue (as some do) that community politics should replace formal representative government? Combined with the resource arguments about the appropriate size for local authorities, the most effective method of accountability could be to go for community-based councils where there is direct participation, and office-holders literally have to live with the consequences of their stewardship of collective resources. Ramm points to the Papua New Guinea experience in East New Britain Province as evidence for the effectiveness of this approach (albeit in a context where the overall scheme of decentralisation has proved a disaster).[27] In Africa, many authors point to the effectiveness of traditions of self-help activity, particularly where there is a well-developed civil society and the support of elite-led community development associations, as in Nigeria, Ghana and other more developed parts of West Africa. Such an approach, however, would have major consequences for most current schemes of decentralisation. The idea that local authorities outside the big towns could make any contribution to economic development (as opposed to improving very small-scale local amenities) would have to be abandoned, and the merits of large-scale, well-resourced government developmental bureaucracies deconcentrated to perhaps regional levels (districts in India) would have to be put back on the agenda.

Community based local government and the market

Devolution to community-based, self-sufficient authorities also appeals to 'New Public Management' writers who despair of the ability of representative, formal local government ever to solve the problems of accountability in a Third World context of endemic corruption, lack of transparency and costly, ineffective financial controls. Tanzi, for instance, suggests that local councils should be wholly autonomous, both financially and politically. In such a system local government spending would be determined *solely* by local revenue-raising capacity or, if central government grants were made, they would be on a strictly limited, 'contract' basis, with no possibility of 'bailing out'.[28] The intention would be to make government decision-makers 'bear the financial and political consequences of their decisions' and force them to internalise costs; that is, they would not be able to shift the cost of services for local beneficiaries on to the shoulders of non-beneficiaries. A further important mechanism would, therefore, be extensive employment of 'user charges' for services directly provided by the local authorities. In this

---

[27] Ramm (1993).   [28] Tanzi (1995); see also Werlin (1992).

way a 'customer–provider' relationship between those responsible for the services and local citizens would be encouraged.[29]

These 'New Public Management' approaches, already extensively used in the industrialised economies since the 1980s, have not been tested very much in the LDC context, although Paul has reported on a World Bank irrigation project in Indonesia which found that villagers who had to pay fees for irrigation services and organise user groups were able to exercise more influence on the performance of the irrigation agency ('no water, no fee').[30] The key problem with the approach would seem to lie in the concept of a direct relationship between providing only services that can be paid for by available revenues or user charges, and the 'consequences' for providers. For most of the countries reviewed in the literature, local politicians and officials have clearly managed for some time to get away with consuming revenues and providing only limited services with few consequences for themselves. Making costs 'transparent' by loading them on to user charges might simply provide another way for local authorities to protect themselves from the consequences of financial disciplines imposed by cuts in central government grant or contracts. Other services would simply disappear if the costs had to met by local taxes or charges, and a process of de-development would begin. Only if local governments were forced to be genuinely self-sufficient would there be real consequences, which would probably lead to the demise of most LDC local governments outside the big towns. Ultimately, therefore, these are arguments against government decentralisation and in favour of the market; and they cannot be applied to deconcentrations unless the intention is radically to reduce the scope of central government as well.

Redistribution and poverty alleviation

Despite the relative success of the Indian experiment, democratic decentralisation should not be seen as a panacea for wider problems of poverty, social inequality or economic stagnation. Even the most successful and responsive of our cases showed little evidence of having been particularly responsive to 'vulnerable groups', the poor or the marginalised, a finding echoed more generally in the literature. The contribution of decentralised authorities to spatial redistribution in Tanzania, for instance, has been strongly contested by Therkildsen and Semboja, and the Papua New Guinea system is notorious for having actually created a new elite of paid local politicians whose excesses destroyed all faith in the ability of local government to provide redis-

---

[29] Bird (1994).   [30] Paul (1994).

tributive development.³¹ It would seem that the strong tendency for decentralisation to reinforce existing patterns of uneven development can only be counteracted by very vigorous and centrally directed financial equalisation schemes such as are reported to exist in Chile,³² or by the determined action of a central government with an ideological mandate, as in West Bengal. The latter is one of the few cases where a researcher with in-depth knowledge of the area argues that decentralisation did provide real benefits to poor peasants and 'disadvantaged'groups such as Scheduled Castes and, to a lesser extent, women.³³ But even here, it is acknowledged that these achievements depended substantially on central funding and on the highly organised actions of the Communist Party at local level; Webster also argues that, because of the importance of temporary 'make work' schemes, there was no real transformation in the economic structure likely to have a long-term impact on the poverty of small farmers. (On the other hand, he does acknowledge that West Bengal's dramatic leap to the status of India's fastest growing producer of food grains was indirectly a product of its decentralised, 'pro-poor' policies, when combined with technological change.)

The social and political context of democratic decentralisation

It is clear, both from the findings presented in this book and from the general literature, that even the most appropriately designed institutions for decentralisation cannot work independently of or even against contradictory forces coming from the social and political structures within which they are embedded. To some extent, decentralisation is a policy forced to carry an unrealistic burden of expectations regarding its ability to transform whole societies dominated by authoritarian or patronage politics. Features of good governance such as accountability through the law, elections and public scrutiny were shown to have been crucial in explaining the success of one of our four decentralisation experiments in India (Karnataka). Unfortunately many of these features are prior or independent rather than dependent variables in relation to the democratisation and decentralisation reforms. In India, four of the essential social prerequisites for accountability mechanisms to work effectively have existed for some time:

(a) Competitive parties: there is little point in executives reporting to elected bodies unless those bodies are prepared to challenge, demand

---

[31] See Semboja and Therkildsen (1994); *contra* Maro (1990); Peasah (1994).
[32] Nickson (1995).   [33] Webster (1994).

Conclusions

information and debate alternative strategies. This is most likely to happen where there is already a competitive party system which can generate pressure in the council chamber from a group of people who want to expose any faults of the administration.

(b) A widely distributed free press: even more important is the existence in India of a free and investigative press, which reports the doings of local politicians and, more remarkably has a presence in most areas, not just the federal and state capitals.

(c) A professional civil service: the willingness of officials to develop a constructive but law-abiding relationship with elected politicians derives partly from a self-confidence built on the long-established autonomy and professionalism of the civil service. Whilst the notorious 'permit raj' mentality of the Indian civil service has its negative aspects, the respect for rules and regulations is also functional in a politically accountable system.

(d) All of these social institutions have combined to encourage the development of a public 'culture of accountability' which is ready to complain about the bad behaviour of politicians or civil servants and to demand accountability. (The protection of human rights through a strong judicial system is another supportive feature for this to flourish.) Such a culture is further reinforced if there is a well-developed civil society in which social interests are organised and vocal.

Whilst aspects of all these social features can be found in varying degrees in other LDCs (although in some hardly at all), it is rare to find them all combined together. It is unlikely, moreover, that decentralisation on its own can create them. The development of genuine forms of accountability and participation at the local level is a challenge to power structures whch can easily snuff them out if they remain isolated. As recent studies of the democratisation process have shown, democratisation – perhaps especially at the local level – is unlikely to succeed where the institutions of social and economic domination substantially overlap with or correspond to those of the power structure or political institutions.[34] It is no accident that the limited modifications of pre-existing patterns of corruption and political manipulation observed in Karnataka occurred in the country where these practices were weakest and where opportunities for civil society to assert itself through representative processes were strongest. There are some parallels here with Robert Putnam's work on the significance of 'social capital' in underpinning the

---

[34] Cf. Rueschmeyer, Stevens and Stevens (1992).

performance of Italian regional governments.[35] We would argue, however, that social capital, in so far as it refers to social networks and habits of association in civil society, is not sufficient on its own to determine the prospects of a democratic decentralisation reform, even in the most promising environment. A culture of accountability springs from an interaction between civil society and appropriate institutions, which generally have to be created by a strong central political force. There is a possibility, therefore, that the institutional devices described above could be used to create elements of accountability associated with decentralisation if they are implemented within a broader context of democratic and governance reforms at the national level. Then a 'virtuous circle' could, at least, be set in motion, in which culture and society could be changed. They are not, after all, immutable forces. Indeed, even at the local level, our research did reveal that, where people at the grassroots were offered the opportunity to participate in decentralised institutions they did so on the whole with enthusiasm and felt (on the evidence of our surveys) that the experiments were valuable and worth continuing. Governments would be wise not to ignore or disappoint these kinds of popular expectations.

[35] Putnam (1993).

Methodological appendix

THE SURVEYS

1. In each of the four countries both a mass and an elite survey were undertaken using, as far as possible, a common questionnaire. In all, 2,030 respondents were interviewed. In Bangladesh a written Bangla (Bengali) translation of the questionnaire was used, and in India a written Kannada version. Both in Ghana and in Côte d'Ivoire the variety of local languages, some unwritten, was such that interviewers used either an English (Ghana) or French (Cote d'Ivoire) version as the basis for their work. In southern Ghana interviewers used mainly the Twi language; some who knew Krobo, Ga or Ewe were used for the very small number of respondents who felt more comfortable in those languages. At training sessions, interviewers practised simulations of the interviews in Twi and agreed on appropriate translations of particular phrases. In northern Ghana, the same procedure was adopted with the Mampruli language, although some interviewers in particular villages used the Bimoba or Konkomba languages.

In Côte d'Ivoire French is very widely spoken particularly in the south. Nevertheless, in the two southern communes, interviewers who could speak Attié or Dioula (the most widely spoken indigenous language in Côte d'Ivoire) were used and agreed translations discussed. In the north, three of the five interviewers were native Senoufo speakers and all knew Dioula.

2. In Ghana interviewers had to be recruited and trained locally in each district. In East Akim, twenty-four interviewers were used (twelve men and twelve women i.e. a pair for each village); about half were National Service personnel (university graduates or secondary school graduates waiting to go up to unversity), the others were teachers and a medical administrator with experience of census and health survey work. In East Mamprusi, the majority of the sixteen interviewers were local school

teachers together with a few clerical staff from the District Education Office.

In Côte d'Ivoire, interviewers were recruited with the help of ORSTOM and ENSEA (the National School of Statistical Studies); a team of eight (four men and four women, mainly students) was used together with a 'supervisor' who works virtually full time on ORSTOM surveys.

In India, experienced interviewers from the Institute of Social Studies Trust in Bangalore were used for the Dharwar District survey, and a similar team from the Institute of Development Studies, Mysore, for the Mysore District survey.

In Bangladesh, two different teams were used: one from the NGO, Proshika, which provided a group of experienced village-level development workers, and the other from the Rural Development Academy in Bogra, which put together a team of village development animators and others experienced in rural surveys.

In all countries, men interviewed men and women interviewed women.

3. The mass surveys were based on representative quota samples constructed as far as possible on the basis of census data for each area, using categories of gender, age, education and, in Africa, occupation. In the South Asian cases, interviewers were instructed to 'balance' occupations informally. The sample was drawn on an area basis by grouping villages into four types – near or far from a main road and near or far from the district capital and then randomly selecting two or three of each type. In the villages, interviewers selected respondents from various sampling points, either public places such as markets, social areas and the like, or by calling randomly on households. In Bangladesh all women had to be interviewed at home.

The elite survey involved selecting opinion leaders of both sexes in the survey villages; the deciding factor here was social/political status and these respondents did not have to conform to the quota categories. In Ghana and Côte d'Ivoire they were selected locally after preliminary enquiries by the interviewers and the principal researcher, and included traditional office-holders (both men and women), traders' and farmers' leaders, ethnic group and religious leaders, sporting and cultural groups, head-teachers and PTAs, and leaders of parties or other quasi-political organisations.

In India and Bangladesh they included not only influential people such as associational leaders, notables and teachers but also landowners and (India only) caste leaders.

4. The Ghana survey

The total number of respondents interviewed in Ghana was:

E. Akim mass: 372 (12 villages)
E. Akim elite: 26   "
E. Mamprusi mass: 256 (8 villages)
E. Mamprusi elite: 32   "
Total: 686

The overall quota categories were based on the composition of the total local adult population, and were calculated from the 1984 Ghana census using the Regional and Local Authority Tables. The categories were applied to the sample in each village, and were as follows:

Ghana: quota categories (% of sample)

		E. Akim male	E. Akim female	E. Mamp. male	E. Mamp. female
Gender	male	50	50	50	50
	female	50	50	50	50
Age	18–29	42	42	40	40
	30–44	30	30	32	32
	45–64	20	20	19	19
	65+	8	8	9	9
Education	none	42	57	82	93
	primary/middle	50	40	12	5
	secondary/technical	6	2	4	1
	post-secondary	2	1	1	1
Occupation	Professional/technical/administrative[1]	9	4	{5	{1
	farmer (large)[2]	10	4	10	–
	farmer (small)	50	50	70	30
	production/artisan	10	10	3	14
	sales/service	3	14	2	13
	student	14	10	5	1
	unemployed/homemaker	4	8	5	41

[1] Includes teachers and clerical (i.e. all 'white collar')
[2] 'Large' and 'small' farmers were identified by the question referring to employment of labour

5. The Côte d'Ivoire survey

The total number of respondents interviewed was:

Mass survey   512 (128 per commune)
Elite survey   64 (16 per commune)
Total: 576

In each commune, sampling points were selected from the quarters of the commune town and one or two satellite villages, as follows:

Yakassé: 3 quarters, 1 village
Affery: 8 quarters, 2 villages (N.B. this was the largest town)
Mbengué: 3 quarters, 2 villages
Dikodougou: 5 quarters, 2 villages

The overall quota categories were based on the composition of the total local adult population and were calculated from the 1988 census (unpublished results by sub-Prefecture) kindly made available by the Census Bureau, Department of Statistics, Abidjan.

The quotas were applied in each commune as follows:

Côte d'Ivoire: quota categories (% of sample)

		Yak m.	Yak f.	Aff m.	Aff f.	Mbg m.	Mbg f.	Dk m.	Dk f.
Gender	male	50	50	50	50	50	50	50	50
	female	50	50	50	50	50	50	50	50
Age	18–29	44	44	44	47	40	42	36	42
	30–44	29	31	30	28	28	31	31	31
	45–64	22	20	20	21	24	21	26	22
	65+	5	5	6	4	8	6	7	5
Education	none	62	84	60	78	86	96	87	96
	primary	24	13	24	17	5	2	6	3.5
	secondary/technical	12	3	12	3	3.7	–	4	0.5
	post-secondary	0.5	–	0.5	–	0.3	–	0.2	–
	Koranic	1.5	–	3.5	2	5	2	2.8	–
Occupation	Professional/technical/administrative[1]	3	0.5	3	0.5	3	0.3	3	0.2
	farmer (large)[2]	1	–	11	–	–	–	–	–
	farmer (small)[3]	81	75	61	77	86	59	82	65
	artisan/sales/service	9	6.5	14	9	7	5	10	4.8
	student/unemployed/homemaker	6	18	11	13.5	5	35.7	5	30

Appendix 309

[1] Includes teachers and clerical
[2] 'Large' farmers identified by question on employment of labour
[3] In Affery 'small farmers' included a sub-category (15%) of agricultural labourers

6. The Karnataka survey

The total number of respondents interviewed was :

Mysore:	mass survey	144 (2 sub-Districts, 4 villages in each)
	elite survey	48
Dharwar:	mass survey	144 (2 sub-Districts, 4 villages in each)
	elite survey	48
Total:		384

The quota categories (% of sample) were as follows:

India (Karnataka): quota categories (% of sample)

	Quota category	Dharwar male	Dharwar fem.	Mysore male	Mysore fem.
Gender	male	50	50	50	50
	female	50	50	50	50
Age	18–29	29.4	31.0	30.6	35.6
	30–44	37.1	29.6	36.1	32.9
	45–64	28.7	31.0	30.6	21.9
	65+	4.9	8.5	2.8	9.6
Education	none	40.3	66.7	54.5	74.0
	primary	22.2	18.1	21.2	12.3
	secondary	36.1	15.3	19.7	11.0
	higher	1.4	0	4.5	2.7

India (Karnataka): occupational breakdown (% total sample)

Occupation	farmer (no employees)	35.3
	farmer (employer)	17.3
	labourer	19.4
	tenant	3.1
	trader/business	2.4
	production/service	5.2
	professional/administrative/clerical	2.0
	unemployed/homeworker/other	15.2

7. The Bangladesh survey

The total number of respondents interviewed was:

Mass survey: 288 (72 in 4 sub-districts, 4 villages in each)
Elite survey: 96
Total: 384

The quota categories were as follows:

Bangladesh: quota categories (% of sample)

	Quota category	Bogra male	Bogra fem.	Mkganj male	Mkhanj fem.
Gender	male	50	50	50	50
	female	50	50	50	50
Age	18–29	38.4	37.5		38.4
	30–44	34.2	31.9		30.4
	45–64	19.2	23.6		21.8
	65+	8.2	6.9		9.3
Education	none	52.1	77.8	61.2	84.5
	primary	20.5	11.1	13.4	8.5
	secondary	16.4	6.9	20.9	7.0
	higher	11	4.2	4.5	0

Bangladesh occupational breakdown (% total sample)

Occupation		
	farmer (no employees)	14.5
	farmer (employer)	3.8
	labourer	9.0
	tenant	3.8
	trader/business	7.6
	production/service	6.9
	professional/administrative/clerical	3.1
	unemployed/homeworker/other	51.2

8. The completed questionnaires were coded in Sussex and Glasgow and analysed using SPSS-PC. A specimen questionnaire is appended.

Appendix

THE QUESTIONNAIRE

University of Glasgow/University of Ghana Research Project on Decentralisation and Democratisation in Ghana

Section A: preliminary contact sheet

Interviewer: Questionnaire No.

1. District:

2: Village/area:

3. Sampling point:

4. Respondent no.:

5. Respondent's gender: Male   Female

6. How old are you?

   (a) 18–24
   (b) 25–29
   _____
   (c) 30–34
   (d) 35–39
   (e) 40–44
   _____
   (f) 45–49
   (g) 50–54
   (h) 55–59
   (j) 60–64
   _____
   (k) 65+

7 What is your level of education?

   (a) none
   (b) primary school
   (c) middle school
   (d) secondary or technical school
   (e) teacher training college
   (f) university or polytechnic

8. What is your occupation?

    (a) farmer or other agric.
        (i) what kind of crops?
        (ii) family or own farm, no employees
        (iii) farm manager
        (iv) caretaker
        (v) labourer
    (b) trader/sales/business
    (c) production/transport
        (e.g. food processing, tailor, seamstress, fitter, driver)
    (d) service business
        (e.g. catering, hotel, hairdresser, maid, watchman)
    (e) teacher
    (f) manager/administrator
    (g) clerical or office worker
    (h) unemployed
    (i) other (e.g. student, homemaker)

9. Where were you born?

    (a) this district
    (b) different district, same region
    (c) different region
    (d) outside Ghana

Section B: Questions on district assemblies, mass survey

1. Can you tell me about any projects or services which have been provided for your village or locality during the past 5 or 6 years, even including those that have stopped functioning or have been abandoned?

[PROMPT WITH LIST AND TICK COLUMN ONE IF MENTIONED]

	Col. 1	2 completed	3 abandoned	4 in progress
(a) Classrooms	__			
(b) Health Clinic	__			
(c) Water: pipe	__			
borehole	__			
well	__			
(d) latrines	__			
(e) sanitary	__			
(f) lorry park	__			
(g) feeder road	__			
(h) transport	__			
(i) agric. project	__			
(j) any other	__			
(k) none	__			
(l) don't know/ can't say	__			

2. Do you know who brought the projects or services which you have mentioned to your village? (e.g. DA/DC, before or after 1989; PAMSCAD; Village Ctte/self-help; Aid agency). IF NOT DA/DC, ASK WHETHER ANY HELP FROM DA/DC, AND SPECIFY KIND OF SELF-HELP

Project
(i)

(ii)

(iii)

(iv)

3. Were the people in the village consulted about the need for the projects, or able to make other suggestions about them? (e.g. suitable site, size, design etc.) SPECIFY, BY WHAT MEANS

   Project
   (i)

   (ii)

   (iii)

   (iv)

4. How satisfied are you with the projects you have mentioned?

   Project (i)
   Very satisfied
   Somewhat satisfied
   Dissatisfied (GIVE REASON)

   Project (ii)
   Very satisfied
   Somewhat satisfied
   Dissatisfied (GIVE REASON)

   Project (iii)
   Very satisfied
   Somewhat satisfied
   Dissatisfied (GIVE REASON)

   Project (iv)
   Very satisfied
   Somewhat satisfied
   Dissatisfied (GIVE REASON)

Appendix

5. Since the election of the District Assembly, have you noticed any changes in the attendance of Council employees at their work? (I mean people like health clinic staff, market inspectors, revenue collectors, teachers etc.)

   Has their attendance at work been:

   1. unchanged   2. more frequent   3. less frequent   4. DK Group:

6. If more/less frequent, why do you think that this has happened?

7. Since the election of the District Assembly, have you noticed any change in the number of transfers or dismissals of the kinds of Council employees we have been talking about?

   1. unchanged   2. more frequent   3. less frequent   4. DK Group:

   7(a) If more or less frequent, why do you think this has happened?

8. In general, what do you think are the most important needs of the people in this area?

9. In your view, is the District Assembly able to satisfy any of these needs with its projects or services?

   A lot?   __
   To some extent?   __
   No, not at all   __
   Don't know   __

10. In your view, has the District Assembly done better than the old District Council?

Section C

Now I'd like to ask about participation and democracy in the District Assembly:

11. Did you vote in the District Assembly elections? Yes __
    No __

12. Do you think the District Assembly elections were fairly conducted?
    1. Completely fair __
    2. Fair, but with some problems __
    3. Very unfair __
    4. Don't know __
    (IF UNFAIR, any particular reasons?)

13. Do you intend to vote in the forthcoming national elections?
    Yes __
    No __
    Don't know __

14. Did you agree with your village or locality being included in the [   ] District? Yes __
    No __
    (If NO, any particular reasons?)

15. Did you campaign or work for the election of any particular councillor in the last council elections? Yes __
    No __

16. What is the name of your present Assemblyman/woman

17. Have you taken part in the activities of any non-official association in the past two years? For instance:
    [READ OUT OR GIVE LIST]:
    village development association: __
    youth association: __
    ethnic/regional association __
    women's association __
    farmers' association __
    farmers' co-op __
    traders' association or business group __

Appendix

professional association __
trade union including students) __
cultural association __
religious group or church __
any other group (e.g. party) __
No group [IF NOT A MEMBER OF ANY GROUP GO TO QUESTION 19] IF YES TO ANY OF THE ABOVE, ASK Q. 18:

18. Were you active in your association before the new District Assembly was elected? Yes__ / No__

19. Have you engaged in the past two years in any of the following kinds of activities EITHER on behalf of your village OR [if an association member] with your association?

    [READ LIST]
19(a) Signed a petition or written a letter to the government or the District Council? Yes__ / No__
    If YES, what was it about?

19(b) Held a meeting to raise an issue or take action about an issue with the District Council or government officials? Yes__ / No__
    If YES, what was it about?

19(c) Taken part in a protest or demonstration over an issue affecting your community or association? Yes__ / No__
    If YES, what was it about?

19(d) Meeting to thank Assemblyman/woman for their work?
    Yes__ / No__
    If YES, what was it about?

19(e) Organised refusal to co-operate with the District Council?
    Yes__ / No__
    If YES, what was it about?

20. Have you personally participated in any *officially* organised local meetings, committees or consultative groups since the District Assemblies were set up?

For instance: Unit Committee Meetings: Yes__ / No__
CDR Meeting: Yes__ / No__
Village or town meeting to hear
Assemblyman's report: Yes__ / No__
If YES TO ANY, ASK:

20(a) Were you able to say anything at the meeting?

21. How frequently does your Assemblyman or woman come to meet you or your fellow villagers at a local meeting or consultation since elected?
once per month or more __
once every 3–5 months __
once every 6–13 months __
other __
never __

22. Have *you personally* ever contracted an Assemblyman or woman about a problem affecting your village, or an association of which you are a member? Yes__ / No__
[IF YES, ASK]: What kind of problem?

Did you find the person contacted: helpful? __
unhelpful __
Did you find the person contacted was 'honest'
and Fair-minded Yes__ / No__

23. Have you personally ever contacted your District Council offices about a problem affecting your village, or an association of which you are a member? Yes__ / No__

Appendix

[IF YES, ASK]:
What kind of problem?
was it before or after the election or the District Assembly?
                                                Before__ / After__
did you find the person contacted: helpful?__ / unhelpful?__
did you find the person contacted was
   'honest' and fair-minded?   Yes__ / No__

24. Have you personally ever contacted other District government offices about a problem affecting your village, or an association of which you are a member?   Yes__ / No__
[IF YES, ASK]: What kind of problem?

was it before or after the election or the District Assembly?
                                                Before__ / After__
did you find the person contacted: helpful?__ / unhelpful?__
did you find the person contacted was
   'honest' and fair-minded?   Yes__ / No__

THANK YOU VERY MUCH FOR YOUR CO-OPERATION

References

Acheampong, E. 1995, *The District Assemblies and Participatory Rural Development in Ghana*, unpublished Ph. D. thesis, University of Cambridge.
Africa Confidential, London.
Africa Report, Washington (monthly).
Ahmad, A. J. M. U. 1988,'Local Government Finance in Bangladesh: A Study of Three Union Parishads', *Bangladesh Rural Development Studies*, April.
Ahmad, A. J. M. U. and Alam, A. K. M. K. 1991, *Interpersonal Relations in Upazila Administration in Bangladesh – a Study on Eight Upazilas*, unpublished typescript.
Ahmed, A. 1990, 'Administrative Development Program and the Emergence of a New Local Government System in Bangladesh', *Philippine Journal of Public Administration*, 34: 43–51.
Ahwoi, K. 1992, 'Decentralized administration: progress, problems and prospects', in S. A. Nkrumah (ed.), *Financing District Development and Administration: Report on 5th Annual Workshop on Decentralization in Ghana*, School of Administration, University of Ghana.
Akhter, M. Y. 1990, 'Decentralization for Development: Experiments in Bangladesh', *Philippine Journal of Public Administration*, 34: 27–42.
Alam, A. M. Q. 1993, 'The Nature of the Bangladesh State in the post-1975 Period', *Contemporary South Asia*, 2: 311–26.
Alam, B. A. 1987, 'Women in Local Government: Profiles of Six Chairmen of Union Parishads', *Journal of Local Government*, 16: 79–94.
Ankomah, B. 1988, 'Elections Extraordinary', *New African*, December.
Ashford, D. 1975, 'Theories of Local Government: Some Comparative Considerations', *Comparative Political Studies*, 8: 90–107.
Attahi, K. 1989a, *Urbanisation, Réformes Administratives et Gestion Urbaine en Côte d'Ivoire*, CRAU, Université d'Abidjan and CUCS: University of Toronto.
  1989b, 'Côte d'Ivoire: An Evaluation of Urban Management Reforms', in R. Stren and R. White (eds.), *African Cities in Crisis*, Boulder, Colorado: Westview Press.
  1992, 'Planning and Management in Large Cities: A Case Study of Abidjan', in UNCHS (Habitat), *Metropolitan Planning and Management in the Developing World: Abidjan and Quito*, Nairobi: UNCHS.
Awotukun, A. M. (ed.) 1995, *New Trends in Nigerian Local Government*, Ile-Ife.
Ayee, J. R. A. 1990a, 'The Implementation of the 1988–89 District Assembly Elections in Ghana', *Africa Insight*, 20: 169–75.
  1990b, 'The Functions and Financial Resources of District Assemblies under

the 1988 Local Government Law in Ghana', *Journal of Management Studies*, 6: 46–55.

1991, 'Decentralization and Local Government under the PNDC of Ghana', unpublished paper presented to CODESRIA, University of Ghana.

1992, 'Decentralization and Effective Government: The Case of Ghana's District Assemblies', *Africa Insight*, 22: 49–56.

1994, *An Anatomy of Public Policy Implementation*, Aldershot: Avebury.

1995, 'Financing Sub-national Governments in Ghana: The District Assemblies Common Fund', *Regional and Federal Studies*, 5: 292–306.

1996, 'The Measurement of Decentralization: The Ghanaian Experience', *African Affairs*, 95, 378: 31–50.

1997, 'The December 1996 General Elections in Ghana: A Post-mortem', paper presented to the Political Studies Department Seminar, School of Oriental and African Studies, University of London.

Aziz, A. 1993, *Decentralised Planning: The Karnataka Experiment*, New Delhi: Sage Publications.

Aziz, A. and Arnold, D. D. (eds.) 1996, *Decentralised Governance in Asian Countries*, Thousand Oaks, California: Sage.

Bakary, T. 1984, 'Elite Transformation and Political Succession', in I. W. Zartman and C. Delgado (eds.), *The Political Economy of the Ivory Coast*, New York: Praeger.

1986, 'La démocratie par le haut en Côte d'Ivoire', *Géopolitique africaine*, 2: 207–30.

1991, 'Le retour au pluralisme politique en Côte d'Ivoire', *L'Année Africaine 1990–1*, Bordeaux: CEAN.

Bangladesh, Government of, n.d. *Manual of Upazila Administration*, vol. 2.

Barkan, J. and Chege, M. 1989, 'Decentralising the State: District Focus and the Politics of Reallocation in Kenya', *Journal of Modern African Studies*, 27: 431–53.

Bastian, S. (ed.) 1994, *Devolution and Development in Sri Lanka*, Colombo: International Centre for Ethnic Studies.

Becker, C. and Selwyn, W. 1975, *The Efficient Organisation*, New York: Elsevier.

Bennett, R. J. 1990, *Decentralisation, Local Government and Markets: Towards a Post-Welfare Agenda*, Oxford: Clarendon Press.

Bennett, R. J. (ed.) 1994, *Local Government and Market Decentralisation: Experiences in Industrialised, Developing and Former East Bloc Countries*, Tokyo: United Nations University Press.

Bird, R. 1994, *Decentralizing Infrastructure: For Good or for Ill, W*orking Paper and Background Paper for *World Development Report 1994*, Washington DC: World Bank.

Blair, H. W. 1987, *Decentralization and Possibilities for USAID Assistance in Bangladesh*, typescript, Dhaka: USAID.

1988, 'Success or Failure in Rural Development: A Comparison of Maharashtra, Bihar and Bangladesh', paper presented at the Association of Asian Studies.

1989, *Can Rural Development be Financed from Below?* Dhaka: NORAD.

Blau, P. M. and Scott, W. R. 1963, *Formal Organisations: A Comparative Approach*, London: Routledge and Kegan Paul.

Blunt, P. 1990, 'Strategies for Enhancing Organizations Effectiveness in the Third World', *Public Administration and Development*, 10, 3: 299-313.
Blunt, P., Richards, D. and Wilson, J. 1989, 'The Hidden Hand of Public Administration in Newly Emerging States', *Journal of International Development*, 1: 409-43.
BRAC 1983a, *The Net: Power Structure in Ten Villages*, Dhaka: BRAC.
1983b, *Who Gets What and Why: Resource Allocation in a Bangladesh Village*, Dhaka: BRAC.
Brett, E. A. 1994, 'Rebuilding Organisation Capacity in Uganda under the National Resistance Movement', *Journal of Modern African Studies*, 32: 53-80.
Brudney, J. L. and England, R. E. 1982, 'Urban Policy Making and Subjective Service Evaluations – Are They Compatible?', *Public Administration Review*, 42: 127-35.
Burkhead, J. and Hannigan, P. 1978, 'Productivity Analysis: A Search for Definition and Order', *Public Administration Review*, 38: 34-40.
Butler, D. *et al.* 1991, *India Decides: Elections, 1952-1991*, New Delhi: UM Books.
Carter, N. 1991, 'Learning to Measure Performance: The Use of Indicators in Organizations', *Public Administration*, 69: 85-101.
Casley, D. J. and Lury, D. A. 1982, *Monitoring and Evaluation of Agricultural and Rural Development Projects*, Baltimore: Johns Hopkins University Press.
Chabal, P. 1985, *Political Domination in Africa*, Cambridge: Cambridge University Press.
Chazan, N. 1983, *An Anatomy of Ghanaian Politics: Managing Political Recession, 1969-1982*, Boulder, Colorado: Westview Press.
CIRDAP (Centre for Integrated Rural Development for Asia and the Pacific) 1992, *Impact of Decentralization on Rural Poverty: An Asian Perspective*, Dhaka.
Cobbe, J. 1991, 'The Political Economy of Education Reform in Ghana', in Rothchild (ed.).
Cohen, J. M. and Uphoff, N. 1977, 'Rural Development Participation: Concepts and Measures for Policy Design, Implementation and Evaluation', *Rural Development Committee Monograph Series*, 2, Cornell University.
Cohen, M. 1980, 'Francophone Africa', in Rowatt, D. C. (ed.), *International Handbook on Local Government Reorganization*, London: Aldwych Press.
Collier, D. 1991, 'New Perspectives on the Comparative Method' in D. Rustow and K. Erickson (eds.), *Comparative Political Dynamics: Global Research Perspectives*, New York: Harper Collins.
Côte d'Ivoire 1980, Ministère de l'Economie, des Finances et du Plan, Administration de l'Étude Régionale d'Education, *A l'Ecoute des ruraux*.
1985, Ministère des Travaux Publics, Direction des Etudes et Programmes, *Préparation du 3ème projet de développement urbain DEP-BIRD*.
1988a, Ministère de l'Intérieur, DGCL, *L'Opération de Communalisation: Deuxième Phase, 1986-1990, Bilan Intermédiare au Titre des Années 1986 et 1987*.
1988b, Direction de la Statistique, *Recensement Général de la Population et de l'Habitat, 1988*.

References

1991a, Ministère de l'Intérieur, DGCL, *Dix Ans de Communalisation, 1981–1991, Recueil des Circulaires etc.*

1991b, Ministère de l'Intérieur, *DGCL, Résultats des Elections Municipales en 1985 et 1990.*

1992a, Direction et Contrôle des Grands Travaux, *Guide Municipale de la Côte d'Ivoire.*

1992b, Ministère de l'Intérieur, DGCL, *Tableau Synoptique des Communes, Exercice 1992.*

1992c, Direction et Contrôle des Grands Travaux, *Projet de Développement Municipal, Commune de Dikodougou, Programme d'Actions Concertées.*

1993a, Ministère de l'Economie, des Finances and du Plan, Direction des Budgets et Comptes, *Annexe à la Loi de Finances, Gestion 1993.*

1993b, Ministère de l'Intérieur, DGCL, *La Politique de Décentralisation en Côte d'Ivoire: Evolution et Perspectives.*

Crook, R. 1989, 'Patrimonialism, Administrative Effectiveness and Economic Development in Côte d'Ivoire', *African Affairs*, 88, 351: 205–28.

1991a, 'State, Society and Political Institutions in Côte d'Ivoire and Ghana', in J. Manor (ed.), *Rethinking Third World Politics*, London and New York: Longman, pp. 213–41.

1991b, 'Economic Management, Institutional Capacity and Agricultural Development', Conference on Governance and Economic Development in Sub-Saharan Africa, May 1991, Queen Elizabeth House, University of Oxford.

1995, 'Multiparty Democracy and Political Change in Côte d'Ivoire: Surviving the Crisis' in J. Wiseman (ed.), *Democracy and Political Change in Sub-Saharan Africa*, London: Routledge and Kegan Paul.

1997, 'Winning Coalitions and Ethno-regional Politics: The failure of the Opposition in the 1990 and 1995 Elections in Côte d'Ivoire', *African Affairs*, 96, 383: 215–42.

Crook, R. and Jerve, R. M. (eds.) 1991, *Government and Participation: Institutional Development, Decentralisation and Democracy in the Third World*, Bergen: Christian Michelsen Institute.

Crook, R. and Manor, J. 1991, *Enhancing Participation and Institutional Performance: Democratic Decentralisation in South Asia and West Africa, Phase One*, Report to ESCOR, the Overseas Development Administration, London.

Day, P. and Klein, R. 1987, *Accountabilities*, London: Tavistock.

De Guzman, E. P. 1992, 'Decentralisation: A Panacea or Bane for the People?', typescript, IDS, University of Sussex.

Delpech, B. 1983. 'Les Nouveaux Abidjanais et leurs racines', *Cahiers d'ORSTOM, sér. sci. hum. XIX*, 4: 567–84.

Dichter, T. 1989, 'Development Management – Plain or Fancy?', *Public Administration and Development*, 9: 381–94.

Dillinger, W. 1994, *Decentralization and its Implications for Urban Service Delivery*, Urban Management Program Discussion Paper 16, Washington DC: World Bank.

Dreze, J. and Sen, A. 1989, *Hunger and Public Action*, Oxford: Oxford University Press.

1990, *The Political Economy of Hunger, Volume Two, Famine Prevention*, Oxford: Oxford University Press.

Dubresson, A. 1990, 'Réforme communale et gestion des villes de l'intérieur en Côte d'Ivoire', *Communication au Colloque Internationale, Ouagadougou*, Université de Ougadougou, Secretariat d'Etat à l'Habitat et à l'Urbanisme, 1–5 October 1990.
Dubresson, A. and Vidal, C. 1991, *Loin d'Abidjan: les cadres, urbanistes de l'intérieur*, Abidjan: ORSTOM.
Dubresson, A. and Jaglin, S. 1993, *Pouvoirs et cités d'Afrique noire*, Paris: Karthala.
Dunn, J. and Robertson, A. 1973, *Dependence and Opportunity: Political Change in Ahafo, Ghana*, Cambridge: Cambridge University Press.
Dunsire, A. 1978, *The Execution Process, Vol. 2: Control in a Bureaucracy*, Oxford: Martin Robertson.
Dutheil de la Rochère, J. 1976, *L'Etat et le développement économique de la Côte d'Ivoire*, Paris: IEP/CEAN.
Faber, M. 1991, *Development Planning in Ghana: What Parts of the System Merit Technical Assistance? An Inquiry with Recommendations to the Overseas Development Administration*, Brighton: Institute of Development Studies.
Faizullah, M. 1989a, *An Examination in the Key Operational Issues of Rural Local Governments with a View to Improving Their Functioning*, Dhaka: NILG.
  1989b, *Towards Effective Local Government in Bangladesh*, Dhaka: NILG.
Fauré, Y.-A. 1989, 'Ivory Coast: Analysing a Crisis', in J. Dunn, R. Rathbone and D. C. O'Brien (eds.), *Contemporary West African States*, Cambridge: Cambridge University Press.
  1991, 'Sur la démocratisation en Côte d'Ivoire: passé et présent', *L'Année Africaine 1990–91*, Bordeaux: CEAN.
Ford Foundation 1992, *Perspectives on India's Development in the 1990s: Overview*, New Delhi: Ford Foundation.
Foster, C. 1996, 'Reflections on the True Significance of the Scott Report for Government Accountability', *Public Administration*, 74: 567–92.
Fraternité Hebdo 1987, *Les Municipalités: la démocratie en actes, édition 1985–90*, Abidjan.
Fraternité Hebdo, Abidjan (weekly).
Fraternité Matin 1988, 'Communes: un pari sur l'avenir', Spéciale Indépendence, déc.
Fraternité Matin, Abidjan (daily).
Fried, R. C. 1980, *Comparative Urban Politics: A Performance Approach*, Englewood Cliffs, N. J.: Prentice Hall.
Gasper, D. 1989, *Multi-Level Planning and Development Administration in Botswana*, Harare: Department of Rural and Urban Planning, University of Zimbabwe.
Gastellu, J. M. and Affou, Y. 1982, 'Un mythe à décomposer: la bourgeoisie de planteurs', in Fauré, Y.-A. and Médard, J. F. (eds.), *Etat et Bourgeoisie en Côte d'Ivoire*, Paris: Karthala.
Gbaka, K. 1992, *Fiscalité Communale: rêve ou réalité?*, Abidjan: PUSAF.
Gboyega, A. 1994, 'Decentralization and Local Autonomy in Nigeria's Federal System', paper presented at the Conference on Democratic Decentralisation in Asia and Africa, Institute of Commonwealth Studies, London, September 1994.

Ghana 1985, *1984 Population Census of Ghana, Special Report on Localities*, Accra.
  1991, *From Centre to the Grassroots*, Ministry of Local Government, Accra.
Ghana National Commission for Democracy, 1991, *Report of the NCD Regional Seminar: The District Assemblies and the Evolving Democratic Process*, Accra.
Graf, D. 1988, *The Nigerian State*, London: James Currey.
Graham, L. S. 1991, 'Public Policy and Administration in Comparative Perspective', in H. Wiarda (ed.), *New Directions in Comparative Politics*, Boulder, Colorado: Westview Press.
Gyimah-Boadi, E. 1990, 'Economic Recovery and Politics in the PNDC's Ghana', *Journal of Commonwealth and Comparative Politics*, 28: 328–43.
Haque, A. S. 1985, 'The Politics of Local Government Reform in Rural Bangladesh', *Public Administration and Development* 5: 205–19.
Harmon, M. and Mayer, R. 1986, *Organisation Theory for Public Administration*, Boston: Little, Brown and Co.
Hatry, H. P. 1978, 'The Status of Productivity Measurement in the Public Sector', *Public Administration Review*, 38: 28–33.
Healey, J. M. and Robinson, M. 1992, *Democracy, Governance and Economic Policy: Sub-Saharan Africa in Comparative Perspective*, London: ODI.
Hegde, R. 1994, 'Local Self-Government in Karnataka: Planning from Below', in M. S. Adiseshiah *et al.*, *Decentralised Planning and Panchayati Raj*, New Delhi: Institute of Social Sciences.
Herbst, J. 1993, *The Politics of Reform in Ghana, 1982–91*, Berkeley: University of California Press.
Holtsberg, C. 1990, *Issues on Poverty Alleviation and Rural Development: Discussion Paper for the Like Minded Group in Dhaka*, Dhaka: NORAD.
Huntington, S. P. and Nelson, J. 1976, *No Easy Choice: Political Participation in Developing Countries*, Cambridge: Cambridge University Press.
India, Government of, 1978, *Report of the Committee on Panchayati Raj Institutions*, New Delhi.
Institute of Social Sciences 1989, *Social Background of Zila Parishad Members in Karnataka, 1989*, New Delhi: Institute of Social Sciences.
  1992, *The New Panchayati Raj in Karnataka: An Evaluation*, New Delhi: Institute of Social Sciences.
  n.d. *Karnataka: Mandal Panchayat Members, Social Background, 1990*, New Delhi: Institute of Social Sciences.
International Monetary Fund 1995, *International Financial Statistics Yearbook 1995*, Washington DC: IMF.
Islam, N. 1987, *Devolutionary Strategies in Sri Lanka: Political Decentralization and Ethnic Conflict*, Faculty of Administration, University of Ottawa.
Israel, A. 1987, *Institutional Development: Incentives and Performance*, Baltimore: Johns Hopkins University Press.
Jabbra, J. G. and Dwivedi, O. P. (eds.), 1988, *Public Service Accountability: A Comparative Perspective*, West Hartford: Kumarian Press.
Jacobeit, C. 1991, 'Reviving Cocoa: Policies and Perspectives on Structural Adjustment in Ghana's Key Agricultural Sector', in Rothchild (ed.).
Jahan, R. 1980, *Bangladesh Politics: Problems and Issues*, Dhaka: University Press Limited.
Jain, L. C. 1993, 'Panchayats', *The Administrator*, 71–85.

Jeffries, R. 1989, 'Ghana: The Political Economy of Personal Rule', in D. C. O'Brien, J. Dunn and R. Rathbone (eds.), *West African States*, Cambridge: Cambridge University Press.

Jeffries, R. and Thomas, C. 1993, 'The Ghanaian Elections of 1992', *African Affairs*, 92: 331–66.

Karnataka, Government of, 1974, *Statistics for Planning*, Bangalore.

—— 1983, *The Karnataka Zilla Parishads, Taluk Panchayat Samithis, Mandal Panchayats and Nyaya Panchayats Act, 1983 and Various Rules Framed under the ... Act*, Bangalore.

—— 1989, *Report of the Zilla Parishad and Mandal Panchayat Evaluation Committee*, Bangalore.

Khan, M. M. 1987, 'The Politics of Administrative Reform', *Public Administration and Development*, 7: 351–62.

—— 1988, *The Decentralized Planning Process in Bangladesh*, Bangkok and The Hague.

—— 1992, 'Policy and "Democratization" in Bangladesh (1971–1990)', in R. K. Arora (ed.), *Politics and Administration in Changing Societies*, New Delhi, pp. 177–85.

—— 1996, 'Local Self-government System in Rural Bangladesh', in Aziz and Arnold (eds.), pp. 42–62.

Kramsjo, B. and Wood, G. D. 1992, *Breaking the Chains: Collective Action for Social Justice among the Rural Poor of Bangladesh*, London: Intermediate Technology Publications.

Kraus, J. 1991, 'The Political Economy of Stabilization and Structural Adjustment in Ghana', in Rothchild (ed.).

La Voix des Communes 1988, Séminaire UVICOCI, oct. 1988, Nouvelle Série 1, Abidjan.

Leitan, G. R. T. 1990, *Political Integration through Decentralization and Devolution of Power: The Sri Lankan Experience*, Department of History and Political Science, University of Colombo.

Leonard, D. K. 1987, 'The Political Realities of African Management', *World Development*, 15: 899–910.

—— 1991, *African Successes: Four Public Managers*, Berkeley: University of California Press.

Leonard, D. K. and Marshall, D. R. 1982, *Institutions of Rural Development for the Poor: Decentralization and Organizational Linkages*, Berkeley: I. S. S., University of California.

Leonard, D. K. and Prewitt, K. 1974, 'Quantification, Productivity and Groups', in A. Adedji and G. Hyden (eds.), *Developing Research on African Administration*, Ile-Ife.

Lesourd, M. 1988, 'La forêt, la machette et le billet de banque', *Cahiers d'ORSTOM, sér. sci. hum.* 24: 73–97.

Likierman, A. 1988, *Public Expenditure: The Public Spending Process*, London: Penguin.

Local Government Information Digest, Ministry of Local Government, Accra (periodical, irregular).

Maddock, N. 1990, 'On Monitoring and Evaluation of Rural Development under Decentralisation', *Third World Planning Review*, 12: 249–60.

Maniruzzaman, T. 1992, 'The Fall of the Military Dictator: 1991 Elections and the Prospects of Civilian Rule in Bangladesh', *Pacific Affairs*, 65: 203–24.
Maniruzzaman, T. and Razia Akter Banu, U. A. B. 1983, 'Civilian Succession and the 1981 Presidential Election in Bangladesh', in P. Lyon and J. Manor (eds.) *Transfer and Transformation: Political Institutions in the New Commonwealth*, Leicester: Leicester University Press, pp. 117–42.
Manor, J. 1977a, 'The Evolution of Political Arenas and Units of Social Organisation' in M. N. Srinivas *et al.* (eds.) *Dimensions of Social Change in India*, Bombay: Allied Publishers, pp. 169–87.
  1977b, *Political Change in an Indian State*, Canberra: Australian National University Monographs.
  1977c, 'Structural Change in Karnataka Politics', *Economic and Political Weekly*, 29 October: 1865–9.
  1980a, 'A Changer of India', *The Economist*, 29 March.
  1980b, 'Pragmatic Progressives in Regional Politics', *Economic and Political Weekly*, annual number: 201–14.
  1989, 'Karnataka: Caste, Class, Dominance and Politics in a Cohesive Society', in F. Frankel and M. S. A. Rao (eds.), *Dominance and State Power in Modern India: Decline of a Social Order*, vol. 1, Delhi: Oxford University Press, pp. 322–61.
  1993, 'India', in D. Butler and A. Ranney (eds.), *Electioneering: A Comparative Study of Continuity and Change*, Oxford: Clarendon Press, pp. 110–32.
  1994, 'Political Regeneration in India', in A. Nandy and D. L. Sheth (eds.), *The Multiverse of Democracy*, New Delhi: Sage Publications, pp. 230–41.
Maro, P. S. 1990, 'The Impact of Decentralization on Spatial Equity and Rural Development in Tanzania', *World Development*, 185: 673–93.
Marsden, D. and Oakley, P. 1990, *Evaluating Social Development Projects*, Oxford: Oxfam.
Mawhood, P. 1991, 'The Politics of Decentralisation: Eastern Europe and Africa', in Crook and Jerve (eds.).
Mawhood, P. (ed.) 1983, *Local Government in the Third World*, New York and Chichester: Wiley (republished in 1993, Pretoria: Wiley).
Mayer, L. 1989, *Redefining Comparative Politics*, London: Sage.
McCarthy, F. E. 1993, 'Decentralization and regime politics in Bangladesh during the Ershad regime', *Journal of Social Studies*, 61:102–30.
Miller, W. L. 1988, *Irrelevant Elections? The Quality of Local Democracy in Britain*, Oxford: Clarendon Press.
Moore, M. 1993, 'Declining to Learn from the East? The World Bank on Governance and Development', *IDS Bulletin*, 24: 39–50l.
Moris, J. 1991, 'Institutional Choice and Local Development', in Crook and Jerve (eds.).
N'gethe, N. 1994, 'The Politics of Democratisation through Decentralisation in Kenya', paper presented at the Conference on Democratic Decentralisation in Asia and Africa, Institute of Commonwealth Studies, London, September 1994.
Nickson, R. A. 1995, *Local Government in Latin America*, Boulder, Colorado and London: Lynne Riener and Westview Press.

Ninsin, K. 1991, 'The PNDC and the Problem of Legitimacy', in Rothchild. (ed.).
Nugent, P. 1995, *Big Men, Small Boys and Politics in Ghana: Power, Ideology and the Burden of History, 1982–1994*, London and New York: Pinter.
O'Loughlin, M. G. 1990, 'What is Bureaucratic Accountability and How Can we Measure it?', *Administration and Society*, 22: 275–302.
Ogutu, F. 1989 *District Planning in Kenya: A view from the Bottom*, unpublished Ph. D. thesis, University of California.
Olowu, D. 1994, 'Decentralization, Democratization, and Development in Africa', paper presented at the Conference on Democratic Decentralisation in Asia and Africa, Institute of Commonwealth Studies, London, September 1994.
Olowu, D. and Wunsch, J. S. (eds.) 1990, *The Failure of the Centralized State: Institutions and Self-Governance*, Boulder, Colorado: Westview Press.
Omara-Otunnu, A. 1992, 'The Struggle for Democracy in Uganda', *Journal of Modern African Studies*, 303, 443–63.
Oquaye, M. 1995, 'Decentralisation and Development: The Ghanaian Case under the PNDC', *Journal of Commonwealth and Comparative Politics*, 33: 209–39.
Ostrom, E., Schroeder, L. and Wynne, S. 1993, *Institutional Incentives and Sustainable Development: Infrastructure Policies in Perspective*, San Francisco: Westview Press.
Ostrom, V. 1989, 'Guidance, Control and Performance in the Public Sector', in Sanda *et al.*
Oyugi, W. O. 1990, *Decentralized Development Planning and Management in Kenya: An Assessment*, Washington DC: World Bank.
Parry, G., Moyser, G. and Day, N. 1992, *Political Participation and Democracy in Britain*, Cambridge: Cambridge University Press.
Paul, S. 1994, *Does Voice Matter? For Public Accountability, Yes*, Washington DC: World Bank.
Peasah, J. 1994, *Local-Level Government in Papua New Guinea: A Study in Change and Continuity in the Development of Liberal-Democratic Self-Determination at the Local Level*, Boroko: National Research Institute.
Putnam, R. 1993, *Making Democracy Work: Civic Traditions in Modern Italy*, Princeton: Princeton University Press.
Ragin, C. 1987, *The Comparative Method: Beyond Qualitative and Quantitative Strategies*, Berkeley: University of California Press.
Rahman, A. 1988, 'The State, Local Power Brokers and Rural Development in Bangladesh: A Study of the Selected Upazilla Chairmen', *Sociology and Development*.
Rahman, H. Z. 1990, 'Landscape of Violence: Local Elections and Political Culture in Bangladesh', *Economic and Political Weekly*, 24 November: 2622–4.
Ramm, J. -F. 1993, *Rethinking Decentralization in Papua New Guinea*, Nagoya: United Nations Centre for Regional Development.
Ray, A. 1991, *Political Participation, Rural Development and Local Government Reforms in India*, Tokyo: Pinter.
Rimmer, D. 1992, *Staying Poor: Ghana's Political Economy, 1950–1990*, Oxford: Pergamon Press.

Robbins, S. 1990, *Organisation Theory*, Englewood Cliffs, N. J. : Prentice Hall.
Rose, R. and Peters, B. G. 1981, 'Memorandum to Treasury and Civil Service Committee', *Third Report from Treasury and Civil Service Committee, Parliamentary Papers 1981-2, vol. 27, No. 236*, Great Britain: House of Commons.
Rothchild, D. 1991 (ed.), *Ghana: The Political Economy of Reform*, Boulder and Colorado: Westview Press.
Rueschmeyer, D., Stevens, E. and Stevens, J. 1992, *Capitalist Development and Democracy*, Cambridge: Cambridge University Press.
Ruf, F. 1985, *Politiques et encadrement agricole: partage des tâches en Côte d'Ivoire*, Abidjan: IRAT/CIRAD.
Saint-Vil, J. 1991, 'Les communes ne doivent pas compter sur l'état Providence', *Fraternité Matin*, 8 January.
Sanda, A., Olowu, D. and Ojo, S. 1989, *Managing Performance in Nigeria's Public Sector*, Ile Ife.
Saqui, Q. M. A. and Mukabber, M. 1988, *Local Resource Mobilisation: A Case Study of Selected Upazila and Union Parishads*, Dhaka: NILG.
Schick, L. 1990, 'Budgeting for Results', *Public Administration Review*, 50: 26-34.
Semboja, J. and Therkildsen, O. 1994, 'Decentralization, participation and spatial equity in rural Tanzania: a comment', *World Development*, 225: 807-10.
Shah, A. 1991, 'The New Fiscal Federalism in Brazil', World Bank Discussion Paper No. 124, Washington DC: World Bank.
Shivaramu, K. and Channegowda, M. B. 1982, 'Perceived Problems of Members of Mandal Panchayats', *Journal of Rural Development*, 11: 1-10.
Slater, R. 1991, 'The New Panchayati Raj - An Alternative Paradigm?', typescript.
Smith, B. C. 1985, *Decentralization: The Territorial Dimension of the State*, London: Allen and Unwin.
Smith, T. 1991, 'The Comparative Analysis of Bureaucratic Accountability', *Asian Journal of Public Administration*, 13, 1: 93-104.
Smoke, P. 1993, 'Local Government Fiscal Reform in Developing Countries: Lessons from Kenya', *World Development*, 216: 901-23.
Smoke, P. and Olowu, D. 1992, 'Determinants of Success in African Local Governments: An Overview', *Public Administration and Development*, 12: 1-17.
Tanzi, V. 1995, *Fiscal Federalism and Decentralisation: A Review of Some Efficiency and Macro-Economic Aspects*, paper presented at the Annual World Bank Conference on Development Economics, 1995, Washington DC: World Bank.
Tay, H. 1974, *L'Administration ivoirienne*, Paris: Berger-Levrault.
Teune, H. 1990, 'Comparing Countries: Lessons Learned', in E. Oyen (ed.), *Comparative Methodology*, London: Sage.
Therkildsen, O. 1993, 'Successful African Local Government: Some Methodological and Conceptual Issues', *Public Administration and Development*, 13: 501-5.
Thomas, B. 1987, 'In Search of Institutional Effectiveness', *International Journal of Administrative Science*, 53: 555-79.
Thynne, I. S. and Goldring, J. 1987, *Accountability and Control: Government Officials and the Exercise of Power*, Sydney: The Law Book Co.

Uphoff, N. 1986, *Local Institutional Development: An Analytical Sourcebook*, West Hartford.
Vengroff, R. and Johnston, A. 1989, *Decentralization and the Implementation of Rural Development in Senegal*, Lewiston, New York: Mellen Press.
Verba, S., Nie, N. H. and Kim, J. O. 1978, *Participation and Political Equality: A Seven Nation Comparison*, Cambridge: Cambridge University Press.
Webster, N. 1994, 'Panchayati Raj and Democratic Decentralisation in West Bengal, India', paper presented at the Conference on Democratic Decentralisation in Asia and Africa, Institute of Commonwealth Studies, London, September 1994.
Werlin, H. 1992, 'Linking Decentralization and Centralization: A Critique of the New Development Administration', *Public Administration and Development*, 123: 223–35.
West Africa, London (weekly).
Widdecombe, D. 1986, *The Conduct of Local Authority Business, Cmnd. 9797*, London: HMSO.
Woode, S. 1989, *Making the District Assembly Work*, Accra: Tema Press.
World Bank 1983, *Bangladesh: Selected Issues in Rural Employment*, Washington DC.
   1989, *Sub-Saharan Africa: From Crisis to Sustainable Growth*, Washington DC.
   1992, *Governance and Development*, Washington DC.
   1995, *World Development Report, 1995*, Washington DC.
   n.d., 'Aide Mémoire: Ghana: Fiscal Decentralization', Accra (unpublished document).

Index

Abidjan (Côte d'Ivoire), 5n, 138, 141, 147, 148, 171, 172, 285
absenteeism, 19, 58–61, 69, 117–18, 132, 281
accountability, 2, 10–14, 19, 20, 21, 30, 42–9, 102–11, 115, 116, 118, 122, 135, 142, 168, 203, 233–4, 240–7, 267, 268, 269, 272, 280, 284, 285, 286, 287, 288, 289, 290, 291, 292, 294, 295, 296, 297–300, 302–4
Accra (Ghana), 206, 212, 213, 239, 242
administration, *see* bureaucracy
Adzopé, 148
Affery, 148, 151, 171, 180, 187, 193–4
agriculture, 3, 136–7, 202
Anglophone practices and perceptions, 3
associations, voluntary, 33–6, 67, 71, 87, 94, 95, 98, 99, 100–1, 153, 160, 203
autonomy, political, 13, 14, 20, 52–6, 58, 70, 89–90, 107, 108, 110, 111–13, 282, 286, 298, 300, 301, 303
Awami League (Bangladesh), 92
Ayee, J. R. A., 237n, 254n, 267n

Bangalore (Karnataka, India), 26, 39, 56
Bangladesh, 3–4, 5, 6, 25, 41, 50, 52, 56, 67, 69, 70, 76, 85–135, 218, 272, 273, 278, 279, 280, 281, 282, 283, 286, 287, 288, 289, 290, 291, 292, 293, 296, 299
Bangladesh National Party (BNP), 4, 92, 93
Bédié, H. K., 5, 136, 137
Bihar (India), 25, 297
Bogra District (Bangladesh), 87–9, 91n, 100, 101, 105, 106, 111n, 122n
Botswana, 297
Brazil, 291n, 293
budgets and budgeting, 3, 9, 13, 14, 18, 20, 22, 52–3, 80–1, 84, 85–6, 110, 111, 119, 146, 173–4, 208, 238–40, 241–5, 285, 288, 292, 298
bureaucracy, 2, 3, 4, 5, 6–7, 8, 9, 10, 12, 13, 14, 15, 19, 22, 23, 27, 31, 32–3, 38, 41, 42, 44–68, 69–70, 72, 73–4, 77–8, 80, 81, 84, 85, 89, 94, 98, 101, 103–9, 112, 114, 115, 116–17, 118, 119, 120, 121, 122, 124–5, 126, 128, 132–3, 134, 170, 202, 203, 204, 205, 207, 208, 209, 210, 217, 220, 223, 224, 230, 233–40, 241, 242–6, 278, 281, 284, 285, 287, 288, 289, 291, 293, 296, 297, 298, 299, 300, 303

campaigning, 7–8, 27, 34, 37, 40–1, 90, 92, 152, 215, 272
castes, 18, 23–5, 26, 28, 29, 31, 33–42, 52, 65, 76–7, 78, 79, 80, 81n, 279, 280, 281, 295, 302
central governments, 1, 4, 5, 6–7, 8, 14, 16, 20, 22–3, 29, 33, 42–5, 48, 51–5, 60, 61, 68–70, 73–4, 76, 79, 80–2, 84, 87, 89–94, 103, 104, 105, 106, 112, 113, 114, 119, 122, 204, 208, 210, 235–40, 282, 284, 285, 286, 287, 288, 290–1, 293, 294, 296, 297, 302, 303
centralised governance, 1, 4–5, 62, 80–2, 89–90, 110, 119, 122, 137, 138, 205, 235–40, 251–2, 262, 265, 290–1, 297
chicanery, political, 29–30, 54–5, 68–9, 77–8, 90–3, 103, 104–6, 121, 133, 134, 213, 234–5, 242, 281, 303 (*see also*, concealment; corruption)
Chile, 299, 302
civil society, 1, 3, 16, 17, 25, 76, 83–4, 86–8, 94, 100, 103, 105, 131–3, 137, 138, 203, 207, 246, 274, 275, 277, 283, 285, 291, 296, 300, 302–4 (*see also*, associations, voluntary; non-governmental organisations; society; unions, trade/labour)
cocoa farming, 136, 196, 200, 212, 277
Colombia, 293
Committees for the Defence of the Revolution (CDRs) (Ghana), 204, 209, 213, 216, 217, 218, 220, 221, 225, 232, 234, 236, 244, 245, 274–5, 296

331

332 Index

communes (Côte d'Ivoire), 4–5, 138–9, 140, 141, 143, 146, 147, 200, 272, 276, 278, 282, 285–6
Communism, 2, 38, 302
concealment, 54–6, 61–8 (*see also*, transparency)
conflict, political, 4, 15, 25, 27, 46, 48, 80, 83–4, 87, 90–1, 100, 104–7, 203, 204, 212, 272, 295
Congress Party (India), 22, 23, 26, 28, 38, 48, 51, 67, 68, 80
constitutions, 4, 73, 82, 204, 269, 295
contacting politicians and bureaucrats, 7, 16, 17, 19, 20, 32–3, 40–1, 94–6, 98, 126, 128–9, 154, 216, 218, 219, 220, 230–1, 272, 276, 278, 284, 286, 290
Convention People's Party, 203
co-ordination, administrative, 45, 49–50, 86, 107, 116–17, 144, 199–200, 210, 237, 264, 268
corruption, 1, 2, 10, 19, 29, 42, 60–8, 69, 72–3, 78, 79–80, 84, 91, 92, 97, 105, 106, 108–09, 112, 118–23, 125, 127, 129, 130, 131–2, 135, 138, 184n, 204, 168, 268, 281, 282, 287, 292, 296, 299, 300, 303
Côte d'Ivoire, 3, 4–5, 6, 17, 56, 70, 76, 87, 136–7, 202, 213, 215, 218, 272, 273, 274, 276, 278, 280, 281–2, 283, 285–6, 287, 289, 290, 291, 294, 299

decentralisation, *see* deconcentration; devolution
deconcentration, 2, 3, 4, 5, 6–7, 13, 14, 86, 143, 204, 208, 233–4, 237–40, 270, 284, 287, 297, 301
democracy and democratisation, 1–5, 19, 26, 32, 83–4, 117–18, 121, 135, 138, 203, 204–5, 223, 226, 268, 276, 279, 282, 285, 288, 298, 303–4
devolution, 2, 3, 4, 6–7, 13, 14, 23, 40, 104, 111, 135, 141, 143, 207, 300
Dhaka (Bangladesh), 86, 87, 88, 89, 90, 92, 104, 105, 106, 107, 116, 132
Dharwar District (Karnataka), 26, 28, 38, 42, 46n, 55n, 59n, 77
Dikodougou, 147, 151, 159, 182, 195, 196
Direction et Contrôle des Grands Travaux (DCGTx), 183, 195
District Assemblies Common Fund, 208, 248n, 269
District Assemblies (Ghana), 3–4, 204–10, 272, 274, 275–6, 277, 282, 284–5
District Councils (Karnataka), 3–4, 22, 27, 28, 31, 32, 35–9, 40–2, 45–51, 53–6, 58–82, 279, 281

East Akim District (Ghana), 206, 211, 214, 215, 218, 219, 221, 223, 225, 226n, 227, 228, 230, 231, 233, 237–8, 239, 240, 241, 242, 243, 246–7, 248, 249, 251, 252, 253, 254, 255, 258, 260, 261, 262
East Mamprusi District (Ghana), 206, 211, 213, 214, 215, 221, 223, 225, 227, 229, 230, 231, 232, 233, 237, 238, 239, 240, 241, 242, 243, 244, 245, 246–7, 249, 251, 252, 253, 255, 257, 260, 261, 264
economic reform, 13, 138, 251, 284, 300, 301 (*see also*, neo-liberal economics)
Ecuador, 293
education, 34–5, 38, 39, 42, 52, 59–61, 75, 76, 81–2, 85, 96, 97, 108, 117, 124, 128, 155–6, 158, 165–7, 190–3, 200, 207, 211, 222, 224, 225, 226, 227, 228–33, 237, 241, 243, 244, 260, 262, 275, 276, 277, 281, 282
effectiveness, 2, 9, 14, 18, 21, 45, 50–1, 52–69, 80, 111–25, 177–83, 247–56, 279, 291 (*see also*, projects, developmental; service delivery)
efficiency, *see* effectiveness
elected politicians, role of, 11–12, 14, 15, 16, 17, 20, 22, 23, 27–31, 38–41, 44–55, 57–70, 73–5, 76, 80–2, 84, 89, 90–5, 101, 102–11, 112–32, 159–62, 173–5, 207–9, 210, 212, 215, 216, 217–20, 221, 222–3, 226–9, 231–6, 242–7, 266, 272, 273–4, 275, 278, 282, 284, 285, 286, 287–9, 291, 292, 293, 294, 297, 299, 301; devices to ensure their encounters with citizens, 29–32, 58, 74–5, 95–6, 163–4, 165–7, 168, 199, 217, 219, 228–9, 274, 277, 278, 289, 290, 293, 299, 301–2
elections and electoral politics, 2, 3, 4, 5, 10, 11, 12, 14, 16, 19, 22–3, 27–9, 35–8, 40, 90–4, 101, 119, 121, 122, 134, 136, 137, 138, 143, 148–53, 198, 207, 213–16, 271–3, 275, 281, 285–6, 287, 289, 290, 292, 294, 296, 299, 302 (*see also*, campaigning; elected politicians)
electrification, 188, 195, 262, 264
elites, 13, 17, 19, 35, 39–40, 75, 79, 86, 99, 100, 105, 111, 114, 118, 126, 129–31, 133, 134, 137, 139, 161, 170–2, 200–1, 202, 203, 204, 207, 219, 223–31, 233, 255–6, 275, 279–80, 282, 285, 287, 294, 300, 301–2
equality, 2, 75 (*see also*, inequality; poor people)
Ershad, H. M., 4, 85, 87, 89, 90–3, 103, 104, 105, 106, 107, 112, 113, 116, 120, 121, 128, 132, 133, 134, 135, 287, 293

fairness, 10, 12, 19, 27–9, 36, 72–3, 79, 90–3, 128–9, 131–2, 134–5, 198, 214, 299

Index

financing decentralisation, *see* fiscal systems and policy; local resource mobilisation; revenue; tax-raising powers
fiscal systems and policy, 2, 12, 14, 20, 50, 52–3, 71, 80–1, 104, 107, 110, 111–13, 114, 116, 118, 126, 127, 131, 132, 135, 140, 145, 146, 208, 237, 238–9, 242–6, 247–8, 253–4, 266, 275, 282, 283, 284, 285, 286, 287, 288, 289, 290, 291, 293, 296, 298, 299, 300 (*see also*, local resource mobilisation; revenue; tax-raising powers)
Fonds régionaux d'aménagement rurale (FRAR), 167–8, 185
Francophone practices and perceptions, 3, 4, 141, 144, 146, 294, 295, 299
Front Populaire Ivoirien (FPI), 148, 151, 160, 170, 194

Gandhi, Indira, 68
Gandhi, Rajiv, 55
Gandhian ideas, 2
gender, *see* women
Ghana, 3–4, 5, 6, 52, 56, 70, 76, 87, 202–70, 272, 273, 274, 275, 277, 278, 280, 282, 283, 284–5, 286, 287, 289, 290, 291, 295, 296, 297, 299, 300

health, 46, 50–1, 52, 59–61, 65, 75, 78, 85, 105, 108, 113, 120, 128, 130–1, 190, 195, 207, 211, 224, 237, 242, 262, 281, 282
Hegde, Ramakrishna, 57n
Houphouët-Boigny, Félix, 5, 136, 138

implementation of policy, 11, 12, 13–14, 18, 20, 27, 42–9, 75, 84, 102, 240–1, 243–4, 246–7, 298
India, 2–3, 18, 22, 34, 35, 68–9, 79, 80, 82, 87, 94, 96, 103, 107, 109, 110, 117, 120, 122, 123, 125, 218, 279, 280, 299, 300, 302 (*see also*, Bihar; Karnataka; Maharashtra; West Bengal)
Indonesia, 301
inequality, 4, 23, 25, 33–42, 78–9, 83, 86–7, 97, 99, 102, 118, 125, 130, 155–6, 162, 202, 301–2
information flow, 27, 30–1, 42–52, 70, 74–6, 84, 281, 303
instability, political, 3, 4, 68–9, 202
interest groups, *see* civil society
Italy, 304
Ivory Coast, *see* Côte d'Ivoire

Jacqueville, 139
Janata Party (India), 22, 26, 28, 39, 54, 66n, 68, 81–2

Jatiyo Party (Bangladesh), 4, 90, 92, 93, 132, 133, 134
Jawahar Rozgar Yojana programme, 55–6, 70n, 288
journalists, *see* press

Karnataka (India), 3–4, 6, 22–84, 86, 94, 100, 103, 107, 109, 110, 111, 112, 115, 117, 120, 130, 132, 135, 271n, 273, 274, 278, 279, 280, 281, 283, 288, 289, 290, 291, 298, 302, 303
Kenya, 296, 297
Korhogo, 147, 160

Latin America, 1, 293, 294, 295n, 299
legitimacy, 1–2, 10, 80, 82, 90–1, 93, 132, 133, 198, 203, 222, 265, 266, 268, 292, 295, 296
levels in political systems, 13–14, 18, 20, 22–3, 39–40, 49–50, 52–8, 84, 86, 87, 104–9, 112, 114–15, 175–6, 199–200, 204–8, 264, 269, 285
lobbying, 7, 16, 38–9, 76, 83, 101
local awareness and knowledge, *see* popular awareness and knowledge
local councils, *see* communes; Mandal Councils; Union Councils
local demands, *see* popular demands
local needs, 1, 19, 42, 49–50, 70–1, 78, 127, 188–90, 257–60, 281, 282–3 (*see also*, popular demands; popular preferences)
local preferences, *see* popular preferences
local resource mobilisation, 3, 8, 10, 12, 14, 49, 53–4, 56, 113–14, 139, 208–9, 218, 220, 221–2, 241–2, 248, 263, 264, 275, 282, 285, 286

Maharashtra (India), 297, 299
Mamprusi District Council, 249, 250, 252, 253, 261
Mandal Councils (Karnataka), 4, 22, 27, 28, 29–32, 35–7, 39–42, 44, 48–51, 53–82, 278–9, 281, 288, 289
Mandal Panchayats (Karnataka), *see* Mandal Councils
Manikganj District (Bangladesh), 87–9, 91n, 100, 101, 111n, 122, 125
Mawhood, P., 298
Mayors (Côte d'Ivoire), 143, 146, 159, 168, 169–72, 185, 287, 194
Mbengué, 147, 179, 194
meetings, public, 16–17, 29–32, 34, 37, 41, 58, 94, 95–6, 98, 101, 153–4, 215, 216, 217, 218, 220, 230–1, 232–3, 272–4, 275, 276
methodology, 5–6, 15–20, 70–1, 210–13, 305–19

Mexico, 293
military, 4, 13, 84, 87, 89, 90, 92, 106, 119, 135, 204, 225, 235, 278, 279, 281, 284, 287, 292
multi-party politics, 1, 4, 5, 1–13, 25, 53, 65–8, 77, 83–4, 90–3, 120, 140, 148, 204, 205, 236, 278, 285, 288–9, 296, 302–3 (*see also*, parties, political; single-party politics)
municipal councils (Côte d'Ivoire), 137, 141, 142, 169
municipality, *see* municipal councils
Mysore District (Karnataka), 26, 28, 38–9, 42, 46n, 59n, 75, 77–8

National Assembly (Côte d'Ivoire), 137, 138, 140
National Democratic Congress (Ghana), 205
Nazir Sab, Abdul, 59n
neo-liberal economics, 1–2, 301 (*see also*, economic reform; structural adjustment)
New Public Management, 300–1
Nkrumah, Kwame, 203
Nigeria, 291n, 293, 296, 298, 299, 300
non-governmental organisations (NGOs), 31, 71, 87–9, 100–2, 133, 297 (*see also*, associations, voluntary; civil society)
Nugent, P., 205n

obligation, political, 32, 117–18, 132, 289
Olowu, D., 297, 298
outputs, *see* projects, developmental

Pakistan, 99
Papua New Guinea, 300, 301–2
Paraguay, 293
Parry, G., 154n
Parti Démocratique de la Côte d'Ivoire (PDCI), 136, 137, 140, 144, 148, 150, 151, 154
participation, 1–2, 5–6, 7, 10, 11, 12, 26–52, 69, 87, 89–111, 139, 148–9, 155–7, 158, 203, 204, 207, 210, 213–33, 271–81, 283, 284, 285, 286, 287, 289, 291, 299, 303, 304; definition of, 7–8; measurement of, 15–20 (*see also*, campaigning; contacting politicians and bureaucrats; meetings, public; pressuring; protests; thanks, expressions of; voting)
parties, political, 12, 22, 26, 27, 28, 29, 53, 65–6, 77, 80, 81–2, 83–4, 87, 90–3, 120, 132, 133, 134, 137, 203–5, 207, 209, 213, 214, 216, 236, 275, 278, 281, 285, 288, 289, 294, 295, 296, 298, 302–3 (*see also*, Awami League; Bangladesh National Party; Congress Party; Convention People's Party; Front Populaire Ivoirien; Janata Party; Jatiyo Party; multi-party politics; National Democratic Congress; Parti Démocratique de la Côte d'Ivoire; Rassemblement des Républicains; single-party politics)
Paul, S., 301
performance, institutional, 5–6, 7, 8–13, 52–80, 111–32, 176–98, 210, 247–66, 267, 271, 281–9, 290, 291, 292; definition of, 8–10; measurement of, 15–20 (*see also*, effectiveness; responsiveness)
petitions, 17, 34, 37, 94, 98, 129, 217, 273–4
Philippines, 130–1
planning, 3, 20, 49–50, 54, 86, 109–11, 143, 205, 207, 208, 210, 216, 239–40, 241–3, 284
poor people, 8n, 11n, 17, 23, 25, 30, 33–42, 71–2, 76–9, 81, 86, 96–102, 114, 125, 129–31, 155, 188, 223–4, 227, 230–2, 257, 267, 277, 278, 279, 280, 282, 283, 301–2
popular awareness and knowledge, 1, 17, 20, 31, 35–7, 40, 61–8, 69, 73, 87, 97, 98, 117–18, 121, 128, 132, 134, 213, 215, 218–19, 273–4, 276, 278, 279, 284, 286, 287, 290
popular demands, 1, 14, 20, 21, 30–1, 38, 49–50, 76, 125, 284 (See also, local needs; popular preferences)
popular preferences, 1, 14, 16, 18–19, 21, 49–50, 69–79, 118, 125, 127, 131, 134, 186–7, 188–90, 233–4, 254–6, 262, 281, 282, 283 (*see also*, local needs; popular demands)
poverty, *see* poor people
Prefects (Côte d'Ivoire), 137, 144, 145, 167, 175–6, 184–6, 196
Prefectoral administration, *see* Prefects
press, 12–13, 32n, 45, 50–2, 65–6, 106, 119, 120, 122, 125, 288, 303
pressuring, *see* lobbying
process, 9, 10, 14, 19, 21, 79–80, 131–2, 197–8, 265–6, 281 (*see also*, fairness)
professions and professional associations, 34, 36, 42, 58–62, 95, 99, 119, 202, 203, 207, 224, 225, 226, 228–33, 246, 275 (*see also*, press)
projects, developmental, 9, 15, 16, 18, 19, 20, 31–2, 39, 46, 52–69, 80, 81, 84, 85, 95–6, 105, 106, 107–9, 112, 113, 116–17, 119, 120, 123–5, 127, 130–1, 135, 165–7, 177–82, 185, 191–2, 222, 242–6, 249–51, 260–2, 267n, 281, 282, 283, 284, 285, 286, 287, 291
protests, 7, 34, 37, 38–9, 41, 44, 64, 91, 93, 94, 98, 100, 109, 134, 217, 220

Index   335

Provisional National Defence Council (Ghana), 203–5, 207, 209, 213, 223, 226, 227, 234, 235, 236, 269
Putnam, R., 303–4

Rahman, Ziaur, 87
Rassemblement des Républicains (RDR), 151
Rawlings, Jerry, 203, 204, 214, 216, 231, 275, 276, 296
recentralisation, 4
religion, 2, 39n, 95, 99, 160, 224, 225, 276
rent-seeking, *see* corruption
representative politics, 3, 7, 8, 11, 12, 14, 17, 18, 20, 32, 39–49, 76, 84, 101, 102–11, 173–4, 199, 204, 213–16, 221–4, 233–6, 276, 277, 278, 286, 292, 297, 299, 303
resource mobilisation, *see* local resource mobilisation
responsiveness, 1, 9–12, 14, 16, 18–21, 29–33, 36, 59–61, 68–79, 80, 118, 125–31, 131, 135, 188–90, 193–7, 256–65, 281, 282, 283, 284, 285, 286, 291, 301
revenue, 3, 4, 7, 8, 18, 30, 52–4, 85, 104, 145, 178, 183–4, 200, 203, 208, 220–1, 241–3, 248–9, 263, 282, 284, 285, 286, 300, 301 (*see also*, local resource mobilisation; tax paying and collection; tax-raising powers)
revolution, 4, 87, 203, 207, 209, 214, 218, 223, 226, 233, 234, 235, 236, 274–5, 276, 296
rural development, 7, 18, 19–20, 22, 25, 52–69, 86–7

Scheduled Castes, *see* castes
Semboja, J., 301
Senegal, 294
service delivery, 7, 9, 14, 16, 18, 19, 46, 52–69, 107–9, 117, 122, 123–5, 131, 207, 211, 253, 281, 282, 300–1 (*see also*, education; health)
Singapore, 296
single-party politics, 5, 285, 292, 296
Smoke, P., 297, 298
society, 11–12, 13, 35, 38–9, 79, 83–4, 86–7, 202–5, 228–34, 246, 283, 288, 290, 291, 295, 302–4 (*see also*, castes; civil society; status, social)
Sri Lanka, 296, 297
status, social and political, 8n, 32–49, 57, 75–6, 77, 231, 277, 279, 285, 288 (*see also*, castes; elites; civil society; society)
Structural Adjustment Programmes, *see* economic reform

Sub-district Councils (Bangladesh), 4, 85–135, 287

Tanzania, 296, 301
Tanzi, V., 300
tax-paying and collection, 8, 19, 113, 146, 167, 168, 183, 185, 198, 200, 220–2, 241–2, 264, 266, 268
tax-raising powers, 7, 53–4, 56–7, 85–6, 142, 145, 207, 208, 209, 299
thanks, expressions of, 34, 37, 41, 94, 98
Therkildsen, O., 301
tiers, *see* levels in political systems
Togo, 211
transparency, 2, 10, 61–8, 79, 84, 121–2, 135, 281, 295, 296, 300–1 (*see also*, concealment)
tutelle, power of, 144, 145, 170, 175–6

Uganda, 296, 297
Union Councils (Bangladesh), 4, 85–135, 279, 280, 287
Union Parishads (Bangladesh), *see* Union Councils (Bangladesh)
unions, trade/labour, 34, 95, 99, 203, 294
United Nations Development Programme (UNDP), 284
Upazila Parishads, *see* Sub-District Councils (Bangladesh)
USAID, 2

violence, 27, 79, 90–1, 92–3, 97, 106, 133, 203, 212
voting, *see* elections

Webster, N., 302
West Bengal (India), 77, 280n, 283, 295, 297, 298, 302
women, 8, 18, 23, 27, 34, 36, 40–1, 67, 68–9, 85, 95, 96, 97–102, 129–31, 156–7, 158, 189–90, 214, 224, 225, 226–33, 258, 259, 276, 277, 279, 280, 302
World Bank, 1–2, 195, 251, 301

Yakassé-Attobrou, 148, 151, 160, 171, 181, 187, 194–5
Yamoussoukro, 139
youths, 34, 36, 95, 96, 99, 188, 209, 226–33, 231, 233, 276, 277, 282

Zilla Parishads, *see* District Councils (Karnataka)
Zimbabwe, 87n, 296, 297

For EU product safety concerns, contact us at Calle de José Abascal, 56–1º, 28003 Madrid, Spain or eugpsr@cambridge.org.